Being a Great Dad

2nd Australian Edition

by Dr Justin Coulson

Being a Great Dad For Dummies®, 2nd Australian Edition

Published by
John Wiley & Sons Australia, Ltd
Level 4, 600 Bourke Street
Melbourne, Vic 3000
www.dummies.com

Copyright © 2023 John Wiley & Sons Australia, Ltd

The moral rights of the author have been asserted.

Additional material authored by Stefan Korn, Scott Lancaster, Eric Mooij, Directors, DIY Father

ISBN: 978-1-119-91028-2

A catalogue record for this book is available from the National Library of Australia

Cover image: © andreswd/Getty Images

Typeset by Straive

Contents at a Glance

Table of Contents

Introduction

The expression 'useless as a chocolate teacup' comes to mind when describing what many fathers in the past felt about their involvement during labour and when caring for newborns and children. Fathers historically have taken a passive role during pregnancy, going about their lives mostly as normal (and wondering what the rules are about pregnancy and intimacy). They've offered a shoulder rub to their partner during childbirth. And when it came to looking after babies and children, history is replete with examples of men avoiding the multiple night-time wakings, feigning strategic incompetence when nappies needed changing, and focusing only on disciplining older children when home from work.

But that was then. These days, an increasing number of guys now want a piece of the baby and child-rearing action, and are rolling up their sleeves to muck in with everything that needs doing — from active involvement in labour to nappy changes and all the fun of toddlers and children as they grow and develop.

The number of stay-at-home dads (SAHDs) is rising in almost all developed countries — a sure sign that the parenting world is changing and that staying home looking after the kids is no longer a reason to hand in your man card. In fact, SAHDs are leading the way for all other dads to show the world how brilliant dads can be at looking after babies and children.

Parental leave in workplaces is changing too. Corporations are recognising that not just mum needs time off when a baby is born, or may need more flexible working options as that baby and child grows older. The organisational trend is towards parental leave for fathers so they can support their partner, bond with their baby, and savour the precious early moments of parenting. And parental leave for dads is happening more and more, even in sectors where the alpha male and his over-the-top commitment to the company have historically dominated. (I'm looking at you, financial sector.)

Moreover, many nations, particularly Holland, Sweden and Finland, actively encourage parents to work a four-day week. Time with family is prized and honoured. Government policy encourages it, and for good reason.

Countless studies by fatherhood institutes around the world show strong scientific evidence for the positive difference a dad makes in the lives of his children. Unfortunately, many of the challenges and difficulties our children experience are linked to absent, uninvolved or unsafe fathers. And while it's true that children raised by single mums can — and do — thrive (because their mothers are phenomenal), there is little doubt that fathers count. In comparison to children raised without the positive presence of a dad in their lives, kids raised by a positive, active, involved and safe dad have an increased likelihood of doing better at self-regulation, delayed gratification, emotional management, social relationships, academic achievement, avoiding unsafe, unhealthy behaviours as teens — the list goes on. Oh yeah, and they're happier and more satisfied with life. Measurably.

The journey of being a dad starts way back at the very beginning, even before conception. It starts with the way you love your partner, the mum of your soon-to-be child. The great news is that more dads are keen to be a positive, active, involved member of the family, and society's conditions are ripe for helping us make it happen.

About This Book

With *Being a Great Dad For Dummies*, 2nd edition, I'm doing my bit to help every new dad or dad-to-be start (and continue) his journey to healthy, safe, active fatherhood. In this book, I focus specifically on pregnancy, birth, and raising your child from a male perspective. The great news is being a healthy, safe, active dad isn't difficult. Dads can do everything mums do except giving birth and breast-feeding. So if you're worried about becoming a dad, relax, read on and know that everyday blokes make fantastic dads.

I'm thrilled to be able to serve as your guide to dadhood. Since 2012, my organisation — *Dr Justin Coulson's Happy Families* — has developed into one of the most recognised organisations promoting, well, happy families — and involved fatherhood — in Australia and New Zealand. In *Being a Great Dad For Dummies*, I share what the very best science has taught us about how you can be involved in your children's lives for better — and how doing so can build a happier life for your child, and for you.

I've spent years talking to hundreds of thousands of parents about this stuff. And I've also had plenty of practice. My wife and I have six of our own kids, so I've got the miles in the legs. I'm race fit and ready to share the research and the practice to make this gig hum for you. And what all of this means is that you can find all you need to know in one place (this book), and don't need to waste time reading lots of leaflets or browsing through hundreds of websites trying to get reliable and practical information from a male perspective. I've packed these pages with plenty of useful information so you can become the best father you can be.

So, why this book? The reasons include the following:

» The Baby Boomer (1950s) approach to having children cast a long shadow into the way we approach modern parenting, but things have changed. Modern dads want to be involved and they want to find out for themselves what they need to know to look after a newborn baby.

» Your kids, your family and our world need strong dads. Fathers have been somewhat absent from childcare and upbringing due to work, family situation or a limited understanding of the role of a father. It's about time we changed that.

» You may find even approaching the topic of pregnancy, babies and parenting hard.

» You may be missing out on the best moments of your life if you feel you don't know what to do with babies and children.

» You have everything you need to be a fantastic dad, but you just don't know it yet. Or perhaps you lack a bit of confidence to demonstrate your dad skills. This book will help.

» Your child and partner are likely to really appreciate all the cool things you know and are able to do when you've read this book.

» By being a positive, healthy, active dad right from the beginning, you make the most significant contribution to your child's life you could ever make — it beats any expensive present, university savings account or inheritance fund your child may receive.

Although I hope you read every word I've written, I understand your life is busy and you want to read only the need-to-know info. You can safely skip the sidebars, which are shaded grey boxes containing text. These provide supporting or entertaining information that isn't critical to your understanding of the topic.

Throughout this book, I also give you the website addresses of a number of dedicated parenting or fatherhood sites where you can find more information on some of the topics I discuss, such as buying sensible baby gear and toys, parenting styles, effective behaviour management, illnesses and special conditions, childcare and child education. Although you don't have to go to these websites, having a browse through them is well worth your while.

Foolish Assumptions

I assume that you're reading this book because you've just been told that you're going to be a dad soon or you've decided it's about time you became one. You may also have been told by your partner to 'skill up' and read about pregnancy and parenting so she doesn't have to do all the work around the baby. Good — because you don't want that anyway. Today's dads can do everything that mums do except giving birth and breastfeeding.

I assume you're somewhat puzzled by the prospects of becoming a dad and would like an easy and comprehensive guide. This book is for you if you're

» Freaked out about becoming a dad

» Concerned about your lack of knowledge and experience around all things babies and children

» Three months into your partner's pregnancy and feel like it's all getting a bit too complicated

» Looking for an alternative to being told everything you need to know about babies by your partner

» On your way to the delivery suite and have missed all the ante-natal classes

I also assume you haven't had much exposure to or experience with pregnant women, newborn babies and children up to now.

Icons Used in This Book

Icons are those little pictures you see sprinkled in the margins throughout this book. Here's what they mean:

CHECK THE NET

The internet is a wonderful place to access information on being a great dad. This icon highlights some helpful sites for you to check out.

REMEMBER

This icon denotes critical information that you really need to take away with you. Considering the state of my own overcrowded memories, I wouldn't ask you to remember anything unless the information was really important.

TIP

This icon alerts you to on-target advice, insights or recommendations that I've picked up over the years.

WARNING

This icon serves as a warning, telling you to avoid something that's potentially harmful. Take heed!

Where to Go from Here

You choose what happens next. This book is packed with information to help you at whatever state or stage you're at on your fatherhood journey. You can go directly to the topics of most interest to you, or you can start at the beginning and take it from there. With the information in *Being a Great Dad For Dummies*, 2nd edition, I'm confident that you can handle any challenges fatherhood (or your little champ) throws at you. Most importantly, this book helps you become a confident and competent dad, and have fun along the way.

1

From Here to Paternity: Conception to Birth

IN THIS PART . . .

Understand being a dad doesn't start the day you meet your newborn child; instead, the process begins much sooner — in some cases, even before your child is conceived.

Prepare for the hurdles you may face on the way to getting pregnant and meeting your baby.

Focus on your baby's development through each trimester of pregnancy, understand medical terms and help your partner deal with common side effects during each stage.

Find out all the pregnancy secrets worth knowing — including which baby gear is actually useful.

Understand what's actually going on at each stage and phase of labour, and know what to keep in mind during what can be quite a drawn-out affair.

Know what to do in the first few hours after birth when you finally hold your brand new baby in your arms.

Chapter **1**

Fatherhood

Right now, somewhere across the globe, someone is becoming a father. He may be suited up in scrubs as his child is delivered by caesarean in a high-tech delivery suite, or holding his partner's hand as she gives birth in a pool at home. He may be pacing at the neighbours' hut in a village somewhere in the developing world as his wife gives birth surrounded only by women, or heading through rush hour traffic to get to the hospital on time. Wherever these dads-to-be are, they all have one thing in common. When they clap eyes on their new little baby, they know life will never be the same.

Well, that's the story the movies tell us. It's a romantic narrative that's completely true for some of us, but doesn't resonate with many. When I became a dad for the first time, I was moved. I cried. I loved my wife more than I'd ever thought possible. And then . . . I really just wanted to get back to the office. I didn't think I could contribute anything further. I felt kind of like the adventure (birth) was over, and now it was time to get back to work — to providing. I had to *learn* to love this new human that I'd helped to create, and that was going to take time.

Regardless of where you fall on the continuum, from awestruck through to blasé, one thing is certain. Change is coming at you faster than an F1 supercar down the straight. For ages, you've been focused on yourself — well, hopefully you *and* your partner: building a career, buying a house, perhaps travelling and seeing the world. You've concentrated on becoming a person and a couple in your own right. But when you have a child, you begin a whole new adventure — one that doesn't end when your visa runs out or the bar closes. And you become a whole new person.

In this chapter, I explore what it means to be a father and talk about the reality of being a dad. The role of fathers has changed a lot in just the generation between our fathers and us. We're more involved, but it feels as though we also have a lot more stress on us. The cost of keeping up means more of us feel overwhelmed with work commitments and financial pressure than any previous generation. Burnout among Western parents is at all-time highs. Becoming a father is associated with increased relationship stress between a man and his partner. It's a tricky time. And we have to contend with information overload, with so many people having so many opinions on how to dad just right.

But fear not — in this chapter and in the rest of the book I keep fatherhood real with practical information, useful explanations and the occasional high-quality dad joke. (Is that an oxymoron?) After all, children are lots and lots of fun, so why make the journey to fatherhood more serious than it needs to be?

Imagining the Dad You Want to Be

I'm going to use a fancy phrase here to set up a bit of a thought experiment. The phrase is 'temporal distancing', which means I'd like you to do a mental time-travel exercise. Psychologists highlight how temporal distancing (imagining a future state) helps us to get clear on who we really are and what we really value. So here goes. Insert your relevant time-travel pop-culture reference (for me it's *Back to the Future* and the flux capacitor), and let's pay a visit to your future.

Imagine yourself 20 to 30 years from now. You're sitting around the outdoor table. You've just enjoyed a tasty BBQ (rib-eye cooked medium rare — or for the environmentally conscious, some tofu cooked however you like it) and the grandkids are playing with some LEGO and other blocks on the floor. (Of course LEGO's are still around!) You're watching *your grandkids* with awe while you listen to your *adult children* chatting about how you were as a dad and how you raised them.

How would you like your children to remember you? What stories are they telling? What do they remember about the way you responded when they made mistakes, got it wrong, laid into each other as only siblings can, and refused to do as they were told (as all kids will from time to time)?

Do they remember you being on the sidelines of their games? Were you in the audience at their recitals or assemblies? Did your face light up when they walked into the room? Did you listen? Were you patient, forgiving and compassionate? Did you take them to the video game arcade? Or to the opera? Surfing? Or to the art gallery? Did you instil values that they appreciate now they're wrangling their own little kids? Did you hold them to a high standard but remain gentle when they failed? And are they grateful that you taught them about the very best music on the planet (yours) even when they wanted to listen to all that modern junk?

I know imagining life as a grandparent when you're in the very earliest stages of dadhood may seem a bit of a stretch. But this activity taps into your deepest desires around what kind of a father you'd like to be. It's about understanding your values. My guess: you'd like to be a deeply engaged and active dad. And while you'd probably like to goof off and get a bit rough-and-tumble at times, I suspect you're also looking forward to those sacred, tender moments where you see the miracle your child is and your heart just about explodes with wonder and gratitude. How good does this sound? A lot of water is still to go under the bridge before you get there, but I highly recommend this approach, and so does so much of the scientific evidence that shows children of involved dads do better in life.

REMEMBER

Fatherhood can make you a better version of you than you ever thought possible. (And it will also show you every one of your failings in glaring detail.) Not all at once. The process takes a while. But if you let it, you'll be refined.

When we refine oil (or water or sugar), we remove impurities and other unwanted material. This might seem a heavy way to start a book about becoming a father, but you should know that fatherhood is life's ultimate course in character development and refinement. If you allow it and seek it, being a dad will change you for the better. You'll learn to be more patient, kind, long-suffering, gentle, supportive, generous — unconditional — than you ever thought possible. (Some dads don't allow it . . . but you're reading this, so that's not you.) You'll learn to be the kind of dad that your child believes really does deserve that coffee mug for Father's Day that says *Best Dad Ever*.

REMEMBER

At the office or in your employment, you're replaceable. The machine keeps churning whether you're there or not. In your child's life, however, no-one can take your place. So long as you can be a safe, positive presence, *you are irreplaceable*. Your child needs you. So does your partner. You make a difference.

So no real downside exists to being an involved dad — and your involvement starts right from the beginning, with taking a keen interest in your partner's pregnancy, participating in the birth of your little one however you can, being a support in the early years, and getting involved as your child grows. That's what this book is all about — enjoying the journey!

Dispelling Common Myths about Fatherhood

In the past, fathers were often effectively cut off from being involved in childbirth and parenting through preconceived ideas, peer pressure or the demands of the modern workplace. Towards the end of the 20th century, however, we experienced a revival of fatherhood and the dawn of a new generation of dads — a generation of dads who were no longer content just bringing home the bacon and playing a supporting role in the rearing of their children.

Dads in the 21st century now have the option to do things differently and show the world they make fantastic caregivers. They want to be up to their elbows in parenting. Some dads are even taking over and sending mum back to the workforce. Something fundamental is changing about how we bring up our children and organise our lives.

However, despite the generation of new dads, many dads are still faced with a few persistent stereotypes that are taking way too long to die a slow death.

These stereotypes include some of the following:

>> **Fathers are completely useless when it comes to looking after babies and children.** I want to say that this suggestion is garbage. But at the start, it's probably true for many of us men. Rarely have we grown up helping our parents raise our little siblings. And teen boys and men in their 20s don't tend to pick up the cute baby at family gatherings, sporting events, church or down at the pub on Saturday arvo so they can have a cuddle or to help burp the kiddo. Men aren't generally recognised for their proactively nurturing natures. This means our experience and skills are often limited at first. But practice — time on the field — is how we get better.

REMEMBER

Research shows that fathers are just as good as mothers at caring for babies once they've had a bit of practice and training. They're great with responding to their baby's needs and temperaments, and learning how to read baby's cues. And getting involved is worth it. Research also shows that children with involved dads do better in school, and are more confident and independent later in life. Yes, dads may parent differently from mums, but male ways of doing things are just as important.

>> **Fathers don't have to do any of the day-to-day care that babies and children require.** This may be true if you want to remain in the dark ages of fatherhood. Twenty-first century dads do care-giving for one important reason: the best way to bond with your newborn child is by taking part in all that day-to-day stuff. Changing a nappy, trimming nails and bathing baby aren't just jobs that need to be completed; they're an ideal way for your baby to spend time with you and get to know you — and for you to get to know your baby. Your child learns that in times of need, you're there to offer safety, help her feel better, and comfort her when she's unwell or just needs a cuddle. Your baby learns words from you as you chat to her while she's in the bath, learns how to put clothes on from the way you dress her each morning, and adopts all sorts of other good qualities simply from the way you are.

REMEMBER

What builds your relationship with your baby aren't the big things, but the countless minor moments you have together. Consistency in the seemingly insignificant but important stuff is what makes you a great dad. Every single one of those 'insignificant' interactions counts.

>> **Mums think dads are incompetent.** This one may be true from time to time. But most mums really want to see dads step up and get involved. And, at the risk of falling back onto stereotypes, women may admire you just a little when you walk into that playgroup with bub on your shoulder. If you get the occasional overly 'helpful' mum in the supermarket who doesn't think you quite know how to handle a crying baby, be confident that you can demonstrate who's daddy by settling your little one with calm and competent compassion. Don't worry — I get to how you do that later.

>> **Fathers don't have a social life.** Wrong — fathers (and all parents) have a *different* social life. You may have to invest a bit of time and thought into how you manage going out or taking part in sports or your other hobbies once you're a dad. Having an extra person in your life takes a bit of getting used to, but that doesn't mean you'll never be able to go out again. Working with your partner as a team and exercising a little creativity — while remaining mindful that your partner likely also wants to have a social life and needs your support to do it — is usually all it takes.

>> **Dads don't have a sex life.** Actually that one is kind of true, but only temporarily. The birthing experience, sheer exhaustion, and practicalities of looking after a newborn can make getting back to your pre-baby sex life with your partner somewhat tricky. And, for the safety of your partner, waiting several weeks (or more — check with your doctor) to help her recover from the birth is essential. The word here is patience. Rest assured: your sex life does return (check out Chapters 6 and 8 for more on this subject), and it will get better and better, even after kids. But you might just have to be a bit more creative now that your little one is in the house.

Knowing What Really to Expect

Asking someone to tell you what being a father is like is a bit like asking 'What does salt taste like?' Simply answering 'salty' may be true, but is unhelpful to anyone who hasn't tasted salt. How do you explain what being a father is like? The only answer is that it's like nothing you can explain — except, just like anyone who has tasted salt knows the taste, anyone who has been a father knows the feeling.

TIP

A good way to get an idea of what fatherhood is like is to spend some time with friends who have recently had a baby. And here's a novel idea for a lot of us men: talk to your parents and in-laws about it. They've been there. Their experience won't be the same as yours, but this can be an incredible opportunity to grow your relationship with them.

Similar to the uniqueness of your child's DNA, every father's experience is different. However, in the following sections, I run through some of the common factors of being a dad, the pros and cons you're likely to face, and some of the lifestyle changes you may consider making.

Understanding the dad experience

Here are some common factors that most fathers face:

>> **At first, you may feel like nothing has changed at all.** Many new dads feel like this. And they can sometimes be really troubled by the fact that they've just held their new baby and now they're thinking about that 'thing' at work that needs attention. Bonding, adjusting and really experiencing the change that fatherhood brings takes time. Truth be told, in the first hours and days after birth, many dads feel overwhelming love for their partner but very little for their baby. It takes time for the relationship to develop. But once it does — and it could take a few months — you can't be who you used to be. You've *become* a dad.

>> **You often feel frightened, scared, overwhelmed and sometimes lost.** Again, this is normal. The emotional change some dads feel as they consider the reality of their new circumstances can really hit them for six. And the practical stuff knocks some dads around too. Just changing a nappy for the first time or getting clothes on a newborn feels awkward and wrong when you're new at it. But that's life, right? We're always stepping into something new, taking on a challenge and trying something we're not ready for. It's what life is about!

>> **Sleep becomes a big issue.** Babies don't understand that day is for being awake and night is for being asleep. Over time, your baby adjusts to what's known as a 'circadian rhythm' and eventually 'sleeps through the night' — the Holy Grail for most parents. But a baby who makes this adjustment before six months of age is rare (and even then, it's typically only about six hours before they need another feed). Babies also need nutrition every few hours to grow, so if your baby is waking up in the night for feeds, consider that she's thriving and growing is a good thing. Chapter 6 discusses feeding your baby and getting her to sleep.

>> **You do things that you never thought you'd do.** You laugh at things that you might have mocked a few years ago. Your less-sensitive and compassionate teenage self would be rolling his eyes at you! And you will almost certainly cry at times that you least expect. You also learn lots about yourself and experience things that you can't experience any other way. Fatherhood is truly an adventure.

>> **Sharing your partner's body with your child before and after birth can feel a bit weird.** Sex during pregnancy can be both brilliant and a bit challenging, depending on how your partner is feeling and how willing she is to get involved with you. Sex after birth can involve tackling some new challenges. See Chapter 3 for more about sex during pregnancy, and Chapters 6 and 8 for more on sex following birth.

REMEMBER

Being a father is a lot about acceptance and going with the flow. A useful mantra to remember is 'This too *will* pass', because every illness, teething episode, period of sleep deprivation or colic will pass. I consistently reminded myself that 'pain is temporary but joy lasts forever'. In the moment, when you're weighed down with exhaustion, worry or fear, you might wonder if that's true. But as a guy who's been there with six kids, and who is now a grandfather, I can promise you: it's true. Every word of it.

The pros and cons of fatherhood

As with every life decision or change, good things and challenges exist. If you want to take a rational approach to fatherhood, consider the following.

On the plus side:

>> Fathers report their lives are more meaningful than before they had a child.

>> Fatherhood can make you a more compassionate, mature and confident person.

- >> You get to be a child all over again. (Yes, you get to goof off, roll around on the floor, wrestle, play with cool toys and teach your child lots of silly tricks.)

- >> You can hand down skills and values from your family.

- >> You may for the first time in your life truly understand your own father.

- >> You get a real kick out of raising a child well and seeing her achieve lots of things.

The challenges:

- >> Until around three months of age, newborn babies are full on. They cry, sometimes for no apparent reason at all, and you feel like the sound is piercing your brain. Chapter 6 provides helpful hints about settling a newborn and coping with crying.

- >> Sleep deprivation is common for all new parents. Fathers of babies under a year old typically have 42 minutes less sleep each night than other men. Doesn't sound like much, but it adds up. For ways to deal with sleep deprivation, see Chapter 8.

- >> You have less time for yourself and making plans really does mean making plans — spontaneity goes out the window a bit at the beginning.

The upsides of fatherhood far outweigh the downsides, especially because most of the really annoying aspects (such as sleep deprivation) get much easier the older your children get.

REMEMBER

A sad reality for a small percentage of Australian fathers is that they may not get the chance to experience all the joys that fatherhood has to offer. Though we don't often talk about miscarriage, stillbirth, premature birth and death in infancy in our society, these are terrible losses for some fathers to bear. Others have to deal with the fact that their child, so full of promise and hope, has a serious illness or disability that forces them to shift expectations of what being a father is all about and what their future brings. This grief can be overcome, and life can still be wonderful — and profoundly meaningful. And other fathers have to deal with relationship breakdown with their partners, which can sometimes result in lack of time with their children. I talk more about these issues in Chapters 17, 18 and 19, and provide information and support for parents.

Letting go of best laid plans

Parenting, for both fathers and mothers, requires a certain amount of letting go. When a baby is born, you no doubt want things for your child — the best of everything, and every opportunity and good thing in life that may come her way. But birth plans don't come to fruition, family holidays turn into exhausting experiences where you just do all the hard parenting stuff at a new location, and you wonder what happened?

Many years ago, a taxi driver started chatting with me about parenting. When he found out that I write books for parents, he asked me, 'How do I make sure my son becomes a pilot?' I was intrigued. 'Does your son *want* to be a pilot?' I asked. He replied, 'I am not sure.' I paused as I considered where to take this conversation, and then questioned, 'How old is your son?' The response came: 'About six weeks.'

Making plans to try to set up your child for success is tempting. But more than anything, particularly in these early stages of your child's life, focus on the here and now. Be in the moment. Stay where your feet — and your child's feet — are. The nights may feel long as you battle sleep deprivation, but be assured, they fly by, and you will miss the laughter that makes your face crack no matter how hard you try to keep it straight, the cheeky smiles that light up your baby's eyes, and the joy that comes from being a dad to a newborn. More good things are coming. What matters here and now is soaking up what's right in front of you.

Trading in your lifestyle (but not the sports gear)

Being a great dad will likely involve some sacrifice — and if it doesn't, check how equal your relationship feels. For most dads, becoming a father is about changing your state of mind and changing your ideas of what's important to you. If you want a baby but don't want to change the way you live your life, you're probably better off waiting for a while to have children (keeping in mind that biology will have something to say if you wait too long).

Once you become a dad, some things inevitably change:

>> **Your work:** If you want to spend time with your family, you may consider working fewer hours, or changing to a flexible working arrangement that you can negotiate with your employer. Most dads don't make big changes, although a trend is forming around this. It's not always possible, but it's worth considering, particularly if you want to be a hands-on dad. See Chapter 6 for more about finding a work–life balance.

>> **Your freedom:** Doing things when and where you want doesn't work when you've got a baby. If the swell is perfect and you feel like going out for a surf, you may have to wait until your baby is asleep, or take her and mum along with you. Cycling with the guys in the bunch becomes trickier. And if you and your partner love the outdoors, that camping trip with the hiking or

mountain biking might have to be postponed a year or two (or ten). Spending time out and about with your partner changes. Going out to dinner and a movie is no longer a spontaneous activity, but one requiring planning. Finding time for yourself alongside work and family commitments is one of the biggest challenges fathers face. Chapter 6 provides ideas for juggling other priorities after your baby arrives.

» **Your finances:** If you and your partner both had an income before your child came along, you're likely to be down to one income for a while. If you lived in a one-bedroom flat, you likely need to find somewhere bigger, and a way to pay for it. Some careful conversations might be necessary as you determine how to enjoy your new life with a baby without breaking the bank.

» **Your friends and family:** Your relationships with friends and family change. If you live away from your parents, you're likely to find yourself having to spend a lot more time travelling to visit them so your baby can see her grandparents (and you get a few hours of free babysitting). Your partner may have a deeper desire to be close to her mum. This is important. If you can assist in making this happen, do it. Your partner's sense of support is crucial to your family functioning well. Some of your childless friends really embrace you having a child and become the fun aunt or uncle your child gets excited about seeing. Others aren't so keen and you see them less as a result.

» **Your holidays:** Going on holiday takes on a whole new meaning. You definitely have to postpone that backpacking trip around South America for a few years, at least until your kids are big enough to trudge alongside you. Family holidays are different — great fun, but unlike any holiday you've had since you were a child. And, ironically, they tend to be a lot of work — which makes them feel less like a holiday.

» **Your lifestyle:** Risky lifestyle or sporting activities such as big wave surfing, remote cycling, base jumping and free climbing are no longer just about risking your own life. You now have to consider the future of your child and family. Some dads won't change a thing. Others will start to think again, and find new ways to get their thrills or stay fit.

» **Your health and behaviour:** A child is one of the ultimate reasons to change unhealthy habits such as smoking, heavy drinking, using recreational drugs, eating junk food and being a slob. Children need a smoke-free environment to breathe in, good healthy food, clean clothes and nappies, and good hygiene to prevent illness. And watch your words too. Coarse language from a toddler might be funny the first time, but can be pretty awkward if it happens repeatedly. With babies and kids the process is pretty much 'monkey see, monkey do' — eventually all your behaviour comes back to you through your children.

Only Fools Rush In

Sometimes you can plan when you have a child, and sometimes nature has her own ideas. Either way, fatherhood is a big deal — fatherhood's not like buying a new pair of shoes or potting a plant. Your child, if you decide to have one, has only one shot at life and she deserves the best start you can give her. A positive, healthy, involved and reliable father is a big part of that. If you're being pushed into having a child by your partner or family members, talk it through with your partner. Don't just go along with it because you're afraid of the discussion. Becoming a dad is an important step in life, so take some time to figure out how you feel about it and share your thoughts with your partner.

Hey, I'm not ready for this

How often in your life can you say you're really ready for something? Not often. Fatherhood, of all things, is probably the most difficult to feel truly ready for. Even if you've been planning to have a child, spent months going through IVF (see Chapter 2 for more about this) and been dreaming of the day you hold your child in your arms, the sledgehammer of reality is likely to whack you over the head when your partner goes into labour and you realise how not-ready you are.

If your partner is already pregnant but you don't feel ready for fatherhood, you've got time on your side. In the coming months, as your baby grows and gets ready for birth, read up on what's happening and what your partner's going through. (Chapter 3 runs you through all the changes occurring for mum and bub in each trimester of pregnancy.) Find out more about the reality of labour, the interventions that might be required and what happens in the first few hours after birth. (Chapter 5 provides some great help here.)

If you're really, truly not ready for fatherhood as the birth approaches, it may help if you talk to someone about your fears. Your midwife or GP can put you in touch with a counsellor.

CHECK THE NET

You can find a counsellor yourself through these organisations:

>> Family Relationship Services Australia, frsa.org.au

>> Relationships Australia, relationships.org.au

TIP

Don't forget to talk to your partner about what you're feeling. After all, you are in this together, so it helps to share your feelings and thoughts with her.

Although having children can be the most amazing and joyous adventure, the strains of work, family and other commitments can put a lot of pressure on a relationship. Unfortunately, many relationships don't survive this extra pressure. In Chapter 19, I talk about how fathers can cope with divorce and separation and still continue to be great dads.

My partner wants a baby

You're faced with a sticky situation — your partner is ready to have a baby, her biological clock is ticking, all her friends have babies and she's eager to join the club. But you're not.

Here's my advice: Rather than fight the idea of becoming a parent, talk about it together with your partner. Explain why you're not ready but, equally, listen to her point of view. Imagine yourself as a dad — how does that feel?

Mull it over. Where do you want to be in ten years? Dad to a litter of children with the rewards that brings? Or still living a childless life with the freedoms that brings? When you look back on your life in your old age, do you want children and family to be part of it?

You may feel like there's never a good time to have children or you just don't feel ready. Perhaps you're quite clear that you definitely don't want children. Cool, but then you also owe it to your partner to let her know.

Timing isn't always everything

Sometimes, despite thinking that you'll wait to have a family until after a big project is completed, you've found a bigger house, or you've been on that trek to Base Camp, nature jumps the gun. Your partner brings home a pregnancy test and you both find out she's likely pregnant. That home pregnancy test needs to be confirmed, but once it has been — you're going to be a dad.

The possible reactions you might exhibit are as varied as the number of men on earth! But . . . think about how you might react ahead of time and how your reaction might be perceived by your partner. If you respond with shock, panic, frustration or any negative emotion, what foundation does that set for discussions moving forward? How does it establish your attitude towards your relationship with your partner? And with your child?

Your response matters. If you're unsettled, pause. Ask for her reaction (remembering she might be wanting to take her cue from you). And, if you can, be excited — or at least upbeat. If the pregnancy is unexpected, let her know that you think it might take a day or two to sink in . . . but you're totally there for her, and for the bub. (Most men I speak to were stoked to know they'd be a dad, although more than a few started to experience nerves and stress a few days later as it began to sink in.)

As for timing, the truth is there's probably never a good time to do something that requires enormous sacrifice or change. But there's always a good time for kindness and empathy — and excitement.

Introducing the New-Generation Dad

Fathers today are a quantum leap from the previous generation of fathers. Twenty-first century dads push prams, get up for night feeds, change nappies, and have tried and tested burping techniques. We do everything — except for being pregnant, giving birth and breastfeeding. As for the rest of it, we can tackle anything. Dare I say it, dads can even do some things better than mums.

Dadhood: A good time to man up

All your life you've had just one person to take care of — yourself. You've made choices, taken risks and shouldered the consequences. But becoming a father is 'the big stuff'. You have a vulnerable, dependent, helpless child on your hands who needs you for the most basic aspects of her survival, such as food, warmth and love. And if everything's gone well, you also have a partner who needs you in a way you've never been needed before. To raise the stakes just a little further, your baby is also watching how you treat your partner — their mum — and the way you do sets the stage for what your child will expect from their partner. A lot is riding on how you do this stuff. Now's the time to stand tall, let go of your stuff, and be there for them — your family. (Does that sound weird? It's actually *your family*!) A real man makes the people around him feel stronger and safer. Fatherhood gives you the opportunity to do this in a way nothing else ever can or will.

Becoming a dad can add a profound sense of meaning to your life. Your views on life, priorities in the world and aspirations for your own future are forever altered. This is a good thing. By becoming a dad, you become part of the circle of life that has been going for eons. You're passing on the baton to your child, packed with all your wisdom and skills, to send your little one off on her own journey. You've got so much you can share with your offspring.

REMEMBER

Children need dads. A Canadian study showed that having a father in a child's life helps her develop empathy. Another long-term study showed that a father's involvement with his child from birth to adolescence helps build emotional stability, curiosity and self-esteem. If you're going to have a child, it will be better for you and for your family if you can be involved, committed and passionate about your new role. Your child deserves nothing less. She will feel stronger and safer if you're in her life in a positive, involved way.

Our children need involved fathers in their lives and, frankly, you owe it to yourself too. If you're going to be a dad, be a 100 per cent dad and experience it all. You wouldn't do other things in your life half-hearted, so get with it and give parenting your best shot. Make an effort, skill up and spend as much time as possible with your child. Doing so with all your heart makes you a better man.

WARNING

Being a 100 per cent dad makes you a better man because it will stretch you and challenge you in ways you can't imagine. That's how we grow — through challenge, trial and adversity. As daunting as that sounds, it's worth it. After all, who doesn't want to make more of themselves than they are now? Being a dad will do that for you.

Exploring care routine strategies

The question of how best to raise a baby is one of the most hotly contested subjects today. The rows of parenting psychology books on bookshop shelves attest to that. Some researchers have made the argument that over the last several centuries we've become disengaged from listening to our instincts. We've medicalised natural processes (such as birth and bonding) and slavishly followed rigid routines and overbearing doctor's orders that demanded that mother's (and even doctor's) convenience came first and baby's needs came second. We've joined the rat race and let work dictate our daily and weekly schedules. And we have sometimes looked beyond the mark in our quest to find happiness and create a healthy family.

If you think all the available parenting information is a bit too much, you're probably right. It's easy to feel overwhelmed by the vast amount of 'expert' advice that everyone is trying to give you about how to raise your child. Reading up on this material can be useful, but choose carefully. And remember, you and your partner are in charge of your child — and you decide how you want to bring her up.

Here are some common care routine strategies you may have heard of as you contemplate fatherhood:

>> **Strict routine.** In our parents' day, a strict routine with feeding and sleeping by the clock was promoted as being the best way to bring up a baby. Today, advocates of this method claim that having a strict routine or schedule establishes good habits early so you can minimise sleepless nights and excessive crying. For some parents, routines work a treat and their baby easily

slips into line. For others, their baby resists and parents end up even more stressed out that their little one won't play by the book. My tip: a strict routine is typically best for parents with twins or triplets.

>> **A routine, but not by the clock.** More common today, a flexible routine recognises that babies need to feed and sleep at regular intervals but, rather than let the clock determine when that might be, in this strategy reading your child's cues is the key to making the routine work. A pattern or routine of waking for a feed, feeding, having a nappy change, some play or awake time, and then back down for a sleep does occur. This pattern continues throughout the day, with no play or awake time at night. Chapter 7 has more about establishing a routine, and this is what I'd recommend for most families (with some exceptions for multiple children or parents with mental health challenges).

>> **Attachment parenting.** This form of parenting mimics parenting styles found in developing countries, where cots, bassinets and strollers are rare. Your child is in contact with you at all times of the day, is carried around in a sling or baby carrier, and sleeps with you at night, so she builds a strong bond and attachment with you. It's built around something called 'attachment theory' — a scientifically based description of how to create connection with your child that leads to positive outcomes. But much of attachment parenting in practice goes well beyond what research suggests, and devotees can become a little extreme.

REMEMBER

Many other strategies for raising a newborn exist. Do you leave her to cry when you put her down in order to teach her to fall asleep on her own (hint . . . definitely not in the first six months, and cautiously after that time), or rock her to sleep in your arms every nap time — which isn't practical either? Do you have the baby sleep in your bed, or have her in a bassinet in her own room? These are questions that you and your partner have to ponder and come up with your own answers to. And remember, there are the perfect 'text book' answers, and then there's the reality. You have to live with whichever strategy you come up with, so the strategy has to work for *you*. Chapter 6 gives you lots of ideas for raising a newborn with answers to these questions and many more.

TIP

Keep in mind that the way you want to run things in your family is up to you and your partner. Whether you adhere to a strict routine, or are a bit more laid back about it, as long as your little one is clean, fed and thriving, happy and cheerful, gets enough sleep, and is shown love and affection, she's going to be okay. Don't get caught in a trap of constantly comparing your baby to other babies; doing so generally leads to insecurity and stress and doesn't help you be a better dad. But ask questions of people who have been there, who have done it well, and who model great dadding. You need great guides. This book is one. They can be another.

REMEMBER

Another minefield you're going to have to get your head around is your child's education. Private, public, Steiner, Montessori, homeschool — these are all terms you're going to hear bandied about as your child gets older. Luckily for you, I've done some of the hard yards in Chapter 15 so you can figure out the educational maze for yourself.

TIP

As your baby turns into a toddler, you'll have to start thinking about discipline. People often think of discipline as the way you punish your child for being naughty. But that's not what discipline is about. Discipline is about creating an environment where your child can learn to adjust her behaviour and understand what's okay and what's not. The process involves teaching, guiding and instructing. Discipline's about clear boundaries, consistency and consequences. I talk more in depth about discipline in the Part 3 chapters.

The Seven Habits of Highly Successful Dads

I've observed certain habits and attributes in amazing dads — and these are traits that each and every man can develop on his journey to becoming a father.

Here are my top seven habits and attributes:

>> **Willingness to have a go:** Feeling truly confident about handling a newborn takes time, but think about it. If you want to learn a musical instrument or a new language, you're going to make a lot of mistakes. Maybe a million! Want to learn to be a great dad? Get your hands dirty (literally, in some cases), knowing you may get it wrong. That's how you learn. And it's also how you build that relationship. Don't feign incompetence and leave it to your partner. Have a crack. Show up. Get it done.

TIP

Can't get the nappy on properly? Have your partner, midwife or child health nurse show you. Then practice it ten times. You'll get it. If it's worth doing, it's worth doing badly until you can do it well.

>> **Selflessness:** After a life of doing the stuff you want to do, letting go of your agenda can be hard. The very best dads don't think less of themselves — but they do think of themselves less. While they are attentive to the needs of their little one, the most selfless thing they do is try to make life better for their partner. They find ways to serve and assist her, and lighten her load. They don't demand she think for the whole family. If you want to be an amazing dad, do stuff without being asked (such as cleaning the kitchen, making the bed, or running the bins to the bottom of the driveway). When she's over-whelmed, take the baby for a walk. This makes your relationship better and helps you be the best dad ever.

>> **They are comfortable in their masculine skin:** The best dads know who they want to be, and how they want to be. They know that real men make the people around them — especially those weaker than them — safer and stronger. This matters, because when your baby is colicky, or wakes every few hours at night, or is teething and cries constantly, you may be at the end of your tether trying to work out how to put a stop to that noise. And without a healthy view of masculinity, being less than your best is tempting. The truth is that often no solution is possible as you endure these challenges. You can't do anything to fix the problem or make a difference. It's just the way it is and you're going to have to deal with it. But understanding that everything in parenting comes and goes — that one day, your little one will sleep through, one day, your child will have all her teeth, and one day, she will grow out of colic — helps you endure the bad times while they last. And it's easier to do this well when you know who and how you want to be as a man, and as a dad.

REMEMBER

The early weeks of a baby's life are a little like one of those *Survivor*-type reality TV shows — except harder because you're dealing with a baby. Just surviving the sleep deprivation, the crying that grips your brain and shakes it about, and the never-ending rounds of feeding, burping, changing and settling can seem impossible. It feels like a marathon. But even marathons end sooner or later. The marathon runner has a vision for getting to the finish line and takes the steps to get there. It's the same with us as dads. You know you want to see that kiddo riding a bike, graduating school, finding a partner and living a good life. You've just signed up for a two-decade marathon . . . so see the finish line and take the steps to get there.

>> **Perspective:** When your child is upset, it's easy to see things from your perspective. You're tired. You're stressed. Mum's falling apart. It's all too much. Why won't the baby just eat, sleep, poo and leave you to live your life? Stepping back and seeing the world from your child's perspective — getting curious, not furious — will be your life saver.

TIP

Something happens when you pause and imagine life through your baby's eyes. Here's this kid . . . your kid. Non-verbal. Can't move. Needs something. Only one way to get it: scream. And while you're complaining, the gas in her tummy is building. Or the poo in her nappy has crawled up her back and it's burning her skin and stinking her out and feeling gross. Or she's got a pain but can't tell you where. And you're upset because you were halfway through that thing that matters to you? You're only human. But remember, now she's getting your negative vibe and starting to feel insecure about herself. A shift in perspective where you imagine — with real empathy — what she must be feeling, is an attribute of the very best dads.

>> **Playfulness:** Immerse yourself in all the tasks that need doing around your baby, toddler and child and make it fun (so long as it doesn't upset bubba). Adding some playfulness means you're likely to develop a passion for being a

dad. Your child picks up on your passion and is inspired to learn, develop and grow with you at an amazing pace. Play is one of the best ways for kids to develop and grow, and research shows dads can do playtime like a pro.

» **Patience:** Patience is a virtue — especially for dads. Patience is your friend and makes things a lot easier when you've got kids around. Without patience, you can just pop with anger — often leading to tears all round, even for you. Most of the learning in the early years (and perhaps even throughout life) is achieved through constant and frequent repetition. As a father, you're in the business of facilitating that learning, which means repeating yourself a lot, such as reading *Where the Wild Things Are* for the 53rd time, or telling your little one not to pour her milk in the fish tank for the 17th time. You can literally play peek-a-boo 400 times and your baby will still want more! As adults, we're often not great at dealing with constant repetition because it feels boring or frustrating, but repetition is just about the only way children can learn. By fostering your own patience you're able to elegantly deal with constant repetition and keep your calm. As a result, your child gets the support and encouragement she needs to learn. By being patient, you also avoid putting unnecessary pressure on your child to achieve something, which helps reduce frustration or feelings of inadequacy on her part.

» **Presence:** Taking time to be with your child and partner as a family is important. How you spend that time with your family is also important. Children have a finely tuned awareness of your attention. They can tell right away if you're actually engaging with them or merely present physically, with your mind miles away. Being present means you devote 100 per cent of your attention to your child and you focus on what she's doing. You don't watch movies online, scroll your social media video feed, or respond to emails at the same time as playing with your child. If you're hanging out with your child, be fully present and 'in the moment'.

To a child LOVE is spelled T-I-M-E. The best dads know this, and find a way to give it freely.

Help, I'm a Dad!

I wrote this book because I was once a new dad like you, starting out with mysterious new babies, literally wondering which way the nappy went on. It is tough at the start. Six kids later and grandbabies on the way, and all of that experience has become pretty handy. But starting out . . . whoa! I was clueless, and I needed a guide.

Being a dad can be scary. But it is more likely to be wonderful, and even awesome. Being a dad will leave you in awe. Your kids will have friends come and go. Even partners will come and go — hopefully the good ones will stay. But they'll only ever have one dad. You.

And for you, this role will become a vital part of your identity. Dadhood is the kind of role that many of us dads will judge our lives on. They say that no other success can compensate for failure in the home. This may seem like tough talk, but something inside us already kind of knows it.

If it matters that much, chances are, you want a guide on the side to help you out of some tough spots here and there.

Asking for directions

Unfortunately, most men don't do vulnerability that well. The stereotype remains mostly true: many men don't like asking for directions. That said, having a map or cool navigation gadgets often helps. That's why I worked with Beyond Blue to create Dadvice — to provide helpful advice for brand new dads.

TIP

You can find Dadvice at `healthyfamilies.beyondblue.org.au/pregnancy-and-new-parents/dadvice-for-new-dads`. Think of Dadvice as your map to fatherhood and this book as your journey planner. So you're off to a good start.

Finding trusted organisations and sources of information

In many ways, the people who know your baby best are you and your partner. You know what she likes and dislikes, what her little quirks are and when something doesn't seem right with her. The thing is that if we feel like we have all the answers, we might miss something important that can really make a big difference. And as hard as it can be to look elsewhere for answers, sometimes someone else may know what your baby needs more than you do. You can find great advice out there. Reading it, ingesting it, and growing with it are worthwhile.

REMEMBER

As adults, we're used to feeling like we're on top of most things; like we're pretty competent and capable. We know how to fix stuff. With babies and children, the situation is different. Many aspects of babyhood and childhood can't just be fixed. Things take time, expertise (sometimes not our own), and a truckload of compassion and humility — compassion for your baby and your partner, and humility for you because maybe you don't know as much as you thought you did. To overcome a particular issue, you may have to try lots of different approaches until you find one that fits.

Your first stop to finding these different approaches will probably be Google. But stick with this book for trusted, empirically sound ideas. You've also got friends and parents (although this can be tricky). And many people find their child health nurse to be a godsend. They have experience with all kinds of children, and can spend some time with your little one getting to know her and finding out what's going on. Another good place for information is the booklets and information you were given when your baby was born. Depending on where you live, your health service gives you a guide for basic baby and toddler care. These booklets often have good strategies for aspects such as starting to feed your baby solid food, coping with crying and dealing with nappy rash, along with local services you can call in times of need. Throwing them away as unnecessary may be tempting, but some can be valuable. Hold onto them . . . just in case.

Internet research

The internet's a pretty handy thing. With just a few keystrokes, you can search for anything your heart desires.

Anyone can build a webpage, run a blog or comment in a forum, but that doesn't mean they have the expertise you're looking for. Gauge the quality of the information provided on websites by checking the organisation or individual who's responsible for it, their credentials, affiliation with recognised authorities and any ulterior motives they may have, such as financial, political or religious reasons.

Once you're happy with the person or people providing the information and opinions, checking out forums where other dads are sharing their problems and offering solutions can be handy. Just don't take as gospel that everything they say is authoritative. And keep in mind that what works for one baby may not work for yours, and vice versa.

As a starting point, you can check the following sites for useful and trustworthy information:

>> **Dadvice** (search for it via Beyond Blue website, www.beyondblue.org.au, or go to healthyfamilies.beyondblue.org.au/pregnancy-and-new-parents/dadvice-for-new-dads): Written by dads for dads, the site contains information about all aspects of fatherhood from newborns to supporting your partner and looking after yourself.

>> **Raising Children Network** (raisingchildren.net.au): This non-profit site is supported by the Australian Government, the Royal Children's Hospital in Melbourne and the Parenting Research Centre. The site has articles on all aspects of looking after kids, from changing a nappy to the tricky questions of spoiling a baby and spotting allergies. The site also offers a special section for dads.

>> **Happy Families** (www.happyfamilies.com.au): Okay, maybe I'm taking advantage of the fact that I've written this book . . . but my website is full of articles, videos and other resources to help dads navigate the challenges parenting throws our way.

WARNING

If your baby or child is sick, avoid diagnosing her by searching the internet. After phoning a health service, a real live GP is your first port of call should you be concerned about your baby's health. For more about common health problems, check out Chapter 14.

Turning to friends, colleagues and family

When you're a new father, people are excited for you, and some may get a bit nostalgic for when their own children were little. They want to share with you their hard-won pieces of advice and may have an opinion on just about every aspect of looking after junior. Some of the advice may make sense to you; other gems are likely to seem bizarre. You just have to add each pearl of wisdom to your pile of approaches to try should you need to. Ultimately, you find out yourself whether or not something makes sense for your situation.

Turning to people who are close to you is an invaluable way to stay sane. If you're struggling, go hang out with a dad who's been through this experience. Looking at dads who've been through the crazy first weeks and months, and then come out the other side and want to have more kids, is a great way to get inspired and motivated for your own journey. You may at first think they've lost the plot but, really, these dads are no different from you. They've survived and, as many dads say, 'every day just gets better'. And, no, they haven't joined some terrible cult and become brainwashed — they've just had children and, one way or another, that tends to have a big impact on everyone.

Not long from now, you may be the one sitting down with a new dad, hearing tips and advice flow forth from your own mouth!

TIP

Don't overlook the power of your own dad. If he was a positive influence in your life, go to him, tell him you want to go a great job, and listen. Learn. Ask him what he wishes he'd known, what he would do differently if it all started again, and what he thinks he completely nailed. If he was a lousy influence and completely blew it, consider what talking to him about your experiences might do. The conversation could blow up and go nowhere. If that happens, though, you haven't lost anything because the relationship was a mess already. But what if you went to him and gently said something like, 'Things didn't work out so well for us. I'd like to talk with you about what you'd do differently, what you've learned, and what I can do so I can break the cycle for me and my little one.' Perhaps closure, forgiveness and new relationships might be possible. (But please enter a situation like this carefully. A wounded or manipulative, hurtful dad may not be good for anyone in your family.)

Starting a dad group

We all know a new dad or someone who's about to enter into the realm of father-hood. Lots of dads meet at antenatal classes and keep in touch after that. Getting together to talk and share your experiences doesn't need to be a formal affair, with chairs in a circle and 'feelings'. It can be meeting for a beer while junior snoozes in her stroller, or a coffee at a cafe with the little ones clamouring over each other on the floor. Getting together can be as simple as a gathering at the park. Finding new dads to join you should be easy, but if you're feeling a bit iso-lated, give your midwife or child health nurse a call to see if your carer has any dads living nearby on the books you could catch up with.

TIP

An easy way to get together with other dads is to use the mum networks. Ask your partner about speaking to other mums about a dad get-together. Before you know it, a BBQ, picnic or stroller walk has been magically arranged and you can take it from there.

Savouring dadhood

Numerous studies have shown that if we truly want to be happy, we need to savour the great stuff in our lives. To savour means we amplify or extend a positive expe-rience. How?

A great steak (or terrific seared tofu if you're a vegan) tastes so much better when you breathe in the aroma of that char-grilled finish, and when you then slowly place it on your tongue, close your eyes, and feel those juices flow through your mouth. Slowing the experience right down and concentrating on every smell and every flavour magnifies the taste. If we're really, truly savouring that piece of food, we often groan in the bliss of the moment.

As a dad, you experience plenty of times when you don't feel like you have anything to savour. Being a dad is hard work. And it will stretch you in ways you didn't know you could be stretched.

But being a dad is something you'll want to savour, especially while you have a newborn. When it comes to being a dad, the scariest part has nothing to do with poo explosions or having vomit on your shoulder — it's that it goes so fast. You may not feel like the hours and days are moving fast when your baby isn't sleep-ing, your partner is exhausted, everyone's sick, and you wonder why you ever thought it was a good idea to have this kid. But time really races by. Before you know it, your baby is crawling, then walking, then heading off to day care, and then big school. You'll look at your partner and say, 'Where did that time go?' So savour those moments. Take lots of photos. And relish every part of the breath-taking cuteness of your newborn baby.

Research shows that when children have an actively engaged dad, they do better. At every level. Your little one needs you. But studies also show that dads who spend more time with their children also do better. It seems you need your little one just as much.

BECOMING A GREAT DAD

In 2002 I was a young dad with a three-year-old and a newborn. And I was failing. I had no idea how to get it right. My temper was worse than my toddler's. My children had exposed some anger issues that I'd never known about before. And my marriage was looking shaky.

With the desire to save my family, I quit my job as a capital city radio announcer and returned to school for what would end up being nearly nine years of full-time study in psychology so I could learn to be a better dad and husband.

That decision changed my life. It helped me to learn how to support my family emotionally and psychologically — not just financially. And it's the reason I do what I do now.

While it involves a lot more, ultimately if we drill right down to the core, being a great dad means you have to be good at just a couple of jobs:

- **Love your kids and partner — and show it consistently.** You won't get it right all the time. No-one can. We're not perfect. But this has to be your number one priority. Do this through powerful connection, where your family feels consistently heard, seen and valued. When you do this, you build trust. They know you're acting in their best interest. And you connect and build trust most effectively when you stay positively, healthily and safely involved in their lives.

- **Work on boundaries together.** This means you act in a way that ensures your kids know you're there to provide protection (and to teach them to protect themselves), and to provide structure. The structure and boundaries you develop with them will make life feel predictable and safe. Focus on working with them when they need guidance, discipline and structure, rather than doing things to them.

(continued)

(continued)

If you can create an environment where you meet these needs, and support them to work things out for themselves (with your gentle input and encouragement), you'll be doing fine. Actually, you'll be doing better than fine. You'll be nailing it!

Unfortunately, you're going to make mistakes. Hey, you're only human. You can bet that, at times, you'll blow up, freak out, and not be the cool dad at all. Sometimes you might reckon it's justified. But remember — the best dads help their kids feel stronger and safer. If you're undermining how strong and safe they feel, you still have work to do.

When you get it wrong — and you will — say sorry. Repair things. Try again. And earn that 'world's best dad' coffee mug you know you're getting from the Father's Day stall at school a few years from now.

Also remember you have as many ways to be a good dad as there are dads in the world. Not all of them are good. But they can be. And so can you.

A good dad loves his kids, helps them feel safe and strong, and gives them the support and guidance they need as they have their hiccups, mistakes, setbacks and difficulties — whether they're emotional, behavioural, neurological, physical, spiritual, social or parental. A good dad is 'there'.

So as you embark on this parenting journey, prepare for the most challenging and frightful journey of your life. It's tough going. But keep your eyes out for the joy, because if you're 'there', you'll see a never-ending stream of tiny joyful glimmers that make it all worth the price of admission.

Chapter **2**

Getting Pregnant

D eciding to start a family with your partner is one of the biggest decisions you can make in your life. (Yes, bigger even than which footy team to support.) For some, starting a family's not even a decision — it just happens. For others, just getting on the starting line of fatherhood is a journey, with the pregnancy and birth still to get through before you earn your dad wings.

Getting pregnant can be as easy as a few rolls in the hay or it can be a long struggle. But the important thing is that you and your partner approach the journey to parenthood together, even if talking about fallopian tubes and sperm counts isn't really your thing.

You probably think you know what's involved in conceiving a child, but my guess is that you're in for a few insights and surprises as you read this chapter. I start off with some useful sex tips, and then outline the journey your sperm makes before reaching his lady-in-waiting, the egg, and the mission that egg undertakes to get to its safe haven, the uterus. You find out tips and tricks to getting pregnant, and what options are available if things just aren't coming together. And, finally, once things are underway, I guide you through the process of getting sorted for the coming months.

Here Comes the Fun Part

You've probably worked out where babies come from by now. Making babies is fun — and so it should be! Not many projects in life start with a little sexy time with your one and only. The rest of the journey may be exhausting, challenging or even frustrating at times, but at least this first step can be all about a good time.

So go on, have sex, and lots of it. Not many manuals tell you to do that, do they? In this section, I run through some tips for conceiving naturally, how to improve the odds, and what to do if conception doesn't seem to be happening. But first, let's talk about sex in the 21st century.

Getting consent — and getting sexy

Here I run through a few tips and aspects to remember about the sex side of things. And they matter. Take note.

Understanding the stages of sex

All kinds of models are available that explain how sex and arousal works. And it's different for men and women. For our purposes, I'm going to suggest sex has five stages: connection, desire, arousal, orgasm and resolution.

Connection is where it starts, particularly for a woman. In fact, if she doesn't feel connected (which I define as feeling seen, heard and valued), no-one's getting any sexy time at all. Smothering her with connection because of an ulterior motive will feel constraining and controlling. Instead, allowing connection to occur naturally and healthily will be the best way to get things moving.

Desire is not typically something men struggle with. But for women, it can sometimes be more of a challenge. Desire is about her mind being focused on *wanting* sexual progress.

Arousal comes next. (Actually, for men arousal is often what kicks off a push for connection and a build-up of desire.) For men, this stage happens quickly. Usually five to eight minutes is enough. Women typically need about 20 minutes of non-erotic touch before they become aroused. Touching breasts or genitals too soon can actually suppress, rather than enhance, arousal. Once arousal kicks off, it's usually going to be another 20 minutes before women move towards orgasm.

Orgasm is stage four. The common fantasy is that both partners orgasm together. This rarely happens, and when it does, researchers have found most people don't rate it that highly. But if we get it right, know this: women can have longer and stronger orgasms than men. And they can have more than one! But they can take a while to come, and it may take a lot of effort, especially compared to a man. Also note, most women need direct clitoral stimulation, and some studies indicate that only 20 to 30 per cent of women achieve orgasm through sexual intercourse alone. My tip: she comes first.

Resolution is the final stage. This is where we hug, stay close, and our body and brain releases all of those feel-good chemicals that bring us together in bonds that make us want to say all those beautiful things to each other. This stage lasts from several minutes through to a few hours, and during this stage further sexual activation is unlikely.

Checking in and asking for consent

The next thing to keep front and centre is this: regardless of the duration or intensity of your relationship, consent is king. And consent is sexy. You may think that because you've been together for a while, consent for your intimate activities is simply given. Not true. Your partner (or you, for that matter) may not always be up for it. Tiredness, stress, a disagreement between you both, monthly menstrual cycles, or any number of other reasons might mean she's not keen. Being in agreement at all stages of your sexy time is vital. But — and this is a big but — don't grovel, beg or plead. If your partner sighs, gives in and says 'fine', that's a pretty low bar. And you're missing out on the most important stages of sex — for you and for her.

TIP

Don't simply ask your partner, 'Do you consent to having sex with me?' Even if she did, she probably doesn't after a question like that. Instead, work consent into your sex. Walk up behind her as she gets ready for bed, for example, and run your hand up her neck and into her hair, massage the back of her neck, and ask, 'Do you like that? Would you like more of it?' As things heat up, check in with the same kinds of questions. Ask 'Would you like me to touch you there?' as you tease. Ratchet up the anticipation by *not* going for a home run (that's penetration, in case you missed the analogy) straightaway.

As you progress, keep gently checking in all along the way. Unless she tells you something along the lines of 'stop asking because you're ruining the vibe', consent is key. And you can turn it into a powerful and flirtatious aphrodisiac all the way along your foreplay and sexual journey. (The kink and BDSM community is *huge* on consent — and whether you're into that or not, you've got to admit that consent doesn't slow them down or get in the way of great sex.)

REMEMBER

Your partner may have some places she just doesn't want to go. Again, because you've likely been in a relationship for a while, you may know each other's no-go areas. But perhaps you're still exploring. A wide variety of sexual experience is waiting to be had, whether that be introducing sex toys or considering anal sex. As always, consent is king. Your partner may or may not like the idea of trying those things out. If she's not keen, pushing, poking and prodding may get you what you want in the short term, but will undermine your best efforts to have a healthy relationship in the long term. Nothing's less sexy than a guy pleading for a sex act his partner doesn't want.

Understanding your partner's build-up

To be clear, this is not a sex manual. But if you are with the woman you love and you plan on conceiving a child, you do want it to be a great experience — for both of you. Understanding that women's bodies prime differently to men's bodies helps with this. The desire and arousal stages of sex can take a long while for many women.

WARNING

Pornography has delivered heterosexual men a script that says women want lots of penetration — and that penetration is staggeringly satisfying, they're always ready for it, and it leads to amazing and orgasmic outcomes. That narrative isn't helpful for most couples, and can actually harm your sex life.

While many men can go from a complete sexual standstill to all done and dusted in no time, powerful, positive sex for a woman can take *at least* 45 minutes. And to be clear, that's not 45 minutes of penetrative intercourse. That's 45 minutes of touching, playing, kissing and so on. Patient and slow building of sexual tension and desire coupled with consent and communication usually leads to her satisfaction. And that, almost universally, will lead to your satisfaction. Making your partner happy by slowing down the process and making it about her will ultimately make it better for you both. So drop the porn script (if you've absorbed it) and learn to tease, taste and test. This will elevate your game with the woman you love, big time.

REMEMBER

A small percentage of women, regardless of their and their partner's best efforts, simply don't climax. If you and your partner need help in this area, seek medical or therapeutic help so you can work together to ensure your intimate lives remain positive and strong in this type of situation.

Knowing your partner's body

Another challenge we men face is that we can have a poor understanding of our partner's anatomy. I talk about female anatomy a bit over the next few pages, and understanding this area of your partner's body can really help as you move through pregnancy and beyond.

Chances are you've never really investigated her 'down there' bits closely. Perhaps some of what you do know comes from pornography, which probably isn't giving you the most realistic understanding. To improve this understanding, take a look at Figure 2-1, which shows the female genitalia.

TIP

If your partner is open to it, you can even do some real-life explorations so you know the difference between her labia and her vagina, and you can determine the difference between her clitoris and her g-spot (which is probably the back end of her clitoris). Let her know you want to understand so you can help her enjoy your intimate moments more. Hopefully, you can have positive conversations that lead to understanding. (But don't go there unless she consents and is comfortable with it.)

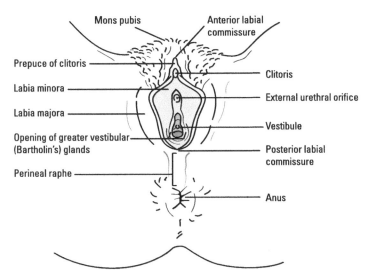

FIGURE 2-1:
Female internal and external genitalia.

Conceiving naturally

Now let's get to the 'becoming a dad' part of sex. In a perfect world, just making the decision to 'start trying' would result in an instant pregnancy. But nature didn't make the process that easy. Lots of barriers exist between your sperm and her egg; in fact, it's a miracle any of us were born at all.

Of the millions of sperm a man ejaculates during sex, only about 100,000 make it past his partner's cervix at the entrance to the uterus, having run the gauntlet of acidic vaginal secretions. (Figure 2-2 shows the female reproductive system.) Of the 100,000 sperm that get past the cervix, only 200 make it into one of the two *fallopian tubes* where a ready-to-be fertilised egg has made its way from an ovary and is waiting for a date — and that's *if* your timing is right and your partner is ovulating (producing an egg). Luckily, many sperm are present to start with because such a small percentage of them survive the journey. In the end, it's a merciless race to see which one of your sperm emerges as the champion and fertilises the egg by breaking into it.

Once the egg is fertilised, it moves down the fallopian tube and into the *uterus* or womb. Cell division starts and the tiny cluster of cells begins nestling into the lining of the uterus wall, also known as the *endometrium* (see Figure 2-3). The cluster of cells then starts another long journey transforming into an *embryo*, and after eight weeks *gestation*, into a *foetus*. Bingo — your baby is on his way.

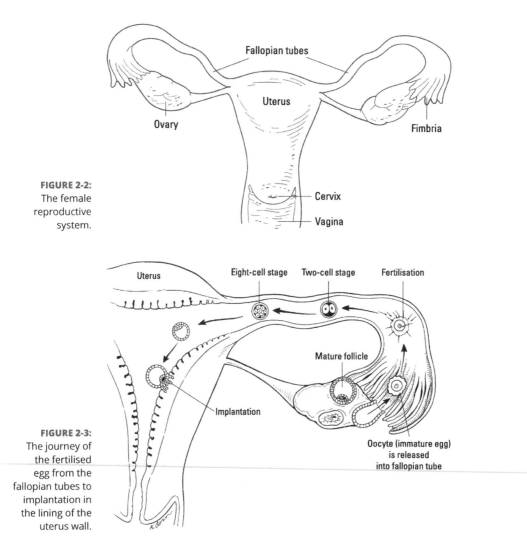

FIGURE 2-2:
The female reproductive system.

Fallopian tubes

Uterus

Ovary

Fimbria

Cervix

Vagina

Uterus   Eight-cell stage   Two-cell stage   Fertilisation

Mature follicle

Implantation

Oocyte (immature egg) is released into fallopian tube

FIGURE 2-3:
The journey of the fertilised egg from the fallopian tubes to implantation in the lining of the uterus wall.

Improving the odds — pregnancy tips and tricks

Like a lot of things, getting pregnant is a matter of having quality equipment and good timing. Nail those and your chances of getting pregnant are pretty good.

But you can help things along with the following:

>> **Being fighting fit:** For prospective fathers as well as mothers, the healthier you are, the better for conception. Now's a good time to stop smoking, lay off the booze and other recreational drugs, get an exercise routine, and eat well.

>> **Staying put:** Try to ensure your partner doesn't get straight up for the 'loo routine' after sex. Your partner can help those precious sperm get to their destination by keeping horizontal with her pelvis tilted upwards. While no scientific evidence shows that lying down after sex will increase the odds that you'll conceive, some evidence exists that standing up and heading to the bathroom can cause gravity to pull sperm away from their journey. The chances of it being an issue are low, but it's good for your relationship to stay put for a short while anyway. So keep some tissues handy, cuddle up, and have some extra skin-to-skin time for about 15 minutes before you decide that it's all over.

>> **Making a date:** *Ovulation* is when an egg is produced ready for fertilisation. The process occurs on approximately day 14 of a 28-day menstrual cycle, with day one being the first day of your partner's period. So plan for that time to be your sexy time. If your partner's cycle is irregular or you just need more reassurance, try an ovulation test kit to tell you if the time is right for lurve. Ovulation test kits are urine tests that detect hormones, like a pregnancy test kit. Getting stuck into conversations around dates and timing can be kind of unsexy, so be intentional about flirting, sending sexy text messages and snaps, and upping the sexual tension so it doesn't turn into a 'just get it done' process. You want to enjoy this together, right?

>> **Making sure your little fellows are in tiptop shape:** Have a health check. Your doctor can check for any signs of sexually transmitted disease, any anatomical problems such as an undescended testicle and any other issues, such as low sperm count, that you may not be aware of.

>> **Checking on medication:** Some prescribed medication as well as over-the-counter drugs can have a negative effect on mum or baby, so check with your doctor before taking anything during pregnancy.

>> **Practising:** Have sex at least once a day when your partner is ovulating. If you feel a little put off by scheduled sexy time, just do it all the time — even in the off season. You never know what might happen. Being 'in the mood' for sex should also help conception! Finally, do some research on positions that aid conception and try them out — now that's an assignment you can enjoy!

REMEMBER

Stress can affect your partner's ovulation, so try not to get too worked up about not getting pregnant straightaway. For some, these things take time. Worrying about it won't make things happen any faster. Wanting to get pregnant is a great excuse for having sex, so just enjoy it for a while.

REMEMBER

Health experts advise your partner takes *folic acid* if you're trying for a baby. Taking folic acid won't improve your chances of getting pregnant but it does improve your chances of conceiving a healthy baby. See Chapter 3 for more information about the effects of taking folic acid on your unborn baby.

Conception's not happening

You've been trying for months. And trying. And trying. But conception's just not happening. You're getting sick of sex — as if you ever thought that would be a problem. But, yep, you may be feeling exactly like sex is the last thing you'd like to do. As they say, too much of a good thing, and so on. So don't beat yourself up over feeling sex-tired.

WARNING

Couples under 35 years of age who have been having regular unprotected sex for a year and haven't become pregnant are said to be infertile, and those over 35 years old are deemed infertile after six months. If this is you, it could be time to talk to your doctor about getting some help. See the following section for more information about infertility.

Understanding What Can Go Wrong

Approximately one in six Australian couples has an issue with getting pregnant. A lot of factors in both partners can cause infertility, but here I just look at what factors could be affecting you. Around one in six guys across Australia experiences infertility, and problems on the male front can account for 40 per cent of 'infertile' couples not being able to get pregnant. Low sperm counts, blockages to the sperm being ejaculated, poor sperm motility (ability to move), and sperm with an abnormal shape account for most fertility problems among guys.

Working out why conception hasn't happened

The following factors can contribute to infertility in men:

>> **Anatomical problems** such as erectile dysfunction or blockage caused by a varicose vein, called a *varicocele*, that connects to the testicle

>> **Exposure to harmful substances** and heavy metals (*not* heavy metal music such as Metallica or Pantera)

>> **Lifestyle**, such as smoking and drug taking, which can slow sperm

>> **Overheating sperm** by having frequent hot baths or wearing tight fitting underwear or tight trousers (be careful with those tight jeans if you're planning on procreating)

>> **Sexually transmitted diseases** such as gonorrhoea and chlamydia.

REMEMBER

In 40 per cent of cases of male infertility, the cause may not be known. Either way, going for a check-up is a good thing to do. So be a man and get on top of this — if a problem exists, at least you know and chances are you can do something about it. This reduces stress overall and your partner will appreciate you even more for having a check-up.

REMEMBER

If the issue is not with you but your partner, be aware that this will most likely be a rough time for her and she's possibly going to be feeling like something of a failure. A lot of women believe that being able to carry and nurture a child is an essential part of being a woman, and not being able to do this may leave her feeling inadequate. As her partner, you're in the best position to help her feel just as whole a woman no matter what. No woman (or man) should feel like they're not enough because of fertility issues. They need support, not condemnation.

Exploring other ways to get pregnant

If your partner is having trouble falling pregnant, the first step is to talk to your doctor. In some cases, lifestyle factors may be what are holding you back and if the problem is a blockage, surgery could help. But in other cases, you may need to consider *assisted reproductive technologies*, otherwise known as calling in the baby-making experts.

Some of the treatments you may want to talk about with your doctor or specialist include the following:

>> **Artificial insemination (AI):** Semen is collected, given a bit of a clean-up, and then inserted into your partner's vagina, uterus or fallopian tubes. And, yes, you'll be the one responsible for delivering that semen sample into a plastic container.

>> **In vitro fertilisation (IVF):** Your partner is given hormone treatments to ramp up her ovulation. When she is ovulating, your partner goes through a procedure where her eggs are harvested. The collected eggs are then mixed with your sperm and given a chance to be fertilised. The fertilised eggs are put

into your partner's uterus, and then you wait to see if they settle into the uterine wall.

>> **Intracytoplasmic sperm injection (ICSI):** Sounds sexy doesn't it? Rather than mix sperm and egg and wait to see which eggs are fertilised, sperm is injected straight into the egg. As with IVF, the fertilised eggs are placed into your partner's uterus, where hopefully one implants.

WARNING

If you use IVF or other assisted reproductive technology, be aware of the increased chance of multiple births. According to a recent report in the UK, on average one in four IVF treatments result in multiple pregnancies, compared with one in 80 naturally conceived pregnancies.

With IVF, sometimes two embryos are placed into the uterus, increasing the chances of having twins. In Australia, some clinics won't allow you to transfer more than two embryos. This is because the chance of complications during pregnancy and birth, such as premature birth or *pre-eclampsia* (a pregnancy complication characterised by high blood pressure), is higher with multiple pregnancies than with a single baby.

REMEMBER

About two-thirds of couples dealing with infertility do have a baby through these kinds of strategies, so medical intervention's definitely worth finding out about. Ask questions, even if doing so can feel a bit embarrassing at the start. By the way, this is good training for going through birth — many more embarrassing moments to come!

ADOPTING

You've been having sex on schedule for years now and had the tests to make sure your little guys are not only plentiful but frisky as well. Your partner has been through multiple cycles of IVF but it just hasn't worked out and all the trauma of not getting pregnant is way past its use-by date. Perhaps you've decided to give up on having a child of your own.

Being unable to conceive a child doesn't have to mean you can't be a father. Adoption is another option you can look at.

Adopting a child means you take on the parental rights and responsibilities of looking after that child as you would if you were his biological father. That's a lifetime's responsibility. Loving your own child unconditionally can be tough at times, but to do so for a child who is not biologically yours might be a stretch for some men. Take this option slowly, but don't wait too long. Adoption policies around age of adoptive parents are quite strict. If you're up for it and have the confidence you can provide the loving support that child needs — and that you can be the dad you hope to be — go for it. Be aware, though, that most (though not all) adoptions these days are open adoptions, which means the child and his birth parents stay in touch with each other.

The number of babies who are put up for adoption in Australia is much lower than it was a generation ago — in fact, it's staggeringly low. In 2020–21, just 264 adoptions were finalised in Australia — including 42 inter-country adoptions and 222 Aussie child adoptions. Often the adoptions are of children already known to the family (through relatives). And adoption numbers have declined by around two-thirds in the past 25 years.

In Australia, each state has different departments that look after adoption services. Check the service in your area:

- **ACT:** www.communityservices.act.gov.au/ocyfs/children/adoptions/adopting-a-child-from-the-act
- **New South Wales:** www.facs.nsw.gov.au/families/adoption
- **Northern Territory:** nt.gov.au/community/child-protection-and-care/adoption
- **Queensland:** www.qld.gov.au/community/caring-child/adoption
- **South Australia:** www.childprotection.sa.gov.au/adoption
- **Tasmania:** www.decyp.tas.gov.au/children/adoptions-and-permanency-services/adoption-services/
- **Victoria:** www.justice.vic.gov.au/your-rights/adoption/adopt-a-child
- **Western Australia:** www.wa.gov.au/organisation/department-of-communities/adoption-and-providing-permanent-care-child

Wow! You're Going to Be a Dad

Okay . . . so you've gone through all of the procreative acts. Conception may or may not have occurred. How will you know it's happened?

Are your partner's boobs sore? Check.

Period missed? Check.

Thrown up for no reason? Check.

No guarantees just yet, but it's starting to sound like pregnancy is on the cards which means . . . that you're potentially going to be a dad (or your partner just had a really stressful week). Either way — don't panic. If your partner is really pregnant, you've got around nine months to sort out your new life. Say goodbye to how you currently live, farewell the days of tidy living rooms, sleeping-in and comfortable hours of self-indulgence, and say hello to fatherhood! So with that in mind, a baby taking around 40 weeks to grow from a tiny cluster of cells into a living, breathing, crying baby is really a good thing. This time allows you to get a few things in order, indulge yourself or do some wild stuff before your baby arrives.

Getting confirmation

Your partner is likely to have raced off to the nearest pharmacy the moment she suspected she might be pregnant. Over-the-counter pregnancy tests can sometimes give inaccurate results, so even if you have a positive result from a test, the first thing you want to do is make sure the pregnancy thing is actually happening.

Make an appointment with your GP, who is likely to give your partner a urine test to see what levels of the hormone human chorionic gonadotropin (HCG) are present — that's the hormone thought to be responsible for the morning sickness and bone crunching tiredness your other half has to look forward to. If the test shows increased levels of HCG (that is, a positive result), your doctor may perform a gynaecological examination on your partner to check the physical signs of pregnancy more closely. But even your GP is only able to provide a definite answer when the pregnancy symptoms are clear, which is around four weeks after fertilisation. So holding off telling the world may be a good idea — in fact, you may want to wait until the first scan anyway. Find out more about ultrasound scans and breaking the news to others in Chapter 3.

REMEMBER

Once you've received confirmation of your pregnancy, a quiet (or loud) celebration with your partner is in order. However, it has to be a celebration unlike most you've likely had in the past because alcohol, cigarettes and other drugs are definitely off the menu. But, hey — you can find plenty of other ways to have a good time. (Sex is definitely still *on* the menu!)

TIP

If you're both drinkers and you've decided that, for the health of the baby, your partner will stay off the drink, you might want to abstain in solidarity with her. The 'pregnant pause' campaign (pregnantpause.com.au), which is run through the Foundation for Alcohol Research and Education (FARE), reminds mums and dads of the risks to baby when alcohol is mixed with pregnancy. The website also provides tips to help you be a great support to your partner by taking time off the grog so she doesn't feel like she's missing out. Go on. It's the least you could do.

Knowing what to do next

Now that you know it's happening, welcome to the exciting new world of *antenatal*, or pre-birth, care. This was once strictly the domain of the pregnant woman and her doctor (usually male for some reason), but things have changed. For starters, you as the dad are going to be much more involved (say 'yes!'). And you also have more choices about who you team up with for the journey to parenthood. Your GP can refer you to maternity services in your area and generally you have the choice of paying for care from a private obstetrician or midwife, hiring a doula or birthing expert, or staying in the public health system with a hospital or independent midwife.

The role of your carer of choice is to guide you through the pregnancy, birth and early weeks of your baby's life. Your carer should have the medical training and ability to monitor the baby's growth and wellbeing, and to check for conditions such as pre-eclampsia and *gestational diabetes*. Your carer also works with you to come up with a birth plan (see Chapter 3 for more details on birth plans), delivers your beautiful new baby and helps you in the first few days after birth. This may include getting your partner started with breastfeeding or helping with basic baby care tasks such as bathing or changing a nappy. In general, your lead maternity carer is your 'go-to' person if you have any questions, health issues or just need someone to talk to during the pregnancy. So check with your carer first before contacting other services or professionals. You may find that you'll work with a variety of people to ensure each of these tasks is taken care of.

REMEMBER

Yes, a lot of attention during this time is on the mum-to-be. But that doesn't mean you can't be involved in talking through the kind of care your partner and unborn child receive. You, as dad, have a very important role in the making of your family, so don't feel embarrassed or afraid to ask about anything you're not sure of. Just remember, decisions about pregnancy, labour and birth are best made by the person most affected by these things. You might have opinions on what happens and when, but you're not the one going through the labour and birthing that baby. If disagreements emerge between you and your partner, get curious, not furious. Explore, don't explode. The best thing you can do is be there, be helpful, and support and affirm her, and encourage safe, healthy living. If you want to be really helpful, do some of the thinking so your partner doesn't have to carry the baby *and* the cognitive load of making the house and relationship function. Use your initiative with the practical stuff — plan dinners, for example, organise outings or make the bed and do the laundry.

Choosing a carer

The childbirth industry is chock full of people and organisations to assist with care for your partner and baby: midwives, birthing centres, doulas, obstetricians and hospitals are just a few. Knowing who does what can help you decide where you would like your baby to be born, and what kind of care you would like to receive during and immediately after birth.

Here's a rundown of the types of mainstream carers you can choose between:

>> **GPs** are your general family doctor. They aren't specialists in antenatal care or childbirth, but in rural settings, they can work with the local hospital to provide maternity care. Even in cities, they'll often be your first port of call for basic medical info.

>> **Midwives** are trained health professionals who give antenatal care, deliver babies, help establish breastfeeding and stick around for up to four to six weeks after the birth to help when you're unsure about your baby's health and wellbeing. Midwives can also ensure the recovery of mums to a healthy state. Midwives take a holistic approach to pregnancy and birth, and often counsel you as a family, acknowledging not just the physical challenges of becoming new parents, but also the importance of your mental and social wellbeing. They see pregnancy and birth as a natural process, not a medical one, and can sometimes deliver your baby at home. While they're trained in their field, midwives aren't doctors and don't perform *caesareans* or prescribe medication (although they can prescribe some specialist drugs). If you choose to go with a midwife and complications arise during the pregnancy or birth, the midwife most likely arranges for you to see an obstetrician in the public health system. Many health systems have you primarily cared for by midwives from conception through till post birth check-ups.

>> **Doulas** are trained supporters who assist your partner before, during and after the birth. They're kind of like a non-medical bestie for your partner — someone who will advocate for her when things fire up during labour. Their job is not to replace a midwife or obstetrician, but to be there to support your partner to have a comfortable labour. They also help with practical aspects such as setting up the home to provide a great environment for bub, and assist with the emotional adjustment that comes with the arrival of your baby.

>> **Obstetricians** are doctors who specialise in *obstetrics*, or the health of women and babies during pregnancy, birth and after the birth, called the *postpartum* or *postnatal* period. They generally work in hospitals and are often the choice of couples experiencing complications during pregnancy, or who have had trouble getting pregnant. If you choose to use an obstetrician as your carer, you have to pay for it. And it can be costly. In Australia, some of the fees can be claimed back through a Medicare rebate. (You'll generally pay for most private health care, but the obstetrician/gynaecologist role is typically the most specialised and expensive.)

If you've chosen an obstetrician as your carer, during the birth, midwives or hospital nurses are on hand to monitor your baby's progress. Typically, the obstetrician arrives only for the late stages and delivery itself. You may have heard stories describing how an obstetrician only showed up *after* the baby was born. These stories can leave some parents wondering if they might be paying a lot for nothing. This isn't the case. Obstetricians are primarily concerned with the physical health of the baby and mother, and don't help you with any non-medical baby care issues after birth. For example, they won't come to your house to show you how to best change your little nipper's nappy.

TIP

I strongly recommend looking around for a birth and labour coach who believes in empowering dads to better support their partners during labour. Most antenatal courses that are hospital run (see Chapter 3) cover the basics but are fairly neutral on how dad can be a great support. In fact, I'd argue that dads can be sidelined, sometimes quite strongly and insensitively. But some people provide powerful strategies for helping mum through labour — while also giving great guidance for dads who want to be an active support rather than a yawning, nervous appendage who stands around like an idiot feeling guilty and inadequate while he waits for it all to end. Do your homework on this. Finding such a carer and coach may end up being one of the most rewarding investments you'll make in your life.

REMEMBER

Talk with whoever you choose as your maternity carer about the options for where your baby can be born: at home, in hospital or in a birthing centre. The availability of birthing options depends on where you live and the carer you have.

Take time to find the right maternity carer for you. As well as getting referrals from your GP, a good place to start is with recommendations from your friends and colleagues. Make sure you're really happy with your carer and that you've got 'good chemistry'. Things can get pretty hectic during pregnancy or birth, so make sure you're in good hands and you're comfortable with your carer's personal and professional style. If you're not happy with your carer, consider changing. Both of you must be 100 per cent comfortable with your choice of carer.

CHECK THE NET

To find out what services and carers are available in your area, check out www.healthdirectory.com.au. To find a private midwife, go to www.midwivesaustralia.com.au/women/find-a-midwife and to find a doula go to www.doulanetwork.org.

Things to do before morning sickness starts

Your life is about to change forever, so there's no time like the present to do some of those things you might have to trade in when your child is born.

To celebrate your impending fatherhood while you're not a father yet, think about the following:

>> Unprotected sex (with your partner) will no longer result in pregnancy — so go for it! (Of course, this assumes you're clear from disease and faithful to her and your relationship. Risks from STIs still exist during pregnancy.)

>> Have the holiday of your lifetime. Holidaying won't be the same for the next 18 years or so (maybe longer, depending on how many kids you have), so make the most of your time now.

>> Ponder your own experience growing up and which things you would like your child to experience.

>> Sleep in late and cook a leisurely brunch for you and your partner regularly.

>> Splurge on something indulgent, such as going to a fancy restaurant or a day spa.

>> Start a blog or scrapbook to document the months leading up to your child's birth and make it a memento to give your child when he's older (yes — plenty of good material for an embarrassing 21st birthday slideshow).

>> Skill up on massage techniques and practise on your partner. Invest in a few good-quality aromatherapy oils and some sweet almond oil.

Morning sickness doesn't affect every woman who becomes pregnant. And life still goes on, even after a baby is born. But the central message is this: savour this time. It's really special. And you'll want to make memories, so long as your partner isn't too sick to eat, have fun and be a little bit active. (If she is, be patient and compassionate. Growing a baby is a big deal.)

Chapter **3**

Pregnancy: A Drama in Three Acts

Pregnancy is a bit like *The Lord of the Rings* trilogy: it has a beginning where the scene is set and a bit of chaos occurs, a middle where things calm down a bit and an end where everything comes to a head. The three distinct parts of pregnancy are called *trimesters* and each has its scary and great bits (just like in the films), such as the first time you hear your baby's heartbeat at a check-up, feel your baby kick inside mum's belly, or see your baby's squashed up body twisting and turning on an ultrasound screen.

The easiest part of becoming a dad is the pregnancy bit. Dads don't get the morning sickness and leg cramps, and we're not the ones who sometimes feel as if we can't get out of bed without a crane. By the end of the pregnancy, you're probably going to be right on top of what aches this week, or what bizarre food your partner has to have *right now*, but the worst pregnancy symptom you'll usually experience is tiredness because your partner is uncomfortable trying to sleep.

But just because you're not dealing with soreness and other ailments doesn't mean you can't do anything during pregnancy. Apart from all the preparations (which I talk about in this chapter and also in Chapter 4), you can do loads with your partner to help her out a bit and to get to know your offspring (yes — before he's even born!). Your partner definitely needs a present and participatory man for the finale: 'birth' (which I cover in detail in Chapter 5).

In this chapter, I take you through the three trimesters of pregnancy and tell you a bit about what your baby is up to on the inside. I also take the mystery out of morning sickness and explain why your partner may experience sore boobs — and everything else.

Act One: The First Trimester

After the initial excitement that you're going to be a dad, the hard yards of supporting your partner through pregnancy begin. Realistically, supporting your partner's not actually 'that' hard, but you get to demonstrate your commitment to your new role when the initial ultrasound scan clashes with an all-important meeting you had arranged for that day.

Eating enough to make a baby

During pregnancy, your partner is literally 'making the baby', so good ingredients are essential for a quality end product, meaning that your unborn baby needs good food. Mum's healthy diet during pregnancy has a profound impact on the wellbeing of your little one even later in life, so work on healthy food choices together.

WARNING

Don't let any diet discussion turn into an awkward 'control' scenario. A bloke dictating his partner's food choices or creating guilt in her by food shaming is an ugly thing.

TIP

The best way to navigate this diet conundrum is to ask your partner how she wants to approach diet over the next 30 to 40 weeks, and go all in with her. For you, this may mean also laying off unhealthy options — because nothing is worse than tempting a pregnant woman with food and drink she can't or shouldn't have.

Mum also needs good food to help her deal with the physical, mental and emotional changes and challenges she faces until your baby is born.

REMEMBER

The 'eating for two' approach is an unhelpful pregnancy myth — no matter what Great Aunt Beryl may tell you. The female body only requires 10 to 12 per cent more energy when pregnant.

So, what is 'good food'? Your partner needs the following:

>> **Six servings of fruit and vegetables:** An apple or tomato is a serving, so is half a cup of salad. Leafy green vegetables are particularly good because they contain folic acid, which helps prevent birth defects such as spina bifida (see Chapter 18 for more about birth defects).

>> **Six servings of grains:** A cup of cooked pasta or rice, or a slice of wholegrain bread or a bread roll makes a serving. Wholegrains are particularly useful because — you guessed it — they contain folic acid. (In September 2009, Australia introduced folic-acid enriched breadmaking flour. New Zealand followed suit in 2021.)

>> **Three servings of dairy:** A large glass of milk, a tub of yoghurt or two slices of cheese are each a serving.

>> **Two servings of protein:** An egg, or two slices of lean red meat, or two chicken drumsticks are one serving. Vegetarians can also get protein from nuts and seeds, legumes and tofu.

REMEMBER

Folic acid, also called folate, is a B vitamin that's important to help prevent birth defects such as spina bifida. Eating folate-rich foods such as wholegrains, chickpeas, leafy green vegetables, and Vegemite helps you reach the recommended daily allowance of 500 micrograms (0.5 milligrams). Your partner can also top up her folic acid intake by using vitamin supplements. Check the recommended amount of folic acid for your partner because some women in a high-risk category need more.

WARNING

Most guides will recommend that mums shouldn't eat certain foods because of the risk of bacteria, such as *Listeria monocytogenes*, to which pregnant women and unborn babies are vulnerable. While some question marks exist about the strength of the evidence for some of these foods, it's better to be safe than sorry. To be on the safe side, don't go treating your partner to:

>> Cold sliced meats (such as hams and salami) or pâté, and any raw meats

>> Pre-packaged ready-made salads that you'd buy in a store. (Instead fresh and homemade salads are a good alternative because the risk of listeria toxicity is far lower when you make it yourself.)

>> Soft cheeses such as brie, ricotta and blue vein

>> Sprouted seeds

>> Sushi

>> Unpasteurised milk

Ask your GP, obstetrician or midwife for a comprehensive list of foods to avoid.

TIP

By the end of her pregnancy, your partner may be really hanging out to eat a good bit of brie again, so a great way to celebrate the baby's birth may be to put together a platter of the things your partner's been missing out on for nine months. Start a 'foods to remember after birth' list.

Dealing with common side effects in the first trimester

For some unfortunate mums, the first three months of pregnancy are a downright drag and can feel like an illness rather than the beautiful natural process of creating life. No glow can be seen and no bump is present to show off. Instead, as your baby makes himself comfy in your partner's uterus, he's making his presence known in other ways. Symptoms vary wildly from woman to woman, so you have no way of exactly knowing what's going to hit your partner. The following sections cover some common complaints.

REMEMBER

Some women don't have any of these issues, and some have them at level 10! Your partner not having strong symptoms isn't a sign of problems. She might just be lucky. On the other hand, if your partner is struggling, think about how you want her to react to you when you have a serious case of 'man flu'. (We all know how serious that can be, and how much pampering we need when it strikes.) Your partner needs that same level of love and care to get through this. But while man flu only lasts a few days or a week at most, for some women this pregnancy sickness can go the distance.

Jokes aside, care during pregnancy is really serious for you, your partner and your baby. In serious cases, these issues can be life-threatening. Be involved, and listen to good quality, specialised medical advice. If you have any concerns, involve your medical professionals.

REMEMBER

During the next nine months, you're going to learn a whole new vocabulary and get to know your partner's insides more than you may want to. The Glossary lists terms to help you decipher what your carer of choice is talking about. If you're unsure of where the various parts of the female reproductive system are located, refer to Chapter 2.

Morning sickness

Morning sickness typically involves feeling nauseous and vomiting. The condition is common and is usually experienced during the first three months of pregnancy. Morning sickness doesn't pose a risk to the baby unless it's very severe. Nausea can come on at any time but is usually worse in the morning because your partner's stomach is empty. At its worst, morning sickness is like having a hangover and being seasick at the same time, so no wonder your partner is off to the bathroom once again. If you're like me, you'd choose death or swimming back to dry land over being seasick, so try to get your head around how rough morning sickness must be! (Bathrooms also become a prominent feature in the last trimester, albeit for different reasons — your partner needs to wee what seems like every ten minutes because the baby puts pressure on her bladder.)

TIP

One thing that makes morning sickness worse is getting up on an empty stomach, so try having a plate of dry crackers or toast with Vegemite ready for your partner to nibble when she first wakes up. Other tips include eating smaller portions more often during the day, increasing intake of carbohydrates and reducing intake of fats, and stimulating pressure points on the inner arm just above the wrist crease.

WARNING

Morning sickness can get so bad that your partner may become dehydrated. The symptoms aren't always easy to spot so double-check with your midwife, obstetrician or GP if your partner is having a really rough time with morning sickness. In particularly serious cases, medical carers may recommend hospitalisation. It can be that bad!

Exhaustion

Your baby is growing rapidly. Believe it or not, it takes a lot of your partner's energy to keep this process moving along. Just getting through a day at work may be more than your partner's up to, so you can score lots of points if you take on more of the household chores, prepare meals and do the things your partner's not up to doing. Bonus points if you do it without being asked.

Heightened sense of smell

Pregnancy does strange things to a woman, not least of all her ability to smell everything. Your partner can walk into a room you left three hours ago and smell your aftershave. She's likely to be sensitive to most smells, especially things such as perfume, food and petrol fumes — they may even make her vomit — so if you're heating your favourite garlic bread (the one with extra garlic), open a window or put on the range hood.

Tender breasts

What was your favourite dessert when you were growing up? Do you remember seeing the dessert, in the fridge or cooling on the bench, hours before dinner, and being told you could 'look, but don't touch'. For many expectant dads, the same concept might now apply in the bedroom. Pregnancy hormones cause your partner's breasts to become a bit bigger, but in some cases they're sore and tender. So while you may be admiring your partner's new wonder boobs, it pays to wait until she invites you to party before gatecrashing her bra.

REMEMBER

Consent, as always, is king. And, in most cases, the tenderness and pain does subside — which means you'll both enjoy several months of booby bliss.

Moodiness

Blame any moodiness during pregnancy on the hormones. Your partner hasn't turned into a grumpy, unpredictable monster — she's just at the mercy of her body. Go easy on her if she's a little ratty right now. Talk to her and figure out a way to communicate when she's feeling emotional or grumpy, because *progesterone*, the hormone responsible for all this, isn't going to go away for a long time yet.

TIP

A gentle way forward is to name or describe how she's feeling (with empathy), and ask if she wants space or company. You might simply say, 'It's been a rough day hasn't it? You're feeling awful. Would you like me to stay and be close to you, or do you just need space?' Note that sometimes the moodiness will be so utterly challenging that she may not know what she wants. If that's the case, hug her until she asks you to leave. But remember that if she does tell you to leave, it's not about you. It's not personal, it's pregnancy. Stay low key. Don't pressure her to cheer up. Just be there until it passes.

ACTIVITIES TO AVOID

Some activities aren't recommended for mums-to-be, such as:

- Going on rides in theme parks (because of the acceleration the body experiences during the ride)

- Extreme sport and adventure sport (such as bungee jumping, parachuting and wild water rafting)

- Dyeing her hair (because of the chemicals used in dyes)

- Travelling on a plane (in case the baby decides to arrive early, although this is mostly relevant towards the end of the pregnancy)

For a comprehensive list of things to avoid, ask your GP, obstetrician or midwife.

Remember: Though your partner's feeling crappy, this is your chance to shine. You can treat your partner and make her feel special in lots of simple ways at this difficult stage. Come home with a little gift (baby socks are great), shout her a pregnancy massage (along with some nice oils to battle stretch marks), or choose a nice movie for the night (stick with rom-coms — action stuff usually doesn't work so well). If your partner bites your head off for trying, don't take it personally. Try again next week.

Finding out what your baby's up to

Between 6 and 12 weeks, your baby grows from 6 millimetres long to 5.5 centimetres long (see Figure 3-1). In other words, your baby has grown 900 per cent in six weeks. No wonder your partner is so tired.

During this time, your baby's organs take shape, with the heart beating from about six weeks. Though neither you nor your partner can feel him yet, your little tadpole (babies look like that at the beginning) is moving around in there. He's floating in amniotic fluid in his amniotic sac. The placenta is developing to act as life support for your baby.

REMEMBER

Your first ultrasound scan, which typically happens between 6 and 12 weeks after conception, is a pretty big deal for a couple of reasons. First, you get to see your baby for the first time ever and it's an amazing sight. Second, in some cases, your doctor may unfortunately advise you that something isn't quite right. This happens in about one in six cases and may result in miscarriage or termination of the pregnancy for medical reasons (see the sidebar 'Dealing with the grief of miscarriage').

REMEMBER

Significant decisions need to be made in relation to aborting a pregnancy, so seek medical advice (and any other advice from trusted confidants) and be sure you and your partner are on the same page. You *don't* want to force issues here. Your doctor typically prepares you before your first scan, but talking about this scenario with your partner before you have your scan is a good idea.

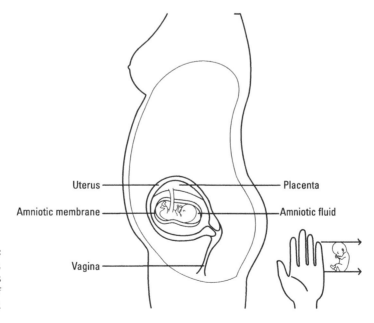

FIGURE 3-1:
At 12 weeks, your baby is about the size of your little finger.

Uterus

Amniotic membrane

Vagina

Placenta

Amniotic fluid

TWO (OR MORE) FOR THE PRICE OF ONE

You've just found out, through the magic of an ultrasound scan, that you're going to be a father of not one, but two babies at once. You're freaking out. Being dad to two at the same time is hard work — but, of course, it's not unmanageable. Being dad to two at the same time is a great opportunity to be twice the man (at least) of what you are today!

Having twins, triplets or more babies at once is called a *multiple birth*. Multiple births happen in two ways. Identical or *monozygotic* twins are formed when the fertilised egg divides into two very early on, and two separate embryos develop. Non-identical twins, also known as fraternal or *dizygotic* twins, occur when two eggs are fertilised at once in the fallopian tubes. Triplets can sometimes be a combination with two identical twins and a fraternal twin, but not always.

In pregnancy, twins are more at risk of arriving prematurely (38 weeks for twins is considered full term) and having a low birth weight. Your carer will guide you through the intricacies of multiple births and will probably monitor more carefully your partner's wellbeing throughout the pregnancy.

Unfortunately, a multiple pregnancy means that the side effects of being pregnant are more pronounced, so morning sickness may be more intense, weight gain faster and earlier in the pregnancy, and things such as varicose veins, heartburn and shortness of breath more pronounced. See the sections on dealing with common side effects for the last two trimesters later in this chapter. See also Chapter 2 about IVF and multiple births.

Act Two: The Second Trimester

The morning sickness is waning, your partner is feeling a little less exhausted and she's beginning to show a bit of a bump — welcome to the second trimester. Weeks 13 to 28 are usually the best period of pregnancy. You start to see your partner's body change as the baby grows, and feel the baby's first kicks by putting your hand on her belly — a pretty amazing feeling.

REMEMBER

Because 80 per cent of miscarriages happen in the first 12 weeks, many parents don't announce they're pregnant until the second trimester. Pregnancies are far more stable after this period.

In this section, I take you through the second trimester, providing insight into what might be happening with your partner and what your baby is up to on the inside.

Enjoying the golden trimester

If everything is going well, most pregnant women feel a lot better throughout the second trimester. As your partner's belly is getting bigger, the reality that you're going to have a child really sets in. Exciting times! Towards the end of the second trimester, your partner probably also starts feeling those first kicks and bumps. Typically, this happens around 18 to 20 weeks. Kicks may be hard to spot at first, as that little foot tries to get in touch with you through all those abdominal muscles, but feeling them for the first time is a magic moment.

You see your partner transform as the baby grows, and she may start planning what to buy (more clothes!) and how to decorate the baby's room. This is called the 'nesting instinct' and you pretty much have to go with it. When purchasing things for the baby, however, dads are important because we tend to 'keep it real'. Many household budgets are under a lot of pressure when the baby arrives and with your partner potentially high on hormones, going shopping together can help avoid a local financial crisis.

REMEMBER

Navigating your communication around budgetary issues is likely to be a source of conflict, so tread carefully. Yes, you need to pay the rent or your mortgage and you need to eat, but don't ever let money become more important than your relationship and the reasonable desires and instincts of your partner. (See Chapter 4 for an overview of what you actually need to buy.)

Around 20 weeks, your midwife, obstetrician or GP may send you for an ultrasound to make sure the baby's bits are all in the right place and that things are progressing smoothly. If you can't wait another 20 weeks to discover the baby's gender, you can usually find out at this scan — unless the baby has those legs crossed! Again, don't feel like this is compulsory. Some people love the gender reveal, but some equally passionate people say you should wait and savour the surprise at the birth. Either way is fine, so don't be afraid to go your own way on this regardless of what others say. (We kept it a surprise for all six of our daughters!)

REMEMBER

Sex during pregnancy is absolutely okay! The second trimester might be the best time to share a bit of passion, although how your partner is feeling throughout pregnancy greatly affects the mood. Stick with consent as your marker and, if you're lucky, the sparks will be flying. If you both feel good about it, pregnancy sex can be a lot of fun. And having sex almost up until labour is not out of the question, depending on how your partner feels.

Understanding more medical stuff

In the second trimester, your carer starts to feel for the baby at each check-up by asking your partner to lie down. They also use a *Doppler* or a foetal heartbeat monitor to listen for the baby's heartbeat, which at a remarkable 120 to 160 beats per minute makes it sound like a dance party's going on in there. Your caregiver will check the *fundal height*, or the length of the uterus as it progresses into the abdomen.

Your midwife, obstetrician or GP may also routinely ask your partner for a urine sample to check for protein in her urine. Blood pressure also gets the once over because high blood pressure combined with protein in urine are indicators of *pre-eclampsia*.

Now is the time to ask about a *nuchal fold test* to check for potential birth defects, especially if your partner is older than 35. A nuchal fold test aims to determine the likelihood of your baby being born with *Down Syndrome*. This can be a big issue to consider with significant ethical and psychological ramifications. Talk with your partner about what it would mean, either way, and make sure you do all you can to be aligned on your decisions here.

REMEMBER

Having a child with any kind of additional needs, disability or non-typical development presents challenges you likely never saw in your future — it will literally change your life — but many parents who experience this say it changed them for the better in ways they never could have imagined. Other people's judgment is irrelevant in situations like this. It's your family, and it's between you and your partner.

Dealing with common side effects in the second trimester

Most changes during this trimester are a result of the growing size of your baby. They include

>> **Back pain:** This is perhaps one of the most common complaints of pregnant women and is caused by the growing weight of the baby, additional strain on the spine and a change in the centre of gravity that the body needs to adjust for.

>> **Constipation:** Yup, it's a shocker but your partner may find it hard to 'go'. The main reason for constipation in the second trimester is an increase in the hormone progesterone, which slows the movement of food through the

digestive tract. Later in pregnancy, the problem of constipation is likely to be made worse by the pressure of the growing uterus on the intestines. Taking iron supplements, which many pregnant women need, can also make constipation worse. Talk to your GP or a dietician for the safe solutions.

>> **Heartburn:** This burning sensation in the middle chest is caused by the hormone progesterone, which softens the uterus so it can stretch, but also softens the oesophagus, allowing acid to come back out. So if your partner complains about heartburn, don't be offended — your cooking isn't the cause. (You are cooking, aren't you?)

>> **Leg cramps:** These seem to plague pregnant women more at night, but no-one's sure what causes them. Blame the hormones, I reckon.

>> **Softening ligaments:** The ligaments in the pelvis stretch, which widens the pelvis to prepare for birth. Softening ligaments can give your partner a floating sensation in the joints and cause sharp stabbing pains when she stands up too quickly or rolls over in bed. This is called *round ligament pain* and is nothing to be worried about, although knowing about this pain is good.

You can't do much about the ailments outlined in the preceding list, other than continue to be a superstar with your support, love and encouragement.

Finding out what your baby's up to now

At 24 weeks, your baby is about 21 centimetres from head to bottom (see Figure 3-2). He also has his calendar full doing these amazing things:

>> **Getting his eyes done:** Pigmentation in the iris develops. If your baby is of European descent, he's born with blue eyes that may change colour in the months after birth. Maori, First Nations Australian, African, Indian, Pacific Island and Asian babies can be born with brown or blue eyes, and eye colour can also change with time.

>> **Having a facial:** Your baby's using the world's best moisturiser, *vernix*, a waxy coating that keeps his skin from getting wrinkled as he floats around in fluid all day. He also grows fingernails, hair and eyebrows.

>> **Listening to music and your voice:** Your baby can hear now, but won't know what he's hearing for a long time yet — though research suggests that babies know their parents' voices when they're born from what they hear in the womb. Amazing, isn't it?

>> **Preparing to rock and roll:** At the end of the second trimester, your baby is almost done growing and developing all external and internal organs.

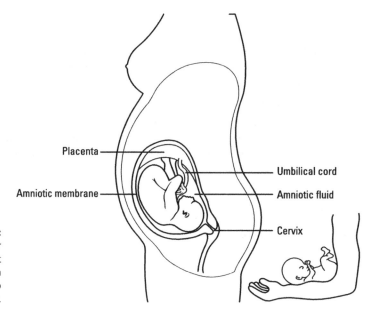

Placenta

Umbilical cord

Amniotic membrane

Amniotic fluid

Cervix

FIGURE 3-2:
At 24 weeks, your baby is about the length from your elbow to your wrist.

Act Three: The Third Trimester

Three is a lucky number, so shouldn't the third trimester be the best of them all? In a way, the third trimester is the best because you end up with your newborn baby, but the period can feel like quite hard work for your partner (and that's even before labour starts).

You may have to go the extra mile during this trimester to support your partner, because things get decidedly uncomfortable for many mums towards the end of their pregnancy. Help with whatever she's asking you to do and put on a brave face. (No whining and moaning allowed — hey, would you want to swap places?)

During this last trimester, your baby has to grow a lot. As a result, your partner's belly gets quite big and a few everyday tasks become quite tricky. Tying shoes, picking anything up from the floor, or even climbing in and out of the car can become major tasks. Meanwhile, you're likely to be busy with all sorts of preparations for the baby's arrival in your house and with preparations for 'B Day'.

In this section, I run through what you need to know about childbirth classes and birth plans, what your baby is up to and how your partner might be feeling.

Looking into childbirth classes

Now's the time to find out about childbirth or antenatal classes. Childbirth education is ideally the perfect place to find out everything you ever wanted to know about giving birth, and your partner is likely to love you even more for taking an interest.

These classes are often a great way to build a support network, because lots of people go on to keep in touch with their antenatal classmates as their babies grow. Plus, you'll often have the chance to ask questions and receive answers that you might not have otherwise been able to. However, sometimes these classes sideline partners, focusing primarily on the birth process and the drug options your partner will have at her disposal, along with the support provision the birth facility provides.

REMEMBER

The hospital system is designed to minimise risk, and to control the birth process from start to finish. This is generally a good thing. But many mothers (including trained midwives going through their own labour) experience birth trauma when they don't feel seen, heard and valued by medical professionals. Attending childbirth education that really teaches you how to support your partner is a powerful way to advocate for her, and to support her in a time of enormous vulnerability.

TIP

Look around for private education providers who offer information that goes above and beyond, helping you to be the best support you can for your partner, and offering solutions and strategies that are safe alternatives to the standard medical practices that many modern mums and dads are unsure about.

A range of public and private providers of childbirth classes exist in Australia. If you're having your baby at a hospital, check if they provide antenatal classes. Ask your carer, check with Medicare or speak to your friends or colleagues who have already been to one.

TIP

Checking with someone who has already attended an antenatal class you're interested in is definitely a good idea. Some classes are more dad-inclusive than others. For example, some providers split the group into mums and dads to talk about specific issues or situations. Having a guys-only session as part of an antenatal class is great because it provides the ideal opportunity for some 'man talk' about pregnancy, babies and fatherhood.

The birth plan

The time's come to start looking forward to The Birth. That baby is going to have to come out. In ye olde days, birth involved fewer choices — woman goes into labour, sheets are torn into strips, water is boiled, a lot of yelling occurs, and then (hopefully) baby comes out safely. Of course, birth in those distant times was far from straightforward — it was a dangerous time, and both infant and maternal mortality were frighteningly high.

These days, significant risks still exist for mum and bub, but with our technology and greater awareness of the anatomy of birth, the risks are greatly reduced. On the flip side, you're faced with a lot of choices concerning how junior enters the world. Home birth or hospital birth? No drugs, or all the drugs you can get? With lots of family, a video camera and updates on Twitter? Or just your partner, the person delivering the baby and you?

Fortunately, the modern world has also come up with an answer to organise all the various options you may want to consider — a *birth plan*. This sounds like an oxymoron, because birth is generally a natural process that you just have to surrender to — more often than not, you have very little control over what happens. But you can still have preferences.

A birth plan is not like a formal contract and may not even be recorded in written format. Most likely, you simply discuss the various pain relief options and delivery methods with your midwife, obstetrician or GP. Your carer can tell you about pros and cons for each option and you can tell your carer which option you're keen on and which you're not. So a birth plan is really just stating your preferences — providing a clear understanding of how you would like things to go so that the person delivering your baby knows your wishes. In the best of circumstances, you then support your partner as the birth plan is carried out.

REMEMBER

Keep an open mind about how the birth may go. If you've planned for a nice water birth at home, be prepared that, if things don't go as smoothly as you would like, you may have to be transferred to hospital in an ambulance with sirens wailing and lights flashing. Or, if you've said absolutely no way is my woman going to need pain relief, she may be yelling for an epidural in the first five minutes. (And let's be clear — it's not for you to be saying what her pain relief decisions will be. It's up to her. Let it go . . . or tie a rope to your testicles and let her strangle the rope every time a contraction hits — and don't think about even taking a Panadol to reduce the pain.) The ultimate aim is delivering your baby safely into the world with the least amount of anxiety and trauma for your beloved so you set off on your parenting path on the healthiest and safest foot.

REMEMBER

If you've decided on a hospital birth, check out your options (if you have several hospitals in your area to choose from) because standards and facilities vary significantly. Most hospitals offer special 'tours' for pregnant couples to see what the facilities are like and where you need to go on D-day. This tour is really useful because you can check out details and take lots of time to ask everything you ever wanted to know about giving birth in a hospital.

Making choices about the birth

Given that birth plans are really about pain relief, let's discuss pain relief options. In recent times, a swing has occurred towards mum having as little medical intervention as possible so she can deliver the baby as naturally and drug-free as possible. That swing is generally more pronounced among mums outside of the hospital setting. Within hospitals, the push for pain-free pregnancy and maximum medical control can be stronger. An obvious tension exists here.

Ultimately, the pain relief options really depend on your partner's preferences. Towards the end of pregnancy, she's probably grappling with the idea of what labour is going to be like and the pressure to be as stoic about it as possible. Supporting her and standing by whatever decisions she makes regarding her body and the birth of your baby goes a long way towards making it easier on her. Don't add to her confusion and pressure by making demands in either direction, unless you're appropriately qualified. (And given that you're reading this book, that likely rules you out.)

Let's have a look at what's on offer in most cases:

>> **Drug-free:** Heat packs, massage, breathing exercises and being in water may help relieve the pain of labour. Keeping active during the birth and avoiding lying on her back can also help your partner manage the pain.

>> **Epidural:** An epidural is a local anaesthetic injected into the spinal column. It blocks out all pain from the injection point down and is often used during caesareans so the mother can be awake when her child is born. Epidurals are usually safe, but some risk exists of side effects and complications. (After all, a big needle is being injected into the spine.) Low risk outcomes include low blood pressure, dizziness, nausea, itchy skin, and loss of bladder control. More serious side effects can include slowed breathing, or even temporary nerve damage. The most serious side effects are infections and permanent nerve damage. In the rarest of cases, fits, severe breathing difficulties, or even death may occur, but I stress, these are extremely unlikely events.

>> **Gas:** A mix of laughing gas or nitrous oxide and oxygen has been used for decades and is a safe way to relieve pain during labour. It sometimes makes women feel a bit nauseous. In rare cases, they may become sleepy. Vomiting is not uncommon after inhaling a whole big lungful of gas. Some women beg for the gas while others can't go near it.

>> **Pethidine:** A strong pain reliever, pethidine can cause drowsiness in both mother and baby. It crosses the placenta and can cause respiratory depression and low AGPAR scores for the baby. (An AGPAR score is a measure of the baby's health after birth, and considers skin colour, pulse, breathing, pulse and reflexes.) This sounds scary, and it should be treated seriously. Fortunately pethidine is usually used without any long-term effects. Pethidine can also cause nausea for mum.

The preceding list runs through the central drug offerings for most labour rooms. Your partner is in charge of what happens to her body.

Another big decision is where and how to have the baby. No doubt your partner has researched all options by now. Unfortunately, the 'I just wake up in the morning and my baby will be here' option doesn't exist. The most common scenarios are:

>> **Birth centres or free-standing birth centres:** Having your baby in a special birth centre run by midwives might provide you with additional options to try particular birthing techniques or varying positions during labour. Note that birth centres often take a non-interventionist, minimally controlling approach and many don't provide epidurals.

>> **Home birth:** This option has been popular for several decades. You will need the support of a community or private midwife. If your partner wants a water birth, you can hire special equipment to facilitate the birth at home.

>> **Hospital birth:** Most women in Australia opt for a hospital birth. Some hospitals provide extra facilities for water births or natural (as in no pain relief) births.

Talk with your carer about your options and discuss the pros and cons of each one. Don't be afraid to ask questions and be sure you know everything you need to be confident about the upcoming birth. As your partner's number one support person, know what's going on just as much as she does.

Your birth option may also depend on where you live and whether you go through the public health system or use private health insurance. In many states in Australia, home birth is available only for low-risk pregnancies and through private health care.

Understanding even more medical stuff

As you head into the home stretch of pregnancy, you have more frequent check-ups with your midwife, obstetrician or GP. Your doula, if you have one, may become more involved.

The checks generally involve examining the baby's position and making sure he's in the right place. During this trimester, your baby usually makes his way head first towards the cervix ready for birth, a process called *engaging*. If he has his feet pointed down towards the cervix, he's in a *breech* position. If he stays breech until the birth, your carer will usually recommend a caesarean birth. They may suggest trying to 'turn' the baby by applying heavy pressure to your partner's stomach in an effort to make the baby somersault. Evidence suggests this can work in around 50 to 60 per cent of cases, but it *is* very painful, and in some cases can lead to complications. Discuss this with your partner and carer.

Your caregiver may also take swabs from your partner's vagina to test for *group B strep*, which is a bacterium that can infect your baby as he's being born. If traces of it are discovered, your carer may recommend your partner is put on an antibiotic drip during labour. This drip takes considerable time to complete, and in some cases labour will be slowed down to allow it to be finalised. Be sure that if strep is discovered, this is attended to speedily. You don't want your partner to labour for unnecessary hours simply because a drip wasn't inserted.

For all the medical stuff you need to know about labour, check Chapter 5.

Dealing with common side effects in the third trimester

By now, the golden glow of the second trimester has often mostly vanished. As your partner nears her due date, your baby is starting to take over her body — literally. Her internal organs are getting pushed and shoved all over the place and her abdominal muscles have split in the middle to make way for that wide load she's carrying. Your partner may even waddle a little, as her relaxed ligaments widen her pelvis. (If you value your life, don't ever point out that she's 'waddling'.)

Some common complaints during this time include the following:

>> **'I've got baby brain':** Pregnant women often feel like they're losing their marbles. They tend to forget stuff, or get a bit vague even during simple or frequent activities. These symptoms are believed to be caused by hormones, lack of sleep and the general toll pregnancy takes on the body. Be patient and compassionate. We blokes can't even conceive of what this does to a woman's body and her life.

>> **'I can't sleep but I'm so tired all the time':** Insomnia is one thing most mothers-to-be in the third trimester agree on. Her joints may be sore and back aching, with a baby that kicks all night and heartburn to boot. Your partner may also need to get up for a wee every five minutes. Lying on her back to sleep can put pressure on the *vena cava*, an important artery feeding the heart, so she has to lie on her side at night, and turning over in bed can take significant effort. You can suggest she try a pillow under her right side, where the vena cava is, which tilts the weight of her body off the artery. But mostly just be patient and compassionate.

>> **'I've got varicose veins, and worse — piles':** The third trimester can be hard on your partner. She's getting rounder by the day, can't be as active as she's used to, she's tired, and not getting enough sleep is making her grumpy. Stretch marks are likely appearing on her pregnant belly. And then

haemorrhoids — also known as piles — turn up and make her feel downright miserable. She's likely not feeling like a radiant mother-to-be anymore — and may even be feeling like a veiny, fat frump. Varicose veins and piles can be caused or made worse by the weight of the baby on her body, so help her to take it easy and rest lots.

>> **'My ankles are swollen and I'm as big as a house':** As well as carrying a rapidly growing baby around, your partner's retaining fluid and has more blood flowing through her body. In hot weather or after standing for long periods, this blood collects in her ankles. Your partner should put her feet up whenever she can and avoid salty foods. A few foot rubs from you wouldn't go amiss, either. Pointing out that she looks 'ready to pop' doesn't go down well — ever, under any circumstances. Even if she's laughing along with you on the outside, she's probably not laughing on the inside.

>> **'Nothing I eat tastes right':** Blame that pesky progesterone — along with everything else, the hormone causes food cravings. Finding anything that tastes just how she wants it to be may be very hard for your partner, and predicting what she needs is almost impossible. Roll with the cravings and keep up your partner's spirits by getting her whatever she asks for — even if it means a late-night takeaway run for another cheeseburger.

TIP

Taking walks together, reading or singing to the baby in bed at night, making lists of potential names together, and taking photos of that burgeoning belly make for a good time and help you support each other as the big day approaches. These are some of the last days that your family numbers just the two of you, so take time to be with your partner right now.

Preparing for Project Push — are we there yet?

Yes, almost! Your baby's just putting the finishing touches on before making his glorious entry into the world. He's been keeping busy by:

>> **Beefing up:** At the start of the third trimester, your baby weighed about 750 grams, but by the end, he's reached his birth weight — on average, 3.4 kilograms. The most rapid weight gain happens in the final few weeks.

>> **Getting in position for take-off:** All going well, your baby is head down with his feet under your partner's ribcage. No wonder she's uncomfortable.

>> **Practise makes perfect:** He's been rehearsing for his big entrance by practising breathing. He's also developing his bones to be ready for action, opening his eyes and sucking his thumb.

Chapter **4**

Preparing for a Baby in the House

Few things change the way you live as much as welcoming a baby into your life. Having a baby is like having a house guest who never cleans up after herself, cries a lot and has more needs than the two of you put together. Adding a baby to the family is not as simple as clearing out the spare room for her to sleep in. She needs stuff: clothes, bedding, nappies, all sorts of things you need to think about that become part of your daily life as a father. (Rest assured, the first few weeks — even months — are usually okay so you can ease into life with baby, but it ramps up big time in short order.)

As you count down to your baby's birth, you need to get things done to avoid hassles down the line — get those bags packed ready for the hospital, get the bassinet and a car seat sorted and be ready to go at a moment's notice. When she arrives, chances are you won't have a lot of time for decorating the baby's room. You'll want the major elements in place so you can be ready.

In this chapter, I explore the ins and outs of what to look for when buying items such as nursery furniture, strollers, nappies, clothes and toys. You find out what nappy rash is and how to prevent it, and how to help your baby when she's teething. I give you lots of checklists for everything you need to do before the birth and what you need to take with you to the hospital or have prepared for a home birth.

Getting the Right Gear

The first trimester is the perfect time to familiarise yourself with the stuff a baby needs. (You have to do it eventually so it's a good idea to get a head start on this task.) The first thing you're likely to notice is that babies need a remarkable amount of stuff. Unless you have unlimited funds available, finding out about what babies need and being rational about buying baby gear is useful. I've done the heavy lifting for you and in the following sections you find out what you really need and what's pure luxury.

TIP

A great idea to keep costs down is to send the word around among your friends and co-workers that you're having a baby. They may have cots, bassinets and strollers they're no longer using. You can completely kit out a nursery for little outlay, or even for free. And places such as Facebook Marketplace, Gumtree or other online pages can be amazing for finding low-cost, high-quality, pre-loved gear. You might want some things to be new, but most items don't need to be, and your baby quickly grows out of much of what you'll purchase, so save money and go second-hand where you can.

Clothes and shoes

Baby clothes come in more shapes and styles than you would have thought possible. Check out what works for you before you spend up big. Truth be told, if your extended family and friends are as excited as most people are about the arrival of your baby, you probably won't need to buy any clothes for at least six months. They'll gift you more than you need! But, for the sake of being thorough, in this section I provide a rundown of what you might have on your list.

As well as the usual T-shirts, singlets, jumpers and trousers that children and adults wear, babies have these kinds of clothes to keep them decent:

>> **Bodysuits** are long- or short-sleeved T-shirts that do up around the baby's crotch with domes (clips or press-studs). They're handy for keeping everything tucked in so bub's tummy doesn't get chilly if a top starts riding up (which is guaranteed to happen when you spend all day lying down). They're also great during the summer months when a short sleeved bodysuit can be worn by itself without pants or as pyjamas. The only drawback with bodysuits is that if your baby is fully dressed and has a nappy leak, you have to take everything off to change her, rather than just her pants. And this stuff can get messy. But the pros vastly outweigh the cons here.

>> **Stretch-n-grows** are all-in-one trousers and tops that either dome up the legs and front, or zip up. They're like an overall with socks. Some dome up the

back, which is really inconvenient — steer clear of them. Most have feet, but you can get stretch-n-grows without feet for summer.

>> **Sleeping bags** are like stretch-n-grows with sleeves but no legs, just a sack covering your baby's legs and feet. They're handy in winter when your child is able to roll over and kick around in bed. Your child inevitably kicks off her wrap or blanket so having her wear a sleeping bag means she doesn't get as cold. Sleeping bags are also good because if her legs are bare under the sack, you can get to her nappy more easily and disturb her less at night.

The following list is a guide to what you should have ready to go for your newborn baby. You can customise your list as you find your dad-legs and suss out which items work well for you. You can also tweak the list to suit the seasons. As a general rule, baby clothes should be loose-fitting, made with breathable and soft fabric, and be easy to open and close. Remember you can go through three to four sets of clothes in a day because of nappy leaks and baby spew and dirt and mushed food and . . . well, you get the picture.

Here are the items you need:

>> Lots of singlets, either cotton or woolly for cold winters.

>> Four bodysuits, both long- and short-sleeved, or long- or short-sleeved tops if bodysuits don't appeal.

>> Four pairs of trousers. Overalls are pretty cute but make sure they have openings in the legs so you don't have to take the whole lot off to change her nappy.

>> Four stretch-n-grows or sleeping bags for night time. Check that they are cotton, rather than polar fleece or microfleece, because those fabrics aren't breathable and she may get overheated.

>> Two jackets for going out.

>> Two cardigans or wraparound jerseys that don't need to go over her head.

>> Lots of pairs of socks — typically one sock of a pair always gets lost.

>> Four hats, preferably made of a lycra-cotton mix so they stretch, or lovely soft wool if they're handmade.

>> Lots of bibs with either domes or velcro. Bibs with ties can prove too fiddly.

>> Two pairs of slippers that have elastic around the heel. These stay on better than other slip-ons. Babies don't need shoes until they're walking.

>> Two pairs of gloves or mittens. Get some that you can tie around the wrist because babies tend to lose them.

Here are some valuable tips for selecting clothes and making dress-up time easy (on you and the baby):

>> Most babies get grumpy at having clothes pulled over their heads. Avoid anything that doesn't have a few domes opening at the shoulder or an envelope-style neckband (two overlapping pieces of fabric that stretch easily when put over her head) to make pulling the clothing over her face painless.

>> When putting on a stretch-n-grow, cardigan or any other top that doesn't go over your baby's head, lay the item on the surface you're dressing your baby on before you lay her down. Then all you have to do is slide her arms into the sleeves, dome her up and you're good to go.

>> Avoid anything that has a back opening. Your baby spends a lot of time lying on her back in the early months and having domes under you can't be comfortable. They're also tricky to get on when you're getting her dressed.

>> Avoid anything that looks too fiddly. Some babies really dislike getting dressed and trying to do up silly little ribbons when she's having a meltdown isn't a good time for anyone.

>> If your baby arrives in winter, look for clothes that have folds sewn into the ends of sleeves — they're actually mittens. As well as helping keep her warm, these are great to keep your bub from scratching herself with those blade-like newborn nails.

>> If in doubt on sizing, buy clothes that are too big. At least you know your baby is going to grow into them. (See the sidebar 'How many 0s can you go?' for information about size labels on baby clothing.)

>> If you've been given a lot of hand-me-downs, be aware that the fire retardant in some clothing may be worn and not be as effective as it is in new clothes.

>> You're likely to be given a tonne of new clothing as presents, so if you find you have too much, don't be afraid to take it back to the shop and swap it for something you can use in the future, like the next size up.

>> Dark colours show baby spew much more than light colours, but light colours show baby poo much more! Just go with what colours you like.

REMEMBER

Handling a baby during the first few months can feel a bit tricky because she can appear really fragile. So think about what steps you need to go through to put on a particular item of clothing. If the clothes seem complicated to close or open, don't buy them. Don't be afraid to try out the garment in the shop with a baby doll.

HOW MANY 0S CAN YOU GO?

If we lived in a perfect, logical world, clothing labels for babies would give an age range to show the size of the item. But because all babies are different, labels show 0s instead.

Until she's one, your little one is going to be less than zero, or many zeros. Here's how it usually works:

- **0000:** Birth to three months, or newborns under four kilograms
- **000:** Three to six months, or babies four to six kilograms
- **00:** Six to nine months, or babies between six and eight kilograms
- **0:** 9 to 12 months, or babies from eight to ten kilograms
- **1:** 12 months, or babies over ten kilograms

If your baby is premature, look for more 0s when you're buying clothes. Clothes are often labelled '00000' or the label says 'premature'.

TIP

Your baby won't need shoes for a while yet. A good time to start looking for shoes is when your little one starts crawling. Studies show that going barefoot is best — but that's not always practical. For a baby who isn't walking yet, soft-soled shoes with an elasticised heel work well and protect toes from being scraped on the floor or ground. But as she starts walking, her footwear needs to change gradually towards firmer shoes.

Here are some tips and tricks for buying your baby's first pair of shoes:

- ≫ Choose shoes with one centimetre of wiggle room at the front and end, but no more than that — she'll trip over her own feet.
- ≫ Look for shoes that are as similar to bare feet conditions as possible. She doesn't need arch support at the beginning!
- ≫ Babies' feet get hotter and sweat more than adults' feet, so choose natural breathable materials rather than synthetics.
- ≫ Soles that grip are important too, because your child needs all the help she can get to not slip when she's learning to walk.

Toys

When your baby is born, all she does for a while is poo, pee, eat, cry, sleep and gaze benignly at things. So she doesn't need an electronic ABC, a racing car set or a mini piano — and she definitely doesn't need an iPad. What she needs are things that give her a real sense of the world she's just come into — new sights, shapes, textures, smells, sounds and sensations. These can easily be provided by spending time with your baby, singing to her, and touching her skin and fingers with textures like an old comb, fabric, your hair, leaves, the cat's fur — you get the idea. As she begins to grasp and bring her hands together, things like a rattle or a chain of plastic rings can keep her fascinated for ages.

TIP

When your baby starts teething, she looks for things to put in her mouth to push against her gums to relieve the discomfort. Many toys double as teething rings and aids.

Some good ideas for baby toys include

>> **Balls and blocks:** Great for giving your newborn an idea of basic shapes.

>> **Cloth books:** Look for ones with flaps or textures sewn into them.

>> **Plastic keys:** For some reason, babies love your car keys, so give your baby her own set. These are great for teething, too.

>> **Play gyms:** Play gyms are mats with arms curved over the top where you can attach colourful objects such as paper flowers, branches from the garden, soft toys and strings with large shells for your baby to look at as she lies on the mat. Just make sure she can't pull anything down that she shouldn't be chewing on. Nothing is safe from her gummy mouth once she's got the hang of her hands.

>> **Rattles:** You can buy rattles or make your own from old plastic containers filled with rice. Ensure the lid is on securely.

>> **Soft toy animals:** Avoid fluffy toys with long hair or fur.

REMEMBER

Less is more when it comes to toys. No matter what the toy manufacturers tell you, nothing beats spending time playing and exploring with your baby. Your baby's brain development is assisted by appropriate stimulation and human contact . . . not by any particular gadget.

WARNING

To make sure toys are safe for your little one, check for any parts that may come off and become a choking hazard, as well as toxins, such as toxic paints. Inevitably your baby tries to put all toys (and most other things) into her mouth, so make sure toys you're providing are safe for when the inevitable occurs.

Strollers, prams and buggies

Prams have evolved into high-tech, fold-at-the-touch-of-a-button contraptions that can double as shopping trolleys, be taken off-road, and cook you lunch (just kidding on that last part). Baby stores are packed with different models of prams and strollers. A pram and/or stroller is often one of the bigger purchases you make in this fatherhood game, so shop around.

TIP

Some research suggests that babies in prams that face towards you rather than out into the world are better — at least for the first nine months or so — because your baby is less stressed. Facing each other also encourages more talking, laughing and social interaction. Many from-birth prams have both rear-facing and forward-facing positions.

Some of the things you need to look out for include the following:

>> Can you dismantle the pram and put a car seat or bassinet attachment on it in the early months, making transferring your baby from bed or car seat easier?

>> Does the stroller come with a fitted sunshade and fitted weather cover?

>> Does the stroller fit through the door of your favourite cafe? Can it be easily manoeuvred through a packed supermarket? If you're looking at three-wheeled prams, make sure the front wheel isn't fixed so you can manoeuvre the pram easily.

>> How easy is adjusting the back of the seat? Can bub lie down flat in the pram for sleeping? Can the back be raised up high for a growing child to see more of the world around them?

>> How easily can the pram fit in your car boot or in your house? Some models can be bulky.

>> How easily does the pram fold down? The last thing you want is to be pulling levers all over the place when you've got a fussy baby to deal with. If you're travelling by public transport, strollers that can be folded down with only one hand are ideal so you don't have to hand your baby to a random person while you wrestle with getting the stroller on board. (Although babies are great for helping you meet new people — everyone loves to cuddle a baby!)

>> How well does the pram support your child's growing spine and neck?

>> How well can the pram survive if you want to take it on unpaved walkways or bush walks?

Car seats

Getting a cute mobile for your baby's cot is optional, buying a stroller that you can take mountain running is optional — but using a car seat for your most precious cargo is not. Yeah sure, you may have free ranged in your parents' car when you were little and lived to tell the tale, but sadly some children haven't. So take advantage of the fact that things have evolved somewhat since 'the good old days' and use a car seat for every journey you take in the car with your baby. Besides, it's the law.

WARNING

Now and then the idea of holding your baby while you drive will seem necessary. She'll be screaming. It will be late. Nothing will be working. Even so, it's not worth the risk.

Different sizes of car seat for the age and weight of your child are available, generally falling into these categories:

>> **Baby capsule:** This is a car seat shaped like a cradle that is used for newborns up to six months or weighing eight kilograms. The capsule is strapped into the car using the car's existing seatbelts and is rear-facing.

A baby capsule can be taken out with your baby in it and attached to the top of special shopping trolleys and some strollers. Baby capsules also have a movable handle so you can carry your bub around in it like Red Riding Hood's basket of goodies.

>> **Child car seat:** From 6 to 12 months (weight 8 to 12 kilograms), babies should still be in rear-facing car seats. Many rear-facing models can be converted to front- facing after bub's first birthday or once they weigh in the 9 to 12 kilogram range. Car seats usually have a strap that attaches to a bolt in the back of the back passenger seat. If your car doesn't have a bolt, they can be purchased and put into the car by a mechanic for very little money. Other harnessing options are available in newer cars. Just make sure your little one is securely fastened to a seat that is also securely fastened.

From 12 months to four years children must use a rear-facing or forward-facing child car seat with an inbuilt harness. Smaller kids are often best to remain facing the rear for a longer period of time.

>> **Booster seat:** When your child reaches 18 kilograms or her shoulders are too wide for her car seat, she can move to a booster seat. Children are required to be in a booster seat with an adult lap-sash seatbelt or child safety harness.

REMEMBER

Using your child's size as a guide, rather than just their age, is always best when considering car and booster seats. Don't move small kids up to the next level just because they're older. Safety matters here. And, as with strollers, so many models of car seats are available that shopping around pays. Luckily you've got a few months to do this!

KNOWING YOUR BUGGY FROM YOUR PRAM

Confused about what's a pram, what's a buggy and what's a stroller? Then read on!

In Australia, most people refer to baby carriages as prams, although the smaller, more compact, lightweight carriages are typically called strollers. In New Zealand and the US most people call them buggies or strollers. Some people say a pram is used for a baby carrier that only allows your baby to lie flat, while a stroller is used for anything that allows her to sit up. Confused yet?

Whatever you call them, some of them are substantial beasts, sometimes with three wheels, sometimes four. Prams and strollers can be quite cosy and comfortable for your child, and usually have an adjustable back that allows your little one to either lie down or sit up (although the more austere strollers typically don't recline so far, are much lighter, and rather than push bars, have two handles to push). Many models allow baby to face out to the world or, alternatively, to face you (with the position being adjusted depending on the baby's age). Many models also have a carry cot–type set-up, so you can instead sling a bassinet on the frame when your baby's still little.

Whatever mode of transport you choose for your baby, make sure that it meets Australian/New Zealand standard AS/NZS 2088:2000. Prams and strollers are designed to move freely, so always ensure that you're holding onto the pram or that the brakes are on when you've stopped moving. In Australia, prams and strollers are fitted with a tether strap to help you keep control over the pram (you can also buy tether straps where you buy prams). The Australian Competition and Consumer Commission fact sheet 'Prams and strollers — safety requirements' provides helpful information on pram/stroller safety and is available on its website (www.accc.gov.au).

As an alternative to buying a car seat, check out Hire for Baby (www.hireforbaby.com), which can also fit the seat for you.

If you're buying a second-hand seat, check the safety regulations with the road safety authority in your state or territory to make sure the seat is up to scratch.

Other accessories

You find most of these things in homes where kids live:

>> **Baby bath or tummy tub:** You need something to wash your baby in and most parents go with a traditional tub that you can have on a table or sturdy

bench. Using a smaller tub means you don't have to fill up a normal sized tub and break your back leaning down into it. While your baby is still really small and unable to sit up by herself, having a bath support can be handy. A bath support is a ramp that baby can lie back on that holds her at a 45-degree angle so her head is safely kept out of the water. Another option for bathing is to use a tummy tub, which looks a bit like a wastepaper basket but is said to replicate being in the womb. Baby 'sits' upright in it and is held snugly in place by the tub's walls. Tummy tubs are pricey, though, so shop around. (Take a look at Chapter 6 for information about bathing your newborn baby.)

>> **Bouncinette or baby chair:** Most kids have spent time in a bouncinette — those ramp-like baby chairs that bub can lie in and watch you go about your day from a better angle than lying on the floor. They're portable, easy to clean and she can even sit outside in one while you're gardening or pegging out washing.

>> **Highchair:** When bub starts solids, you're going to need somewhere she can sit and be fed. A wide range of highchair models are available, from chairs with an ergonomic design made of timber that hasn't been treated with chemicals to chairs with more levers and straps than a space shuttle. Having a detachable tray that you can take off and clean regularly (after every meal!) is handy, as are safety straps so you can be sure bub isn't going to wriggle her way out and get hurt. As an alternative to a highchair, you may want to use a model that attaches to your table. Later on, you can use little booster seats that you strap to a normal chair.

Making Room for the Baby

Our society has done something a little weird when it comes to sleeping arrangements in the last couple of hundred years — and it flies in the face of our species' long history. We've started sleeping in separate beds, and even in separate bedrooms! For most of human history, people didn't think twice about crowding family (and even friends) into the same bed. In fact, the historical record is full of examples of men, women and children sharing whatever beds were available with whoever was needing a place to sleep (and without any kinky stuff going on). As just one example, in September 1776, two of Western history's most influential men, John Adams and Ben Franklin, famously shared a bed in New Jersey. Their room had one small window. Adams wanted it closed. Franklin wanted it open, saying he needed the fresh air. (Adams won.)

Parents slept with children right up until the late 19th century. Prior to that time, kids sleeping separately to parents happened literally nowhere. Then two shifts occurred. First, people began to accrue material possessions, and having more beds meant you looked wealthier. Privacy and individualism elevated the idea further. And, second, religious prudishness dictated morality, which was further exacerbated by people's desire to *not* sleep like 'the savages'.

So don't stress too much about creating your baby's first room. Sleeping in her own room will happen eventually, but all sharing the same room might be in your little one's best interest, at least in the early stages.

Even so, in the following sections I cover what you need to arrange at some point in time.

The nursery

Whether your baby shares your room or not, you'll want to set up a room that will eventually be hers. And you'll use it straight off the bat too, because most of us can't fit all the kid gear in our room along with all of our gear. I'm talking about a cot, bassinet, drawers, change table, rocking chair, bookshelves — the nursery is one place you can spend a whole bunch of money on all new stuff if you're not careful. Here are some of the basic items you need to set up a nursery.

Somewhere to sleep

For the first few months, most bubs sleep in a bassinet or Moses basket in your room. A bassinet is like a basket on legs. If the bassinet is on wheels, you can move it from room to room easily during the day for naps (babies can sleep anywhere when they're newborns) and wheel it into either your room or the nursery at night. When your little one has outgrown the bassinet, she can graduate to a cot, where she sleeps until he's about two, or has worked out how to climb out of it.

REMEMBER

If you're getting a second-hand cot or bassinet, check it thoroughly to make sure nothing can fall apart and injure your baby. To find out more about ensuring your baby's safety when sleeping and reducing the risk of SUDI (sudden unexplained death of infants), check out Chapter 17.

Another increasingly popular option (that I wish I'd known about when my kids were newborn) is a co-sleeping crib that affixes to the side of your bed, allowing your baby to be within arm's reach all night long. These bed extensions are usually cheap and easy to use. Keep in mind that some experts argue any co-sleeping practice includes a degree of risk, so do your reading and research and stay with what feels comfortable for you and your partner.

Somewhere to be changed and dressed

A lot of nurseries have change tables — tables at the right height so you don't have to lean a lot to change bub's nappies or get her dressed. Some experts advocate that babies should be changed on the floor to avoid the risk of baby rolling off a change table, but others just stand by the rule that baby is never left on the table unsupervised — even for a second. Whichever you choose, having a change mat or a load of cloth nappies under her to catch any rogue pees and poos is essential.

TIP

Cloth nappies are in and out of favour, depending on the year. For me, I think they are an essential accessory — and not only for covering your baby's bum. They can act as change mats, be put over your shoulder to catch any baby spew when you're burping her, be put on the floor during nappy-free time to catch any accidents and can be slung over the handle of a baby capsule to act as a sun shade. They're inexpensive, washable, very hardy and every nappy bag should have one. See Chapter 6 for more on the pros and cons of using them for their intended purpose — as nappies.

Somewhere to store clothes

You would think that so small a person wouldn't need much room for her clothes, but she grows so big so fast she needs room to store not only the clothes she currently fits, but also the ones she grows into. Hand-me-downs and presents from well-meaning friends and family usually mean clothes are rarely in short supply. Child-sized hangers for her wardrobe can be bought from a homeware or discount store.

TIP

If you're given too many hand-me-down clothes, having a system in place for sizing stops you feeling overloaded. Have designated boxes for each size and store them in your baby's wardrobe. As your baby grows out of one size, you've got another size ready to go. This is a great job for dad when your partner feels like she has too much on her plate — and too many hormones whizzing around — during pregnancy or after birth.

Bits and bobs

Other things that are handy to have include

>> A nappy bucket with tight-fitting lid for soaking soiled clothing, bedding and cloth nappies. Although baby poo doesn't smell at first, it gets smellier as your baby gets older — so this is a useful investment!

>> A rocking chair or armchair where mum can breastfeed or you can give the last bottle of the day before bed. An armchair or rocking chair is also

somewhere to share stories, songs and cuddles as your baby gets bigger. Some mums find chairs without arms most comfortable, so trial a few options and choose the one your partner likes most.

>> A pedal rubbish bin with a lid — big size if you're using disposable nappies. Yes, the pedal is essential!

>> Something to house books (and toys, even though you won't need many — or any — for a little while), such as a bookshelf or toy box.

>> A lockable medicine box where you store health items, such as pain relief, a thermometer and nail clippers.

Decorations

Decorating your baby's room is another way to clean out your wallet in a hurry, because thousands of things are available to put in a little person's room. Instagram and Pinterest only make it more challenging for us penny-pinchers as some expectant mums can be tempted to get carried away, so you may have to work together to establish your shopping budget.

Babies spend a lot of time gazing into space when they're really small, as if they're tuning into a radio show you can't hear. They like looking at high-contrast objects around them, such as black and white shapes. Keep the decorations simple. As your baby develops her taste and her needs change, transforming the nursery into a little child's room won't be a drama.

Here are some tips for keeping your decorations on point:

>> Keep the colours neutral, so that the room can easily be redecorated as your baby grows. Use colours with a very light and calming shade — so that your baby isn't constantly alarmed by the fire engine red on the walls, for example.

>> Use pictures of close friends and family on the walls so your baby can grow up knowing who the important people are.

>> You or your partner may want to make something special for the baby's room, such as a painting or piece of embroidery.

>> Mobiles hanging from the ceiling don't need to be fancy. A string of shells hanging from driftwood can entertain a newborn baby for hours.

>> Use removable decals on the walls, so they can be easily taken off as bub grows up and won't damage the wallpaper or paint.

Animals in the house

A few years ago, you may have bought a puppy or kitten when you and your partner were first thinking about having a baby, but weren't quite ready to take the plunge. Perhaps you called it 'practice for the real thing'. Now that your real baby is on the way, you're about to find out that it probably wasn't even close . . . but you also need to think about what's happening to the pets in your house with a little human on the way. Your fur baby is likely to find itself a long way down the pecking order once your baby is on the scene, and having to put up with pulled fur, fingers in eyes and other orifices, and being chased and ridden.

While this is not so necessary with a newborn, you'll want to keep in mind that kids aren't always wise in the way they approach and respond to animals. Once they're big enough, show your child how to be gentle with animals and people from the get-go, as well as how to approach dogs with caution. A child should always hold her hand out for a dog to smell and stay still when it comes near so the dog doesn't see her as a threat.

TIP

Teach your child not to touch strange animals (almost impossible until she's a bit older) and to wash her hands after touching pets in the house because animals can carry all sorts of nasties in their fur. Keep in mind, however, that having a pet in the house — particularly a dog — can be helpful in preventing food allergies and other allergic reactions.

The reverse issue may be even more important. Don't leave your child alone or out of sight with pets. They're animals, and even when they're trained and domesticated, they can be unpredictable and unsafe. Never leave your child unattended with a pet nearby. Keep animals out of baby's room (and cats out of the cradle).

REMEMBER

Dogs and cats can feel neglected when a new baby joins the family, so spend time making them feel settled and happy. Don't move your pet's special sleeping areas or toys away to make room for baby. Try to keep your pet's routines as settled as possible so it doesn't feel left out.

GETTING IN ON THE BABY SHOWER

Baby showers being all about mum, where a bunch of women sit around drinking tea and playing games like 'guess what mess is in that nappy', is no longer strictly true. Dads are getting in on the act, too. No, not sitting around eating sandwiches and oohing over Aunty Vera's knitted booties, but getting together to mark your transition into fatherhood. The event could be a game of pool with mates, a day out fishing, a game of tenpin bowling, a joint occasion with mum's mates, or a boys' night out on the town. So by all means, have a 'man shower' or 'daddy shower' to celebrate the occasion.

Finding the Right Consumables

A whole aisle of the supermarket is dedicated to baby stuff for a reason — your baby needs a lot of baby-specific things on a regular basis, and a lot is available to choose from. Parents also make for really easy prey for marketing people. A few sleepless nights and sheer desperation does amazing things to your shopping habits. So having a good nosey round all the stuff you can buy before the baby arrives makes the shopping-in-a-hurry experience easier on you later on. Don't worry about buying the wrong nappy cream, teething gel or nappies. You go through lots of them and have plenty of opportunities to try out different options. But the following sections help you get a head start.

TIP

Check out Chapter 12 for some great money saving tips for homemade versions of baby stuff.

Nappies

Until you discovered you're about to become a dad, you probably never looked at the nappy aisle in the shops. But in a short time, you'll know it better than any other section of the supermarket. You'll know how much nappies cost, how many per packet, and what a good sale price looks like. Get used to nappies . . . they become your friends, because they're between you and a whole lot of pee and poo. And stock up. You're guaranteed to go through them.

You can select from three main options when choosing what to wrap your baby's bottom in — cloth nappies that can be washed and used over and over, disposable nappies that you throw away after each change, and hybrids where you throw away some bits and wash and re-use the main bit.

You can aim for nappy-free and practise *elimination communication*, if that's your thing (see Chapter 6), but you're a braver man than me if you go down that road.

I mention earlier in this chapter that cloth nappies fall in and out of favour — and for good reasons. The basic, standard cloth nappies can become scratchy, leaky, bulky cloth things that require a degree in origami to fold into the right shape and are held together with safety pins. But the luxury ones come already shaped with domes and velcro to make putting them on and getting them off as easy as a disposable nappy. Whichever way you go (cheap or fancy), you'll be helping the environment.

Close to 4 million disposables are used daily in Australia and New Zealand and, according to the experts, about one cup of crude oil is needed to make each one of those nappies. That's a *lot* of landfill, and a big environmental impact. While cloth nappies still require cleaning — and so still impact the environment — they have a few things going for them. First, they're cheaper over the long run because they can be used and reused. Plus the environmental impact is lower — it's some energy and some detergent. And they don't have chemicals in them, or contain harmful plastics.

CHECK THE NET

Australia's Clean Cloth Nappies (cleanclothnappies.com) provides information on how to use and wash cloth nappies. You can also check out the Australian Nappy Association (www.australiannappyassociation.org.au), which represents cloth nappy manufacturers and promotes cloth nappy use.

WARNING

But if you think just changing a nappy is gross, having to scrub that dirty nappy in the laundry sink or bathroom may be a step too far for you. Up until this point in your life, you've probably avoided getting too much crap on your hands. Cloth nappies need cleaning. Manually. You can't just stick that dirty stink bomb in the washing machine without giving it a scrub first, and it's not fair to leave it to 'someone else' to look after — so, for some, that's asking too much.

Disposable nappies mean you never have to clean a nappy. They can be a better option if you're on holiday, or for use in the day-to-day nappy bag — so if your baby needs a change when you're out and about, you don't have to carry a dirty nappy around until you get home. A handful of eco-friendly disposable nappy brands are on the market in Australia. They're available in most supermarkets at comparable prices to the major brands. They're typically made from corn starch and other sustainable resources, and often don't contain any of the chemicals that keep babies dry but which may cause nappy rash, as well as being bad for the environment. All in all, a sound alternative.

Hybrid nappies are made of a washable underpants part and a disposable pad. Hybrid nappies generally require upfront investment in the pants, but tend to work out cheaper in the long run.

TIP

Disposable nappies may be right for you if you live in an area where water is scarce. Cloth nappies use a lot of water in rinsing and washing.

If you're pragmatic and you don't mind doing the dirty work, you'll probably opt for a nappy solution that's a mixture of both cloth and disposables, depending on where you are and what you're doing on any given day.

Crème de la crèmes

Nappy rash is a big concern for most babies from time to time. The condition occurs when the ammonia from bub's poos and wees irritates her skin, making it red and tender, and making her pretty unhappy with life. The easiest way to stop nappy rash in its tracks is to *change that nappy frequently*. Even then, you'll still probably have the issue of nappy rash at some point. A healthy way to reduce nappy rash is to expose baby's bottom to air and sunlight for a good half an hour each day — but not in the middle of the day when sunburn will be a concern. (No baby wants either nappy rash or a burnt bum.) Using a barrier cream protects her backside from a nasty rash, too.

Like all things baby, you can find an enormous range of nappy creams on the market and your partner might have a few ideas of what to get. Don't feel over-whelmed by the vast choice of products available. At the end of the day, anything from the supermarket that has zinc oxide in it does the trick. Castor oil and zinc oxide cream is effective and cheap, but it can be thick and sticky, so you might want to use it at night and have a lighter cream in the day, or use a powder with zinc oxide in it. You can also try out Vaseline as a barrier cream.

REMEMBER

Manufacturers want you to buy all sorts of other creams to make your little one smell good, have nice skin, fall asleep better, be more successful in life, and so on. By all means, try them out and, if you find one that works really well, keep using it. In general, I recommend keeping your choices simple and using natural oils, which are cheap and effective. Olive or almond oil have been known to be partic-ularly effective for most temporary skin irritations and even cradle cap (see the following section).

Shopping for your baby's health and first aid

Having an arsenal of potions and lotions on hand in the early months and years is essential. Here's what every dad should have in his baby fix-it kit:

>> **Almond or calendula oil:** Your baby doesn't need moisturisers or scented lotions. If she has dry skin, pure oil is best because it doesn't have all the toxins and fillers big companies use to preserve their products. Calendula oil is really great for massage, and almond oil is great for dry skin and *cradle cap*, a condition common in babies where flakes form on the scalp like baby dandruff.

>> **Antibacterial cream:** Stop infections in cuts and grazes by treating them with antibacterial cream.

>> **Arnica cream:** As she grows, your baby is going to get her fair share of bumps on the head and knees. Arnica cream applied to the bruise can assist with the healing.

>> **Child's sunscreen and insect repellent:** Essential if you live in tropical climes, but the best form of protection is clothing and keeping out of the sun. Babies'

skin is a lot more sensitive than adults' skin so your baby can burn even when she's in dappled shade and not exposed to direct sunlight. Mosquito nets can be bought to go over the cot or bassinet, too.

» **Digital thermometer:** If your baby is sick with a cold or flu, you can tell when to whip her off to the doctor by using a digital thermometer to check her temperature. Take your baby's temperature by putting the thermometer under her arm and checking what's called the *axillary temperature*. 'Normal' temperature is 36.7 degrees Celsius. Your baby has a fever if the temp is above 37.2 degrees Celsius. Unfortunately, some babies don't enjoy having a thermometer stuck under their arm for long enough to get an accurate reading. If your little one is like that, you may want to consider getting an ear thermometer, which takes the measurement in seconds.

» **Karvol, Vicks Baby Balsam and Euky Bearub:** Karvol is a decongestant that can be applied to the baby's clothes to clear nasal passages as she sleeps. Vicks Baby Balsam and Euky Bearub are applied to the chest and back when she's congested. Check these medicines are suitable for your baby's age.

» **Nail clippers or baby nail scissors:** Babies can scratch themselves easily so you need to keep their nails short and neat. This is easier said than done. Try small nail clippers or special baby scissors to see what works best for you.

» **Pain reliever:** Children's Panadol or Nurofen for Children can be used for pain and fever after immunisations and teething, and fever when your baby has a cold. Use a plastic syringe with measurements marked on the side to dispense the medication and check with your doctor for the correct dosage (which is worked out by baby's weight). Aspirin is not suitable for young children.

» **Teething relief:** Teething powder and gels such as Bonjela can help soothe a teething baby's gums.

WARNING

Check with your GP before giving your baby pain relief medication if she's younger than six months old. Always check the labelling on any medical product (or any product, in fact) to make sure it's suitable for your baby's age. If you're unsure whether it's suitable — for your baby's age or for the condition you're hoping to treat — check with your GP.

TIP

Be prepared to keep adding to your household first-aid kit with bandages, Band-Aids, ointments, scissors and tweezers as your little one gets older and encounters more little accidents.

BIRTHING EQUIPMENT FOR HOME BIRTH

If you're having a hospital birth, you don't need to bring anything to the delivery suite other than your beloved and her hospital bag (which in some instances can be pretty big indeed). But if you're having the birth at home, you need some bits and bobs to prepare for the big day.

Consider getting the following together if planning a home birth:

- **A birthing pool:** These can be hired or purchased from private companies or through your local homebirthing association. Some can even be used as a paddling pool for your child afterwards.

- **A container for the placenta:** You may not be aware that after the baby is born, another process is required — the delivery of the placenta. Known as the *third stage of labour*, safe delivery of the complete placenta is vitally important for your partner's wellbeing — retained placenta can be fatal. And delivering the placenta can make some mess (because childbirth is messy). Be prepared with somewhere to put it, such as a bucket.

- **Towels:** For cleaning up and wrapping the baby after birth, and for mum and dad if you've both been in the pool.

- **Waterproof mats to cover your carpet:** A tarpaulin covered with newspaper and an old blanket or sheets should provide enough protection.

Your midwife can give you a full list of everything you need to have prepared.

Checking Off Final Items

You have so much to do and only nine months to do it in. Along with watching your partner's belly grow and preparing for the biggest change in your life yet, you still have a few last things to organise and check as the big day closes in. The following sections provide some ideas.

Transport

You've no doubt seen movies where Ms Pregnant goes into labour and Mr Pregnant drives like a crazy man to get to the hospital before the baby's born. If you're having a hospital birth rather than a home birth, some variation of the movie scene is likely to happen to you — without the driving like a crazy man part, of course. Instead, you can do some preparation now to help ensure you get there calmly and safely.

Depending on how far away you live, you may want to check some time in advance of the birth on how to get to the hospital. Some people even do a test run to see how long the drive takes them — and that's not as over-the-top as it seems. The more familiar you are with exactly where you're going, the more calm you both are on the ride in — and the more you can focus on the things that matter, such as safety and your partner's comfort and contractions.

When you do your hospital tour, ask the staff if any special parking is available for families in the maternity ward. This could save you time — and a long, uncomfortable walk for your partner — when the big moment arrives. Unlike the movies, a parking space isn't likely to magically appear right outside the delivery suite doors (although they likely have a drop-off zone nearby), so doing a little investigative work before the big day about where you can park is worthwhile.

TIP

You might also want to think about the following transport considerations:

>> Is where you park the car at home accessible night and day, or is your car blocked in by other cars at certain periods?

>> If your car doesn't start (think flat battery), do you have someone you can call as a back-up?

>> Do you have enough fuel in the tank to get you there?

>> Have you got a capsule or car seat to transport your baby home? Is it fitted correctly? Do you know how to use it? (That is, take out the capsule to carry the baby, place the capsule into the holder, and so on?)

The hospital bag(s)

The old conundrum of knowing what to take on holiday and what to leave behind is nothing compared to the quandary of what to take to the hospital when your baby is on its way.

Packing the hospital bag is often broken down into three sections — things needed for mum during the birth, things needed for mum after the birth and things needed for the baby. Things needed for dad often get a bit neglected, because fathers have a little more flexibility and capacity to look after their own needs (if and when those needs arrive).

REMEMBER

Chances are you won't be thinking about what you need once the labour kicks off. So in your final preparations and bag packing, focus on the needs of mum and bub.

In the following sections, I outline what to pack in a mum- and baby-friendly hospital bag.

What the parents need during the birth

You need some or all of the following items for the big event:

>> **Appropriate clothing:** Mum's feet might get cold in an air-conditioned hospital, so pack a pair of nice comfy soft socks. Work out what she wants to wear while she is in labour, and make sure it's in the bag — though be aware that clothing becomes an annoyance for many women in labour, and she may decide to take most of it off. If you're having a water birth or plan to use the shower during labour at the hospital, you might want to pack a pair of shorts so you can get in the pool or shower, too.

>> **Mobile phone and charger:** In this day and age, this probably goes without saying, but I'll say it anyway. Remember your phone charger. Your phone is going to get a workout during these next few days.

>> **Headphones:** In your partner's downtime during recovery, she may want to close out the world and have some quality screen or music time on her phone.

>> **Snacks and drinks:** Some labours can take a long time (24 hours is not unusual), and mum doing all that pushing and dad doing all that supporting is hard work. Hydration and energy are the two things most needed by a labouring mum. To keep fluids up, offer water, juice or ice. Hydration assists the muscles to do their work and they need it.

TIP

The digestion process almost stops as labour progresses. Your partner's body has too many other — and more important — things to focus on rather than digestion, so the easier food is to digest, the better. Easy to digest foods include fruit such as grapes, ripe bananas or whatever is in season, and juices. Pack some snacks for yourself as well — you don't want to be marauding hospital corridors during the night when you're hungry, and the food in the hospital hallway vending machines is not particularly sustaining.

WARNING

Plan to minimise your phone use during labour. Watching Instagram reels or sports on your phone while your partner is in labour doesn't go down so well. Instead plan to have your phone turned off most of the time — the main game is what is happening right there in front of you and the more you are 'present', the stronger the connection you will have together. Pain and discomfort are very personal things, but someone being there 'with you' and doing what they can for you is a world away from having them watch something funny on YouTube or grab a sports update.

Your partner likely won't want loud noises or strong smells (such as candles or incense) with her in the birthing room, so no need to pack these.

What mum needs after the birth

In all likelihood, after the birth you ideally spend a few hours with your new baby, call everyone you want to call and feel a little giddy. You probably head home for a shower, something to eat and a sleep. But mum needs at least these things to help her settle into her stay at the hospital:

» A change of comfortable clothes for coming home — just make sure you don't pack pre-pregnancy clothes, because your partner's body won't usually completely re-adjust straightaway

» Lanolin nipple cream that doesn't need to be washed off before breastfeeding

» Maternity bras and nursing pads for leaking breastmilk

» Maternity pads (though these are sometimes supplied by the hospital)

» Pen and notebook for recording a few things after the birth

» Pyjamas or a nightie that opens at the front for breastfeeding, a dressing gown and slippers

» Soft cotton undies

» Toiletries your partner uses regularly, such as a toothbrush, shampoos, cleanser, deodorant, moisturiser, lip balm, contact lens supplies, hair bands and brush, and any medications

What bub needs after the birth

The little person you're taking home needs

» **Disposable nappies:** Even if you're going to use cloth nappies, *meconium*, the sticky tar-like poo your baby expels in the first few days after birth, is best handled by disposable nappies because meconium can be hard to get out of cloth ones. Many hospitals don't give away free nappies anymore, so be prepared and take a few extra.

» **Bottle feeding equipment (if applicable):** Undoubtedly, breast is best — the empirical research supporting breastfeeding is overwhelming. It's good for mum and it's good for your new baby. But sometimes breastfeeding is not feasible, and sometimes — even with the best intentions — it just doesn't work out and can't be done. You should feel no shame if this is the case, and in Australia we're fortunate to have an alternative if breastfeeding can't be done. Formula (labelled 'from birth'), bottles, teats and sterilising equipment are all necessary if you're going to bottle feed.

>> **Muslin wraps or blankets:** Hospital air-conditioning can be chilly, and wrapping (or swaddling) your newborn helps her feel more secure.

>> **Something to wear:** A couple of newborn-sized all-in-ones with feet and long sleeves, some hats or beanies, and some socks or booties will also be useful. Newborns are used to being in a nice warm womb and aren't great at controlling their temperature yet, so even in summer they need to be kept warm. You may also have a special 'coming home' outfit picked out.

>> **Wipes and nappy rash cream:** These items are needed for cleaning and protecting your baby's bottom while changing her nappies.

WARNING

Don't be tempted to throw in a dummy (or pacifier) when packing for bub. While a dummy is probably one of the most commonly known baby accessories, lactation consultants may not be that happy about you giving your little one a dummy — especially if you're experiencing breastfeeding difficulties. This is because dummies are believed to cause 'nipple confusion' in some cases. Dental experts also argue pretty strongly against them because of the pressure they put on newly formed teeth down the track. Additionally, in a couple of years' time when it's time to ditch the dummy, you're going to find your little baby has a strong opinion about keeping it around. The removal process can get pretty ugly. My advice: avoid a dummy if you can. This may create some short-term pain here and there, but the disadvantages are overwhelming in comparison.

TIP

If you want to go the extra mile to ensure you've got everything you could possibly need for your newborn, check with a midwife. And check with a lactation consultant for any breastfeeding equipment, aids or remedies your partner may need.

Checklists

In all the excitement of becoming a father, forgetting stuff is really easy, so devise a comprehensive list of everything you think you're likely to need and put this list somewhere you can't miss it. Don't leave getting ready up to your memory — you're bound to forget something.

Your checklist should include

>> **Car seat:** Have you got a car seat sorted and know how to fit it into your car?

>> **Home birth list:** Mats to protect floors, home birth pool if you want it, towels for yourself and the baby, and anything else your midwife requires.

>> **Nursery:** Baby has somewhere to sleep and bedding to sleep in, baby has clothes to wear, you have something to store clothes in, baby has nappies and bum protection, and you have something to change baby on.

>> **Pet care:** Who can look after any pets during the birth while you're not at home?

>> **Phone list:** Have a back-up list of emergency numbers, and numbers for your lead maternity carer, maternity ward, friends, family and work (as well as having them as contacts on your phone).

>> **Your hospital bags:** For during the birth, for the hospital stay and for bub.

>> **Your transport:** Ensure your car has petrol, you know your way to the hospital, and you know where parking is.

IN THIS CHAPTER

» **Getting ready for labour**

» **Knowing what to do during labour**

» **Supporting your partner to deliver your baby**

» **Cherishing the moment your baby arrives**

» **Enjoying the first few hours and days with your baby**

Chapter **5**

Birth

B eing born is, ironically, the most dangerous thing you probably do in your life. In developing countries, just having a baby is still a precarious thing to do. That said, infant mortality rates are at the lowest in history and constantly dropping. In Australia, problems during birth are rare and plenty of help is available if things get a bit tricky.

But that doesn't mean you can take everything for granted. You need to know what's going on during birth. Knowledge is power, so I've built this chapter to turn you into a support superstar for the pending birth of your baby. Of course, no two births are the same and no-one can tell you what's going to happen during the birth of your child. The process may seem a bit random and very drawn out, but usually that's just part of the journey to dadhood.

In this chapter, you find out about the different phases and stages of labour, when real labour starts and when to call your carer or get to the hospital. You discover strategies for making labour less of a pain for your partner and how to keep both of you sane during this trying time.

I also cover some medical issues you, your partner or the baby might experience during labour, and guide you to welcoming your baby to the world. Finally, I give you some useful information on how to get through the first few hours and days with your newborn baby.

The Final Countdown

Finally, the big moment is here — you and your partner have probably been thinking about the time when your baby is born for most of the pregnancy. The somewhat unpredictable nature of the onset of labour adds to the excitement. Going through labour is a bit like doing your first parachute jump — except that someone pushes you out the door whether you're ready or not. So enjoy the ride!

Discovering what you need to know about labour

You can't be too prepared for labour. And because you're number one in the support crew, understanding what's going on is essential. Like all good things in life, labour happens in three stages, as follows:

>> The **first stage** is when your partner's cervix softens, then widens (*dilates*), making space for the baby to transition from the womb (uterus) down the birth canal and out into the world. The uterus contracts at regular intervals (contractions), slowly opening the cervix (the entry to the uterus), which will eventually allow the baby to come through. As the labour progresses, the contractions become increasingly painful. The cervix is fully dilated to facilitate the baby's birth when it reaches ten centimetres (which is another way of saying the opening from the uterus to the birth canal is wide enough for the baby's head). For a first birth, the first stage takes an average of 6 to 14 hours (but can take a day or more), so you can see that your presence with a strong shoulder, lots of reassurance (and ice to sip), plus heat packs (to soothe) really helps. Not all of this time in the first stage of labour is spent in 'active labour' — more on this later.

>> The **second stage** is the bit where your partner pushes the baby out. The second stage is also helped along by contractions that are different in feeling and intensity to first stage contractions. Second stage is when mum is actively engaged in pushing the baby down the chute, rather than focusing on 'getting through' the contractions of the first stage — when her job was to relax and let her body do its thing (open her cervix). In the second stage, your partner becomes more actively involved with using each contraction to help your baby come down through the birth canal and out into the world. Second stage is complete when your little one arrives!

>> The **third stage** is a little less glamorous (as if birth is at all glamorous) and involves the placenta, that lifeline to your baby, being born. The placenta is also called *afterbirth*. Delivering the placenta takes between five minutes to an hour. Most women are too knackered by this stage — or energised by finally

meeting their baby — to notice much about expelling the placenta. Many births have delivery of the placenta assisted by an injection given into the mother's thigh as the baby's head is birthing at the end of the second stage. This causes the vessels connecting the placenta to the uterine wall to close off and reduces the risk of haemorrhage, so if you see this injection happening, don't be alarmed.

Think that's all there is to it? Nuh-uh. You have a ways to go yet in getting prepared for labour.

REMEMBER

The more you understand, the better you are when crunch time comes. Because you understand what is happening in each stage, you can recognise progress and that things are generally following a well-trodden path. Being able to communicate this progress will be a critical support for your partner when the going gets tough. So the more you understand and see the progress, the more you can be that steadying, reassuring influence to your partner and give her the strength to keep going.

The first stage also progresses through three phases. Your partner may be too caught up in the moment to recognise them as they happen to her, but signposts can be spotted along the way. The following outlines the three phases of the first stage and some of the ways you can identify them:

>> **Latent phase:** This is the very beginning of labour. Contractions begin and are 5 to 20 minutes apart and usually last from 20 to 30 seconds. Generally, these contractions are felt as small waves, often described as moderate tummy cramps. Progression is slow and steady at this stage and continues to be until the cervix is at around three centimetres dilation.

REMEMBER

Life can go on pretty much as normal during the latent phase. If this phase starts at night, don't get caught up timing contractions and watching the clock. Get some sleep. The best thing you (and especially your partner) can do during this phase is to relax, rest and snooze. If it's happening during the day, just get on with things. (My wife had a haircut while she was in the latent phase of two of our six pregnancies. She wasn't trying to look good for the birth . . . she just happened to have hairdresser appointments that day!)

All you need to know is that things are starting and that the contractions become more frequent as the labour progresses. (You won't know exactly what the cervix is doing but the contractions indicate when things are revving up.)

>> **Active phase:** This phase is characterised by the cervix dilating from about three centimetres to ten centimetres, known as *fully dilated*. Contractions increase in length and intensity and come every three to five minutes. Your

partner is now becoming more inwardly focused. She may be less communicative and not have the headspace to be thinking of what's going on 'out there'. This is where you become 'active' as well — ensuring what she needs is there for her.

TIP

Keep an eye on the timing of these contractions and make sure you're *really present* for your partner through this phase. Be ready with the ice in cups and back rubs. And actively check in, thinking *for* her and providing reassurance — unless she tells you to stop it already!

>> **Transition:** This is the point just before the pushing starts (as part of second stage labour). Contractions are very intense, sometimes overwhelming and your partner may say things like, 'I can't do it!', 'I want this to be overrrr!', 'Get me out of here', or 'I want an epidural!' — plus a whole lot of swear words I don't need to list here. She may also be hot, sweaty, feel nauseous and make sounds you have never heard before. Remember, this is normal for transition. See the sidebar 'Understanding the drama of transition' for more on why.

UNDERSTANDING THE DRAMA OF TRANSITION

Transition is where the real drama of labour and childbirth occurs. It's the part of labour almost everyone remembers and talks about. Transition doesn't last as long as the other parts of labour (thank goodness), but it is the most memorable in terms of your partner (and you) being taken to the edge. It helps to know why.

As labour progresses, everything will feel pretty smooth and almost predictable, until transition. Even though the contractions are painful, things will make sense. You'll be timing contractions, and noting what time they each start and how long they are lasting. You'll likely be feeling as if things are under control and progressing. And — this is the critical thing — your partner won't be feeling any real urge to push. It's not there. Not a bit. She knows the baby is coming psychologically, and she wants it to happen, but no physical urge is felt yet to actually deliver the baby.

When your partner is dilated to around seven centimetres, a huge shift happens. Until this stage, everything her body has been doing is directed towards her body opening up (dilating). Her cervix has been contracting upwards toward her abdomen — it's literally been pulling *up* the uterus so the opening to the birth canal is wide enough for the baby to pass through safely.

When your partner hits the seven-centimetre dilation mark, her body lifts momentum to a whole new level. Hormones such as oxytocin and endorphins are pumping, and things are picking up in a big way. A transition is taking place — it's almost time for the baby to come down the birth canal and one contraction at this point does the work that many contractions were doing before. It's intense. It's called transition as movement turns downwards so the baby can be pushed out. Everything was about moving/opening up. Now, it's about bearing down (while it still has to open another three centimetres.) Only someone experiencing this contraction can understand how it feels — and that's not blokes. So now's the time when you need to be the calm in the storm. This, more than any other time, is the business end of childbirth.

REMEMBER

One of the more obvious signs that things are about to kick off is when your partner's waters break (that is, the membranes of the *amniotic sac* rupture). This sometimes happens in the most inappropriate situation — but, hey, it's all natural. However, your partner's waters breaking doesn't always mean she's in labour. She may be but, in some cases, labour starts up to 24 hours after the waters break. Either way, calling your midwife or doctor to inform your carer that the waters have broken is a good idea. Read about more signs of the first stage of labour in the section 'When you think you're in labour', later in this chapter.

WARNING

If you spot any blood or meconium (poo) when the water breaks, contact your midwife or doctor and seek immediate medical attention.

Understanding your role in labour

Supporting and being there for your partner is really important. So what does 'being there' really mean? Ask a lot of dads who've been through the birth of their children and the answer that might spring to mind is something like, 'Stand around like an idiot and feel guilty and inadequate'. Feeling sidelined is possible when the focus is on your partner and she's in kind of a crabby mood with you — which you would be, too, if you had three kilos of person coming out of an orifice. She's focusing on what her body is doing, listening to the coaching and advice of her midwife or obstetrician, and coping with pain, hormones and emotions you can't even begin to imagine (or don't want to).

In general, your partner relies on you to sort out a long list of support tasks, which you can do with dignity and humility. So, if your partner needs a shoulder to hang onto for leverage when she's pushing, give it to her. If she needs a drink in a cup with a straw and three ice cubes, get it organised. If your partner says she can't do it anymore, tell her with conviction that she can. Being there means taking care of your partner when she needs you to and, most importantly, reassuring her that it will all work out when she needs you to.

Labour can be totally overwhelming for your partner and she's vulnerable to every emotion in the book. She's also vulnerable to being intimidated by the hospital system: a nurse who suggests pain relief even though your partner wants to have a natural birth; an obstetrician or midwife who wants to set up a drip to speed things along (and increase stress and pain levels with it) because it might make things go faster but not tell you the downside; or an over pushy *lactation consultant* who's stressing out your exhausted partner. If something doesn't feel right, you have to make a decision for the good of your partner and baby and advocate on their behalf. The health and wellbeing of mum and baby are *always* top of the list, but if the baby isn't showing signs of stress and mum wants to keep trying for the birth you and she have discussed, then give her the encouragement she needs and advocate for her preferences. The decisions involve your family so you get to be 'the man who calls the shots' when push comes to shove.

Dads can really make their role count during labour by being

>> **Thoughtful and connected:** Help out where you can by making sure your partner is as comfortable as she can be, is well stocked with snacks and water, and is warm or cool enough. She may not notice she's thirsty until you offer a drink to her. She may need to be gently prompted to go to the bathroom every 40 minutes or so to empty her bladder. (The walk will help labour along and emptying her bladder will be helpful when the pushing starts — nothing impedes progress like a full bladder.) Gentle reminders with clear direction work best. And be aware of your timing — during the contraction is not the time to suggest anything except that the contraction is doing its work and will be gone soon. (Say things like, 'This is good, and it's helping your body open up. 20 seconds to go. Stay with it. Nearly there.') Once the contraction is over, let her know how well she's done and then suggest what you think she may need. Don't take offence if she shuts down a suggestion — she doesn't have the headspace for small talk. Let her know you have her back and her front and everything else. This is about being there for her and looking out for her when she is at her most vulnerable.

>> **The rational calm voice in the hustle and bustle:** Even when things get stressful or hectic, try to keep your cool on your partner's behalf and advocate for her if things are slipping out of control. Medical staff will be open to requests by you when you are respectful of them. As long as they see what you are asking is in line with what your partner wants, they'll go along with it. A nod from her is always helpful.

>> **A link to the outside world:** Let friends and family know what's going on — because they're likely to be anxious to hear how the birth's going. You can also be the first to announce to the world that your new son or daughter has arrived — a very special thing to be able to do! But make sure that your focus is on your partner first. Tell everyone to leave you alone. 'Don't call us, we'll call you' is the best way to deal with excited family and friends.

REMEMBER

Once labour kicks off, take your cues from your partner. Her needs are pretty specific and she lets you know about them. But don't try to tell your partner you know how she feels, because you don't. Any complaining (to her) of any sort from your end is more muppet and less man. Don't be a muppet, no matter how sore your shoulders and arms are from all that massage or holding her up in the shower.

TIP

Have a standby support person in case labour goes on for a long time, or you desperately need some rest. Talk about who would be suitable with your partner. Perhaps her sister or mother could fill in for you while you have a meal or take a breather.

iPhone APPS DURING LABOUR

A wide variety of applications have been specifically designed to monitor the duration and frequency of your partner's contractions during labour. I suggest a few here, but be mindful that such a list dates quickly. So first keep in mind the following when you search online for an app that can offer you support as you track labour progress:

- **Expert development:** You really want the app to have strong expert engagement — and I'm not talking about expert tech development (although that will be useful). Research-backed medical expertise is what you're chasing here.

- **Data saving/sharing:** Some time after the baby is born, you might be surprised to hear yourself saying, 'Do you think we should have another baby?' (Not too soon. Tread carefully.) If you've been able to save the info from your first birth, you have data on what happened. If you need to consult with medicos for your second pregnancy, you can tell them exactly how it happened the first time around.

- **It's all in the reviews:** Take a look at what people are saying. The app reviews are usually going to be a pretty useful guide.

- **Customisability:** It's just more fun when you can upload images and go a bit 'goo goo' at pics of your baby.

At time of publication, the following apps are useful to consider:

- The Wonder Weeks
- What to Expect
- Sprout Pregnancy
- Lorestry

Getting ready — last minute preparations

As you count down the days to your partner's due date, you could be feeling all sorts of things — excitement about meeting your baby for the first time, or absolute terror about the reality of your new responsibility. Anything you're feeling is okay; all expectant dads have been there.

You may also be a bit worried about how you're going to handle the birthing process, about your role in it and how well your partner is going to cope. Worrying is okay and, while it's uncommon, occasionally guys will pass out or even throw up during labour, which is all part of the journey. Nearly everyone ends up being emotional — and, yes, crying. Preparing for birth has been a long, hard ride. Having a baby enter the world is a big deal. Basically, just ride it out and remember it doesn't get better than this moment. This is life at its most complete.

Before the fun starts, double-check (or triple-check) a few things, such as ensuring you've

>> Arranged for someone to look after your pets/plants and clear your mail. You may be gone some time.

>> Briefed people at work, or left handover notes or contact details if you need to leave suddenly.

>> Got the hospital bags packed and ready to go, even if you're planning a home birth, in case you need to transfer to a hospital in a hurry.

>> Made sure the car seat is ready to go and practised putting it in and taking it out of the car.

>> Stored phone numbers of friends and family from both sides on your mobile phone and ensured the phone's charged with plenty of credit if you use a prepaid model. (Remember to take your phone charger with you when you leave the delivery room.)

The checklists provided in Chapter 4 can help you remember anything you may have forgotten.

BRING IT ON!

Though only around 5 per cent of babies are born on their due date, passing that magical day without a babe in her arms will probably weigh on your partner's mind. She may have been viewing the due date as the finish line and to go over it without a result may push her to the end of her tether. By now, the less desirable effects of pregnancy like fluid retention, heartburn, insomnia, weight gain, shortness of breath, waddling and having that baby kick her insides won't be such a novelty. Your partner wants her body back and your baby out.

You can try certain techniques to help bring on labour, and some can even be fun, but none can guarantee results. No doubt everyone you meet who has asked you 'Is the baby here yet?' will follow up with one of these ideas:

- **Drink castor oil.** Drinking castor oil may help stimulate contractions. I don't recommend drinking castor oil because it makes the contractions pretty nasty, but no doubt someone will recommend it to you so be warned and, really . . . stay away.

- **Have acupuncture or acupressure.** Some people swear by the results of having acupuncture needles or pressure applied to certain points of the body. Others think it's coincidental when labour naturally happens soon after the procedure's done.

- **Have sex**. The *prostaglandin* in your semen may help to *ripen* the cervix, making it ready to dilate. Some say it makes no difference. Others say it does. Check with your partner (consent is king), and recognise that at this point in the process, it's not going to be the most fun you (or her) have ever had.

- **Make your loved one a spicy meal.** The aim is give your girl diarrhoea, which can start contractions. It may just give her more heartburn. It's a lousy suggestion, but it keeps coming up.

- **'Sweep the membranes' or 'strip and stretch'.** Sometimes called having a 'sweep' done, during this rather uncomfortable procedure the midwife or doctor puts their fingers inside the cervix. Once inside, they stretch open the cervix and strip membranes away from it.

- **Take a walk together.** The rocking motion may help stimulate contractions. The downward pressure can help too. This is the least invasive and most natural option, and — so long as your partner is happy to walk — the one I most recommend.

Your partner isn't considered overdue until 42 weeks and three days after conception. If labour hasn't happened, you can discuss with your carer when or if to induce the baby. This involves using prostaglandin to ripen the cervix, rupturing the amniotic sac and using *syntocinon*, a synthetic form of *oxytocin*, to start contractions. The medical establishment loves to control things and can be very much pro-induction. As much as you both want that baby out, go gently and wait if you can.

Action!

Your partner thinks something may be happening. Don't panic. It may be launch time, or it may be a false alarm.

When you think you're in labour

You can have the following signs that the birth of your baby is not far away, but it can be days or weeks before full-on labour really starts.

Here are some indicators that things are about to get interesting, but you shouldn't get too excited yet:

>> **A bloody show or mucous plug:** Most people simply call this 'the show'. The mucous plug that blocks the cervix during pregnancy comes away, along with blood from broken capillaries in the cervix.

>> **Braxton Hicks contractions:** These are mild contractions, similar to strong period pain or cramps. They're not 'real' contractions, but may be confused with them.

>> **Intense or increasing back pain:** This can also be a sign that things are beginning to happen.

>> **Loose bowel motions:** A few days before labour, the body releases prostaglandins, which help soften the cervix ready for dilation. Prostaglandins also cause things to be a bit loose in the bowel department.

REMEMBER

Don't worry if none of the things in the preceding list happens before the contractions start. Every labour, birth and woman is different, so call your carer if you're not sure about what's happening.

When the first stage of labour begins, your partner may feel like birth is really happening, but it isn't yet. The difference between the latent phase (also sometimes called *early labour*) and the active phase (sometimes called *active labour*) of the first stage of labour is the length and intensity of contractions. If you're still a bit confused about the various stages and phases of labour, check the definitions provided in the section 'Discovering what you need to know about labour', earlier in this chapter.

REMEMBER

If you and your partner aren't sure whether labour has commenced, or whether your partner is in the latent or active phase, call your midwife, obstetrician or GP for support. Your carer can give you guidance on whether you need to grab the car keys, or if you can settle in for the evening.

When you're really in labour

First things first. You know your partner is in labour because

» Contractions are regular (one every five minutes), lasting 45 to 60 seconds, and increasing in frequency. (If baby is in the *posterior* position — back against mum's spine — contractions will be a lot less regular, with more back ache and less regularity with the contractions.) How long contractions last and how strong they are is key to knowing things are moving along.

» Contractions are getting longer, stronger and closer together, and your partner may not be able to speak during a contraction.

Time to call your carer or head to the hospital (safely) if you haven't already. And once contractions are strengthening and your partner is actively labouring, help her ride the wave of each contraction — increased intensity for 15 seconds followed by strong pain for 30 seconds, and a slow receding of the contraction for 15 seconds (roughly). Talk her through the contraction (so long as she's open to your coaching). Remind her it's happening perfectly so this baby can arrive. And encourage her to rest as much as possible between contractions.

TIP

If your carer hasn't already, alert the maternity ward that you are on your way in (using the number you've already stored in your phone). Let them know what is happening regarding contractions — including length and interval — and how far from the hospital you are so they can be ready for your arrival. Stay calm — your mind will be clearer, and you'll give certainty to your partner, who needs it right now. Plus you'll get there safely.

WARNING

Don't go driving fast or tearing around corners like a Formula One driver — after all, you want to all arrive in one piece at the hospital. This is not the time to be the hero in the car. Fast driving won't make your partner feel good — and, let's face it, she's probably already a little stressed. Very little upside can be gained, and huge potential downside. Keep it together and drive safely.

Helping Your Partner through Childbirth

Get buckled in, because you're in for a real treat. Lucky you — you get to be part of your baby's story right now. The high of seeing a child born is like nothing on Earth — and you're about to meet your own child. How cool is that? In the following sections, I take you through supporting your partner through all the stages of labour, including if any medical intervention is required.

First, though, let's slow down a little at phase one of the labour, the latent phase.

Offering supporting during the latent phase

Many women spend the *latent phase* of labour at home, where they're more comfortable and have lots of room to move around. Even if you're planning a hospital birth, staying at home for as long as is feasible is usually best. Some mums who go to the hospital too early tense up because they're at the hospital (which can slow down labour), and they may experience fatigue earlier than if they'd stayed at home for longer. Plus, it can get boring at the hospital if you're there half a day (or more) early.

REMEMBER

Once in a hospital setting, the focus is fully on the labour. When you and your partner are at home, you can feel more relaxed and the emphasis isn't just on those contractions.

During this latent phase, especially if it's at night, focus on rest. Your partner can sleep between contractions or even through them — they'll wake her up if they start moving along. Relaxation really is the key to the dilation (opening) of the cervix (which is often why labour begins at night). Now is not the time for mum to feel like she needs to vacuum the house so everything's ready for her return (and a modern man like you is going to have that taken care of anyway).

Depending on what time of day it is when labour begins, however, some activity is good, and an easy walk can stimulate contractions and help progress things if contractions are off to a sluggish start. The emphasis, though, is on ensuring you are both in a good space physically for when things move along later on. So whatever promotes calm and relaxation is best.

Contractions during the latent phase shouldn't be unmanageable and you can try these techniques to relieve whatever discomfort your partner is feeling:

» Apply a heatpack or hot water bottle to where your partner feels the most pain — for example, your partner's bump or lower back.

» Give your partner a gentle back rub with some massage oil.

» Run a bath or turn on the shower for your partner — warm water soothes, and a bath can soften the strength of the contractions. If her membranes have ruptured (that is, her waters have broken), a shower is the better option (and no sex if waters have broken!).

» Keep your partner moving (as long as it's not the middle of the night). Movement can help labour progress and gravity means the baby's weight puts pressure on the cervix, helping it to dilate.

>> Turn down the lights.

>> Offer drinks and snacks as needed.

REMEMBER

Your partner may not want food but having it on standby is always good. Offer it when you think she might be open to having something. Make her your focus — you may have to suggest she drinks something or show her the different foods at times when you think she may be hungry. She'll let you know very quickly what she needs or doesn't want.

Ramping up into active phase and then second stage

As contractions get stronger and you move into the active and transition phases of the first stage of labour, and then the second stage of labour, you can continue with the pain relief techniques outlined in the preceding section. Let your partner guide you as to what she needs. At certain points, your partner won't have the ability to do anything other than ride out a contraction, especially in the second stage when she's putting everything into pushing the baby out. Holding up your partner's body and letting her lean on you in whatever way she needs is a great help to her during this demanding time.

REMEMBER

During the active phase of the first stage of labour (when the cervix dilates from four to seven centimetres), contractions build for about 20 to 30 seconds. They peak for between 15 and 30 seconds and then they gradually come down as the uterus uses up the oxygen in the muscles and needs time to build that up again. After a total of around 60 seconds, that contraction is over. Some are slightly shorter. Some fizzle and do nothing. But most will be consistent. Your job is to support your partner through those contractions and facilitate her rest when they're over.

TIP

To support your partner best during the contraction process, talk her through each contraction. Remind her that contractions are like a wave. Once the contraction is over, the focus is to rest, regroup and relax. Offer ice. Every 40 minutes, see if your partner needs to empty her bladder or to stand and walk. (This applies downwards pressure in a healthy way.) Watch and see if any areas need a strong rub or gentle massage. Reassure your partner that relaxation continues to be the key to dilation, and that riding the contractions instead of resisting them is how they work at their best.

As the birth gets closer, the body increases the contraction rate and intensity — particularly during transition (when the cervix dilates from seven to ten centimetres). It's almost time for the pushing to happen. Contractions build quickly and peak for longer with less time between them. Each contraction still lasts for about 60 seconds, but the build is only 10 seconds, the peak is 40 seconds, and the slow-down is shorter.

This is really an 'all hands on deck' time. You can ride that contraction wave with your partner by talking her through it. Reassure her that it's doing what it should. Encourage her to take a deep breath as it begins and to relax into it, knowing it's doing its job, and opening the cervix for the baby to come out. As you see the intensity start to ebb, confirm with her it's going. Reassure her everything is okay and happening as it should. Unless she tells you to 'just stop talking', your coaching is the best support she can have. This is a powerful time of relationship building as she learns to trust you to be her guide during the hardest thing she's ever done.

TIP

Between contractions, you might find your partner becoming anxious about the next contraction. This is where you remind her to use this 'down' time for what it's meant to be for her: a time to relax, breathe, rest and recover. Acknowledge that another contraction will come, and that you'll work together through it — and then it will go and the baby will be that much closer. But also acknowledge the current calm. Your coaching as contractions come and go like waves will keep you both present and focused, and will become an experience that binds you together.

Being calm in the eye of the transition storm

By the time transition from phase one to phase two of labour arrives, your partner is often kaput. Labour is long and physically taxing. It seems to regularly happen at night, so exhaustion can become overpowering. This is the time when you bring your very best you to the support-person role. During transition, your partner may cry. She may tell you she wants to give up and it's all too much. Or you might cop a barrage of verbal abuse like you've never heard before. Those hormones are screaming through her body and she can feel like it's all too much. Rationality can disappear.

At this point, *you* may also wonder what's going on. You may feel helpless and want it to stop. You'll be hearing her say she can't do it anymore and you may question yourself about what right you have to encourage her to keep going. Can you do anything that will really help her?

The answer is a definite 'yes'. The greatest thing you can do when she is at her lowest is to become her strength when hers is failing. You are the one who can see the progress made when she's caught in the middle of the storm. You are the one who knows that each contraction *will* end and huge progress is being made with each mountainous contraction.

You may feel like you have no right to say it, but tell her with intent and conviction:

>> 'I'm here. You can do this. I believe in you.'

>> 'Just get through this next one. I'm here with you — we can do this.'

>> 'You'll have a break after this next contraction. Just relax — I'm so proud of you.'

>> 'You're doing so well — you're almost there.'

Let her know you're there. Reassure her of how brave she is and that she'll be okay. The transition phase is when you see the unspeakable sacrifice a woman makes to bring a child into the world. If you're lucky, witnessing this will humble you in ways you didn't know were possible, and will make you love your partner to a depth you weren't aware existed. If you're man enough, this is the time you tell her all of that and more. And it's the moment you realise just how strong this woman you love actually is.

Remembering it's not about you

Labour can take a long time. You may get a chance to have a breather between contractions, or you may not. Giving all your energy to your partner is exhausting, *but this is not about you just now* — and the exhaustion you're feeling is nothing compared to hers. Your partner needs you. She needs to know you are there, that you believe in her, and that she can rely on you to coach and guide her, gently, through this.

Perhaps you've heard stories of soon-to-be dads who watched a game of footy while their wife laboured. Or they closed a business deal, went to the pub for a drink with the boys, or did some other stuff that made for a 'great story' years later. But these kinds of actions (and stories) are neither cool nor manly. They are not what makes your partner feel supported. I'll say it again: this process is not about you. Paradoxically, the more you make it about your partner and her comfort, the better the experience actually becomes for you — particularly when you look back on it years later.

Acceptable things for dads to do during labour include

>> Crying (actually, sobbing) when the baby arrives and you see your partner as the most impossibly strong human on the planet

>> Doing some stretching exercises to keep fresh and fend off sleep

>> Drinking water or juices to keep yourself in good condition for the ride ahead

- » Eating snacks

- » Fainting (although you really don't want to do this; try to keep it together and savour the experience)

- » Getting some fresh air (but minimise your time away; if you're all-in, you won't want to leave)

- » Going to the toilet (as long as it's not too often and doesn't take too long)

- » Leaving the room because you're feeling unwell or faint (again, don't be away too long)

The following actions are really in stark contrast to the future super dad you're aiming to be:

- » Bringing your office work to do on your laptop

- » Inviting people (including family and friends) into the delivery suite

- » Joking with the staff instead of giving your partner your focus

- » Playing video games on your mobile

- » Sneaking into the vacant birthing suite next door to have a kip or snoring in a recliner in the birthing suite

- » Talking to others on the phone or in the room while your partner's contracting or needs you (which is most of the time)

- » Telling your partner how tired you are

- » Watching your favourite show or sport on your phone

Unfortunately these stories are told, often with accompanying laughter, all too often. My response: be a man, not a muppet.

Giving nature a helping hand

Sometimes during labour, nature needs help to get your baby out into the world. Lots of reasons exist for this: the baby may be in distress, your partner's health is in jeopardy, or your partner's exhausted and wants the baby out now! None of the interventions covered in the following sections can really be anticipated. Keep in touch with your partner and, if she's adamant she doesn't want any intervention, be her advocate. But don't be the decision-maker. It's her choice, not yours, and hospital staff (or the midwife if it's a home birth) will want to hear what she wants — not you. Talk together if you have time and options, and help her make the decision that is best for her and the baby. You can be the rational and kind part of the decision-making process.

REMEMBER

Being open to what medical staff are telling you is important. In spite of your best laid plans, sometimes intervention is the only way the baby (or your partner) might survive. Don't be rigid. Be her advocate, but recognise that sometimes pragmatism wins out.

Ventouse

A *ventouse* is a vacuum extractor that helps pull the baby out of the *birth canal*. A ventouse is used when the baby's head is low in the birth canal but needs an extra bit of oomph to help him along. The baby's heart rate may indicate he's in distress, or his position may be making it tricky for him to be born naturally.

A suction cup is put onto the baby's head and your partner may have to have an *episiotomy*, which is a cut to the vaginal opening, to make room for the cup to go in. A ventouse can cause swelling to the top of the baby's head, but usually causes little or no trauma to the mother and baby. Episiotomies are easily stitched up by competent doctors and, while your partner will be tender for a while, won't have any impact on long-term comfort (or your sex life) going forward.

WARNING

Don't get involved in medical decisions if an episiotomy is required. Let the medical professionals do their thing and trust that it will be okay. (And please, PLEASE, don't be that guy who tells the doctor to 'stitch things up tight'. It's completely unacceptable and inappropriate, and makes you look small and selfish. You may think even including this here is in poor taste, but I've heard too many men speak specifically about that idea, and I have to mention it. Be better than that.) Let the experts do their job and look after your partner's needs professionally.

Forceps

Forceps look like a scary pair of tongs. They are used to grip the baby's head on both sides and pull him out of the birth canal. Forceps aren't used as often as ventouse these days because of the risk that the mother's insides (including her pelvic floor muscles) can be damaged, not to mention the bruising and risk of damage to the baby's head. An episiotomy is routinely required with forceps use as well.

Emergency caesarean

The big daddy of medical interventions during labour is the emergency caesarean. These kinds of caesareans are called 'emergency' to distinguish them from elective caesareans, where you opt for birth this way. All caesareans take place in an operating theatre, and you have to wear a gown and cover your hair. Your partner is given an *epidural* to numb pain (although, in some cases, the caesarean has to be performed under general anaesthetic), and an incision is made in your partner's belly, usually near the pubic bone, known as a bikini cut. The abdominal muscles are parted and the *peritoneal cavity* is opened to make way for the uterus. The uterus is then opened, and the baby and placenta are brought out.

Having a caesarean isn't an 'easy' way of having a baby; the procedure is major surgery, and you may not want to look behind the sheet that stops your partner from seeing her insides come out. (Partners are rarely allowed in the room anyhow.) Having a caesarean also means your partner takes weeks to recover, and she isn't able to drive or lift anything heavy for up to six weeks. She's also on pain medication and has to rest a lot as she recovers, and stays in hospital for four or five days.

REMEMBER

If your partner had her heart set on a vaginal birth, or a natural drug-free birth, and the birth hasn't worked out that way, she may be feeling disappointed and upset with herself. Add this to the hormones rampaging through her body and you have one sad little mummy. Give her all the love and support you can muster right now — she needs you.

The Big Moment's Arrived

The moment your child is born is a peak experience that's difficult to describe — unique, beautiful and out of this world. Enjoy it. You may find yourself a sobbing mess when the baby is delivered, particularly if you have ridden every contraction in support of your partner. Cherish this snapshot in time because the moment you clap eyes on your child for the first time can't be rehearsed or repeated.

Cutting the cord

After the placenta is born and your baby is coping on his own without help from mum, the umbilical cord is clamped and set up to cut. This small task can take on several significant meanings for your new family. For your partner, cutting the cord can represent the end of her pregnancy and the start of motherhood. For you, the process might symbolise your part in your new family. Most importantly for your little one, cutting the cord symbolises a point in time where all life support systems from mum are cut off and his body has to sustain him.

REMEMBER

Not every dad wants to cut the cord or sees it in the ceremonial way I've just described it. Some dads are uncomfortable with anything medical, don't like the blood, or perhaps they see cutting the cord as the cutting of the literal tie that bonds mum to bub. You cutting the cord is not a requirement, and if you don't see it as your thing — or you're too overwhelmed and involved in comforting your partner and staring at your baby — don't feel like you need to do it. Of all the things you can be involved in during the birth process, this one is not going to be the thing you remember most.

When time stops — meeting your baby

So you're looking at your child for the first time. The experience can be incredible, scary, bewildering and amazing, all in the space of a few seconds. Time seems to stop as you feel all these emotions washing over you.

Take a moment now to have a good look at what's been cooking for nine months — little fingers, little toes — because mum may have her hands full being taken care of by medical staff right now.

Notice all his little features and enjoy the amazing sight of a newborn baby. Typically, you aren't rushed anymore once your baby has been checked and is handed to you. So you can easily take some time out to make your first acquaintance with the little one. What a great start to a lifelong bond. As dad, you're probably eager to hold that baby close. But usually mum gets first dibs for skin-on-skin time. This is important for mum and bub, and not interfering with that time is best. You get plenty of opportunity soon enough.

Keeping your cool

It's been a long day (or two). You've let your partner and your midwife or doctor guide you through the process and you have to admit to yourself you've been a pretty damn awesome support crew. You've advocated for your partner, you've kept her well stocked with food and drink, massaged till you thought your arms would fall off, and she's right now looking forward to a cuddle with your baby and a good rest. But you may find the demands of the system — the midwife needs to zip off to another appointment before you're ready, or you can't be transferred from the delivery suite to the ward because of paperwork — overrides you right now, so keep advocating for your partner and child if they need it.

Welcoming Your Baby to the Real World

Once bub has finally arrived, thinking that the hard yards are over may be tempting. You may be gazing blissfully at your new baby, enjoying video calls with family, or may be tempted to dash home for a couple of hours' sleep. Cool it for a few minutes more because you have more stuff to get through yet.

What happens immediately after birth

Making sure your new baby is in good health is top priority. Most likely, your baby has come out a rather scary shade of blue or grey, but within a few minutes of breathing actual air, he starts to take on a rosier complexion. He's covered in vernix, the waxy coating that protected his skin in the womb. Your baby may even have a pointy head, caused by his soft baby skull plates moving as he came down the birth canal. Yes, babies can be a bit of a sight when they first emerge into the world! Some babies howl the house down when they're born. Others just like to take things a bit more quietly and have a look around first.

If your baby needs a bit of help breathing, your carer may massage his back with a warm cloth, or suction some fluid from his mouth or nose. Don't worry, he'll be good as gold soon.

At one minute and five minutes after birth, your carer does an Apgar test on your little one, giving him an *Apgar score* on a scale of one to ten, with one being lowest and ten being highest. (It's called an Apgar test in honour of the doctor who invented it, and saved millions of babies lives as a result.) Your newborn has five criteria to jump through: colour, pulse rate, reflexes, muscle tone and breathing. This test alerts your carer to any concerns about the baby's health.

After — and perhaps even before — his first test, your carer dries your baby and hands him over to mum for some skin-on-skin time. (Baby may be placed straight onto your partner's abdomen with a blanket covering while the first test is performed and then moved up to her chest.) This skin-to-skin contact is super-important so, tempting as it may be to try to hold your little one right away, leave him lying on mum's chest for as long as you can. This is their time to bond. Yours will come later. You have a whole life to live with this baby. But right now, let mum hold that little one and soak it in. Be in the moment and make it theirs, not yours. (And grab a photo or two. These moments are precious.)

TIP

If you and your partner have discussed dad also having skin-on-skin contact with bub, wait patiently and, once mum has had her time, you can have yours. Let the carers know this is something you have both discussed when the timing is right. Then close your eyes, hold that baby close, and soak it all in.

While all of this is going on, your carer measures your baby's length and head circumference and weighs your baby. Ideally, they do this sensitively while allowing for that skin-to-skin time for mum and your little one. Those details go into your child's personal health book. Some practitioners in some states take a footprint as well. Check with your carer if you would like one to keep.

TIP

While bub is having a snuggle with mum (or dad if mum's too knackered), your carer puts a plastic band around her ankle with your names, date of birth and weight. These can become mementos of your baby's birth when they come off a few days later.

The first few hours

Once all the commotion has died down, a few practical matters must be attended to. Have you started ringing friends and family yet? Sending a photo to your social feed/timeline with the time, date and basic info is always a quick and easy way to get the message out to family and friends. (Get your partner's approval before you post it though!) Making a quick call or have a video chat with closest family is also good form — they prefer a direct call to finding out on social media, and they've normally been anxiously waiting for this moment.

Meanwhile, mum and bub usually have their skin-on-skin time and start to get to know each other a bit, and then bub has some food. Yep — feeding your baby is going to be mum's number one priority for some time, so they may as well get stuck into the process now. Your carer helps mum and bub get comfy with a first breastfeed or, if bottle feeding is a necessity, helps with the mechanics of getting your little one taking her bottle.

Once that's all taken care of, getting bub dressed and getting mum into a nice warm shower are next on the agenda. Your partner is likely to be pretty well done by now, so you may need to give her a hand standing up and getting about, or you may have a chance to get to know your baby a bit better while your partner's busy. Skin-to-skin contact between you and your baby might be best to happen now.

REMEMBER

Baby needs to be kept warm. Keep your baby close during skin-to-skin time. Your warm hands will also help or the hospital may have a baby blanket to drape around bub, depending on the protocols.

The first few days

Many parents can be lulled into thinking their baby is an angel in the first 24 hours. Babies can be very sleepy and settled for the first day, and you may be fooled! But this period is also a very busy time, getting feeding established and finding your feet in your new role as dad. Your baby should be having about six feeds in a 24-hour period to start off with, so supporting mum by taking care of nappy changes, burping or anything else that needs attending to can help her out a lot. If mum is still in hospital, you can be a real hero dad for spending as much time as possible with the baby so mum can rest some more.

Meconium

Your perfect, cute little bundle produces the foulest, stickiest, goopiest poo imaginable in the first few days of life. This black tar is called *meconium* and it's perfectly normal. Meconium is nature's way of flushing out all the various fluids and contents of your baby's intestines. The meconium is gone within a few days. After that, if fully breastfed, your baby's poo should turn to a strange orangey-yellow colour. The great news is a newborn's poo hardly smells, easing you gently into the changing soiled nappies routine.

Going home

If your baby was born in hospital, your carer and the hospital decide when your partner and baby can go home. For some new mums, going home can't come fast enough — and if everyone is healthy and everything is in order, discharge can be arranged within about four hours of birth! Other mums may feel they need longer in hospital taking advantage of the support a 24-hour, on-call midwife brings, or they might not feel physically up to leaving hospital, depending on how the birth went. Don't let the hospital push you out if you're not ready for it. But if your partner feels like home would be more comfortable, get the all-clear and go for it. If you have any concerns, talk them over with your carer — but keep in mind that you can't stay in the relative safety of the hospital forever!

Blues

About day three after birth, mum may feel a bit low. This is perfectly normal and does pass. Your partner may burst into tears for no reason (that she can tell you, anyway) or just feel overwhelmed by responsibility. Chances are, your partner is also sore in all sorts of places, and performing simple personal hygiene tasks or even just going to the toilet can be really tricky. Do your dad thing and try to support your partner by helping out, telling her she's awesome and enjoying your baby. Know that this will usually pass as her hormone levels adjust. Be kind and helpful, and be glad it's not your body going through all those huge changes.

The initial post-birth blues have nothing to do with postnatal depression, which is likely to come later if you or your partner ends up experiencing it. See Chapter 7 for more on postnatal depression.

REMEMBER

2

The First Year

Find out everything you need to know about baby care, routines and your baby's every need — when your baby is completely vulnerable and dependent on you for everything.

Understand the key health risks your baby is exposed to during the first few weeks and months, and how to maintain a healthy home.

Recognise developmental milestones and understand how to stimulate your baby's learning through play.

Learn about the help and support organisations you can rely on during your fatherhood journey.

Chapter **6**

Being Dad to a Newborn

Your baby is finally here. Does being a dad feel 'real' now? If not, don't worry. The first few days and weeks after birth can feel surreal. For some dads, having a child feels life-changing. For others, it's almost like the birth happened and now life resumes. Work commitments pile up. The world keeps spinning. Whether it's an earth-shattering change or life-as-normal, becoming a dad will create changes for you, and if it's been 'no biggie' so far, you can rest assured that the times, they are a-changing.

If you felt a bit left out during pregnancy and birth, now is your time to get stuck in. Your baby is here and needs time with dad as often as possible. Realising that your baby is an actual person and that you're responsible for her now can also be quite daunting for some new dads. (At the other end of the continuum, some dads take it all in their stride.)

In this chapter, I give you some shortcuts on your journey to being a great dad with guides to the practical aspects of baby care, such as changing nappies, and dressing and bathing your baby. You get the lowdown on feeding, sleeping, burping and dealing with crying. I also talk about how having a baby shakes things up in your life like nothing else can, and look at ways to cope with that change.

Dealing with the Aftershock

Starting out with your new baby — a vulnerable, unfathomable being — can be a scary experience. Placing the baby into the car and driving home from hospital may be the first time you've been nervous behind the wheel of the car for a long time. Stepping through the door with your little bundle as you come home from the hospital, or waving goodbye to the midwife if your baby was born at home, are momentous steps on the path to becoming a family. You may feel a little daunted flying solo with your partner and the new baby, but that's quite normal. Every parent in the world has probably felt the same. Don't stress and simply take each day as it comes.

It's life but not as you know it

Remember last week when you slept in on Sunday, had a leisurely brunch with your partner and then went for a walk taking just the house keys and some money to stop off at the shop on the way home? You're going to be able to do that again, but not for many years. Getting your head around how life works now can be a struggle, but that's where dads can shine once more. As dads, we're great at adapting quickly to new situations and making the best out of any challenge we face (say 'YES!').

Looking after a newborn is literally a 24-hour, seven-day-a-week job and for most new parents, it is exhausting, even for dads. Expect your baby to sleep a lot in the first couple of days, but she needs a feed every two to four hours, so even at night she wakes up. Even if mum is breastfeeding, you don't get out of night duty. You can help by doing any nappy changes and burping so mum doesn't feel she's doing everything. If you're bottle feeding, you can take turns so at least one of you gets a decent stretch of rest.

You may already be tired from supporting your partner after a long labour and birth and, because your baby is waking every few hours, you're not getting a good eight hours sleep like you used to. You can't catch up on the sleep you've missed, but you can minimise your own exhaustion by resting when the baby sleeps. This goes for both you and your partner in these heady first days. Getting used to the idea of taking turns for everything is worthwhile. While one of you is busy, the other should rest or catch up on some much needed sleep. Here's a perfect opportunity to shine as a dad by sharing the load with mum.

Of course, you may have really strong reasons for *not* being able to be supportive in this way. Perhaps you have work commitments that demand you work nights, or maybe you have a job that requires a particularly high level of performance. If this is the case, explore ways that you can support your partner in ways that work for both of you. The most important thing is that you're there so that the exhaustion doesn't turn into something more serious.

REMEMBER

Apart from breastfeeding, dads can do everything around a baby and no natural disadvantage or disposition exists. You're just as qualified at handling a newborn as mum. In other words, you both don't know much and are learning as you go.

Any information you've read about caring for babies tells you lots of chores have to be done in the first weeks. That's not necessarily true. On days where everything goes smoothly — baby wakes, has a feed, is burped, gurgles cutely for a bit and then goes down for a nap without a whimper — you may wonder what all the fuss was about and sit around twiddling your thumbs. But not every day goes smoothly. And not every cycle of feeding, burping and sleeping goes smoothly in a day. At any point, the following may happen:

>> Bub's nappy overflows or leaks.

>> Your baby shows symptoms you decide to have checked by a midwife or doctor.

>> Your baby spills (vomits) — called *posseting* — after a feed.

Events such as those just listed mean you suddenly have to deal with something unexpected and your plan for the day is disrupted. They're typically minor interruptions and if you have a relaxed attitude, it won't be much of a big deal. But . . . have you noticed that when you're tired and sleep deprived, little things become big things? That's the real challenge here.

In a nutshell, you need to get used to minor disruptions because they happen a lot with children. Life becomes a lot less predictable and plans go awry. But you can see this unpredictability as a good thing, and you can enjoy it rather than choose to be a victim of it. Expect to have to change your baby's clothes (and yours) frequently, clean the carpet or furniture, or visit the after-hours clinic. Your baby also may have days when she just refuses to sleep or cries incessantly — which is a special kind of torture — and you can end up spending an entire day or night rocking her, walking her in a stroller or carrying her in a sling just to get some peace. If you can count on one thing with newborns, it's to expect the unexpected.

REMEMBER

Your baby isn't doing any of this to make your life miserable. The kiddo isn't waking up in the middle of the night thinking, *Yes, this is my chance to destroy my parents' life!* Your baby, instead, is completely ill-equipped to manage herself right now. She needs you to be at your best — patient, compassionate, patient, kind, patient, understanding . . . and did I mention patient?

TIP

Take offers of help whenever you can. Having a person close to you whom you can call when things are trying — and who understands you're running on empty — is very handy. You could ask friends to drop over a meal for the two of you, take over pushing the stroller while you sit in the backyard away from the crying, or hang out the washing. A few hours, break from the baby can make all the difference.

If you feel you're at the end of your tether, don't despair. Get someone to give you a break for a couple of hours and chances are you'll feel much better.

At home with your newborn baby

Falling into the trap of letting mum take care of everything to do with the baby can be easy. Some mums have a tendency to 'take over' and secretly or unconsciously harbour the belief that dads are somewhat inadequate when it comes to dealing with babies. Of course, this is not so. No competition is taking place to see who's better at looking after bub. In some cases, you may have to tell mum to go away and do something else while you look after the baby.

TIP

Take care of bub early on so you become more and more confident at handling your baby. Confidence comes from competence. You can consider yourself 'graduated' from dad school when you are perfectly happy to spend an entire day alone with bub (although that may be a while down the track if mum is breastfeeding).

If you develop a mindset of seeing your baby as a developing person who needs your help every step of the way, rather than a source of work and chores, you're already onto a winner in becoming a future super dad. If you've decided to adhere to a strict routine, or the baby is unsettled or unwell, seeing her as a problem that needs to be fixed, or a timetable that needs to be met, can be tempting. She may seem like a blob that just eats, poos and sleeps, but a lot's going on inside that little baby right now. Although she can't show you quite yet, she's getting to know you.

Hierarchies at home

In the first months of life, your baby is going to develop a special kind of 'attachment relationship' with the people she is most involved with (usually you, mum, and perhaps a grandparent). That attachment simply represents the quality of the connection your baby shares with people around her. Here's the thing that can be hard to take for every new dad: no matter how much you try, in most circumstances an attachment hierarchy is going to develop, and you'll probably be number two on that hierarchy, and maybe even number three. But — and this is the critical aspect — the more time you spend engaging with your little one, the more comfortable she becomes with you caring for her, even in the absence of mum (who really needs a break now and then).

In the early weeks, your newborn stares at you, sussing out your face, learning the sound of your voice and snuggling into you for snoozes. These are important bonding times. Attachment relationships are being established. Mum bonds in a way we can't (if breastfeeding), and mum also has a 40-week head start on this relationship thanks to pregnancy! But do this stuff well and your baby will be smiling up at you in no time.

REMEMBER

Babies don't usually smile with intention and control until six weeks — although they can appear to be smiling (grandma will tell you it's just wind), which is nice even if it is uncontrolled. You know when the smile is intentional. She looks you in the eye and her face lights up like you're the best thing she's ever seen (which, of course, you are). At that point, you just melt inside and you may think that being a dad is the coolest thing you've ever experienced. And it confirms that you're definitely on that attachment hierarchy.

When your baby holds your gaze and checks you out in detail, a lot of developmental work is happening in her brain. Give her every opportunity to look at you. Breastfeeding mums have the advantage that this happens naturally during feeds, so you need to carve out some extra time with bub to get your fair share of baby time. Your baby's eyesight is quite limited in the early weeks and months. They see best things that are around 20 centimetres away — which, cleverly, is about the distance from mum's boob to her face. That's the distance that builds bonds in the early days.

TIP

Be a 100 per cent dad. Do the full spectrum of care tasks — changing your baby's nappies, bathing her and wiping spew off your shoulder — in the first few days because that's how your baby bonds with you. Performing these tasks tends to give you a different perspective on life and, after a while, you might find that little dramas like baby poo on the carpet are really no big deal.

YOUNG DADS

Being a father, no matter the age you become one, is about commitment; commitment to being there for a new young life, and guiding that new person towards adulthood and independence. For young men who find themselves becoming fathers, the commitment is no different — although, without the advantages of age and maturity, fatherhood can be even more of a challenge.

In addition, for young dads (teens or even very early 20s), your relationship with the mother may not be a stable one, your parents may think you're too young and,

(continued)

(continued)

therefore, not prepared to be a father, and tension may exist between your family and the mother's. Some people may think not having the baby at all is the better option.

But the more you show you're committed, the more people respect your determination, and the more your baby feels the love and security having a father brings. You can show your commitment by being involved with your baby from the day you find out your partner is pregnant. Go to pregnancy check-ups and antenatal classes, start making arrangements for how you're going to financially support your partner and child, and show that you're man enough for this very important job. Enlist the support of both your and your partner's families. But don't overdo it. If you become too controlling it may be interpreted badly. It's a fine line. Walk it with concern for your baby and her mum, and over time you'll prove to everyone including yourself that you've got this.

To be legally recognised as the baby's father, you need to have your name on the child's birth certificate. Doing so makes having access to your child easier if your relationship with his mother breaks down.

For resources for young dads, take a look at MensLine Australia (`mensline.org.au/being-a-dad`). The service also provides professional counsellors who can provide information and support for all father and parenting issues. You can call them on 1300 78 99 78.

You've got the blues

Expect mum to shed some tears in the first week. Hormones are playing war games in her body right now and she's likely to be up and down like a yo-yo. Sometimes the best you can do is to listen, remain calm even if she has a go at you and stay positive at all times. These are just clouds passing and chances are her mood will change in a few hours. So don't sweat the small quarrels, emotional outbursts or little annoyances.

What you may not know is that dads can get the blues after birth, too. At these times, communicating well with your partner about what you're going through is really important.

REMEMBER

Sometimes the blues can morph into postnatal depression (PND), a serious mental health issue for new parents. Have a look at Chapter 7 for more about PND and how it affects mums and dads.

Looking after a Newborn

So now that you've got the baby, what do you do with her? How do you look after her? Feeling responsible for a new person can be hugely overwhelming, but babies are pretty straightforward. All they really need is love, food, warmth, sleep and a clean nappy.

In general, newborns exist in a 24-hour cycle of sleeping, feeding, being awake and sleeping again. Your baby tires very easily and is awake for only about an hour or so at a time. A large chunk of that time she's being fed, burped and changed if necessary, but time is available for a bit of interaction with dad, like story time (tell her anything you want — she loves to hear your voice), a few songs or even a walk outside together before the next nap time. The amount of wake time she enjoys will change quickly, so savour the sleepiness while it lasts. As she grows it becomes a whole new ballgame.

REMEMBER

Depending on where you live, your midwife or carer visits you or you visit her in the first few days and weeks after the birth to monitor your baby's growth and your partner's wellbeing, and to see how you're getting on in your new lives as a family. You then pass into the care of your child health nurse. So, if you ever feel you don't know where to turn or who to turn to, your carer, midwife or child health nurse should be your first port of call. You have regular appointments to visit your child health nurse as your child grows, and in some cases they can come and see you. The hospital where your partner gave birth may also have day clinics where you can take your little one if you're having problems in a particular area, such as sleeping or feeding.

TIP

Help from a registered nurse is available at all hours of the day and night through healthdirect on 1800 022 222. Most states also run a nurse-on-call service, so check with your carer what's available, and have the numbers saved in your phone.

Getting your hands dirty

In your dad role, you get to master a few practical jobs that are probably entirely new to you — until now.

Nappy changing 101

No magic is involved in changing a nappy; they're actually really easy (see Figure 6-1). Being prepared before you start is the key, as is keeping cool when the nappy you're taking off is fuller or more odorous than you thought it may be. To change a nappy, you need

>> A change table or change mat on the floor, bed or sofa where you have lots of space around you and good access to your baby lying in front of you

>> A clean nappy, changing mat

>> Barrier cream or powder

>> A nappy bag (small plastic bag) to put the soiled nappy in (for the rubbish bin if disposable or, if it's a cloth nappy and you're out and about, for storing the nappy until you can take it home and put it in the laundry tub, ready for cleaning — by you)

>> Baby wipes or a bowl of warm water and some cotton wool or cloth standing by to wash down bub's bum

>> Towels or extra cloth nappies within reach just in case a last-minute explosion or leak occurs while baby's nappy is off

REMEMBER

To minimise the risk of your baby falling from the bed or change table while you change her, either keep a hand on her at all times, or change her on a mat on the floor.

Complaining about how bad bub's nappy stinks doesn't win you any extra points with your partner. Keep it together, get the job done without complaint, and watch the way she admires you for your willingness to step up to the plate.

TIP

If you're a gadget dad, you may want to check out baby wipe warmers. Often baby wipes can feel really cold to a baby so these devices help to warm the wipes.

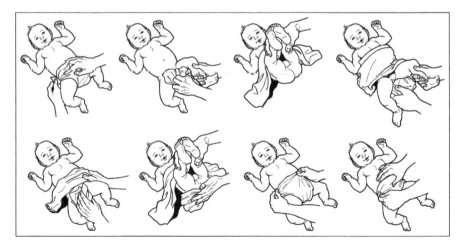

FIGURE 6-1:
How to change
a nappy.

As I talk about in Chapter 5, your baby's first poos are called meconium and they're unforgettable — sticky, greenish-black and tar-like. Your baby's poos gradually change colour as her digestive system is cleaned out and she adjusts to her new food.

The colour of your baby's poo depends on the type of food:

>> Breastfed baby poos are runnier than meconium, and are an orange-yellow colour.

>> Formula-fed baby poos are firmer and a green-mustard colour — and most people agree that they stink more.

If you're reading this before you've had your baby, talking about the colour and consistency of baby poo may seem very odd. But you may find poo discussions become part of your new social chitchat with your partner and other parents.

REMEMBER

To help prevent nappy rash, give your baby some nappy-free time each day. Allow the skin to be exposed to the air and sunlight (but not in the middle of the day — protection from UV rays is important). Use a barrier cream or powder when she has a nappy on to protect her skin.

ELIMINATION COMMUNICATION

The practice of elimination communication (EC) means dispensing with nappies and reading your baby's cues telling you when she needs to relieve herself. You simply learn when junior needs to go and pop her on the potty. Using sounds like 'ssss' and getting her used to specific places where she can 'go potty' can also act as cues that trigger your child to relieve herself.

Those who practise EC say the method empowers children by letting them take charge of their own toileting, encourages a stronger bond between parent and child as you learn to understand your child's needs and cues better, and makes your baby feel more secure because she knows you're going to take care of her when she needs you to.

Practising EC doesn't mean you have to go the whole hog and be nappy-free completely — many parents try EC only when they're outdoors, or only during the day. Others encourage potty use at set times of the day, such as right after waking up or before or after a bath. If you're interested in giving EC a go, take your time and see what works for you. Being watchful and conscious of your child's cues is the first place you need to start. Be prepared with a potty and some old cloth nappies to take care of accidents. And be aware that it's a pretty challenging process for many parents, but plenty of people swear by it.

Take a look at www.nappyfree.com.au for more information.

Bathing

Babies don't need baths every day, but a regular clean around their bottoms to prevent nappy rash, and around the face and neck where dribbled and regurgitated milk can collect is a good idea. Some babies don't like to be naked for long; others love being in the water.

TIP

For babies who aren't fond of a bath yet, 'topping and tailing' is an option. This practice is when you wipe baby's face, neck, hands and bottom with damp cotton wool or a soft cloth instead of giving her a full bath.

Holding your newborn securely at all times when you're bathing her is important. The best way is to place your arm under the shoulders so that your forearm is supporting her head and your hand is holding the shoulder and upper arm furthest away from you. Hold on securely — she can be a wriggly little monster even at this young age, and soapy skin gets slippery.

Here are some tips for bathing your little one:

>> Check the temperature of the bath with both hands (immerse them to a point above the wrists) and be sure to agitate the water to remove any hot spots. The water should be lukewarm — that is, if the water feels hot, it's too hot; if it feels cold, it's too cold. You can also check the temperature with a bath thermometer.

>> Ensure the room temperature is quite warm. Your baby is naked and wet, so she can feel quite cold even when you feel perfectly fine in your clothes, especially when her head is wet for extended periods (try washing the head last).

>> Collect everything you need before you start — including a cloth or cotton wool and a towel. Bub shouldn't need soap, shampoo or cleanser yet; let the natural oils in her skin do the work.

>> Gunk can collect in all those rolls she's sporting on her legs and arms, so give the creases a wipe. The same goes for your baby's hands, so unfurl those little fists to wipe her palms.

Pay particular attention to the neck. Spilt milk rolls down the neck and can sneak into that chubby triple chin she's got at the moment.

>> Wash her face, hair and neck where milk often collects with a soft cloth or cotton wool.

>> When cleaning baby girls' bottoms, wipe from front to back.

You don't need to pull back your little boy's foreskin to wash underneath.

>> When wiping your baby's face, wipe her eyes from inner to outer using cooled boiled water and cotton wool. This helps prevent an eye infection. If she has a sticky eye, as is common in the first weeks after birth, you can also use this technique. You may want to do this before giving her a full bath, while she's still got clothes on.

TIP

Take a phone with you when you bathe your baby. Sometimes you may find you've forgotten something or need help, but you should never leave a baby unattended in the bath. Not even for 5 or 10 seconds. (Babies can drown in a few centimetres of water.) A phone is really handy if you have forgotten something and your partner or another person is elsewhere in the house.

TIP

Your baby sports a little stump of *umbilical cord* for about five to ten days after birth. The stump is kind of shrivelled and not that appealing to look at, but it needs to be kept dry and clean to prevent infection. All you have to do is wash it with cotton wool and warm water when bathing baby or changing her nappy and pat it dry. Fold down the front of her nappy to stop the nappy rubbing against the cord and irritating it. If in doubt about the cord, call your midwife or doctor.

Dressing

Newborns aren't big fans of getting dressed and undressed, so keep clothing simple. Sleepsuits with domes or a zip down the front are perfect for these early days when bub is in and out of bed or having her nappy changed a lot during the day.

In general, your baby should be wearing one more thin layer than you. If you're not sure how hot or cold your baby is, put a finger down the back of her neck. She needs to feel warm rather than too hot or cold.

TIP

If your newborn seems irritated by something, the source of irritation can be as simple as a scratchy label rubbing her neck or a thread wrapping itself round her toe. Cutting off labels, especially if they feel rough or scratchy, is a good idea — but be sure to get the whole thing. That little edge can be a big irritant.

Feeding

Feeding your baby to help him grow and be healthy is an absolute given. But how do you feed him and when?

Breast or formula?

The World Health Organization recommends breastfeeding as the best way to provide nutrition for a baby. Breastmilk's the ideal food for your baby for at least the first six months of her life, providing targeted nutrition for her age and boosting her immunity. Breastmilk's always at the right temperature and generally readily available. Breastfeeding encourages bonding between mother and baby and can help with mum's health too. Last but not least, breastmilk's free. (For more on the benefits of breastfeeding for mum and bub, see Chapter 17.)

However, this isn't an ideal world and sometimes the situation just doesn't allow breastfeeding to work. Breastfeeding may not work for your family for many reasons. That's okay — an alternative to breastfeeding is available. Formula is a milk powder with added vitamins and nutrients to support growth and development, and plenty of babies thrive on it.

Whatever you and your partner decide to feed your baby, pros to both breastfeeding and formula exist. In some cases, both breastmilk and formula can be fed to your baby, which means dads get more time in the feeding seat. Breastfeeding mums can also express milk using a breast pump, which means you can help with the feeding even if a can of formula is nowhere to be seen.

REMEMBER

As a dad, you can get out your advocating shoes again and support your partner in whichever method of feeding she needs or prefers. If your partner's given breastfeeding her best shot but it hasn't worked out, the situation can be tough emotionally for her. Your partner may feel like a failure, or less like a 'real' mother to her child. She may be sensitive to the opinions of others around her, family and health professionals included, who don't understand the decision. Don't worry about the opinions of others; you don't have to justify yourself to anyone. Be confident that you're doing the best for your family.

TIP

Before deciding what and how to feed your baby, get as much information as you can so you're fully informed of the choices and their implications.

Bottle feeding

If you're bottle feeding, you need the following gear:

>> Bottles and teats

>> Something to clean the bottles and teats in, such as a bottle steriliser unit for use in the microwave, a large bowl and sanitiser tablets, or a large pot that you can boil everything in, and a bottle brush

Formula should be made up right before a feed according to the instructions on the tin or packet. Have a supply of bottles and teats ready to go for when your baby's next feeling peckish to save you mucking about.

TIP

Even if your partner's breastfeeding, getting the bottle feeding equipment anyway is a good idea. Your partner may wish to express breastmilk, so you need the equipment included in the preceding list for bottle feeding. Bottles and feeding equipment used with breastmilk need to be sterilised and cleaned just as thoroughly as feeding equipment used for formula.

REMEMBER

Feeding your baby is about creating a nurturing relationship between you and your child, as well as food. Your baby is held close when being breastfed and the same should go for bottle feeding. You can hold your baby in the same loving way as if she were breastfed, sing to her or have a little chat while she feeds. You find she gazes up at you adoringly and checks out every little nook of your face.

How much and when?

Newborn babies love to eat. They grow rapidly and their stomachs are small, so they need regular feeds to keep them tanked up. Having regular feeds also encourages milk production. If your partner is breastfeeding, her milk supply adjusts to meet baby's demand.

Your baby tells you when she's hungry by:

>> Opening her mouth and thrusting her head to the side, as if rooting around to find your partner's breast

>> Sucking her fists or clothing

>> Crying, which is a late sign of hunger and means feed me now or else!

A good sign that you're on the right track with feeding your baby is that she's putting on about the right amount of weight for her age. Babies usually lose weight in the first two weeks after birth. After the first few weeks, bub generally gains around 200 to 300 grams per week. Don't worry — this rate slows as she gets older.

REMEMBER

Newborns usually need to be fed every two to three hours, or about eight to ten times in a 24-hour period. You know your baby is getting enough to eat because she has at least six to eight wet nappies per day, her wee is light yellow, not dark, and her poos are soft. If you're concerned, telephone your child health nurse, midwife or doctor.

Burping

Bringing up a good hearty belch may come naturally to you, but for bub, who can't sit up or stand and whose digestive system is still immature, a bit of air caught in her tummy or gut needs help to come out or it can be very painful. Usually a gentle pat on the back or a gentle rub anticlockwise (again on the back) does the trick. Your demure little princess comes out with a burp to make you proud.

You can use three good positions to burp your baby (see Figure 6-2):

>> Lying on your lap, with bub facing down

>> Sitting on your thigh, facing out

>> Over the shoulder, with bub's head held upright on your shoulder

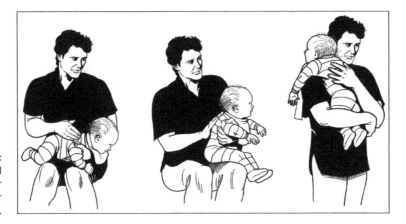

FIGURE 6-2: Three good positions for burping your baby.

Don't forget to support bub's wobbly head. To protect yourself against any posseting (white milky spew), drape a flat cloth nappy or muslin cloth over your shoulder or lap.

And, finally, if you haven't been pooed, peed or vomited on yet, you're not trying hard enough! Man up and get stuck in with the baby care tasks.

TIP

If your baby is difficult to burp or seems uncomfortable, try getting her upright and moving around a bit. Putting her into a baby carrier and taking her for a walk (gently bouncing your baby with each step) can help all the trapped air escape and smooth the digestive process — and can be a great baby and dad bonding time.

FEEDING IS ALL A MATTER OF STYLE

When you feed your baby can be just as controversial as *what* you feed your baby. Many experts and organisations advocate *demand feeding,* which is letting the baby determine when she is fed rather than feeding her to a schedule. A wide range of books is available with feeding plans to match your baby's age. These books are controversial and most feeding experts recommend a more child-centred approach, but not every family can do that. An exhausted or depressed mum, or one with twins or triplets, are two examples of where a more structured approach might be needed.

Sleeping – you and the baby

Newborns wake regularly in the night and day for food, so getting a good eight-hour stretch of sleep is unlikely at this stage. As she gets older, your baby sleeps for longer chunks at night and stays awake for longer in the day.

Your baby tells you she's tired by

>> Grizzling

>> Making jerky, tense movements

>> Rubbing her eyes

>> Staring into space

>> Yawning

Crying is a late sign of tiredness and may mean your baby is overtired. When bub is overtired, she may be more difficult to settle because she's wound up about being tired.

Teaching your baby about night and day

Babies don't have a sense of day and night when they're born, but the good news is that so long as you have a reasonable rhythm to your sleep/wake cycles, your baby will eventually fit right in. Humans have evolved, naturally, to sleep at night.

Babies usually follow a cycle of sleeping, feeding, burping, changing, playing and sleeping again during the day, but you can leave out the playing at night. Where you're animated and chatty in the day, you're all business at night, keeping the room dimly lit for feeds and nappy changes, and putting baby straight back to bed when you're done.

Having a bedtime routine can help signal that night is on the way and that's the time for sleeping.

Settling your baby

How you get your baby to sleep is perhaps the most controversial topic out there. And everyone has an opinion about it — and will judge you for the approach you take! Strategies range from the *cry-it-out* approach, where you put your baby down for a sleep in a bassinet or cot and offer limited comfort to her cries until she falls asleep, to the *attachment parenting* philosophy of keeping bub in close contact with a parent in a sling or pouch to sleep and having her sleep in bed with you at night.

Other parents use a technique called *controlled crying*, where baby is left to cry for a short period of time — say, a couple of minutes — before being soothed and comforted, and then left for a slightly longer period. The length of time between visits is stretched out and eventually baby goes to sleep.

WARNING

Methods such as cry-it-out or controlled crying should not be attempted before baby is six months or older. Research evidence on these strategies is mixed, although generally suggests they should be okay after six months. But be aware, even with some evidence supporting the use of these strategies — and no evidence showing they are harmful — strong moral arguments against it do exist. People *really* care about this topic.

Some parenting experts warn against rocking your baby to sleep or doing anything where she falls asleep as a result of parent intervention, because bub becomes dependent on that technique to sleep. Putting your baby down sleepy but awake and letting her fall asleep on her own teaches good sleep habits.

REMEMBER

The baby-sleep challenge is literally one of the hardest things you will navigate as a new dad. It creates a level of stress that is previously unimaginable. Be aware that no-one is at their best when they're tired, so working out a way through this becomes a high priority early on.

Being never-endingly responsive to every whimper is ultimately unhelpful to your little one's sleep challenges, because it exhausts you and leaves you less able to be a great dad (and same goes for mum). But it can be distressing for everyone involved when the baby is screaming, it's late, and everyone is bone tired. Leaving the baby to cry it out is a heartbreaking approach for most parents, and doesn't seem to do much good for the bub. Plenty of ink has been spilt as people have debated how to deal with this challenge, so let's keep it simple here.

When your baby is whimpering, you can probably wait a few minutes and see whether she settles or becomes more upset. If your baby starts crying, you might want to briefly wait to see if things escalate. Sometimes stepping quietly into the room and giving her a pat or a short cuddle is all it takes. If your little one escalates things, check the nappy, see if she's hungry, try burping, and spend more time soothing. And remember that every child eventually sleeps through the night. It will pass.

TIP

Reach agreement with your partner before deciding which settling technique, method or routine to follow, because using different approaches tends not to work. Consistency is key.

REMEMBER

If you're having severe trouble settling your baby for days or weeks on end, call your midwife, child health nurse or community health care organisation. Sleep schools are also available throughout Australia, where a specially trained nurse guides you through the process of training your baby to sleep. A range of different programs are usually available for parents to attend, from two-night intensives, to five- or seven-night stays. These schools usually promote approaches that aren't consistent with more 'gentle' or 'attachment' parenting. They typically go with cry-it-out approaches, so go in with your eyes open.

Swaddling

One technique for helping babies to sleep is swaddling, which involves wrapping a light blanket around the baby to keep him snug (see Figure 6-3). Swaddling also helps control the *Moro reflex*, which is when your little one seems to startle or jump out of her skin for no reason at all!

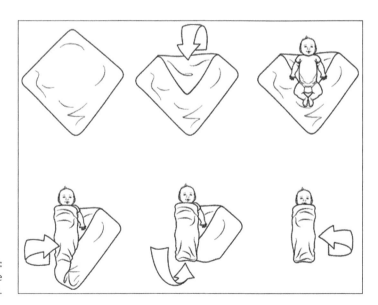

FIGURE 6-3:
How to swaddle
a baby.

Crying — you, your partner and the baby

At some stage, crying is bound to take place in your household. A healthy baby may cry for several hours per day (or more). Crying is your baby's way of telling you she's hungry, lonely, tired, in pain, gassy, too hot or needs a nappy change. Sometimes she cries for no apparent reason at all.

Trying to figure out what the problem is while your baby howls can be stressful. Sometimes you may find yourself wanting to stop the noise whatever way you can. Crying can make you feel angry and frustrated, and you may want to lash out physically. Emotions can be contagious, so take a breather and stay in control.

TIP

If you feel the crying is getting too much for you, put your baby in a safe place such as her bassinet or cot, and then take a few minutes to calm yourself outside. A very short but demanding exercise can help get rid of some excess adrenaline as well — so 'get down and give me 20'.

Whenever your baby starts crying, get into the habit of checking three things: is she hungry, has she got a dirty nappy, and is she comfortable and well (does she have a high temperature, are any signs of vomit evident, and are any other obvious signs of a health problem apparent)?

After you've checked your baby, do one (or all) of the following to try to calm and comfort your baby:

- » Burp her to help her bring up wind (if she's just had a feed).
- » Cuddle and sing to her in a calm soothing voice, or put on a playlist of gentle lullabies.
- » Give her a warm bath.
- » Put her down for a nap — she may just be tired (no kidding).
- » Put your baby in the car and go for a drive around the block (not the most environmentally friendly alternative, but sometimes driving's the one thing that works).
- » Switch on a household appliance that makes a monotonous sound, such as a hairdryer, vacuum cleaner or washing machine. Or download some 'white noise' sounds from the internet and play the noise to your baby.
- » Take her for a walk in the stroller or baby carrier (at any time of the day or night).
- » Try a gentle soothing massage (see Chapter 7 for tips on baby massage).

REMEMBER

Sometimes your baby is upset and you can literally do nothing about it. The feeling that comes from not being able to control everything is horrible. But keep in mind that getting mad won't make things better. No baby ever looked at a cranky dad and thought, *Well, since you're so upset about things, I'll calm down for you.*

Under no circumstances should you ever hit, shake or lash out at your baby, regardless of how tired you are or how long the baby has been screaming.

Daddy time

Spending time with your baby doesn't have to be all work and no play. Every nappy change is an opportunity to have some fun with your little one.

Besides the usual chores and jobs you do with your baby, you can hang out together in other ways that are just good old-fashioned fun. Try these out for size:

» **Bathe or shower together.** Bathing together can be a little nerve-racking at first. Make sure mum is standing by with a towel when you're ready to get out. Hold the soap — you don't want things to get slippery!

» **Enjoy some tummy time.** Tummy time is where your baby lies on the floor on her stomach and tries to lift her head, which helps develop junior's neck, shoulder and core strength.

» **Have a chat.** Babies coo from a few weeks old and delight in having their sounds repeated back to them.

» **Read to your baby.** It's never too early to turn your baby onto reading. She can delight in the experience of being near you and seeing magical shapes and colours in the pictures.

» **Sing to your baby.** You can sing numerous good songs to your baby, but you can always make up your own. And bub doesn't care if you can't hold a tune. She just adores you more for it.

» **Take a trip to the park.** Your champ's a little too young for slides and flying foxes, but she loves sitting on your lap with you on the swing for a gentle swing back and forth. She also loves being outside and around other children.

Juggling Your Other Priorities

Before your baby came along, you were a partner, son, brother, friend, employee or boss and a member of your extended family. Now that bub has arrived and your priorities have changed, fitting in all those aspects of your life can be a struggle.

You can not only jeopardise the relationships you have with people in your life by letting fatherhood take over everything, but also lose your relationship with yourself and find your own wellbeing at risk.

Making time for yourself

You don't stop being the person you were before bub came along. You still need to take care of yourself so you can be the best father — and partner and so on — you can be for a long time. Just as mums need time to themselves, dads deserve some time off too. Having a chat with your partner about continuing to fit in sport or time with mates is important.

REMEMBER

Making time for yourself may make you feel a little guilty and can be tricky to manage, but you need to take care of yourself before you can take care of anyone else.

Looking after your partner

Some childcare organisations have a tendency to hammer the message 'baby comes first', which is, of course, important.

However, taking care of your baby can't be at the constant expense of your relationship. After all, if your relationship goes down the drain, a lot more trouble is ahead.

If you're the primary caregiver, you know what it means to look after a baby all day and sort out the household at the same time. Being primary caregiver is a lot of hard work, so get your partner to help out when she gets home.

If you're the main provider, make sure you chip in and do whatever needs to be done when you get home. Yes, working all day and then helping out at home while looking after the baby is tough, but you can get through it. Looking after a baby and child does get easier over time — promise!

Above all, you and your partner need to have 'us' time and spend quality time together. You can do this by getting friends or family to look after the baby for a few hours while you go out, or even making a big deal out of a special occasion and celebrating at home when bub is asleep.

Here are some more ideas to keep your relationship alive and kicking:

>> Invite some friends (especially those you're both friends with) over to cook dinner for you (or with you). Yes, inviting people to cook you a meal is cheeky

but most people are only too willing to help out. This way you two get to see your friends, have a classy meal and don't have to do any work!

>> Surprise each other with little gestures such as leaving messages, buying a little treat or present, or finding a movie you both will love.

>> Take a walk together with bub asleep in the pram. That way, the two of you can get some gentle exercise and spend time together.

We are family

Your newborn isn't just your pride and joy, but also the pride and joy of your entire extended family. Nothing is like having a child to help you realise what your own parents went through when you were a kid. They undoubtedly want to be part of your new child's life. So share the love!

Having a lot of interaction with her grandparents, cousins and other close relatives is invaluable for your baby — the more love coming at her, the better. Having your baby feel comfortable and safe with family members also means having a lot of babysitters and extra pairs of hands when you or your partner are finding things tough. Interacting with different people also helps your baby develop her social skills and builds confidence.

DEALING WITH VISITORS

They say it takes a village to bring up a child. When your baby has arrived, you might realise that at least half of that village wants to drop in to check out the new addition to your family. Apart from your immediate family, expect to see neighbours you didn't know you had, uncles and aunts you haven't seen since you were a kid, old colleagues, acquaintances and, of course, all your and your partner's friends. Although you may want to show off your greatest creation, the demands of looking after a newborn (the sleep deprivation, the unfolded washing, the plates that are piling up everywhere) and your own anxiety about parenting don't make a great mix for entertaining. But you can turn a horde of visitors into an army of helpers with the following:

- Don't serve tea or coffee when visitors come over. Point them to the kettle — or the vacuum cleaner or washing machine.

- If someone rings and says they're coming over, get them to pick up any supplies you're too busy or exhausted to get from the supermarket yourself.

(continued)

(continued)

- Make the most of offers — people love to help and contribute in any way they can.

- Put a sign up on your front door with something like 'Parents and baby sleeping, please phone to let us know when you're coming over'. Screen calls — that's what answering machines and voicemail are for.

- Don't be afraid to say 'no' when you just don't feel like having people over. People are generally quite understanding, especially if they have children themselves.

Managing the work–life balance

Managing your commitments at work and your life outside paid employment is often a tricky one in this fast-paced society. Technology that allows you to work and be contactable 24 hours per day doesn't help you separate work from leisure time. Even before becoming a father, finding time to do the things you love may have been a stretch. Now you have the extra demands of a family, you may need to readdress your work–life balance and take some steps so you don't burn out.

In Australia, *flexitime*, or working more flexible hours, is becoming more accepted, especially for men. The after-effects of the COVID pandemic have improved things in this area enormously. In some workplaces, you may be able to design your own hours, bank up hours worked to take days off in lieu, or add a no-overtime clause to your contract. And the opportunity for parental leave is increasing in many organisations, allowing you to savour these early days with baby. Take advantage of this if it's available. It's a good thing.

CHECK THE NET

To find out how to go about setting up flexible working hours and what rights you have, go to www.fairwork.gov.au and search 'flexible working arrangements'.

Sex

Having a little sexy time is probably the last thing on mum's mind for a few weeks (or months) after birth, and this can be rough on a new dad. The lack of lovin' isn't because you smell bad or have suddenly become repulsive. Blame it on the hormones, lack of sleep, leaky breasts and the time it takes to recover from birth.

REMEMBER

Most doctors recommend waiting at least six weeks after birth before having sex. That's the length of time it takes for the uterus to get back to pre-baby size after a vaginal birth — and for your partner's body to recover from the labour.

Women who've had a rough labour and some kind of intervention such as ventouse or forceps should wait longer and may not want to resume intimate activities any earlier than 8 to 12 weeks after the birth. A tear or an episiotomy (refer to Chapter 5) can take six weeks or more to heal.

On top of that, your partner may not feel very sexy after going through the birth and taking on the new role of 'mum'. Your partner may feel self-conscious about her postpartum body. The right mental attitude is also required for having a sexy time. The memory of what birth felt like may last longer than the stitches, making the idea of sex unappealing. So you need to be a bit patient.

But things get better. Your partner is really just taking time to heal, get her head around things and regain some of her mojo. It may take a few months, but her appetite for sex does return. So, in the meantime, continue to support and love her, and show intimate affection for her in other ways with massages, foot rubs and cuddles.

REMEMBER

When you're both ready to resume 'business time' again, take it slowly. Let your partner control the pace and position, so things are comfortable for her. You should be prepared to spend at least 40 minutes on foreplay, allowing her body plenty of time to prepare for intercourse. And check in consistently to be sure she's okay, particularly during penetration. Take things slow and steady, be gentle, and use plenty of high-quality natural lube. And don't forget contraception. Breastfeeding preventing another pregnancy is a myth — and are you really ready for number two yet?

Chapter **7**

The First Three Months

Pregnancy didn't really require a great deal of you if everything went to plan. Labour demanded you lift your game. Now you're through the birth. You know which end of your baby the nappy goes on. And you have an idea or two about how things are shaping up in your new family.

The first three months of real life parenting are some of the most challenging times you'll face in your new role as dad, as you come to grips with a vulnerable new human who is slowly learning more about his world and (hopefully) learning that you are there for him all the way.

In this chapter, I deal with chores that need to be done to maintain your baby's health and hygiene, and tackle some problems that you may be facing, such as colic and reflux. I explore your baby's rapid development and how you can make the most of these important early learning stages. I also revisit postnatal depression and who you can turn to for help.

Getting to Know Your Baby

Dollars are the currency that runs our economy. Ideally, lots of dollars are flowing, and we have a healthy economy. And connection is the currency that runs your relationships. All of them. Ideally, you have lots of connection, and a healthy relationship.

But what's connection? My definition is that it's feeling seen, heard and valued.

As a new dad, two connections are key to keeping the economy of your relationship thriving: first is connection with your baby's mumma. It's essential. Nothing else comes before it. Ask yourself regularly, 'Does my partner feel seen, heard and valued?' Second is connection with this new baby. And for that, no substitute exists for spending time with your baby and getting up close and personal.

Babies are funny creatures and grow faster than you expect. They are kind of blobby one day, and all cute and big-eyed the next. You'll be stunned at how much they change in the first three months. Relish in the uniqueness of this child. If you slow down and pay attention, you'll get lost in tiny things — such as the way he yawns, the way his face lights up with a smile (after six weeks) when he sees your face, and the way his hair sticks up like an orangutan's. These are all special things that will probably disappear as he grows up (except the face lighting up, we hope), so make time to absorb them as much as you can, because they won't stay like this for long.

REMEMBER

Everything in your baby's life is new and he doesn't have the experience to interpret situations or sensations. Watching your baby feel sand under his feet or see a dog for the first time can be a delight. Things that we take for granted are totally new and bizarre to your little one. Spending time with your baby is a great way to rediscover the world and research shows that it can lift *your* spirits when you've had a rough day at the office.

When your baby was born you probably didn't feel particularly competent. Changing a nappy was manageable, but bathing the bub? That required practice. Now, though, you know which way he likes being burped, his favourite toys, the best times of day to go out and about, what songs he responds to and the best methods for settling him at night. And the better you do it, the more of a man you probably feel you're becoming! How satisfying — and oddly manly — it feels to settle your little one off to sleep is hard to put into words.

If you don't feel you're getting any more of a grip on fatherhood and still can't get him to sleep or bring up wind, don't worry. Good things take time and babies can seem quite random. Sometimes what works one day won't work the next.

Don't give up being an involved father if you haven't had the amazing experiences I describe in this book so far, or if your efforts are a bit haphazard. Your baby hugely benefits from every moment you spend with him, whether you feel you are making progress with him or not.

Groundhog day

Because life is so new to your baby, routine is essential. It creates a sense of predictability, and predictability builds a feeling of security. While doing the same thing day in and day out is boring for adults, babies love it. Because everything is new to a baby, routine feels safe. And this is good.

If you haven't established some sort of routine or rhythm to your day with bub, establishing a routine soon is a good idea. Without being over the top about it, develop a structure to your day so you and your little one know what's coming.

A pattern of sleeping, feeding, changing, having some playtime or awake time, and then back to sleep is pretty standard. You don't have to run things on a clock — and I wouldn't recommend it, particularly in those early months. But moving flexibly towards routine will make a difference for parental sanity — yours and your partner's.

As he approaches his three-month birthday, your baby can stay awake for about one and half hours before getting tired and needing a sleep (again, every baby is different so I'm going by averages here).

Here are some thoughts about routines and how they may work for you:

>> Anticipate how long you have out and about before bub gets tired and grizzly.

>> Arrange visits from friends and family around your schedule, not theirs.

>> Organise your day around your baby's naps, including getting some sleep while he does. This is even more important for mum.

>> Schedule time away from the baby each day, or time together as a family.

>> Work out when to do those pesky chores, such as laundry and cooking, going to the doctor or baby's check-ups around when you think bub will be awake, asleep or needs a feed.

TIP

Even if your baby is on a strict schedule and seems to have settled into his timetable well, try to take each day as it comes. Babies love to keep things interesting by filling their nappy as you step out the door, spewing just as you've got them into a smart new outfit, or demanding an early dinner when you're out without mum or a bottle to give them. Try not to see the world falling down around your feet if they don't conform to your idea of what they should be doing. Take a deep breath and get used to life on bub's time. Things will settle down again into a new routine soon.

Practical solutions to common problems

Babies are generally reasonably predictable. But it takes a little while to learn their signals and communication methods. They can't talk, so if something is wrong, they can't tell you straight out what's going on. Remind yourself often that your baby has a different, unfathomably fragile body compared to yours. He's sensitive to things you probably don't even notice, so can suffer from 'problems' different from adults. By taking time to get to know your baby, you get more of an idea about what makes your infant tick. You may even have solved the mystery of what kinds of cry your baby makes to communicate with you. Trial and error is often the only way to work out what's going on with your baby, or what to do to achieve a particular outcome.

The following sections outline some suggestions for dealing with common problems experienced by babies (and parents) during the first few months of your baby's life.

Jaundice

A common condition in newborns, *jaundice* refers to the yellow colour of the skin and whites of the eyes. Jaundice clears naturally in around one to two weeks. If the jaundice continues for any longer, your carer may recommend phototherapy, which is treatment with a special light that helps rid the body of bilirubin (the cause of jaundice) by altering the bilirubin and making it easier for your baby's liver to get rid of it.

Wind

Your baby lets you know he has wind by wriggling after a feed or arching his back. He may get upset and cry too. See the three main burping positions in Chapter 6 for starters. (Some people will swear by something called *gripe water* but note that no scientific studies support its use for relieving any baby issues, including wind.)

Colic or infantile colic

We expect tears with babies, but some babies cry a lot. They're healthy. They're clean. They've slept. They're fed. But they keep crying. If your baby is doing this, your GP or carer might suggest that you're dealing with a case of colic. It typically happens mostly in the evening. It kicks off around two to three weeks of age, and peaks around the four- to six-week mark. But the thing about colic is it's not really a medical issue. It's not a physical order or disease. Colic is more of a behavioural observation where a baby cries for extended periods. (Pretty dissatisfying to read that, huh?)

Doctors often disagree about what causes infantile colic or which parts of the body are affected. No blood test is available to test for it. Experts don't agree on how to treat it either! Some doctors say colic's caused by trapped wind; others say a nerve condition's to blame. You will know if your baby suffers from colic. Your little one usually gets pretty ratty in the evening, crying inconsolably for around three hours — so from about 7 pm till 10 pm. Of course, the crying could be a little early and go a little later — but it's basically at the point where you're at your most exhausted. It's a particularly cruel and horrible experience.

The big challenge is this: while a fussy baby is calmed by love and cuddles, a colicky baby screams more and more, louder and louder, longer and longer. This is the kind of stuff that can trigger some adults, leading them to either leave a baby alone in a room to scream or, in an even worse-case scenario, shouting, hitting or even shaking a baby. None of these options will help. Parents should never do any of these things.

Instead work through the following by asking:

>> Is baby hungry?

>> Is baby wet or dirty?

>> Is baby overstimulated?

>> Is baby full of gas and dealing with digestive issues (or even reflux)?

>> Is baby stressed because his parents are stressed?

>> Is baby constipated?

>> Is baby allergic to something?

Excessive crying from a colicky baby can cause personal stress, marital and relationship stress, and in some cases is associated with postnatal depression, mum giving up breastfeeding, and physical harm. It's a serious issue. But remember that it's temporary. Get support from your health nurse, family members and experienced parents who aren't as exhausted or inexperienced as you. And seek medical attention in case it's something else.

TIP

Some babies seem to be comforted by being held tummy down on laps or forearms. Colic doesn't seem to have any long-lasting effects on the baby, but hearing their baby scream night after night can be terribly traumatic for parents.

REMEMBER

If the crying is getting too much for you, put baby in a safe place such as his cot or bassinet and have a breather. You can also call your community child health nurse or your state's nurse-on-call service. Or just ring your mum or another trusted and experienced adult who can help you relieve some of the pressure.

Surviving colic is really hard on parents, but the love and patience you show during this time won't be forgotten by your little one. Hang in there.

Cradle cap

Cradle cap is a kind of baby dandruff, a condition in which flakes appear on the scalp. Cradle cap's not harmful and won't cause your little one any distress. You can get rid of cradle cap by massaging the scalp with almond oil or olive oil and rinsing with water. Cradle cap can sometimes become dark or crusty, or spread to the face, in which case you should talk to your community child health nurse or doctor about more treatment options.

Reflux

The valve where your baby's oesophagus and stomach meet should close to keep food and stomach acids inside. In babies with reflux, this valve doesn't close properly yet. Most feeds end with your baby's milk and stomach acids coming back up again, either by being vomited up or catching in his throat and hurting him.

Your baby may have reflux if he:

>> Has sour smelling breath

>> Has a wet sound in his throat, or has wet-sounding hiccups (caused by regurgitated milk in his throat)

>> Writhes, arches his back, vomits and cries after feeds

Parents of babies who suffer from reflux worry if their baby is getting enough to eat, or if their baby is suffering a lot of pain from the reflux. Here are some ways you can minimise reflux symptoms:

>> Avoid bouncing your baby.

>> Change your baby's nappy by rolling him to the side rather than lifting his legs higher than his head.

>> Feed your baby in an upright position, to help the milk stay down.

>> Give your baby a dummy to suck. Sucking a dummy can help him swallow and clear the milk from the oesophagus.

>> If using formula, try one of the anti-reflux varieties on the market. Talk to your doctor before trying anti-reflux formula.

>> Keep baby upright as much as you can to help gravity keep the milk and stomach acids in his stomach where they should be.

>> Put bub in a baby chair at an angle rather than placing him flat on the floor under a play gym when he's awake.

>> Raise the mattress in baby's bed so his head is slightly higher than his stomach and the mattress is on a slight angle. Don't raise the mattress too much or he will slide under the covers, which may be dangerous.

Reflux can be the result of an allergy to cow's milk protein. In some instances, having mum change to a dairy-free diet if she's breastfeeding, or switching to a non-dairy formula such as goat or soy, may help. Speak to a medical professional or a dietician first.

Treatments for reflux include thickeners that hold milk down, such as infant Gaviscon. You can also ask your chemist for specialised anti-reflux formula. Medication may be prescribed if your baby's case is particularly severe and he isn't putting on as much weight as recommended.

Keep in mind that reflux is a medical condition, but the doctor won't be able to do much beyond diagnosing it. Just like colic, allowing nature and development to run their course is your only option. In the meantime, hang in there and support one another as much as you can. These challenges will be some of the biggest and toughest you'll have ever experienced. Parenting is not for the faint-hearted.

TIP

Your baby will remember the love and comfort you give him as he deals with reflux long after he's forgotten how reflux felt.

See www.reflux.org.au for more on reflux management and support networks.

CHECK THE NET

Colds

Even though you've bundled up your little precious and protected him from everything you can think of, he'll still fall prey to a common cold. Until he's two, you can't do a lot for a baby with a cold except give him infant pain relief (always check the right dosage for your little one's age), extra feeds and lots of cuddles. You can also try the following:

>> Regularly clear the mucus out of your baby's nose with wet cotton wool rolled into a cone. Don't use a cotton bud because a sudden movement from bub can cause the cotton bud to get stuck up there and may cause damage. Use a fresh piece of cotton wool for each nostril.

>> Keep up the feeds so he doesn't get dehydrated. If he's been sleeping through the night (which would be a miracle at this age) expect him to wake up more, so top him up with more breast milk (or a bottle) when he does. (Don't give him water until he's much older.)

>> Saltwater drops can help unblock his nose and sinuses. Dissolve some salt in warm water and apply up his nose, drop by drop, from some dampened cotton wool.

>> He may have to stop to breathe when feeding if his nose is blocked, so take your time and let him control how much he takes.

>> Use a humidifier to moisten the air, which can reduce baby's congestion.

>> You can also try a nasal bulb, which is a plastic bulb attached to a nose piece which goes up baby's nostril. You squeeze the bulb before inserting the nose piece and let the bulb go when the nose piece is in the nostril, sucking out mucus. In most cases, your baby will sneeze a lot, which clears the mucus, so you don't need to get overly zealous about clearing your baby's nose with a nasal bulb. A nasal bulb is just handy when you can see that some mucus is stuck in the nose and you can't get it out any other way.

REMEMBER

If your baby suddenly comes down with a fever, or your instincts tell you something more than a cold is going on, call your local health hotline or get down to your doctor. If anything, a trip to your GP can rule out anything more serious and put your mind at ease. A temperature of 36.4 degrees Celsius taken under your baby's arm is normal.

Infant acne

Some babies develop a pimply face the first days and weeks after birth. The spots are caused by hormones from the mother and fade away once those hormones are out of your baby's system. You can't do anything to make them go away, but keep baby's hands under wraps (for example, in mittens) to stop him scratching the spots accidentally. A gentle wash of warm water will keep the spots from becoming infected. Pat dry afterwards.

Nappy rash

Nappy rash is a flat red area on your baby's bum or genital area caused by ammonia from his wees and poos staying on his skin. Nappy rash is very uncomfortable and you may meet some resistance at nappy changing time if your baby has nappy rash.

The best cure for nappy rash is prevention, so make sure the bottom is washed with warm water and a soft cloth or cotton wool *every* time you change his nappy. Gently pat everything dry and apply your barrier cream or powder before the nappy goes on. Give him some time each day without a nappy to expose his skin to the air and sunlight.

If your poor bub should come down with a case of nappy rash, a cream like zinc and castor oil or calendula cream can help heal the skin. *Be vigilant about bum and genital hygiene.*

Wash cloth nappies in hot water and dry them in the sun to kill any bacteria lurking in the fabric. Some babies react badly to disposable nappies, others flare up at the sight of a cloth nappy, so be flexible and experiment with different products in your nappy routine until you figure out what works for your baby.

Nappy rash tends to flare up when your baby is teething, but not all babies experience this.

TIP

If nappy rash persists despite all your efforts, see your GP or child health nurse for more advice and treatment.

Teething

Most babies younger than three months old haven't started teething, but some babies are eager to grow up and may have a few teeth bothering them. Some babies are even born with a few gnashers!

See Chapter 9 for tips on helping bub deal with teething.

Skin irritations and scratching

If your little guy's skin is dry or he's scratching himself, soothe his skin with olive or sweet almond oil and put some mitts on his hands. You can get shirts and sleepsuits with fold-over ends that become mittens.

Non-trivial care jobs

Like you, babies have growing nails and snotty noses, and get stuff in their ears and eyes. Babies need ongoing body maintenance. Funnily enough, that's often when frustrated mums hand baby over to dad. By the way if, as part of your fatherhood journey, you haven't been vomited on, had poo squirted on you, or been christened with pee yet, you're not trying hard enough.

A compilation of jobs for dads include:

>> **Administering medicine.** After vaccinations or during an illness, your baby may need paracetamol or antibiotics. Medicines for babies are usually

prescribed as a liquid suspension and are most easily given in a plastic syringe (no needle attached). Dosages are typically measured in millilitres (mL) and getting the dosage right is important. Get your GP or nurse to show you the correct dose when your baby's given his vaccinations or he's prescribed medicine.

» **Cleaning ears.** Earwax is a good thing because it protects the ear canal, so don't get too worked up about it. Wiping the outer ear and neck area where milk can collect should do the trick, but be careful not to get water in the ear canal. If you're concerned about the cleanliness of your baby's ears, leave it to the professionals and see your doctor.

» **Mopping up bum explosions.** Every baby has at least one bowel motion that truly tests the limits of what you thought a small person could excrete. Babies also get the odd bout of diarrhoea if they eat something that disagrees with them (through mum's milk, of course) or if they catch a gastrointestinal bug. The result is the mother (or father) of all poos — also called the 'backsider', as poo goes all the way up the nappy and into the bodysuit, sometimes escaping out the top of his neck! If your little one has a tummy bug or diarrhoea, you can minimise the mess by doubling up on nappies, so if he's wearing a newborn size nappy, put a nappy the next size up over the top. That should contain any unforeseen leaks. You may want to invest in an apron to protect your clothes at these times.

» **Trimming finger and toenails.** Get yourself one of those dinky little manicure sets for children, which include a pair of scissors with rounded ends, a tiny pair of nail clippers and some emery boards. Approach your baby when he's asleep or feeding so he's not focused on having his fingers dealt with. The clippers are probably easiest to start with, but failing that try special baby scissors. If you've done a pretty rough job, smooth off craggy nail edges with an emery board so he doesn't scratch himself with them. This job is likely to get harder as your baby gets older, so get some early nail cutting training in while he is still pretty helpless and can't move about much.

» **Wiping away sticky eye.** Many babies have a build-up of mucus at their eye corners, and this can be easily removed by wetting a piece of cotton wool with lukewarm water and wiping the mucus gently away.

Hands-on Dad

The days of fathers coming home from work and disappearing behind the evening paper while mother tended to the baby are a relic of a bygone era, and for good reason. Twenty-first century dads are rolling up their sleeves and are fully involved in all things baby, which doesn't just include chores. In this section, I explore ways to have fun with your new playmate and pick up new skills along the way.

Baby massage

I'm not talking about being pummelled by a masseuse, but a gentle rub with a light oil, much like a hairdresser shampooing your hair or giving you one of those funny head massages. Baby massage has lots of benefits, not least of all getting his skin nicely moisturised. Touch is the most developed sense in a newborn and sensory receptors in his skin help him learn about his body. He's not really aware of where his hands, feet and tummy are yet.

REMEMBER

Baby massage is a gentle way to express care and nurturing for your baby and is a time for you to engage and chat, or sing a song. Baby massage is total bliss for your little one and helps his development tremendously. So if you can give your baby a massage a day that's fantastic (but even one a week is a good deal)!

A good time to massage your baby is after his bath and before bed. He'll be warm from the bath and massage will further relax him for a good night's sleep (fingers crossed).

Here's how to massage your baby:

>> Make sure the room you're in is warm and that your hands are warm as well.

>> Set up a flat, comfortable surface, such as a change table or firm mattress.

>> Use a massage oil like calendula, sweet almond or olive oil. Warm the oil in your hands by rubbing your hands together before touching bub.

>> Take your time. This isn't a chore like washing nappies or getting dinner on the table. Use this time to connect and enjoy being with your baby.

>> Have a chat or sing a song, but keep the tone of the massage calm, peaceful and low key. You can also name the body parts you are massaging. Although speech development is a long while off, naming the body parts establishes vocal patterns your baby will recognise over time.

>> You can roll baby over and rub his back. First, roll bub onto his side, and then put a hand under his torso and the other hand on the leg closest to you. Ease him onto his chest by removing your hand as he turns over.

>> To massage feet, have bub on his front and use slow gentle circles on his feet.

>> To massage legs and arms, hold baby's foot or arm with one hand while massaging the limb in one long, gentle stroke with the other from the hand or foot and up.

Avoid massaging bub straight after he's eaten. Pressure on his belly might not agree with him.

Try to have one hand always touching your baby while massaging, even when reaching for more oil.

Baby activities

You can encourage brain development by playing with your baby. Try these activities:

» **Lying him on his tummy.** Also known as 'tummy time', a few minutes a couple of times a day on his tummy helps strengthen his back and neck muscles. On the floor, you can do some visual activities such as blowing bubbles or slowly moving a ball in front of his eyes. Place some objects such as toys just out of reach. He'll try reaching them as he develops his physical skills.

» **Moving him around.** Movement is good for getting those *synapses* or brain connections firing and linking with other parts of the brain. Try some gentle rocking, or have him lie on your lap facing you as you move your legs up and down. Or you can have bub on your shins while you lie on the floor. Hold his hands and lift your legs. He'll love it.

» **Reading to him.** You can't start the book habit too early. Picture books with clear contrasting colours are a big hit.

» **Talking to him — a lot.** He can't understand your words, but he's listening and learning and picking up language faster than he ever will again. You don't have to discuss Shakespeare or politics, just talk about what you're doing or seeing.

Even a mundane task such as changing a nappy is an opportunity to learn for your baby. Repeating phrases like 'lying down' or 'off comes your nappy' each time connects the words and action for your child. As his language skills develop, you may find him pointing to his nappy, or lying down when you ask him to.

Keeping baby safe and sound

Right now your baby is helpless physically, and he's oblivious to danger. Keeping bub safe is up to you. The buck stops with the parents; nobody else keeps your baby safe for you. So keep up the good work by always:

- >> Checking the temperature of formula by sprinkling a little on your wrist

- >> Ensuring your baby's breathing isn't obstructed by objects such as blankets pulled too high or bumpers in his cot (remember to keep your baby's face clear and his face up when putting him down for a sleep)

- >> Having a smoke-free home and car

- >> Keeping a hand on him when he's on elevated surfaces such as a bed or change table

- >> Keeping your cups of tea, coffee and other hot beverages well clear of the baby

- >> Providing age-appropriate toys, remembering babies really don't need toys at all, and even toddlers and bigger kids don't need too many toys. (Be mindful that toys for older children have small parts that may break off and choke your little one.)

- >> Supervising the baby when he's in the bath, even if he's using a bath support

- >> Using a car seat for car trips

Right now, he can't move or prod his fingers into electrical sockets, but you can get a head start and baby-proof your house for when he's on the move. See Chapter 8 for some ideas.

Your Baby's Development

Watching your offspring transform from a curled ball of wrinkled, angry-looking baby into a wide-eyed smiling bundle of delight is a joy. In the first three months of life, your baby changes so fast, you may have forgotten what he was like in those first days.

Growth and weight

Newborns typically lose up to 10 per cent of their body weight in the days immediately after birth, but can put that back on in the following one to two weeks. Your midwife or child health nurse will keep track of your baby's weight and plot it on a growth chart, usually found in your baby's record book. Unless bub is not putting on any weight, is distressed, lethargic or seems undernourished, weight is not usually a cause for concern, but is a useful way to track his growth.

Babies usually have growth spurts at around 6 and 12 weeks, when they wake more at night for feeds and take more food during the day.

During the first three months, your baby will:

>> Blow lots of dribbly bubbles

>> Coo, baby's first form of non-crying verbal communication

>> Learn to lift his head without help — the result of all your tummy time endeavours

>> Reach out and try to 'bat' objects in his vision

>> Smile — the first heart-melting smiles usually appear around six weeks

Hearing, sight, taste, smell and touch

Your baby's senses, just like the rest of his body, need time to develop. He learns by experiencing the world and interpreting what's going on, using his senses to gather information. Here's the short version of what your baby can sense already and what you can do to encourage further development of his senses.

Hearing

Your baby can hear from before he's born. Already he's had months listening to mum's stomach gurgle and the distant rumble of you talking to him. Your baby may settle to the sound of the vacuum cleaner or washing machine because those noises are similar to the white noise of being in the womb.

TIP

Your baby will respond to the high-pitch 'motherese' or 'parentese' of baby talk, which you may find yourself automatically using when you talk to him. (Some say we are genetically programmed to speak this way, so don't worry about handing in your man card when you hear yourself talk in a high-pitched tone.)

Your little one can't understand English yet, but he can understand your tone and is soothed by soft gentle sounds. He listens when you speak so, even though your speech is gibberish to him for now, keep going, because talking is good for his language development. You might even start reading cardboard picture books nice and early (but keep screens off for as long as you can).

If you live in a household where more than one language is spoken, your child is in for a treat. Not only do children with a multilingual upbringing often perform better academically (across all subjects), but seeing a child master two or more languages with proficiency is also great. In some cases, multilingual children come in very handy as translators between various parts of the family. So by all means speak to your child in as many languages as you can. A baby can produce any sound of any language in the world. If he's exposed to a particular language before he reaches about nine months, he'll be able to speak it like a native tongue.

Your child health nurse or midwife does a simple hearing test during the first few weeks. If for some reason this hasn't happened, have your child's hearing tested right away because hearing problems can be diagnosed early. As your child grows, hearing checks are important, because hearing loss can be caused through things such as ear infections, trauma and high noise levels.

Sight

The world is fuzzy for a newborn, whose eyes are only just working out how to do their job. Your newborn sees best at a distance of 20 to 35 centimetres, which is a good distance to check you out when he's in your arms. In the early weeks, he'll gaze at contrasts like the folds in your curtains or car lights shining on a wall as they pass your house. He'll look at something for a short time and then look away. Looking at something for a long time — apart from you and his mum — is hard work for newborns. You and your partner are your baby's favourite sight.

In these early weeks, your baby learns how to focus both eyes and follow a moving object, and likes to look at contrasts rather than similarly coloured objects.

TIP

You can help your baby's vision by showing him a variety of brightly coloured and contrasting images. Use one item at a time so he isn't overloaded. A nice game to play is to move in and out of your baby's focus range. He'll smile when you come into focus and concentrate on your face.

TIP

The saying 'out of sight, out of mind' is particularly true for babies up to the age of around four to nine months. If bub can't see something, it doesn't exist, which comes in handy when he wants something, such as a toy, but you need him to focus on something else. Hide the toy and you're good. However, bub eventually works out that things continue to exist even when they're not in sight. This signals the beginning of establishing a short-term memory. For example, if mum leaves the room bub starts crying because he remembers his mum and she's no longer there. This phenomenon is referred to as *object permanence*. It's a major developmental milestone and, while it comes with some drawbacks, it's a big deal.

Smell and taste

Bub comes equipped with a pretty developed sense of smell and taste. He knows you by your smell as well as your voice and what you look like, and can recognise changes in the taste of breastmilk or a different brand of formula. Bub can already taste salty, sweet, sour and bitter flavours. When he's introduced to solids in a few months, you'll learn even the blandest foods can taste wild and exotic to a baby.

Touch

At birth, your baby's sense of touch is fully developed and he loves to be in close contact with you as much as he can. Your baby's favourite thing is to be cuddled or snuggled by you and you can't cuddle him too much. Your baby's sensitivity is also why baby massage is such an effective tool in bonding, nurturing and settling.

One of the first ways your infant discovers the world of touch is through his mouth. Even in these early weeks, he investigates rattles, blankets, his fingers and all manner of objects by gumming and lolling them in his mouth.

TIP

The flipside of this incredible sensitivity is that babies can feel pain and are sensitive to scratchy clothing labels, temperature and uncomfortable nappies, so if bub is upset check if he is uncomfortable or overheated because of his clothing. A baby's skin is several times more sensitive than an adult's skin so an unintentionally firm grip can be quite painful. Rugby dads — watch the pressure you apply.

Your baby's amazing brain

By three months of age, your baby is almost unrecognisable from the helpless little bundle you first met at birth. As new connections, called *synapses*, form between different parts of his brain, he displays new skills and understands more of what's going on around him. Synapses are formed very quickly in the first six months of life, but as the brain works out which are worth hanging onto, those synapses that aren't used frequently are abandoned. Repetition of words, songs, sights, sensations, routines, movements, sounds and tastes helps your baby's synapses develop and make sure they're retained.

Research shows that stimulation in these early months and years of your child's life enhances brain development. Conversely, a lack of stimulation leads to a loss of brain function. But you need to find a balance. You can overstimulate your baby and this doesn't help. It hurts.

You may have heard about the 'nature versus nurture' debate, which is concerned with how or how much you can stimulate or influence your child's development. Nobody knows how much influence *nature* (the genes your baby has inherited) and *nurture* (parental input and the learning environment) have. However, neither nature nor nurture is 100 per cent responsible for your child's development; they both have a certain degree of influence.

TIP

Researchers who study brain development found that brain development happens in patterns but not at the same pace. The researchers generally talk about 'development windows' being open for a particular period. The best way to support your baby's healthy development is to keep screen time to zero (especially in this early period), make lots and lots and lots of eye contact, and talk to him all the time (yep, even in that sing-song voice). Beyond that, it's about being kind and patient, with lots of skin-to-skin touch, big smiles and closeness.

Stimulating your baby's brain is easy. Give him lots of safe opportunities to explore what he's interested in and keep offering new experiences. See the section 'Baby activities', earlier in this chapter, for ideas to get your baby's brain's abuzz with new information.

REMEMBER

Babies learn new skills at different stages and ages, so don't worry if your baby isn't doing what everyone else's baby in your coffee group is doing — he'll get there. If you're concerned, talk to your child health nurse.

The next few months are about your baby discovering that he has a body. Newborns don't recognise their limbs or body as their own. Hands are a particularly big part of your bub's life in the coming months. Make sure any toys he has contact with are suitable for his age because toys for older kids may have parts that can break off and become a choking risk. Toys with different textures and surfaces expose your baby to different sensations when he plays with the toys in his hands.

Between one and three months, your baby is probably:

>> Discovering his hands, perhaps sucking his thumb or fingers

>> Smiling in response to your smile

>> Uncurling his fists to grasp a rattle

REMEMBER

While your baby might be able to grasp a rattle, he probably won't be able to look at the rattle at the same time, as he won't connect what his hands and his eyes are doing yet, and the rattle may be too close for his eyes to focus on.

Male and Female Postnatal Depression

Feeling 'the blues' is one thing; being in a black hole is another. That's how some people describe postnatal depression (PND). The condition is associated with mothers for the most part, with an estimated 10 to 15 per cent of mothers suffering from postnatal depression. What's less well known is that 3 to 10 per cent of fathers can suffer from PND too.

While many men report feeling left out of their partners' lives as mothers deal with the constant needs of their babies and their own exhaustion, others feel overwhelmed by the demands of work and hectic situations at home. At worst, you may even have negative or guilty feelings about your baby and feel you're a bad father or partner.

Other contributing factors can include:

>> Not being able to bond with your baby

>> Attitudes towards fatherhood and masculinity — thinking you can't talk about how you're feeling or ask for support, or fearing that you'll be seen as a 'failure' if you're not coping

>> Changes in your relationship with your partner, which can lead to feelings of resentment and exclusion

>> Worries about extra responsibilities, financial burdens and managing the stress of work

Knowing about and recognising some of the signs of PND can assist you to seek help for yourself or someone else with PND. Some of the signs of PND to look for include

>> Anxiety or panic attacks

>> Feelings of hopelessness

>> Frequent crying spells

>> Loss of energy and appetite

>> Loss of enjoyment in everyday activities, and in your baby

>> Loss of sex drive

>> Mood swings

>> Problems sleeping even when baby is settled

>> Prolonged feelings of sadness and hopelessness, with nothing to look forward to

>> Suicidal thoughts

Every case is different. If you feel you or your partner may have PND, talk to each other about how you're feeling and see your GP.

If your partner has PND, supporting her may seem like a pretty impossible task and you may feel out of your depth. You can help in lots of ways. Try some of these ideas:

» Arrange things so you can spend time together with your partner — alone. Regular 'us' time helps de-stress both of you and helps you to find and share some common ground again.

» Let her talk while you listen, or involve a friend she feels comfortable talking to.

» Take over more of the housework and baby care, and try to let her get some sleep. If you can't take on everything, call in some support from family and friends so you're not swamped as well.

» Treat her in some way — for example, with a night at the movies, a massage voucher, a bunch of flowers or a special gift.

» Visit your doctor and get professional guidance.

Postnatal depression in men, though not as common as PND in women, is just as serious. Admitting a problem exists is difficult. You may find the following helpful:

» **Find support in your community:** In Australia, talk to PANDA (www.panda. org.au) on 1300 726 306 or Beyond Blue (www.beyondblue.org.au) on 1300 224 636.

» **Get some exercise:** Feeling fit and active can lift your mood. Around 30 minutes of daily activity is all you need to release mood-enhancing hormones.

» **Talk to family and friends:** This step can be a biggie, but you're likely to be amazed at how keen people are to help. Chances are some of your mates have gone through the same thing.

» **Talk to your doctor:** Your GP can offer you a range of options, including counselling and medication.

Postnatal depression is temporary, and you can find a way through it. If you feel lost, take stock and get some help.

Do you feel like screaming?

If everything's getting too much for you and you need time out, here's a tip. Take time out from your partner and baby, go into another room or leave the house for a bit and let it all hang out. Scream the room, house or street down if you want. This works wonders at releasing tension and you're likely to feel like a new dad. Doing a quick, high-energy exercise such as push-ups to release excess adrenaline can also be really useful. Listening to a baby crying is one of the most stressful things you can expose a human body to (nature's cunning way of making sure the offspring is well looked after and gets priority treatment). So don't be surprised if the baby is stressing you out.

On the flipside, finding moments of awe where you remember how small you are and how big the world is — or how miraculous your baby is — is associated with peace and serenity. From the majesty of an ocean or mountain to a tiny baby's ear, take the time to get lost in moments of awe and watch what it does for your wellbeing.

REMEMBER

You are a rock star in your baby's world, and this kiddo is entirely and completely dependent on you. When things are getting tough, you're sleep deprived, damp nappies are hanging on the clothes rack, it's 2 am and bub won't settle, remember that your baby isn't crying for the hell of it. Take a moment, breathe, and then get in there with kindness and a desire to help. The last thing you want to do is add to your little baby's pain . . . so remind yourself of that in the moment, and you'll do great.

Support organisations

For practical advice on fathering go to the Dadvice website (healthyfamilies. beyondblue.org.au/pregnancy-and-new-parents/dadvice-for-new-dads). Other good support places to start include the following:

>> Beyond Blue: 1300 224 636

>> Lifeline: 13 11 14

>> Mental health services in your state or territory: Go to www.healthdirect. gov.au/crisis-management for a list of crisis line numbers for your state or territory.

>> Post and Antenatal Depression Association: www.panda.org.au or call 1300 726 306

>> SANE Australia: 1800 187 263

Chapter **8**

Months Three to Six

Congratulations — you've survived the first three months! By now, things in your household are probably settling down a bit, and the thrill of the first weeks is dropping away behind you — although hopefully you still gaze in awe and wonder at this human you've played a part in creating. By now your baby is spending longer periods awake and is engaging with you and her surroundings. And she's starting to respond to *you* as well as mum, like she knows you or something!

The next three months are a period of great change developmentally, as your 'helpless' three month old, who can barely hold up her head, transforms into a six-month-old bundle of activity, capable of moving around, downing solid food and using her hands for all sorts of things (some of which you don't want her to do).

In this chapter, you find out what you can do as a dad during the next three months to interact with your little bubble of energy. You also learn about any paperwork required for your baby, doing things with your partner as a couple and what you need to know before you can leave your baby with others.

Your Growing Baby

Your baby is changing — and fast. Commonly, at around three months, she undergoes a growth spurt. If she's been suffering from colic or other problems with digestion, these may (mercifully) start to subside over the next few months. Check out Chapter 6 for more information about burping a baby and Chapter 7 for more about digestive problems.

Baby's new tricks

Over the next three months, your baby will start to:

>> Clasp objects, bring her hands together and reach for toys

>> Develop stronger neck muscles and be able to hold her head up more steadily

>> Gnaw on everything she can get her hands on

>> Make babbling sounds

>> Recognise familiar objects and people, and start to look for toys

>> Roll over from her back to her front

>> Sleep for longer stretches at night (in some cases)

>> Smile (intentionally) and squeal

If your baby isn't doing these things, don't panic. All babies are unique and develop at their own pace. If you're concerned with delayed milestones, talk to your doctor, check with your midwife or talk to the community health organisation in your local area. Table 8-1 lists community health organisation contact details.

THE THREE-MONTH MARK — A MILESTONE IN BALINESE LIFE

When Balinese babies reach the grand old age of 105 days (three months in the Balinese calendar), they undergo the ceremony of *Tutug Sambutan* — a naming ceremony. The ceremony is a big deal in Bali, where the locals practise a unique form of Hinduism. During the ceremony, the baby's hair is cut for the first time, but not on the crown, which is left until the baby is a year old. Also, the Balinese bubs touch the ground with their feet for the first time, and have their feet blessed to help them learn to walk faster. Celebrated with family, friends and even the entire neighbourhood, this event can take weeks to prepare.

TABLE 8-1   **Community Health Organisations**

Australia		
Australian Capital Territory	Australian Capital Territory Health Services	www.canberrahealthservices.act.gov.au/services-and-clinics/paediatric-services
New South Wales	New South Wales Department of Health	www.health.nsw.gov.au/kidsfamilies
Northern Territory	Northern Territory Department of Health	nt.gov.au/wellbeing/pregnancy-birthing-and-child-health
Queensland	Queensland Health	www.qld.gov.au/health/children
South Australia	South Australia Health	www.cafhs.sa.gov.au
Tasmania	Department of Health	www.health.tas.gov.au/health-topics/child-and-youth-health
Victoria	Victorian Department of Health	https://www.health.vic.gov.au/primary-and-community-health/maternal-and-child-health-service
Western Australia	Department of Health	www.cahs.health.wa.gov.au

New challenges for dads

After the first three months of #parentlife, you and your partner are probably more confident parents and are getting your heads around how your new family works. But, as with every stage of being a great dad, there are always a few more hurdles to jump.

Experiencing postnatal depression

In Chapter 7 I discuss that *postnatal depression* (PND) affects dads as well as mums. Postnatal depression is a form of clinical depression that can affect women and men following childbirth. Being mindful of this issue is super important, even though you're now three months in. Sometimes symptoms can show up late and unexpectedly — and it's essential that you get help if they do.

Helping your partner survive postnatal depression

Riding out the storm of your partner's depression can be tough, so your patience, communication and support are vital. She may be irritable — mad at you one minute for trying to do too many things with the baby, and then mad at you for not doing enough. Other signs might emerge as well: apathy, hatred for your little baby, an unwillingness to participate in life. Remember, this is not your partner. It's the depression.

Right now your motivational pep-talks aren't going to help. Nor will chiding her for her lacklustre performance. And trying to cheer her up? No dice.

Instead, step up. See it for what it is. Take the baby off her hands for a while, even if she protests. And be patient. Encourage her to talk to you and others, and essentially to find professional help from her GP. This can sometimes literally be life or death. And even when it doesn't come to that, the toll it takes on your relationship can be enormous. Be gentle with her. And seek help.

Dealing with sleep deprivation

Even if your partner is breastfeeding and you're not getting up at night, you may still wake up when she tends to the baby. So, broken sleep remains almost certain for dads in these early months when your baby is growing and feeding like she's insatiable. If your partner is the main caregiver and you're back at work, having to get up in the morning as well as spending eight hours with a new boss when you haven't had a good night's sleep can really get to you. You need to do something about this situation (other than drinking lots of coffee, which will realistically only get you so far), so get organised. Take turns, sleep when the baby sleeps during the weekend or sleep at a friend's house for one night. Don't forget to give your partner a break as well — things often start to look up after you get a decent night's sleep, and they look up even more when she does.

REMEMBER

Your baby waking in the night for feeds is a good thing — she needs fuel to grow. The trade-off is coping with the lack of sleep, which is temporary. Bub sleeps for longer during the night as she gets older.

Missing out when you're at work

The first time your child rolls over, works out a toy or takes some other momentous step towards independence is probably going to happen when you're stuck at work. Life is like that sometimes. It's unpleasant, but it's reality. The great news — and it really is great — is that even though you know it happened (because your partner contacted you and told you about it, or sent you a video of it), you'll see it for yourself, live and in-person, later that night. And the sensational part of that is that it will *still* knock your socks off.

So, while it's a thrill to see progress happen the first time and in the instant that it happens, it's also a thrill to see it the second and third, and even the fourth time. In fact, you'll probably stay stoked about tiny little moments like this a week or two after they've happened.

New adventures for dads

Now that your baby is spending less time sleeping or napping, you, dad, get to 'lift the game' and have some fun with her. Okay, you may have to wait a few more years until you can kick a ball around the backyard or practice WWE smackdowns together, but you have plenty of things that you can do together right now.

Research shows that playing with your baby, even when she's this size

>> Develops her social skills

>> Enhances her relationship with you (and vice versa)

>> Helps with hand–eye coordination

>> Raises her self-esteem

>> Stimulates her brain development

Best of all, playing with your baby is surprisingly great fun!

Some ideas for spending time with your baby include the following:

>> **Moving around:** Movement helps your baby establish and grow connections between different parts of the brain. These connections are vital in fine-tuning your child's senses, learning new physical skills and developing the ability to think and reason.

A good way to do simple movement is by rolling your baby over. Help your little one to roll over from her back to her front by lying her on her back, and crossing one leg over the other so she slowly rolls onto her tummy. Ideally, do this on the floor on top of a blanket so she can't fall if she rolls suddenly. Make sure her head is supported if she's still a bit unsteady.

>> **Singing!** With your baby in a bouncinette or baby chair, she loves being sung to along with lots of touch. Songs like 'Twinkle twinkle little star', 'Incy wincy spider', and 'Head, shoulders, knees and toes' can delight your little one. (She's probably not going to love your music just yet — or whatever's hot on social media — so stick with simple melody and fun lyrics.) Make corresponding movements when you sing; for example, touch her 'shoulders' when you sing that word.

TIP

One thing you never have to worry about with all babies is your level of vocal talent — they enjoy any attempt at singing. Humming or whistling is also a great alternative.

>> **Stretching and growing:** Blowing bubbles during tummy time helps your little one's eyesight and gets her looking up, strengthening that neck. You can also place toys just out of her reach so she looks up or stretches her body trying to reach them.

>> **Taking tummy time:** This activity is about lying your baby on her tummy so she can learn to push up and lift her head. This exercise is important because it strengthens the muscles in your baby's back, neck, legs and arms in preparation for crawling and walking.

TIP

Some babies really don't like tummy time — and can heartily let you know about it — so try lying down and having her on your tummy facing you. Or raise her up on your shins as you hold her hands.

TIP

The best place for your baby (and you) to play and explore is the floor. Being low makes it very safe from falls and floor contact teaches your baby about her body because she can feel a firm surface at each touch point.

Adjusting to your baby's changing needs

Looking after your baby or child can be great fun — but growth happens fast at this stage of life and it will seem that every time you master a particular situation, she moves on to the next challenge. Welcome to nature's way of ensuring you're not bored as a parent! Now that you're through the first three months, keeping up with your baby's development and adjusting your parenting skills accordingly is very important.

Looking a bit famished?

As your little one gets on towards the six-month mark, you will probably notice she's chowing through the milk and starting to look for something a bit more substantial. Your baby may be ready to start eating solid food. Until now, breast-milk or formula has sustained her, but now her digestive system is more developed and her growth needs have a bit more oomph.

Your baby's probably ready for 'solids' if:

>> She's taking quite an interest in *you* eating. Look for little chewing motions or for her to be reaching out for your food on your plate or fork.

>> She's able to take food onto her tongue from a spoon and swallow it. **Note:** She's not ready if she pushes food away with her tongue.

>> She still seems hungry after a milk feed.

>> She's a bit more unsettled at night, maybe requesting an extra night feed.

Be patient with introducing solids and don't 'force' feed ever. You can try introducing the same food several times over until your baby likes it. Don't offer too many different foods at a time — stick to a few over a period of two or three weeks.

See Chapter 9 for more on first foods for your baby.

The same old routine?

Most experienced dads agree on one thing — just when you think you've got a handle on things, everything changes. Got the baby going for a nap every three hours? Sleeping through the night? Don't get used to it — it's bound to change! Growth spurts, mastering a new skill or teething can unsettle your baby, and just as she gets ready to start eating solids, she may wake more often at night.

Your baby loves predictability — it gives her a sense of comfort to know what's coming up in her day. So if you haven't got your prince or princess into a routine, introduce one now. You don't have to do everything by the clock, rather, just have a cycle (or a rhythm), so that your baby knows what's coming up next. Repetition is a primary mechanism for how babies learn, so routines help on many levels.

If a strict schedule stresses you out because you don't work like that or your baby doesn't adhere to it, relax and do whatever works for your situation and your family. Trying to introduce some structure to your baby's life is a positive step, but not at the cost of your sanity.

Having a flexible but structured bedtime routine can help settle your baby for a good sleep pattern at night. The most popular version of a bedtime routine goes something like this (and if mum's not breastfeeding, you can be in charge of the whole thing):

>> **Bath:** A nice warm soak in the bath can lull most adults to sleep and on babies it usually works a treat. Your little one will like it even more if you're in the tub with her for some good ol' skin-on-skin time — make sure the bathroom is nice and warm. Hold your baby on your chest or tummy, or on your propped up thighs so she can get a good look at you. Babies are slippery little beings, though, so hold on tight — and make sure mum's on hand to scoop up your little one when it's time to get out. (Some dads might be uncomfortable with this idea, so wear your boardshorts if that makes you feel better. Bath/shower time is a treat for baby, regardless of whether it's with mum or dad.)

>> **Massage:** Babies love touch — it's the first sense they develop — and spending a little time soothing your baby with massage, and engaging them with smiles and songs can be a pretty magic time of the day for both of you. Make sure her room is warm and be ready with the sleepwear so she can be

wrapped up cosily soon afterwards. Natural oils such as almond, olive or calendula are great to use.

>> **Top-up feed:** This is where you need mum if she's breastfeeding. If your little one is onto formula, get in touch with your nurturing side, and grab that bottle and tank them up for a long sleep. Another slice of 'dad time' your baby can't help but love.

>> **And into bed:** With a little song, a kiss and a final wrap (if you're into *swaddling* — a form of snug wrapping to restrict the movement of your baby's limbs), your baby soon learns that after a bath, massage and a last feed, it's always time for some serious sleeping.

REMEMBER

A bedtime routine works even when you're on holiday, going to friends' houses or staying at grandma's.

You can adjust your bub's sleep-time routine as she gets older, with reading stories, taking favourite toys to bed or singing a special song together. It's never too early to read or sing to her. (You'll be amazed at what she picks up in the early days and 'plays back' at you when she's a bit older.)

Toys, toys and more toys

No doubt your baby was given mountains of toys when she arrived. Now that she's a bit older, she may enjoy playing with them even more. Make sure you keep some all-time favourites handy:

>> Fabric books or Lamaze toys

>> Rattles, squeaky toys and bells

>> Small balls and hoops

>> Stacking toys, boxes and wooden rings

REMEMBER

You don't need to buy lots of toys — less is definitely more at this stage. Make sure your baby is exposed to different materials and surfaces. Plastic toys and battery operated toys should be last on your list because they typically don't offer a variety of textures and don't encourage inventive, open play. They're also expensive and you then need to buy batteries constantly. And you definitely, *definitely*, don't want to be giving your baby a screen of *any* kind at this age and stage.

TIP

Many objects your baby will be interested in at this stage can actually be found in your household. A set of keys on a key ring, empty cardboard boxes, wooden clothes pegs or fruit and vegetables can keep your little one entertained for hours. Save your money!

Getting On with Life

Life doesn't stop just because your sweet baby has joined the world. You still need to go out, visit friends or frequent the odd café from time to time. The more people your baby meets, places she sees and surroundings she experiences, the better for her rapidly growing brain. So, get out there!

Out and about with your baby

Choosing the gear is, of course, an area that lots of dads enjoy! You get to choose from a wide range of options for carting your baby around, and you can try all of them, depending on your situation. Popping the munchkin in a sling can suit a quick stroll to the shop for the paper, but a jog through the park may be better taken with bub in a pram.

Strollers and buggies

During the first three months, your baby lies reasonably flat in the pram. Ideally you'll have a pram that allows her to face you while you walk. Now that she's a bit older, you can prop her up a bit and face her forwards so she can see what's happening while you walk. You may also want to invest in a lightweight umbrella stroller, which is great for short trips and travelling. Check the model to make sure it's suitable for your baby's age. Check out Chapter 4 for the lowdown on getting the right gear.

Slings and baby carriers

If you haven't already, check out baby slings and baby carriers. They're great for short trips around town. Proponents of baby-wearing swear by the benefits of having their baby in a sling or baby carrier. Babies carried in slings often sleep wherever you go and you don't have the potential hassle of trying to find a spot to park the stroller in a café or shop.

TIP

A tonne of different baby carrier models are out there, each with different pros and cons — so shop around. Get your salesperson to fit them correctly to ensure you're not squashing your precious bundle and that your back isn't damaged.

The most common types of slings and baby carriers include the following:

>> **Frontpacks** are similar to the backpacks you take hiking, only you put a baby in them! They have lots of padding and are usually made of canvas with adjustable straps. They can be worn with your bub facing in to you or out to the world.

>> **Open and close tailed ring slings** are adjustable and fit over one shoulder.

>> **Pouches** are pockets of fabric worn over one shoulder, and are very easy to get bubs in and out of. They aren't adjustable though, so can only be worn by the person they fit.

>> **Traditional slings** are a rectangular shape with straps around both shoulders that can be worn in front or behind.

>> **Wraps** are a three to five metre piece of fabric that ties around the body. They take some getting used to, but are said to be more comfortable in the long run than other slings.

Ask yourself these questions when choosing a sling or baby carrier:

>> How well is the weight of the baby spread over my back and shoulders? Will I get tired after wearing it only a short while?

>> Will it just be me using the sling, or is my partner getting in on the act?

>> How easily do I need to be able to get junior in and out of the sling?

Travelling by car

In general, when taking your little person with you in the car, you need to use the rear-facing capsule position until your baby is at least 12 months old (or your baby weighs more than ten kilograms). Check the instruction manual for details of your model.

Check out Chapter 4 for more information on safely travelling by car with your little one.

Finding activities to do with your baby

So you've got the latest stroller, your baby is in her flashiest gear and you're all keen to go. What can you get up to together?

Consider the following:

>> **Music and movement classes**, like Gymbaroo, are great for getting those brain connections going, but can be expensive.

>> **Playgroups** are community run groups of parents who get together to let their kids play while the adults mingle. Some have music sessions, and provide lots of books and toys. They can be invaluable for perking you up on a bad day — having other people ooh and aah over your baby goes a long way

to putting a big grin on your face. Depending on the organisation that runs the course, expect to pay anything from a gold coin donation to around $20 per class.

>> **Story time and music sessions** at your local library are another tonic for isolated parents, and babies adore them. There is nothing like sitting among 30 other parents and babies singing 'Twinkle twinkle little star', and having all 30 babies laughing in delight (no . . . seriously). And these sessions are usually free.

REMEMBER

Don't be intimidated by any perceived female dominance in some of these social settings — you're just as good a parent as the next mum. So wear your 'dad and I'm proud of it' face and enjoy the attention.

Baby-proofing the house

Your baby is only just beginning to get her moves on, but watch out — in just a few short months your little person is going to be crawling and pulling up on everything, and open season will be declared on cupboards, bookshelves and cables. What was out of reach one day is fair game the next. So now's a good time to take baby-proofing to the next level and ensure everything dangerous and precious in your house is either locked down or locked up. You'll be sure to miss a handful of things. Don't worry — your baby will point them out to you once she starts moving!

TIP

A good place to start is to get down on your hands and knees for a baby's-eye-view of the terrain and see what jumps out at you as potentially dangerous.

Table 8-2 provides ways to help you rectify any trouble spots.

IT'S ONLY MONEY

Babies and children have a unique way to expose you to different points of view. For example, you're sure to come to a different understanding of what's valuable to you, mostly because your baby may eat, destroy, wee on or draw on something that you hold dear. When that momentous event happens (and yes it is 'when' not 'if'), remember not to blame your little one. Until she's much older, your baby isn't going to understand the concept of material value — so if something is really, really precious, make sure you keep it out of reach (using a bank vault isn't a bad idea!). And remember: people matter, things don't.

TABLE 8-2   **Baby-proofing room by room**

Room	What to do
Living areas	Secure bookshelves and other unstable furniture to the wall with anchors to stop them toppling on your baby.
	Put childproof locks on china cabinet doors to prevent your sweetie getting into granny's heirloom china.
	Use a guard around your fireplace or heater. Teach your child to stay away by saying 'hot' when she is near the heat source.
	Tuck cables away or put cushions and furniture in front of them. Hide any remote controls you don't want slobbered on.
	Once the baby is mobile, consider barriers across any stairs or steps.
Kitchen	Keep appliance cords from hanging over the bench or stove. Your baby could easily pull a kettle of hot water on herself.
	Keep pot handles tucked in over the stove.
	Use guards on your stove elements and around the top of your stove to prevent hot food spilling onto your child.
	Forget using table cloths with really small children — one tug and everything goes overboard.
	Keep cleaning products and detergents in a cupboard with a childproof lock, preferably in a high cupboard.
	Never store poisons in food containers. A baby can't tell the difference between disinfectant and a bottle of juice.
	Use a childproof lock to secure any cupboard or drawer that has precious china, knives or equipment you don't want becoming one of your baby's favourite toys.
Laundry	If you use a nappy bucket, make sure the lid is securely fitted and is always stored out of bub's reach.
	Keep cleaning products and detergents in a cupboard with a childproof lock, preferably in a high cupboard.
	Make sure all buckets are left empty.
Bathroom	Make sure your hot water thermostat is set to less than 50 degrees Celsius.
	Keep all electrical appliances out of the bathroom to prevent accidental electrocution.
	Consider getting a lock or keeping the lid down on your toilet to prevent anything, like your car keys, being deposited in the toilet.
	Keep a lock on the medicine cabinet, and keep cleaners and detergents — even your shampoos — in a locked cupboard, preferably out of reach.
Outdoor areas	The law requires that pools and balconies are fenced. Make sure you have a pool safety certificate for any permanent pools. And when impermanent structures are erected, never ever — ever — let the baby out of your sight.

Baby-proofing your home has a serious side, all jokes aside. Every year many children in Australia are injured in preventable household accidents. Child safety is something to take seriously.

You can never take your child's safety for granted:

>> Keep any potentially lethal substances such as pet litter, garden fertilisers, cleaners, pest poisons, alcohol, fire starters and paints in a high cupboard with childproof locks.

>> Young children can drown in a small amount of water, not to mention the hygiene risk of touching dirty areas such as the toilet, so you're best to keep the bathroom out of bounds.

You may not think so now, but when your baby is crawling and walking, she can move very, very quickly, and get herself into trouble fast. The time spent baby-proofing your house (continuously) can save your child's life or prevent her being seriously hurt. (*Note:* It's not a one-time thing. You'll spend the next several years working through different phases of baby-proofing, and the next two decades wondering how you're going to keep everything tidy.)

Wading through the necessary paperwork

By now you most likely have registered your baby's birth, but you still have other bits and pieces of administration to take care of.

Insurance

Give some thought to getting life insurance if you haven't already. If something happens to you, you're going to want your family to be taken care of financially. Shop around for the best deal and to understand the various types of personal insurance. You can try your bank or home insurer as a first approach. And superannuation funds often offer well-priced solutions too.

Give your insurance broker a call to add your baby to your policy.

Savings accounts

Many parents set up bank accounts for their new child, and start saving for big purchases such as a new bike or school fees, or for far-off expenses such as university fees or a deposit on a first house. Most banks have savings accounts for children with low or no fees as well as bonus interest for smart savers.

Tax and benefits

Depending on your income, you may be able to claim a Family Tax Benefit or some other financial assistance from the government as part of financial redistributions and welfare. Check in with Centrelink to see if you qualify.

Wills and guardians

Make sure both you and your partner have updated your wills to take into account your new status as parents, and have thought about who can look after your baby should something happen to you. When thinking about who should be guardian if you and your partner dies or is unable to look after your baby, make sure you ask the person(s) first before naming them in your will, and check whether they're equipped financially and emotionally to add a new child to their family.

You may want to make special mention in your will of any sentimental belongings that you want to hand down to your child, like special clothing, photographs or family heirlooms.

Immunisation records

Keep a record of your baby's immunisations — they may be required when your child starts childcare, kindergarten or school. Medicare keeps a central immunisation record that you can check online at the myGov website. Just go to www.servicesaustralia.gov.au or google Australian Immunisation Register. At the site, you'll be asked to log in with your myGovID and then you can simply follow the prompts.

Doing things together: You're still a couple

Your relationship as a couple affects your little one. Happy parents, happy baby, they say. As a role model to your child, the relationship you have with your partner will ultimately act as a guide when she embarks on her own romantic endeavours in a couple of decades. But all your energy these days seems to go into bub, and with the lack of sleep going on right now, just collapsing on the couch at the end of a long day may seem like the easiest way to recharge. And, with all the attention your new bundle is getting from mum, you may not be feeling 'the love'. So both of you have to work hard to ensure your relationship isn't forgotten about.

Make an effort and make time for each other. Schedule some time in the evening when bub is asleep and prepare a special dinner, or hire a babysitter and head out for the night. It doesn't have to be Bollinger and foie gras; just do something you both enjoy. Keep screens out of your time together and really connect. (And hopefully the grandparents are available, supportive and encouraging for you to do this at least weekly.)

IT'S THE (OTHER) LITTLE THINGS . . .

Sometimes, simply doing things together is what helps you feel good. Here's a list of suggestions:

- Foot massages and back rubs
- Takeaway dinner for two in the park
- Taking a shower or bath together
- A slow, quiet walk
- A catch-up and drinks/games with friends
- A drive to a favourite lookout, and a simple picnic (that you've prepared, not her) while you savour the view
- A night 'in' where you focus on one another, and nothing else

You may be wondering when sex returns to your relationship. Chances are you're both pretty knackered most days or the baby is actively preventing you from getting it on. Your partner may also not feel like being physically intimate at the moment. The aftermath of the birth on her body combined with leaky boobs and that all-consuming tiredness may leave her feeling less than 'booty-licious' right now. Well — basically, you just have to take it easy. Definitely bring up the subject and ask her how she feels about sex. Ask her to let you know when she's ready to resume 'relations' again. You may have to be a bit patient but pressuring her is unlikely to speed things up. The best thing you can do it be present, be connected, and make sure she feels seen, heard and valued. And when things do start to heat up again in the bedroom, remember to take it slowly. Her body will likely be responding differently post-baby.

Leaving Your Baby with Others

Inevitably the time comes when you and your partner need to hand over your precious baby to others. You may just need a break from the baby routine or you may want to get back to working. This is a big deal and many dads feel unsure about leaving bub with someone else (even grandparents or close relatives). Often mums feel even *more* nervous. Don't panic — you can put your mind at ease (or at least you can try) with advance planning.

As with most things, the key to making this process work is effective communication. A key principle is to make sure the person who looks after your baby knows how you want things done.

Let your baby's carer know:

>> Your baby's routine, generally

>> Your baby's bedtime or naptime routine, including any songs or stories that are part of putting your child down to sleep

>> Which foods are allowed and which aren't

>> Any specifics about your little one such as tired signs, signs that junior's got a full nappy or is overstimulated (you're an expert on this, after all)

>> What creams or powders you use (and, of course, any medication if applicable)

>> How you deal with the baby crying

>> Any safety issues around the house

The reality is that if mum is still feeding, you probably won't go out until the baby is asleep. (Or a trusted babysitter might bottle-feed expressed milk, or formula if breastfeeding isn't happening.) Your outing will likely be reasonably short. And the whole time you'll probably be stressing about getting back before the baby wakes. This is all normal. And frustrating.

TIP

Don't push this agenda too hard. If it doesn't feel right, just don't go yet. Wait a while. But if you need it, the ideas provided in this section will be useful in guiding you to better outcomes. Just make sure the babysitter knows to call you if the baby needs you. And make your outing close to home.

Family and friends

Those closest to you are possibly the easiest choice of carer if you need to take some time out and/or attend appointments. Make sure you feel totally comfortable with this arrangement, and be sure to brief them in the same way you would with non-related helpers. Family members are most likely going to be stoked to spend some time with the baby, and some one-on-one time is a great way to build an attachment with relatives. Just ask the relos how often they may want to do it, because you don't want babysitting to become too much of a chore for them.

Nannies

A nanny is a professional who is trained to look after children in your home, and hiring one can be expensive — you're paying the person's income. Some nannies look after multiple children in the one house, so you can team up with friends and split the cost.

TIP

Look for a nanny via a reputable agency that has done all the necessary checks on the potential care. The agency should be able to guarantee your nanny has any required qualifications, basic first-aid and has been vetted by the police. If in doubt, ask to see your prospective nanny's paperwork. Most importantly, check references.

A nanny should

>> Take care of your child's physical, intellectual, emotional and social needs — that is, feed them, play with them, and be someone they feel safe and secure with

>> Take care of your child's (not your) laundry, cloth nappy cleaning, cooking, and bottle washing

In Australia, nannies can ordinarily work without any specific qualifications. So you can use online services to find a nanny. You're still best to read up on the Australian Institute of Family Studies Child Protection Clearinghouse website (www.aifs.gov.au) about police checks and references for nannies.

Some agencies can also provide nannies from abroad (in some cases they're referred to as 'au pairs'). However, au pairs usually stay with you for only up to 12 months, and you may not be able to relate their qualifications, training and references to Australia.

REMEMBER

While nannies are experienced carers, make sure you leave special instructions about your baby and the house. Also, nannies aren't maids — so don't expect them to do your washing and cleaning or to look after your household at the same time unless you're paying them for that as well.

TIP

When choosing a nanny, interview the person with your baby there, and see how they interact together. Watch to see if the nanny spends time chatting and playing with your child as well as talking to you.

Consider asking prospective nannies some or all of the following questions:

>> What's your family situation?

>> What are your qualifications?

>> How do you feel about me working from home from time to time?

>> Why do you like children?

>> What do you dislike about looking after children?

>> What is your philosophy on boundaries and discipline?

>> What is your philosophy on play and stimulation?

>> What do you do when a baby is sick, and you can't wake them up? (Correct answer — call an ambulance!)

Babysitters

Babysitters are different from nannies in that they usually just look after children for a few hours — that is, a morning, afternoon or evening. The majority of sitters are cheaper, too, than nannies. Expect to pay an hourly rate of $15–$25 an hour in Australia. If you go through an agency, you have to pay a placement fee.

In most cases, you don't need to worry about being late back (but check beforehand) — after all, they're paid by the hour.

TIP

Teenage babysitters might be cheap but they should still have access to adult help and a car with an approved safety car seat restraint.

Interview your prospective babysitter just like you would a nanny (refer to the previous section). You're leaving this person in charge of the most important person in your world!

Day care centres

Sending your mini-me off to day care can be a heart-breaking experience for a dad. It can be really hard on mum, too, so be there with a cuddle and some reassuring words if she's upset.

You're essentially entrusting your child to strangers in a strange place, so don't hold back from getting to know your centre well. The more confident you are about the place, the more confident your baby is likely to be as well. Make sure to visit the centre more than once to get a good feel for it.

You can find a range of different types of childcare facilities — community, not-for-profit and commercial.

The standard of Australian child care is considered reasonably good by world standards. The federal government's National Quality Framework, created in partnership with key stakeholders, demands that centres must have special programs for each age. Some take babies from six weeks old, and others don't take under-twos. Some have half-day attendance, others don't. Some provide meals, others don't. Shop around for what works best for your family.

REMEMBER

Childcare is expensive, and it's also in high demand. While many parents opt-out of work so they can stay home with bub in the first months (and even the first few years), not everyone can afford to do that. So register your interest early if you want to make sure of a place for your little one when you need it. Waiting lists in bigger cities or popular neighbourhoods can be up to two years.

TIP

You may be eligible for some government assistance. Contact Services Australia to see whether you qualify for the Child Care Subsidy. Call 131 272 or visit www.servicesaustralia.gov.au/child-care-subsidy.

Here are a few things to look out for with day care centres:

>> Do their opening hours work with your schedule?

>> Do they charge if you're late picking up your child?

>> Do they check a permissions list for whoever is picking your child up? Do they ask for identification?

>> Do they open during holidays and, if so, how much do they charge?

>> What are the teachers like? Are they bubbly and fun to be with? Do they have a rapport with the children, and communicate with them well? Is one particular teacher assigned to look after your child more than the other teachers?

>> What qualifications do the teachers have?

>> What philosophy does the centre have on activities, play, discipline and behaviour? How do they handle children's behavioural problems such as hitting other children?

>> What medicines do they have on the premises, and what is their policy on giving medicines to children? What happens if your child is hurt?

>> Does the centre have fire extinguishers, exits, alarms and smoke detectors? What are their policies in case of emergencies such as earthquakes or fire?

>> What foods are the children given? Can you request special food, such as gluten-free or organic? Is the centre nut-free?

>> What happens at sleep time? Does the centre have a policy on dummies (pacifiers), or special blankets and toys? What happens to children who don't have a nap? Most centres usually have a dedicated sleep room, with a teacher checking on children every few minutes. Some centres provide bedding; others encourage you to bring your own.

>> Do they provide a service for picking up children?

>> What activities are available at the centre?

>> Does the centre take the children on trips outside the centre?

>> Are under-twos kept separate from the bigger kids, or do they all muck in together?

>> Who should you speak to if you have any concerns?

>> How do teachers keep track of your child's progress? Most centres have a book with stories and pictures of your child's activities, and many provide daily updates and photos through an app.

TIP

After a few weeks, assess how well your child has settled in. Is she forming bonds with any of the teachers, and is she generally happy? Also, drop in unannounced to see what your child is up to. Make a regular appearance at lunchtimes — most centres offer days where parents can come in to eat with their children.

In-home care or family day care

In-home care with a trained carer looking after several children at the same time is a different set up from a day care centre but, in principle, you can still ask the same sorts of questions. With *in-home care*, also known as *family day care*, your child is usually placed with one carer, who looks after your little one (and other babies/children) in the carer's own home.

Because you're dealing with just the one carer, you can often get to know the person better than the teachers at a day care centre, and can be a little more flexible in hours.

REMEMBER

To avoid both you and your baby feeling anxious about the daily routine and other issues, you're best to take the time and energy to build rapport with the carer.

TIP

Go with a reputable company when choosing in-home care; they will have vetted your carer's house for safety, given them training, and done police checks.

So what's important when choosing in-home care? Consider the following:

» Does your child get one-on-one attention?

» What learning program is in place?

» What foods are provided?

» What are the sleeping arrangements? (Single bed, bunk beds, floor space: Be sure you're happy with the safety aspects.)

» What are the other children under the carer's wing like?

» What happens if my carer gets sick?

» What happens when my child is sick?

» What happens if I'm late picking up my child?

Chapter **9**

Months Six to Twelve

You're now six months in. Family life is generally making sense. You've got a handle on this fatherhood business now. Things that used to scare you no longer do. And while you continue to marvel at the amazing growth your baby is experiencing — and you're almost certainly still tired — life with a baby is mostly predictable. But, you guessed it . . . a change, it's a comin'. The next six months are all about your baby becoming more aware of his body and using it to get around, from rolling on the floor to getting up on his feet and doing that amazing thing babies do, walking. Witnessing your small, vulnerable child set out on the path to independence is amazing.

Of course, he needs you, his dad, to hold his hand as he makes his way. And if you're like most dads I've talked to, you can't wait to see what happens next.

In this chapter, I show you how to cope with your baby's ravenous appetite and what you need to feed him now that milk's not cutting it anymore. And speaking of cutting, I let you in on tips so teething is less of a trauma for your baby. I show you the amazing changes your baby is going through to become a mover and shaker, and how to manage a trip or holiday with bub in tow. And, last but not least, I conclude this chapter with a little party — your child's first birthday. This is one party where you can all but guarantee your kid will end up a total mess, and it might be the only time you'll be thrilled about it.

Keeping Up with Baby

If you thought your baby changed a lot in the first six months, hold onto your burp cloth, because things don't slow down just yet.

Your baby's changing diet

Until now, breastmilk or formula has been all the food your baby needs. In terms of breastfeeding, hopefully mum has been able to keep up a steady supply and it's been a positive bonding experience for them. Even if bottles have been used, this has been a time of closeness and connection if everything's played out just right. But to keep up with his growth, he needs to move onto solid food. Most health professionals and childcare organisations recommend waiting until bub's around six months old before trying solids, which aren't really that solid, more puree and mush. But you may find your little one is ready to start a few weeks earlier than the six months mark. This is sometimes a controversial decision and some people have super strong opinions about it, but you'll know when it's time.

Your baby gives you some signs he's ready for solids by:

>> Looking a bit famished after a milk feed — he's waiting around for more

>> Paying attention to what you eat, perhaps following your fork going into your mouth and making little chewing faces

>> Pointing at food on the table or trying to grab food that's within reach

You'll also know that the physical development necessary for solids has occurred around the time that your baby can hold his head up for long periods at a time and is able to take food onto his tongue. If he's not ready for solids, he'll push the food out again, called the *extrusion reflex*.

REMEMBER

At this early stage, your baby's digestive system is still pretty undeveloped and he doesn't have any teeth with which to break down food. This means that first solid foods have to be pureed or mashed thoroughly so they're almost runny. Some good first foods to try include the following:

>> Cooked and pureed apple, pear, apricot, peach, carrot, pumpkin, potato and sweet potato

>> Iron-enriched baby cereal or baby rice — use breastmilk or formula to mix these

>> Uncooked and mashed banana and avocado

Here's how to feed solids to your baby for the first time:

>> Give your baby a milk feed first. Solid food comes after milk feeds until about eight months of age.

>> Try one food, such as baby cereal, for three to five days in a row to make sure your baby has no reaction to that food.

>> Try that first food when baby seems relaxed and happy, not when he's super hungry, tired or grumpy. Lunchtimes or early afternoons are often good times.

>> If he's not into the cereal at first, that's okay. Try again tomorrow and if he's still not into it, give him a few days before trying again. Your little one discovering his passion for a particular food can take 10 attempts.

>> Let bub decide how much he needs to eat. Force feeding him is not likely to make eating vegetables something he looks forward to. Let his appetite guide you. It may be only a few teaspoons at first. Small tastes are really all you're looking for at this stage.

And here are a few things to remember about feeding solids to your baby:

>> A baby's sense of taste is very sensitive and he won't need salt, sugar or spices to flavour a food.

>> Some people insist on heating their baby's food, but this is more a matter of adult taste than baby's. If you do heat your child's food, test it yourself before spooning it up to him to make sure the food's not hot.

>> You'll need a highchair, a lot of bibs and some sort of protective plastic matting for your floor — unless you like orange patterns on your carpet.

>> You can buy plastic feeding spoons that are gentler on baby's gums and smaller than teaspoons. They look huge compared to your little one's tiny mouth.

>> As your baby gets older, food can become more textured and less runny.

Once your baby has the hang of solid food, try mixing different foods for a range of flavours. Introduce meat into his diet, because at six months old he needs more iron than you to support the growth of his rapidly developing brain.

WARNING

You might be trying a vegetarian or vegan diet. If this is the case, be *very* careful with your dietary decisions and consult an expert. While such diets can meet your baby's nutritional needs, they also present some unique risks for babies and toddlers. You can probably manage just fine for the baby's first year, but after that, your baby's going to need a lot of nutrients that aren't so easy to provide without expanding his eating options. (See Chapter 10 for information on feeding kids over the age of one.)

Try adding these foods to the menu:

>> Cooked meat such as beef mince, chicken and lamb. Meat must be pureed, minced or served as a broth so it's soft and fine enough for an infant to eat. I'm talking super soft and zero chunks.

>> Cooked parsnips, broccoli, courgettes/zucchinis, green beans (but watch out for the stringy parts because they can be a choking hazard.)

>> Egg yolks (from a hard-boiled egg)

>> Uncooked melon, plum and nectarine

>> White toast, rusks and crackers

REMEMBER

Try each food out for three to five days to make sure your baby isn't allergic to it. If he is, he'll have a bloated tummy, a rash or a hard time breathing. Call your GP or an ambulance right away if he's having a severe reaction.

WARNING

Honey is potentially lethal for babies up to 12 months of age. Honey can contain bacteria that release botulinum toxin, a neurotoxin that can lead to severe food poisoning. Honey is safe to eat by toddlers from about one year of age because their digestive system is fully developed and can neutralise the toxins.

After eight months you can introduce these foods into baby's diet:

>> Cooked creamed corn, peas, silverbeet, cabbage and spinach

>> Fish, unless your family has a history of fish allergy, in which case wait until your baby is a year old

>> Pasta and rice

>> Smooth peanut butter, unless there's a family history of nut allergy — tread carefully here, but note that researchers believe early exposure *can* eliminate the allergic reaction

>> Soy foods such as tofu and tempeh

>> Uncooked kiwifruit, orange, berries, pineapple and tomatoes

>> Yoghurt, cheese, custard and ice-cream, unless there's a strong family allergy to dairy, in which case wait until your baby is a year old

At eight months, your baby can also start exploring finger foods such as slices of soft fruit, cooked vegetable pieces, slices of toast, grated cheese, cooked pasta pieces and crackers. Avoid anything small and hard that may choke your baby, such as hard nuts, popcorn and lollies. And to the extent that it's possible, minimise processed foods and keep it all fresh (or cooked vegetables).

After eight months, solid food takes on more importance in baby's diet and can be given before a milk feed. Move your baby onto three meals a day, with breastmilk or formula snacks at morning and afternoon tea time.

Encourage family meals from the start. Pull the highchair up to the dining table so the three of you can enjoy your meals together. Your baby learns the mechanics of eating from you by copying, and you teach him that eating is about sharing a meal and eating healthy food together.

Don't forget the toothbrush

In the coming months your baby gets his first teeth (see the section 'Teething', later in this chapter, for more information), so you need a new piece of equipment — a baby toothbrush. You can instil healthy oral hygiene early by making tooth brushing time good fun.

Special low-fluoride toothpaste and soft toothbrushes for babies are available. You need only a pea-size dot of paste at the moment, if for nothing else than it provides a bit of taste for baby to think about while you brush his growing teeth.

Brushing teeth with the little one is another perfect dad job. If you're a working dad you can integrate brushing teeth into your champ's bed routine. That way you get even more daddy–baby time in your day.

Your little explorer

From rolling over, to crawling, to pulling up, to cruising to walking — the next six months are characterised by your baby's growing mobility and all the challenges that brings for us dads. Of course, you followed those baby- proofing instructions in Chapter 8 to the letter, and your house is a place where your baby can free range and explore to his heart's content once he's mobile . . . right? But you can't just let him loose on your house to do his exploring. Instead, help his exploration by exposing him to all sorts of different materials and textures. Use plenty of chatting about what he's experiencing to help develop his language at the same time.

The routines, they're a-changing

All babies are different, but you may be surprised to wake one morning and find the sun's up and bub hasn't even made a whimper. This can be terrifying — you rush into his room to make sure nothing is wrong, to be met by a sweetly sleeping baby who wakes just as you enter and greets you with a smile. Yep, your baby has slept through the night — a miracle!

REMEMBER

If your baby hasn't slept through the night after six months, don't worry. This stuff takes time. Kids taking a while to mature to the point where they can manage is developmentally normal. Also bear in mind that sleeping through the night can mean from 10.00 pm to 5.00 am. Don't get stressed about getting your baby to sleep for 12 hours at a time — this may or may not happen with your little one.

You may also notice that baby is awake more and more during the day, and is settling into having two naps a day, one in the morning and one in the afternoon. At six months, your baby needs about 14 hours of sleep in a 24-hour period. By one year of age, he may be giving up one of his naps in favour of a nap in the late morning or early afternoon. Let him decide when he naps by reading his tired signs.

REMEMBER

A change in routine can be messy and may result in things being unsettled for a while, but if you roll with it and remember that everything is just a phase, things settle in no time at all. Some health professionals say that pretty much any routine can be changed over a period of two weeks (consistency is important), so don't worry that you're being locked into a schedule you can't change.

With the rate of development your baby is going through right now and all the new skills he's picking up, you may find he's too excited for sleep and tries out his new party tricks at sleep time, such as pulling up on the side of his cot or crawling around his bed. Some babies pull up on their cot and find they can't get down again, so they cry out for your help. Be attentive. It's so important to know you'll be responsive. If he's crying, head in to wherever he is and ease him back down with your well-practised settling techniques, and wait for this phase to blow over. One sure thing about parenting and dealing with babies and kids is that things change frequently.

Discipline

Now and then your little one is going to drive you bonkers. Whether it's a lack of sleep, throwing food on the floor, chucking a huge tantrum, or even lashing out a little and hitting you, it's all but certain that your kiddo is going to push your buttons at some point.

I talk about discipline more in Chapter 10 but, for now, keep this in mind. Your little one does *not* need any form of pain, punishment, consequence or adult-determined trouble for being mischievous. I promise you that, despite the way it feels, this baby is not waking up in the morning thinking, *How can I ruin my parents' day today?*

At this point in his life, he literally has no coping skills, no regulation skills, and such limited ability to communicate clearly that it would be grossly unfair to get him in trouble for doing what 6- to 12-month-old babies do. What he needs is a patient, compassionate, attentive dad who has one interest, and one interest only: how can I help this little one feel better?

You're good at this

Have you seen the way your baby responds to you these days? With smiles and squeals? He knows without doubt you're his dad and he thinks you're a bit of a rock star.

Perhaps you'd like to take the reins for the day and spend a day alone with your baby. Send mum out for the day, or let her have a day lounging in bed while you and your little one get your groove on together. You might even surprise yourself with how naturally being a dad comes to you now. Isn't it amazing how far you have come on your fatherhood journey? Pat yourself on the shoulder and enjoy your new skills.

Playtime with Daddy

The second half of your baby's first year is characterised by his growing mobility, which is great news for dads. Soon you'll be at the park on slides and swings, or kicking a ball around. But you have to learn to walk before you can run and you can help your little one get the strength he needs to be on his feet.

Sitting, crawling, walking

All babies are different and develop at different rates, but generally you can expect your baby to be:

» Rolling over from his back to his front between three and six months

» Sitting unsupported between six and eight months

>> Crawling between 8 and 11 months

>> Walking between 11 and 17 months

Each stage of mobility is pretty exciting. Show encouragement and enthusiasm as he figures things out, one step at a time. Your presence, your smiles and your delight will be all the motivation your baby needs to keep pushing those limits, keep growing and keep those healthy developmental milestones under control. Activities and games you play together at all these different levels of mobility encourage your baby's strength and learning.

REMEMBER

Your baby is a little parrot and loves to mimic you. You help him move and learn just by being there and having time to play. He watches you sitting, getting up and walking, and wants to copy what you're doing.

Some activities to help your baby get the strength to reach these milestones include the following:

>> **Sitting:** To sit, your baby needs good head control and good balance, both of which are encouraged by tummy time. By lying on the floor on his tummy, he instinctively lifts his head to see you or any interesting toys nearby. You can encourage his balance with some gentle rolling, which helps develop the *vestibular system* in the ear, which is responsible for controlling balance.

>> **Crawling:** Once your baby is sitting unsupported for a while, he'll start to want to reach out for things around him and then work out how to get back onto his tummy. From here he'll work out how to move his body forward and commando crawl by almost slithering along the floor! As he builds strength in his arms and legs, he'll get up on all fours and work out how to propel himself forward and voila — he's crawling.

You can develop your baby's strength by putting things out of his reach that he can move towards, such as blocks, or by rolling a ball near him. When he is crawling confidently, challenge him by giving him tunnels to climb through or chairs to crawl under. Get down on your hands and knees and chase him along — babies love to be chased! Don't forget to give hub lots of different textures to try out — for example, crawling on grass, lino, your bed (supervised, of course) or at the beach.

TIP

Don't stress if you child's style of crawling or getting themselves around looks a little strange. A couple of hundred years ago, babies were not allowed to crawl. Hygiene and safety factors meant parents did all they could to keep their little ones off the ground. Crawling was considered unclean and animalistic. And it turned out, babies at the time didn't need to crawl before they could walk. Kids went from being immobile to walking back in the day.

The good news is that kids these days get to do both — in whatever style they like. (And don't stress about hygiene factors. Think of crawling as an immune-system booster.)

>> **Walking:** As he gets stronger, your little guy will figure out that he can pull himself up to standing on solid objects such as walls, his highchair or in his cot. He may want to hold your hands and walk everywhere, using you for balance. After some months of practising, he'll have the confidence and balance to stand by himself and take a few wobbly steps on his own.

REMEMBER

No doubt he'll have a lot of falls and there will be tears, but falls and tears are all part of the learning process and he will gain confidence, balance and strength. Be there with a kiss and a cuddle for those bumps and scrapes. And plenty of encouragement.

People may say to you that once your baby's walking he'll be into everything and you won't get a moment's peace. That's a very limited view of parenting, because him walking has a huge upside. Your baby can now explore much more of the outdoors, kick balls around in the yard and explore just about everything much more easily without being dependent on you. This is a huge step towards independence and should be celebrated. When your child is walking, they can do things like greet you at the door when you get home from work, or hold your hand as you walk together to the park. Of course, this new freedom does come with a need for extra vigilance from parents.

REMEMBER

Not all babies develop in the same order. Some miss crawling and shuffle along on their bums, or go straight to walking. If you're concerned about your baby's development, talk to your child health nurse.

WARNING

When your child is walking, be prepared for him to run away (and expect you to chase him). Be vigilant — he can disappear in a flash when your back is turned. You'll be amazed at how quick they are once they're mobile. Take extra care around roads, dogs and water.

Talking the talk

Just as the first year is shaped by baby's growing mobility, the second year is shaped by language and emotional development. But just because your little one isn't talking yet doesn't mean he can't understand you. In fact, he's soaking up what and how you're saying things to him. When he's figured out how to get his lips and tongue and mouth co-ordinated, language tumbles out of his mouth.

Your baby's babbling and raspberries, shouts and whoops are all attempts to communicate although he hasn't mastered language yet. Observing his attempts at language is often hilarious. He may turn to you with a serious face and deliver a speech in what sounds like Mongolian or Serbo-Croat that you can't make head nor tail of. If you respond with 'Really?' or 'Is that so?' he'll keep going and eventually words you recognise start emerging. This is great for helping your baby with confidence, and with the process of learning to speak and understand.

REMEMBER

Babies learn by repetition, so reading the same book over and over, or using the same phrases for activities such as changing a nappy or making his cereal, all sink in. Your little one is learning to associate words or phrases with activities, objects and situations. So don't be surprised if you hear him say things exactly the way you do. (That goes for everything, so if you don't want your child to use certain words, hold your tongue when he's around.)

Talk to your child and let him know what is happening today: 'Today, honey, we are going to see Grandma, and then we are going to the supermarket and then home for tea'. He may not say anything in response, but he's soaking up those words.

Children use different speech sounds at different ages. When your child will make certain speech sounds depends on how difficult they are to make. For example, some sounds such as 'm' and 'b' are easy to say and these will probably be some of the first sounds your infant makes.

Remember, even though I'm introducing the idea of speech and language here, you'll only get those first few words at this stage of their development. The real conversations kick off from around 18 to 24 months. But your child will start to vocalise at the 12-month stage. So enjoy it. It's a delightful time and is almost impossibly cute.

WARNING

Along with 'duck', 'ball' and 'dog', your baby will pick up the less savoury words that he hears around the house. Censor yourself early on — you don't want your innocent little child announcing to the world he can swear like a sailor when grandparents come to stay. This also goes for what you say about other people. Kids have a remarkable way of remembering all the things you said about Grandma a few days ago and telling Grandma about it when she's visiting next.

Staying safe in the water

One of the joys of having a baby over six months old is that you can go swimming at a public pool together! Before then, his immune system is probably not up to it, he's not able to control his temperature well and his neck muscles aren't strong enough to allow him to control his head. Public pools often have separate pools for babies and toddlers.

Because Australia is an island — and it can get pretty hot around here — I recommend every parent enrol their child in swimming lessons as early as you can. It's all-but-compulsory in my book. It will give you and your little one confidence around water, and it can be the coolest bonding time together as you climb into the chlorine pool with him and goof off while he learns to swim. Don't miss this opportunity.

Most swim schools will require you to buy special swimmer nappies that hold in any wees or poos your baby may do while in the pool.

If your baby has had diarrhoea, keep him out of a public pool for at least two weeks. If bub has eczema, chlorine and water may irritate it, so put the swimming on hold until the eczema's cleared up. Avoid going to the pool altogether if your baby is unwell, particularly if he has an ear infection.

Instilling a sense of confidence around water in your child now is a good idea, so start teaching basic water safety. Always supervise your child around water, remembering a child can drown in only four centimetres of water. See `kidsafe.com.au/water-safety` for expert advice and resources.

These tips can help keep your child safe:

>> Empty the bath or paddling pool as soon as you've finished with it.

>> Fence your pool. It's the law. Check with your local council to check the fencing meets local planning requirements.

>> Because we're talking about kids up to the age of one, always stay within arm's reach of your child in or near the water. If the phone rings when junior is in the bath, either ignore it or take your baby with you to answer it. Don't leave them unattended near the water. Ever.

Playgroups

No matter how much fun you're having with your baby at home, you will have days when you just have to get out and see adults. Going along to a playgroup can be a good way to entertain your little one and get some much needed adult company at the same time. One of the great things about playgroup is that a whole range of ages and stages are catered for, and you have plenty of other dads and mums to talk with about what's happening in your little one's world and what's coming up next.

Playgroups are usually a group of parents getting together in a community centre or other public space where children can play safely and parents can meet other parents. You can get as involved in the playgroup as you like — taking on responsibilities for running the group or just turning up for a coffee and a chat. You could even start your own playgroup if one isn't in your area. Some playgroups organise musical sessions, have arts and crafts available, and provide morning or afternoon tea for a small donation.

Children love being around other children, even if at this age they don't really interact with each other. Playgroups often have bigger toys, better books and lots more activities than you could fit into your house — all good things for challenging your little one.

Before you join a playgroup in your community, ask yourself these questions:

» Are there activities suitable for my child's age?

» How safe are the facilities?

» Is the playgroup convenient for me? Does it suit bub's sleep time, is it easily accessible for buggies/prams, does it cost much?

» What is the policy for dealing with other people's children? Am I allowed to pick up another person's child? How is conflict between children handled?

» Who is running the playgroup? Is there a commercial interest behind it?

CHECK THE NET

Check out www.playgroupaustralia.com.au to find a playgroup in Australia.

Toys you already own

If you like gadgets, you'll love the toys that are on the market these days. You may find yourself piling up the shopping cart with battery-operated products that do all sorts of funny stuff or claim to turn your child into a genius. As well as the toys you buy, toys also turn up as gifts, your baby inadvertently steals them at playgroup, or you receive toys free with some other baby-related purchase, so you may find gadgetry piling up in your house.

However, apart from the few toys I mention in Chapter 4 — cloth books, soft toys, teething toys such as plastic car keys and rattles — your baby doesn't really need most of the battery-operated toys for his development. Save your money (and the environment) and stick with the basic stuff at this point.

You certainly don't need to buy a lot of toys at this age to stimulate development, because you already have lots of really cool toys in your house right now. You just may not realise they are toys.

Here are a few examples. Babies love things that they can

» **Explore**, such as wrapping paper, pieces of cloth, a set of keys (best to use keys you don't actually need) or old books to gnaw on or rip apart

» **Make noise with**, such as pots and pans — give bub a wooden spoon and let him drum happily away

» **Mouth**, such as wooden pegs, wooden spoons and those plastic spoons you're feeding him solids with (be vigilant about choking hazards)

» **Shake**, such as a plastic container with a tight-fitting lid half filled with rice, or a plastic milk bottle with pasta shapes inside — you can glue the lids on with hot glue or Superglue

» **Stack**, such as food containers — small cardboard boxes or plastic bottles (which you can fill with confetti, rice or pasta) can also be stacked

TIP

Many babies find everyday objects, such as remote controls and mobile phones, far more interesting than their toy version. A toy version will be thrown aside for the real thing any day. Take the batteries out of an old remote, or give them an old phone, and let your little one push all the buttons he likes without risking a call to Brazil.

WARNING

Toys with small parts are still off limits for little ones. Anything with parts smaller than a fist are considered a choking risk, so wait until your baby is at least three years old before letting him play with toys with small parts.

Here Come Some Milestones

As you approach the end of the first year, the stay-at-home parent sometimes returns to work as obligated under the terms of their employment. This can also be a time to sit back and reflect on the past year as your baby approaches his first birthday and becomes a toddler.

Preparing to return to work

Parenting and work arrangements are increasingly flexible and increasingly varied across our society. While many dads stay home to raise the kids while mum works, the two dominant forms of family/occupational structure are dad bringing home the bacon as the primary earner, and mum working for a supplementary wage to keep the family afloat (either part-time or full-time depending on career preferences and work options).

If you're lucky enough to have enjoyed a few weeks or months of parental leave, chances are, it's already over, or it's coming to an end quickly. You're focused on returning to work, and this matters for many of us. Work brings purpose and meaning, and makes us feel like we're contributing in useful ways. (Check out Chapter 16 for more on stay-at-home dads.)

Before you and your partner get back into the rat race, though, think about these things:

>> How will you manage days when your child is sick and can't go to day care?

>> How will you manage your time? Will you have time to juggle work and family? Will you have time to spend with your partner?

>> Who'll take care of the baby? Refer to Chapter 8 for more about other people taking care of your child, such as day care and nannies.

>> Will the costs of childcare outweigh the benefits of going back to work?

TIP

Waiting lists for day care can be up to two years long, so phone around and get yourself on waiting lists as soon as you can. For more about day care options, refer to Chapter 8.

Keeping work and family time separate is a struggle in our high-tech age, when employees and business associates expect to reach you 24/7. However, you can set a few rules for yourself so that you're not burnt out by work, or short-changing your family. Make it a rule that if you have to bring work home, you wait until your baby is in bed before bringing out the work, or that your phone and email are switched off when you walk through the front door at night.

Likewise when you're at work, the more productive you are the less likely you may be to have to bring work home. Keeping in mind that time spent working is time you can't be with your child helps to keep you focused and to value the time the two of you have together. This challenge has no easy solutions. Awareness and boundaries are going to be central to your success.

Going on holiday

The idea of taking on holiday a demanding, pooping, sometimes crying child who is wholly dependent on you for his survival sounds a little like an oxymoron. Nothing is holiday-like about looking after a baby! Holidays aren't the same with children. You basically go away and then do all the same chores in the same sleep-deprived state that you'd do at home, but the view is nicer! Despite this, at some stage in the first year you may want a break from staring at the same old walls.

Going on a short trip isn't such a big deal, but if you're going anywhere farther away than a couple of hours drive, you need a few strategies to stop everyone going mental on the journey.

Driving

Imagine if you were strapped into a car seat with a full harness at the front. You'd get pretty uncomfortable after a couple of hours, and if you couldn't stretch and move around of your own free will, you'd get a bit grumpy too. So will your baby if you don't stop every now and then to let him have a breather, some food or a nappy change.

Here are some more ways to manage a long car trip with your baby:

» If you're travelling during summer, keep bub lightly dressed because he can get pretty sticky on his back or anywhere he's touching his car seat. Use visors on windows to keep glare out of his face and to protect him from the sun. Make sure bub has a cup or bottle of water on hand to stop him becoming dehydrated. Avoid driving in the heat of the day if you can.

» Make sure you've got some snacks prepared for the trip. You wouldn't want to get caught out miles from anywhere with a hungry baby who won't be satisfied with a breastfeed or bottle. It also means you've got food for bub should you break down, heaven forbid.

» Plan your trip around when bub is due to have a sleep because inevitably the motion of the car sends him off to sleepyland.

» Take plenty of toys or objects to keep your little one entertained while awake. Books or his favourite teddy bear are also great. If you can, organise a new toy or something he hasn't seen before. That way you can keep him interested for longer.

REMEMBER

Drive safely at all times. Your most precious person is in the back with you, so don't take any chances.

Flying

The idea of air travel with a baby can strike fear into the most experienced dads. The perils of confined space and air pressure issues coupled with having to sit within smelling and screeching distance of other passengers aren't to be taken lightly, but they're manageable.

Babies don't have the capacity to equalise their ears, which means that as the cabin is de-pressurised as it descends, it creates a build-up in his head that creates so much discomfort and pain that you're all but guaranteed to experience a whole lot of screaming as you come in to land.

Here are some ways to make flying with your baby easier:

>> Have plenty of books and toys to keep him entertained. Organise new things that your little one hasn't seen before. A great strategy is to wrap toys, books and other things your baby is used to as if they were presents. Unwrapping the 'present' is fun and adds to the excitement.

>> If bub's restless, take him for a walk up and down the aisles. Seeing other people cheers him up and gets you out of your seat as well.

>> If other parents with babies are on board, make contact with them. They may come in very handy if you need an extra pair of hands or for keeping an eye on bub while you eat or go to the toilet. Most parents of young children are quite helpful as they know what travelling with babies is like.

>> If you're travelling on a long flight, book the cot position (called the bulkhead seat) that most major airlines offer when booking your flight. If he's not sleeping in the cot, you at least have extra leg room for him to play on the floor at your feet.

>> Pack a drink because the swallowing action helps your baby equalise his ears. If mum's on hand, breastfeeding during take-off and landing can help too. (Sometimes cabin crew can be pretty difficult to deal with on this one because of the necessity of having your kiddo buckled into a seatbelt. Don't make a fuss. Go with it and do what you can.) If mum's not available, give your baby something to drink or eat during take-off and landing.

>> Stay calm. If you're calm, baby will most likely be calm too.

>> Take a fully packed nappy bag with nappies, change mat, wipes, plastic bags for dirty nappies, nappy cream or powder, spare clothes and snacks or jars of baby food.

>> When you check in, ask to hold onto your stroller/pram until you get to the gate (some airlines let you do this; it mostly depends on the size or model of the pram). Navigating through airports and departure lounges and carrying all the bags is a lot easier when you've got a safe place to put bub. Usually airlines can put your stroller in the hold just before you board.

If you're travelling overseas, your baby needs his own passport.

If you're staying overnight somewhere you need:

>> A cot for baby to sleep in, with appropriate bedding. Most hotels and motels have portacots, but check when you make your booking. They'll almost always charge more for this.

>> A mini first-aid kit of teething remedies, pain reliever and any lotions and potions your baby needs

>> A stroller or baby carrier depending on how much walking you plan to do

>> Nappies and nappy changing accessories

>> The usual clothes, toys and books

Wow, that's strange: Addressing your concerns

By now, you know your baby well enough to know when something's not quite right. You may discover something unexpected, such as a rash, your baby might make a fuss at something specific, or something just doesn't feel right.

Father knows best

Sometimes it may be easy to put up with the problem — ignore it and hope that it goes away. Or you can upskill and deal with your concerns. This doesn't mean buying every book in the store about childhood illness, but observing your baby's body and moods and acting accordingly.

Nobody expects you to know everything about your baby, but you are the best judge if something's not right. Trust your instincts and don't be afraid to ask for help if you need it. Child health nurses and GPs are there to provide help.

TIP

Get involved in your child's health care. If something's wrong, don't leave it to mum to work out or take him to the doctor, get in on the act as well. You'll be prepared for when the problem happens again.

Teething

Baby teeth usually emerge between 6 and 10 months of age. I might provoke some big reactions here, but teething should not generally be a problem for your child. We have a huge cultural expectation that teething is a really big deal, but health professionals are increasingly indicating that the emergence of baby teeth does not cause pain, does not cause diarrhoea, and does not cause fever.

If your baby does present with any of these issues, chances are it's not his emerging teeth that are causing the pain, fever or illness. Instead, it could be a response to immunisations, being overdressed, being overstimulated or an infection.

Teething does *not* cause a loss of appetite, nor does it cause a runny nose or coughing. And it certainly doesn't cause vomiting. If your child is experiencing any of these symptoms see your GP and look for other causes.

Oh, and teething doesn't cause drooling. In fact, your baby doesn't really learn to swallow saliva effectively until somewhere around the age of 18 to 24 months!

Stay off the painkillers (paracetamol and ibuprofen) and look for other things that could be creating pain or discomfort for your child. Teething is a natural process and usually the emergence of new teeth will arrive without gum infection or irritation. Expect it to be a non-event. You'll usually find that new teeth in the baby's mouth take you by surprise.

REMEMBER

You can bond over the routine of cleaning gums even before teething, and especially after the arrival of new teeth. If your baby seems irritable and uncomfortable during the teething period, you can offer clean washers or teething rings for chewing and enjoyment. The tactile feel will be fun, and also a productive distraction for your little one. If your baby's gums around the new teeth show signs of infection such as bleeding and swelling (very rare) see your dentist.

Use of medication (analgesics such as ibuprofen or paracetamol to relieve pain) or oral gels (topical anaesthetic) over the gums is not needed. If you're worried, seek professional medical or dental advice.

How time flies

Now you're a dad, time seems to evaporate in front of your eyes. Fatherhood is like a whirlwind tour of your favourite places in the shortest time possible. If you don't take photos and keep a diary, you soon forget the journey. So much happens in the first year. Not only does your baby transform into a toddler, you and your partner are transformed into completely awesome parents.

So how can you capture this first year?

>> **Keep a diary.** You could even do it online to share the joy with your family and friends.

- >> **Remember pictures paint a thousand words.** Take lots of photos of your little one. You really can't take enough. And once they're more than a few weeks old, it's incredible how quickly we forget to take those pics.

- >> **Start a book for your child.** You can record her first words and foods, and the dates when she first rolled over, crawled and walked. You can also keep photos and mementos in the book. They're available all over the internet so browse until you find the one that looks right for you.

REMEMBER

None of this makes any difference if you're not interested in recording these memories. Be interested in contributing to a diary and your photos and spend loads of time having fun with your baby when you take them. When your child becomes interested in his past, he'll really appreciate the effort you put into recording him as a baby.

One today!

What, already?! Your baby isn't a baby anymore — he's a toddler now. How did that happen? Didn't you only just bring him home from the hospital brand-new, like, last week?

Congratulations to you and your partner. Marking this milestone is just as much for you, the parents, as it is for your child — in fact, probably more! One year ago your baby was born and turned your lives upside down.

So gather your family and friends and celebrate your baby turning one. A celebration is an excellent way to thank those around you for all the support they've given you over the last year and to cement your child's place in your family.

Your baby won't remember or even understand today's his birthday, but if you want to mark the day with a child's party, here are some tips to make it memorable:

- >> Plan well in advance to allow yourself enough time to get everything done.

- >> Plastic cups and plates make cleaning up easier and with little ones around make breakages less likely.

- >> Provide food for adults as well as safe food for children. Avoid nuts and hard foods that may choke little ones. Have a balance between healthy and treat foods.

>> Take lots of photos! Bub won't turn one again.

>> Time the party around sleep times. You don't want the superstar of the day to be grumpy because he should be sleeping. Other parents will be working around their children's sleep times too so expect people to be late and leave after only an hour or two.

>> Expect that your baby is going to put both hands deep into that cake and mush it through his hair. Grab a photo and recognise that this baby knows how to party!

TIP

Start the day with quiet family time so you, your partner and your child can look back on the past 12 months and marvel at what you have now in front of you.

3

The Toddler Years

IN THIS PART . . .

Cherish special moments as your toddler speaks real words for the first time, and attempts real skills such as putting on shoes.

Understand your child's development, and how to help them cope with new emotions such as frustration, anger and tantrums.

Work out how to set boundaries and rules to match, and help your child understand right and wrong.

Consider whether to have another baby and how your household might work with more than one child.

Chapter **10**

Toddling Towards Two: Months 12–24

Raising a toddler is a genuine challenge. However, the second year of life is also a delightful age. Language, social and motor skills are all developing, and toddlers can surprise you with what they understand and repeat back to you as they grow. Your toddler will remember where you hid the biscuits, can figure out what the remote control does, and will mimic your gestures and movements in such a sweet, naïve way that it will make you crack up with laughter.

Your child's first words may be a little predictable — Mum, Dad, ball, dog, more. But somewhere between 18 and 24 months be prepared for some unexpected words — noisy, heater, dinosaur, or even toothbrush. Kids this age are often called sponges, sucking up knowledge like you wouldn't believe. The kid who just celebrated her first birthday is going to be quite a different child when she turns two.

In this chapter, you find out all about your child's development, as well as how to cope as she deals with frustration, anger and all manner of emotions she can't figure out. I also take you through the changes in your child's eating, sleeping, and health and safety needs.

Hey, You've Got a Toddler Now

Once your child starts to walk, she magically transforms from a baby into a toddler. Toddlers have a reputation for getting into trouble but don't buy the stereotype — and don't fall for the line that your child needs to 'get in trouble'. Your challenge is to guide your little one with care and gentleness, bearing in mind that you're in for some tricky times. Tantrums are all but guaranteed, regardless of how patient you are. And they'll get bigger as she does, although we're still not at the terrible twos (which aren't as bad as everyone makes out). But what that really means is that she needs her dad every step of the way. She also wants to do things her own way, thank you very much, which creates some tension . . . but it's nothing you can't handle. You've been on top of things so far. This is just the next phase in her (and your) development.

REMEMBER

If your toddler suddenly starts resisting nappy changes, getting into her car seat or having to sit in a shopping cart, she hasn't turned into a monster. She's just continuing her struggle to become an individual and use her own free will. I talk later on in this chapter about how to deal with taxing toddler behaviour.

Sleeping update

Most dads by now are enjoying a good night's sleep more often than not. The baby is usually no longer getting up for feeds in the early hours. That said, don't expect bub to sleep through every night. Wet nappies, being too hot or too cold, or simply needing a cuddle will still have her calling out for you in the night. Often this is just temporary and you'll be getting 40 winks again in no time. Some toddlers will also start to have nightmares and occasionally even night terrors, where they will wake up screaming or lashing out at you. Be there with a cuddle and some soothing words. Make bed a really happy, attractive place to be with soft toys and special blankets, which toddlers can get very attached to. Make sure bedtime involves lots of love and good feelings.

Around this age a lot of toddlers start to really, *really* want to sleep with you. They don't want to be alone. If you've been doing some form of co-sleeping you probably won't mind so much. But the reality is that toddlers can move a lot during the night, and sometimes it will feel like you've been kicked out of your own bed. And the bad news is that sometimes this won't change for a couple of years no matter how you try.

Most toddlers go through some sort of *separation anxiety* in the first year and it comes back in the second. If you've had your little one sleeping in a separate room, your toddler may cling to you more, need more reassurance and object to you leaving the room.

You have a few options here:

>> Pat your toddler off to sleep and hope she stays asleep all night without you there

>> Move her cot into your bedroom so she's close and feels safe

>> Let her sleep with you or her mum in the big bed and you (or your partner) moves into her room

>> Another creative approach that you feel satisfied with, and is kind to your child.

REMEMBER

Sleep challenges are, for many parents, a source of perpetual difficulty. Keep in mind that humans have slept in groups for thousands of years. Only in the last couple of hundred years have we starting this whole 'sleep in your own room' thing. This separation can be really disorienting and frightening for babies. Patience and compassion will work way better than hardline approaches (which usually involve lots of screaming). A flexible low-key approach so everyone stays calm is going to be far more adaptive and will likely lead to better results for your family than rigid, hard-core demands on a baby who doesn't have the developmental capacity to understand why you'd be asking such hard things of her.

Consider the following about your toddler's sleep routine:

>> **Do you have sleep time about right?** You want to put her down about 15 minutes before she's ready to sleep so she can snuggle, nestle and feel safe.

>> **Do you have the sleep routine dialled in?** This could include a song, a story, a prayer or meditation, and special quiet time together.

>> **Do you have sleep hygiene sorted?** This means the room is not too hot or too cold, not too dark or too light, and not too loud.

Be prepared because this period of your life is sometimes about as hard as it gets. These tips will put you on the path, but often trial and error (and loads of patience and compassion — which I may have mentioned before and which I may mention again) might be necessary.

Daytime sleeps start to change around this time too. At about the one-year mark, many children go from two naps during the day to one nap, which is usually taken in the middle of the day. Let your child work out how much sleep she needs by watching for her tired signs — yawning, becoming a bit clumsy, gazing into the distance and becoming grizzly — and putting her down for a nap then. At some point, she will start missing a nap, needing only one. Sometimes she may seem tired in the afternoon but will resist going for a sleep and by early evening will be exhausted, so you could try moving her bedtime forward a bit until she gets used to her one-nap-a-day routine. It gets tricky because sometimes the afternoon nap goes way too late and you realise you'll be up until crazy o'clock. Again, trial and error (and loads of patience and compassion) are what will eventually solve these problems.

REMEMBER

Your partner is likely exhausted, and relying on you to steady the ship. Be the support she needs so she can be great when you start to feel the pressure and need that support too. You're a partnership. You're in this together. Carry the load where you can.

Eating update

The start of this year will see a change in your little one's diet. As she grows more teeth, she's able to handle a bigger variety of foods, and foods with chunkier textures. With her digestive and immune systems maturing, your toddler can handle foods that were once off the menu such as cow's milk, honey and egg whites. Keep high-fibre foods such as bran and wholegrain bread until after her second birthday because they tend to clear the gut too much, stopping nutrients from being absorbed.

WARNING

Small, hard foods such as popcorn and nuts are still off the menu until your baby is at least three years old because of the choking risk.

TIP

Offer your child a variety of foods. What she doesn't like one day she may love literally the next so keep trying with things she's turned his nose up at before.

A typical toddler needs:

>> At least five servings of fruit and vegetables a day. A serving is the amount that fits into your child's hand. Vitamin C helps your child absorb iron, so include some vitamin C-rich fruits such as citrus fruit or kiwifruit.

>> Iron from red meat, chicken or fish, or vegetarian options such as silverbeet, slivered almonds and broccoli.

>> Dairy, but not low fat. Young children need fat to grow (but keep the hot chips and other fatty foods for special treats). Toddlers need about three cups of dairy a day — 600 mL may be given as milk, cheese or yoghurt, but not so much that they fill up on dairy and miss out on other nutrients. (They tend to *love* the white and yellow foods and gravitate to them, so keep that in mind and ensure plenty of colour and variety in all her food.)

>> Breads and cereals, such as bread and Weet-Bix, but not heavy wholegrains or bran until she's at least two years old.

WARNING

Limit the number of sweet snacks such as dried fruit, lollies and biscuits because of their tooth-damaging sugar content. Try slices of fresh fruit, sandwiches, rice crackers and vegetables instead.

Now that your toddler is able to experience more texture and variety in her meals, she can have toddler versions of your meals and eat with you. It's probably still a little early to try teaching your child about the social aspects of eating with all of you around the table talking about your day, but you can start to model it. At this age, though, she's really all about touching the food, playing with the food, mushing the food, and eventually eating the food (you hope). Expect it to be all over the highchair, all over the floor, and all through her hair. This is standard infant and toddler eating practice. Don't get upset about it. Just make sure enough of it goes into her mouth. The 'choo choo train' and the 'aeroplane' tend to be useful ways of getting her to open wide, chomp down and swallow.

TIP

Make sure the TV is off so she doesn't develop the habit of requiring distraction from a screen to get food in. And just hang out together as a family. Seeing you eat good healthy meals encourages your child to eat healthily too.

Health update

Try not to forget that your child, even though she's not a baby anymore, still needs to keep up to date with her immunisations. Check the immunisation register for your child to make sure you're up to date by logging into Medicare via your MyGov account. Google 'immunisation schedule' to find out when your next immunisations are due, or simply talk to your GP.

If your child is now at childcare, she's likely to pick up every germ on the planet, and will have several colds a year, as well as a diarrhoea bug now and then. Even kids who aren't in childcare are vulnerable to the viruses flying around and it may sometimes seem as if your child is only just getting over one cold before another one comes along. Children have the same symptoms of a cold as adults — runny nose, cough, fever, headache, sneezing and swollen glands. She'll probably wake up more often in the night for comforting and be a bit miserable during the day. Unfortunately, you can't give your child any cold medication (most of which isn't particularly effective anyhow), but you can give extra fluids, the correct dosage of paracetamol or ibuprofen (by age) and cuddles to help her feel a bit less miserable.

TIP

At this age, your child is still going to be heavily reliant on you to stay on top of that runny nose. She doesn't have the fine motor skills she needs to coordinate the use of a tissue properly, and even if she did, her ability to blow air and snot out of her nose intentionally will be close to zero.

REMEMBER

You can use non-medicated means to lessen your child's discomfort and congestion. See Chapter 7 for some tips.

Mingling with other children in the wider community also brings your little one into contact with germs that are nastier than the common cold. You may find she's come down with one of the following infections:

>> **Bronchiolitis:** An inflammation of the bronchioles (lungs' airways). Your child will have a nasty cough and may have trouble breathing. Take her to your GP.

>> **Chickenpox:** Starts with a fever and cold symptoms. After a day or two, your child gets red, itchy blisters on her skin. You can calm the itch with calamine lotion or other lotions available from your pharmacy and give your child lots of soothing baths. A vaccination is available to prevent your child getting chickenpox. Talk to your GP about having her vaccinated.

>> **Croup:** A cough caused by a viral infection. It starts out as a cold but becomes a pretty nasty and wheezy cough similar to a barking seal that comes on suddenly. Go to your GP.

>> **Ear infection:** If your child has an ear infection she'll be grizzly and tug at her ears, or rub them. A trip to your GP to check your child's ears thoroughly is in order. She may need antibiotics to treat the infection.

>> **Gastroenteritis:** Most children have a 'tummy bug' at some stage, which usually involves a lot of vomiting and diarrhoea. A number of common nasties could be responsible for your child's illness. Gastro bugs can cause dehydration, so make sure your child gets plenty to drink. Gastro bugs can take a week to disappear, but if you're concerned, see your GP.

>> **Strep throat:** Your child may have a high temperature and be vague and exhausted. Go to your GP.

TIP

If you're at all worried about how unwell your child is, take her to your GP. Checking with a health care professional is best, especially if she's running a temperature that doesn't go down after giving her paracetamol or ibuprofen.

To take care of a child with a fever (a temperature over 37 degrees Celsius), try the following:

>> Give her a dose of children's paracetamol or ibuprofen suitable for her age

>> Keep her clothing light, and use only a sheet to cover her in bed

>> Give her lots of fluids

>> Keep her bedroom cool but not cold

REMEMBER

If her temperature stays high, or you're worried about her illness, see your GP. You know your child best, so if she seems not to be her usual self — for example, she's less active, quiet or sleepy — checking with your GP is a good idea.

Safety update

The baby-proofing is a process, as I suggest in Chapter 8. What was once a hazard no longer interests her, but she's now more mobile and she's also taller. All these new options have come into play! Keeping your child safe is a long-term challenge, so stay on top of it. Now, though, you're dealing with a new safety issue: she's walking.

Once toddlers find their feet, they're off — and fast. Leaving the front door open may spell disaster as your child can be out of the house and down to the road in seconds, literally. Many parents have had the horrible experience of vacuuming one end of the house only to find that the munchkin has snuck out the front and gone to visit the neighbours (or, worse, started to walk around the block).

TIP

Make sure back and front yards have toddler-proof fencing, and that any rooms you don't want your child visiting are closed off and out of bounds — at least until she can reach the door handle. I don't tend to recommend safety gates for stairs because kids need to learn to navigate stairs, which means exposure is a good thing (within reason). Some parents find a playpen handy at this age, but be aware that an 18-month-old can learn pretty quickly how to get out of a playpen.

In the first half of her second year, your little one will be canny enough to use other objects such as chairs, fan heaters, boxes and large toys to climb and get into cupboards, benches and other places you assumed were out of reach.

WARNING

Pay particular attention to your kitchen. A curious toddler can pull a kettle of boiling water on herself by fiddling with the kettle's cord. She can also work out how to grab at pot handles, so keep handles tucked in towards the stove and away from inquisitive little hands. And a quick tip for when they're older: instant noodles are responsible for the overwhelming majority of hospital admissions for child burns. Keep that hot stuff out of reach for a long time yet.

REMEMBER

From 12 months of age, your child will be able to sit facing forward in her car seat. Depending on what model you have, she may even need a bigger car seat.

Need-Supportive Fathering

As a parent, you have the choice to find out and educate yourselves about your children, or to not bother and rely on what you know from your own parents. Previous generations can pass on some hard-won wisdom when it comes to child-rearing. But you'll want to be discerning. In some cases, relying on the knowledge of the previous generation may not be such a great option. Science has helped us improve our parenting in some powerful ways in more recent decades.

You may have heard about *conscious parenting*, and *gentle parenting.* Perhaps you've also heard of *helicopter*, *tiger*, *free-range*, *slow*, *positive* and *attachment parenting*. The parenting conversations of today are a far cry from parenting conversations when you were growing up. But what's the best way to parent?

As a dad, it's important to think about what sort of parent you want to be and what you want for your children. It's also important to consider *why* you want that.

Parenting research shows us that dads who actively and intentionally learn about how children are developing and get intentional about being there for their kids tend to raise children who do better in life than kids whose dads are less present, involved and intentional. Being actively involved in your child's life is important so you can understand and manage the different stages she's going through, rather than being dumbfounded by her behaviour.

REMEMBER

You no doubt realise that learning to walk is a great developmental achievement, but so is having a tantrum. Understanding what's behind these developmental milestones makes all the difference. Reacting appropriately to your child's behaviour is much easier when you know what's going on.

If you look at your toddler's new tricks (especially the challenging behaviour) from the point of view that this is a phase of her growth and development, managing the way your child behaves is much easier and less stressful for both of you. That said, the environment and situation plays a big part in your toddler's behaviour as well; for example, toddlers and young children will act up and be difficult to manage when they're tired, hungry, or in pain or discomfort — just like most adults.

For motivation, wellbeing and resilience, children need:

>> **Connection**: This means your child feels seen, heard and valued. To really connect, your little one needs to feel that she matters and that she belongs. You can build up this sense of connection by talking, playing, listening, singing, and being a steady and consistent positive presence in her life.

>> **Structure** (which you might call limits and boundaries): This means that you run things to a schedule. But it also means you create limits and boundaries for her. Sometimes this will be to keep her safe. More often, however, this structure will help her feel competent and capable so she can expand those boundaries and explore the world more. Structure is about both safety for development *and* the steps necessary to become safer in a bigger, wider world.

>> **Autonomy** (which doesn't mean total freedom, but the chance to figure things out herself): Study after study shows that when we get controlling — telling our kids to 'do it like this, not like that', and forcing them to do things our way and in a hurry — their development is negatively affected. Children can't be given total freedom and flexibility. That's irresponsible. But they do best when we allow them to explore, play, grow, figure things out and, yes, even when they can choose from a select range of options.

Let me repeat: give your child loads of love and connection, clear limits and boundaries to keep her safe and help her grow competence and confidence, and a sense of autonomy where possible (within reason — she can't stay up all night and eat ice-cream!). These are the three things most associated with positive developmental outcomes in kids.

REMEMBER

Your toddler is learning that she has her own will and can assert herself. She's a curious little creature who doesn't know yet what the rules about living are, and she needs you to show her what her boundaries and limits are — kindly, gently, patiently and with compassion.

A Busy Year for Your Little One

Remember how much your child changed in the first year of life? She may have slowed her rapid rate of physical growth, but not her development. She's speeding towards ever-increasing abilities, skills and independence. By the age of two, she'll be half her adult height!

Toddler development

This year is characterised by your little one taking her first steps and speaking her first words, and also by her social and emotional development. By the time she's two, she'll be able to say about 50 words, if not more.

At this time, she's developing the following physical skills:

>> Being able to see into the distance and spot things such as the moon, planes and birds in the sky

>> Climbing objects such as ladders, steps and chairs to get higher! (She'll almost certainly want to go up the slide rather than the ladder . . . and you should let her.)

>> Feeding herself with a spoon, then a fork, then adding a knife to the equation with much more dexterity and skill than before

>> Making attempts to run, albeit with knocked-knees

>> Performing little tasks such as 'find dad's slippers'

>> Stacking objects on top of each other, such as blocks and little chairs on tables

>> Taking her clothes off and putting on some simple clothing, such as her hat and jacket

>> Throwing and kicking a ball (however, catching is pretty advanced)

Her language skills are growing too. During this year, she's learning to:

>> Listen to and understand conversations

>> Say approximately 50-plus words, although not clearly and perhaps not in coherent sentences, but rather like 'Daddy gone' or 'sock where?' (called *telegraphic* speech)

>> Understand simple instructions

As for her social and mental development, you'll find that she's:

>> Able to feel jealous, and may object if you and your partner show affection for each other, or if you're close to other children.

>> Able to remember things, and may talk about them or find things that she's left somewhere (see Chapter 7 for more information about object permanence).

>> Able to say 'No' more often than you'd like (she probably learned it from you if you missed the part about autonomy on the previous pages) and she can be possessive of favourite toys.

>> Excited by presents or events, or the anticipation of seeing someone special such as grandparents.

>> Incredibly curious and wants to be involved with everything that you're doing.

>> Involved for longer periods with specific toys. Give her some transition time/reminders when you want to start a new activity, such as changing her nappy, because she may not object so loudly then.

>> More interested in books, and will want you to read them over and over again. Repetition is good for children's learning, so even if you've read her *Guess How Much I Love You* 500 times already, just keep reading it if she asks. You may find she also knows the words off by heart and will pull you up if you skip phrases or pages.

>> Objecting to changes in her environment or activity. If she's really enjoying playing with blocks, she may object to having a bath, even though she loves bathing.

>> Perhaps afraid of dogs, water, heights, the dark and all manner of things, including things she used to enjoy.

>> Recognising herself in a mirror, as well as family and friends in photos.

>> Showing more determination to do things her way or the highway. She's also showing her independence by refusing your help with tasks.

>> Well bonded to mum and dad, and will get upset if you leave her alone.

Playing with your child at this age is really fun. Unlike a baby, your toddler can make full use of playgrounds, and go outside and explore the landscape, and you can really talk to each other!

Here are some simple things you two can do together that your child will really love and that will encourage the development of skills:

>> Building blocks fascinate toddlers and help develop fine motor skills. Try making some towers or castles together.

>> Get outdoors. Climb a tree together, get on your bikes (well, she'll be on a trike or balance bike, or on your bike with you), or head to the park or playground.

>> Let the music play. Some toddlers really love listening to music and dancing. She wants to do everything you're doing, so dance along with her. It doesn't matter if the neighbours see you.

>> Let your toddler explore. If she gets into your wardrobe and tries on your shoes, let her go for it!

>> Play chase around the house. Stay just a little bit out of her sight so she has to catch you.

>> Play in the sandpit. Sandpit play helps your little one develop fine motor skills and dexterity, as well as allowing her to experience sand running through her fingers.

>> Play with water. Toddlers love pouring water into objects, so if you're washing the dishes, she can 'help' by standing on a chair at the sink with you and pouring water from one cup to another.

>> Read stories together, sometimes dozens of times over. Read as much as you can because it's so good for kids. You can change things a bit by reading the story in a silly voice, or asking your child questions about what's on each page as you go along. Voices are really important. And read slowly. Comprehension is tricky at this age. (Picture books at this age. Fewer words are best.)

>> Roll around on the floor together. This helps with your toddler's sense of balance and prepares her for rough and tumble play when she gets a bit older.

Toddlers can get pretty excited when rough-housing or playing and forget themselves, so you and mum need to set some rules around play. Some suggestions include no throwing balls in the house, no hitting and no snatching toys from other children. However, children don't fully understand the concept of sharing and inflicting pain until they are much older (around four to five years old when 'theory of mind' kicks in), so they will still snatch toys and hit other children. Be patient and consistent. When things get a bit out of hand around the playground, remove your child from the scene, distract her or give her a cuddle as a simple intervention.

REMEMBER

Talk about everything that you and your little one are doing. Her mind is a sponge and she'll soak up every word.

TIP

If you announce what you're going to do next or what you'd like your little one to do next, you'll probably encounter less resistance. We all want to feel we're in control (at least a little bit — refer to 'Need-Supportive Fathering', earlier in this chapter, for more on autonomy) and know what's happening and toddlers are no different, so commentate everything you're doing and tell her what's going to happen next.

Say 'daddy'

Hearing your child talk for the first time is like hearing angels sing from the sky. For the whole of your child's life she's done nothing but coo and babble and cry, and then voila! Words! Some of the first words she'll say won't sound like much until a light goes on in your head and you recognise 'ball' or 'truck' or 'dog' — an amazing moment.

Communicating is more than just about words and speech. It's also about body language, gestures and the tone of your voice when you speak, which is how you can help your toddler connect ideas with spoken words. For example, the way you say 'hot!' in a sharp tone indicates to your child that hot things are to be avoided, and the way you say 'good girl!' with applause and a kiss helps to connect those words with good feelings. Toddlers understand pointing, gestures and tone before they understand words, so you can help expand your little one's language by connecting those things with words. Try to describe what you're doing so she connects that action with the words you're saying.

Unlike when you tried to learn a language at school, picking up language is really easy for young children. All your child really needs is lots of talking from you and help to connect ideas, such as pictures in books and actions like getting dressed, with words in order to get those language synapses firing.

Toddlers typically go through a *word spurt* from 18 months onward, where they may learn a word from hearing it only once. Children who have been through their word spurts already can deduce or *fast map* what the word for a particular object is by eliminating objects they already know. Show your child three animals, such as a duck, a lion and an animal they've never seen before. Ask her which is the duck, which is the lion and which is the aardvark, and she'll be able to pick the aardvark because it's the animal she doesn't know.

Enthusiasm is infectious. If you're talking about how gorgeous your little petal is, or how well she's put away her toys, your tone communicates how you feel about her, and that's what will hold her attention and motivate her to work out what you're saying.

TIP

Repetition of words and phrases is important, so keep pointing at the rabbit picture and saying rabbit. Any day now you'll hear your kiddo mumble 'wabbit' when you point at the picture.

Dad, I need a wee

Toilet training is a subject close to the heart of many fathers — those who are cheering for an end to nappy changing and those who can't bear the thought of having to clean poo out of the carpet again.

Toilet training is another of those sticks that people measure their children's success by. Most children are nappy free between 18 months and four years old. That's a wide timespan, and it needs to be because kids develop at different rates. Some parents may brag that their superstar child was toilet trained by two years as if that's some mark of her genius, but some perfectly normal bright children aren't ready to go potty by themselves until they're four. Try not to get too hung up about toilet training by a certain age. Like other milestones such as rolling over and walking, your child will toilet train when she's ready. You can lead her to the toilet but you can't make her wee. On average, kids are usually around 28 months old before they're toilet trained, with plenty of kids either side of that average.

You know your toddler is ready to give the toilet a go when:

>> She's interested in watching you go to the toilet yourself.

>> She has dry nappies for a couple of hours or more. This shows she can 'save up' wee in her bladder.

>> She has the language skills to tell you she has done a wee or a poo, or can tell you she wants to do a wee or a poo.

>> She starts to dislike wearing a nappy and tries to take it off.

>> She can pull up and pull down her trousers or tights.

>> She can walk steadily and sit long enough to wee or poo.

>> Her bowel movements are soft, well formed and fairly predictable.

REMEMBER

Your child doesn't need to demonstrate all these signs to show she's ready to toilet train. Like starting solids, starting toilet training is something you can judge and try out. If it doesn't work, just wait and try again when more signs pop up.

TIP

In France parents believe you shouldn't start toilet training before the child can walk up and down stairs upright and unassisted. Apparently this means the child's muscles are ready to control bowel movements. See if it works for you!

Some tips for starting toilet training are:

>> Choose a settled time in your child's life to begin toilet training, not the week your parents are coming to stay or an immunisation jab is due.

>> If your child has a regular routine, find a time to try the potty that can become part of that routine.

>> Be prepared for toilet training to take a few months. Have patience if things go backwards. There will almost certainly be setbacks but, like everything, setbacks are just a phase. If toilet training isn't working after about a fortnight, stop and wait a month or two before giving it another shot.

>> If she's watching you use the loo, tell her what you're doing.

>> Let her push the button to make the toilet flush to reduce the fear that comes when she hears the flush.

>> Go slowly. Don't expect her to be dry at night for a while after she's got the hang of the toilet in the daytime. Night time toilet training is actually about hormones, and doesn't typically kick in for a while yet (although, like all things, early and late developers happen there too.) Daytime accidents will occur too, so be a patient dad.

>> Encourage her to eat fruit and drink fluid to avoid constipation.

WARNING

Forcing your child to toilet train when you want her to is bound to fail. Let her guide you to when she's ready developmentally to go to the toilet.

Here's how to start toilet training:

>> Get a plastic potty or a toilet trainer that sits on the toilet seat.

>> At a specific time of day when you think she needs to wee or poo, put her on the potty with her nappy and clothes on so she can get a feel for the potty. Keep in mind that kids are most likely to need to go after food or after a bath.

>> When she's used to being on the potty each day, try it with her nappy off.

>> Change to training pants or a combination of training pants and nappies for night time. Training pants are designed so that your child feels wet even though they're still holding that moisture in (mostly). The idea is to help your little one develop a cause–effect link between a soiled nappy and the muscles in her body that are responsible for making a wee or poo.

>> Give a big cheer when she wees or poos in the toilet or potty. (I suspect you'll do this naturally because it's such a relief to know the nappy days are almost done!)

REMEMBER

Don't forget to show your little one how to wash and dry her hands after using the toilet. You may as well start as you mean to go on.

It's All about Me, Dad!

The newborn who didn't recognise herself in the mirror and had no idea she even had hands has left the building. Your toddler not only knows who she is, but also thinks she's the only kid on the block, and will act like nothing else matters — not the instructions you give her, or the cat she's chasing. A lot of parents start to want to get serious about discipline somewhere between 18 months and two years old.

Understanding discipline

Toddlers don't know the rules to the game of life yet, so you have the opportunity to teach the rules to your children. Another word for this is *discipline*. Discipline's not about laying down the law and punishing your child when she doesn't conform, but about giving your kids the tools to know what's right and wrong and helping them on the way to becoming independent young people.

If you look up discipline in the dictionary, the first definition is *punish.* But the older meaning of the word is quite different. It's teach, guide and instruct. (Incidentally, punishment means to exact retribution, or to make someone pay a price. Not sure about you, but I don't like the idea of exacting retribution from my two year old.)

Developing a warm, loving relationship with your child where she feels safe and secure with you is the best place to start, because she'll know you're always there for her and love her, even when she's just painted her room with toothpaste.

In the section 'Need-Supportive Fathering', earlier in this chapter, I cover three needs children have: connection, structure and autonomy. Structure (boundaries and limits) is essential for socialising your child so she knows where she stands — and knows the consequences of crossing those lines. Children are often challenging because many of them have a part of their nature that wants to push those boundaries.

Some tips for making discipline work include the following:

>> **Be consistent with your boundaries.** If biting someone or snatching a toy from a friend is not okay one day, but okay the next, your child will be confused. She needs to know from day one that biting or snatching are not okay. At the same time, you want to teach her gently and kindly, using warmth, talking, guidance and encouragement so she doesn't feel alienated as a result of her behaviour. Distraction and some time-in with you when things are getting ugly can be helpful here.

>> **Be realistic about what your child can do.** Children can't do everything perfectly straightaway and can't control their emotions or understand their bodies the way adults do. We get grumpy when we're hungry or tired, and so do children, but children don't know how to control those emotions yet — and if they *feel* lousy, they're almost certain to *act* lousy.

>> **Remember children model the behaviour they see from their parents.** If your child sees you punching the wall when you're annoyed, in all likelihood she'll repeat that behaviour when she's annoyed. Saying sorry to your toddler encourages her to say it too when she needs to.

>> **Communicate with your toddler, even if she isn't really speaking well yet.** Showing her the rules may take a few explanations, but she'll get there. You don't need to give complicated explanations for why hitting the cat is not okay. Simply telling her he may scratch her is enough.

>> **Understand it takes time for toddlers to learn their boundaries and to understand consequences.** Try to be patient with your child. Think how long it takes to learn to speak, or tie a shoelace. Regulating emotions and behaviour is way more complex, and it takes a long time to learn how to get this right.

>> **Keep in mind kids aren't naughty for the sake of it, or to wind you up.** There's usually a reason. Your toddler is trying out new things every second of the day, like throwing bits of banana around the car, for the experience of it. She may also be less well behaved when she's tired or hungry, frustrated or shy. Work with your child's routine. Don't go shopping at lunchtime, for example, or to a busy crowded place at nap time.

>> **Remember that your child just wants you to love her and to please you.** This may be hard to do on a day when she's thrown bits of banana around the car. Be patient and use distraction to divert her attention while removing the banana from sight.

>> **Reward good behaviour with lots of love and praise, but try not to withhold love when she's behaving badly.** Let her know you love *her* (the little person), not the behaviour.

>> **Say more positive than negative things to your child.** Reword phrases; for example, 'no running in the house' becomes 'slow down, please'.

>> **Work out with your partner what action to take when your child is doing something undesirable.** Note that new science shows the old-school discipline strategies such as time out (the naughty chair) or smacking undermine those needs your child has (connection, structure and autonomy). If you're hurting them, that ruptures the relationship, removes autonomy, and makes them feel awful about themselves. Distracting your child from a behaviour, showing her how to clean up if she's made a mess, or talking things through to help her understand what's going on are all techniques to discipline (teach, guide and instruct) a child. Smacking a child is not acceptable. More than 60 years of evidence has shown that smacking is ineffective in changing behaviour and it confuses children. How can dad love me when he hits me?

I recommend using a framework for effective discipline that starts before any issues arise. It goes like this:

>> Be consistent and explain expectations

>> Establish limits and boundaries

>> Listen and understand her

>> Show love and warmth to your child at every opportunity

REMEMBER

Discipline starts at this point, and the result of discipline done well will be a structured and secure environment to grow up in.

If your child is really pushing your buttons with her behaviour, yelling at her won't make things any easier. In fact, it may just make things worse. So try to be calm, take a deep breath and sing a song, like 'Incy wincy spider', to yourself.

TIP

When you feel yourself getting really wound up, check with yourself how you're feeling and what your day has been like. It may be that the behaviour of your little one isn't actually that bad, you've just had a tough day. It might be a good idea to remove yourself from the situation to let off some steam, or lift your spirits by listening to a good song in the car. Kids do badly when they're hungry, angry, lonely, tired and stressed (HALTS). So do we as dads.

REMEMBER

Understand the difference between discipline and punishment. Discipline is derived from 'disciple' and refers to a particular code of conduct given to a person to follow. Punishment is the practice of imposing something unpleasant or aversive on somebody. Punishment doesn't involve any instruction or code of conduct and as a result it is typically not effective in changing behaviour. Use discipline with your children rather than punishment.

Tantrums, biting and hitting

When you first met your seconds-old baby all those months ago, you probably didn't imagine that she'd be having a full-on hissy fit in the middle of the supermarket over not being able to grab a bottle of bleach from the shelf. But it happens to even the nicest babies, with the nicest, most nurturing parents. Not only do children have tantrums, but they also hit other children (or you), pull hair, bite and scratch because they aren't yet able to control their emotions, frustrations and physicality.

Tantrums

Although two year olds are famous for being tempestuous, even children under two have tantrums. Tantrums can go on into the fifth year and beyond. (We all know plenty of grown-ups who still have tantrums, right?) You've probably seen a child mid-tantrum in the street or shop, with an embarrassed, stressed out parent standing nearby, trying to reason her little one out of it, or ignore the whole thing. You probably said that your kid would never do that. But tantrums are almost inevitable. And I hate to say it . . . but your kid will almost certainly do that!

Tantrums happen when your child is overloaded with stress or frustration. She has an idea of what she wants to do, such as running around like a crazy thing in the supermarket. If you want her to do otherwise, such as staying by your side as you shop, she's going to get pretty fed up with you holding her back, and she'll have a tantrum.

She may also be tired and hungry, or feeling vulnerable or insecure, which makes everyone's tolerance for things they don't want to do much lower, even you big grown up fathers. The HALTS acronym from the previous section is relevant again here: hungry, angry, lonely, tired and stressed. It happens a lot with toddlers (and their parents).

Here are some pointers on how to stop tantrums happening:

>> Make sure your child isn't tired or hungry before setting out on an activity.

>> Talk to your child about what you're going to be doing or who you'll be seeing so there aren't surprises for her.

>> If you're at the playground and it's nearly time to leave, let her have plenty of time to get used to the idea, so she understands when it's time to go. (Remember, she doesn't understand what 'five minutes means', so use that, but also let her know that five minutes is when you finish singing this song, or after 10 big pushes on the swing.)

>> Get your child involved in what you're doing so she's engaged with you rather than wanting to behave in a way that requires you telling her off. Involvement and fun are the key.

If a tantrum is on its way, the best strategy is to come in close to your child and go for a hug or distraction (and if you guess wrong, it will probably be too late). Some parents think they shouldn't give any attention during a tantrum, but if your child is demanding attention, she probably needs it! Offer it to her. It might make all the difference.

Once the tantrum starts, though, you can't do much. High emotions usually mean low intelligence, particularly for little ones. Here are the steps that will work best most of the time (but nothing works every time):

1. **Offer hugs and closeness.**

   If she says 'yes', you already know it's going to be fine. But it's unlikely.

2. **If your hugs and closeness are rejected, say 'okay', and then say 'I'll just wait over here until you want a hug'.**

   Offer another hug before moving. Any self-respecting toddler will say no (actually, she'll yell at you).

3. **Take a few steps away and wait about 10 seconds before offering another hug.**

   If she says 'yes', hug her like crazy and restore the relationship with love and kindness.

4. **If your next offer is rejected, say 'okay', and then say 'I'll just wait here until you want a hug'.**

5. **Move a little further away (or maybe step out of the room if you're at home), count to 30 seconds (maximum) and then check in again to see if she wants a hug.**

   Usually by this stage your child has had enough time and space to calm herself down. Or she's recognised that she needs a hug and you happen to be right there with a big embrace and a whole lot of love.

REMEMBER

You're not rewarding bad behaviour here. You're offering support when her emotions are so big she can't control them. You're teaching her to co-regulate.

Here are some other ideas that will help when co-regulation is needed:

>> Lower your body position. Get down on your child's level.

>> Lower your voice. Soft sounds promote soft feelings.

>> Soften your facial expression. Soft eyes create soft hearts.

>> Model deep breathing.

>> Walk outside. Nature is fuel for the soul.

>> Find a preferred sensory activity. A crinkly leaf or a slippery piece of ice can be a powerful distraction and emotion regulation tool.

>> Dim the lights and reduce sensory input.

>> Stop talking altogether.

>> Change how close to your child you are.

Trying to reason with or distract your child is usually pointless during a tantrum. You can't get logical with someone having a tantrum whether they're two or 52. They won't listen because they're too emotionally flooded. Just let her get it all out and when the tantrum's over, give her a cuddle and a kiss and keep on with what you were doing. Don't get upset, because that usually just intensifies the tantrum. Keep breathing!

TIP

Chat to your partner about how you plan to manage tantrums and activities that may involve tantrums, such as shopping, long car rides or visiting people. Consistency is important, so the two of you need a consistent approach to handle tantrums or discipline in general.

Hurting others

Having your child come home from day care with a bite mark or scratches on her face is horrible. When your child's the person doing the biting and scratching it's also horrible . . . in a totally different way.

Your toddler hasn't got the hang of *empathy* (the ability to feel how others are feeling) yet and her hitting someone else hasn't registered on her list of things on the 'not okay' list. It will take another couple of years for this to really get through.

Hurting others is often a sign of some underlying emotion, such as anger, fear, frustration or feeling insecure. Sometimes, it's simple experimentation at a young age. Ideally, you'll spend time finding out what is behind this behaviour so you can address the problem directly and let her know plainly that hurting another person is never okay. But, sometimes you'll never know the reason. Little ones don't communicate so well just yet. This means ongoing patient teaching. Again, you'll need to teach your child most of this stuff dozens of times — maybe hundreds — before it really sinks in.

Your little one doesn't necessarily grasp that her hitting or biting hurts the other person. Empathy is a complex concept that most children only master when they are around five or six years (or older).

TIP

Labelling your child as a 'biter' or 'hitter' leads to more biting and hitting. Your child is a person, not a behaviour. And a quick warning: if you think hitting or biting your child to teach them a lesson will work, think again. It won't. It just hurts your child, hurts your relationship, and makes your child think she's a bad kid. (Sometimes it actually models the very behaviour you're trying to stop!)

Here's how you can deal with your child hitting or scratching another child:

» Acknowledge how your child is feeling — 'I know you're angry . . .'

» Explain that's not how we deal with problems — 'but we don't hit people when we're angry. Hitting hurts people.'

» Give her an alternative — 'If you're mad, you come tell me and we'll hug and work it out.'

» Show her how to touch people with kindness rather than anger.

Bear in mind that your child is still crazy young. These past few pages have been a crash-course in child discipline, but the reality is that most of it will go over her head until she's at least three. Your central focus up until that point — as hard as it will be sometimes — is to be patient and gentle, and keep showing her a better way to handle conflict or frustration. This is another area where you can be a shining example as a dad — show her how it's done.

Sharing — what a nice idea

Toddlers are territorial creatures whose favourite word after 'no!' is 'mine!' Your sweet little girl doesn't yet understand the feelings of others and thinks only about herself. Sounds awful, but it's true.

Even kids who are best buddies at day care or cousins who adore each other's company will fight over possession of a favoured toy, and lay claim to what they think is theirs. Play dates, playgroups and childcare can be rife with conflict. This conflict is all part of your toddler becoming independent and learning she has some control over the universe.

At this stage of your child's development, don't sweat it. Don't emphasise it. Just let it go. It's not developmentally appropriate. In Chapter 10, I start to walk through some basics of sharing, but under the age of three it's not going to happen (and when it does, it's a fluke.)

Setbacks

Dealing with setbacks is a part of fatherhood. All great fathers have setbacks. Your little angel has been glorious company for a week, but one day you come home from work to find she's transformed into a monster, ignoring everything you tell her. Letting fly with a few choice words may be your default option but it won't help anyone.

You'll face a few setbacks on your fatherhood journey, and you're guaranteed to have moments when you're not the dad you hoped you'd be. Maybe setbacks are nature's way of keeping life interesting for parents, or perhaps they're part of a greater plan designed to help us become the best version of ourselves we can. Development and progression aren't linear. In most cases, no logical explanations seem to exist for why setbacks occur, so you have to take them as they come. Learn from these situations so you can continue to improve, and remember that while your baby is developing (in a two steps forward, one step back kind of way), so are you. Don't be distracted by temporary setbacks.

These strategies can help:

>> Breathe.

>> Get some advice from your partner.

>> Spend some time involved in a favourite sport or pastime to create some distance.

>> Imagine what a parent you really look up to as having it all together might do in that situation.

>> Imagine an audience is watching you parent, and act accordingly.

>> Imagine your child talking to you about this incident 20 years down the track. What would you want them to remember?

>> Remember that it's feeling big right now, but it's really a small thing. You've got this.

REMEMBER

You're always going to have setbacks — they're part of being a father. Your child, even though she's acting like a demon, really only wants to be loved and to make you happy. Try to remember that when she's smearing jam or snot on your suit jacket.

Chapter **11**

Charging Towards Three: Months 24–36

N ow that your little one is two years old, he's no longer an infant, but a fully-fledged toddler. At the end of this year when he's three, he'll graduate from toddlerhood and become a pre-schooler. Your little human may have been through a whole lot of firsts in these two years — first smile, first step, first word — but so have you. And while the challenges change, so do the opportunities and thrills as you see your youngster develop, mature and take on the world in new ways. Between two and three, you can have your first kick around, first conversations and a whole range of other firsts.

But be aware, two is also a challenging age. In Chapter 10 I step through a range of issues you'll face when it comes to discipline. Things were ramping up in your past few months, but now . . . well, you're going to get it full blast. It's part of the territory and it has been through the generations and across cultures. Two-year-old children, for a host of reasons, have some strong opinions about things and they don't hesitate to tell you about them — although the only expression he knows for 'I'm not very fond of this' may be very similar to a full-on scream. Tantrum alert. It's coming, ready or not.

Luckily for you, in this chapter I'm here with tips for talking to your toddler in ways that may bypass the whole tantrum situation. I also provide ideas to encourage his interests with play indoors and out, and to keep on top of discipline. And I look at kindergarten and changing your work to fit your lifestyle.

Exploring the World with Dad

Your toddler is quickly getting better on his feet and now's the time he comes alive in terms of his physical capabilities. He'll be up for more sliding, swinging, bike riding and everything physical. This increased physical ability is great. It builds confidence, promotes learning and creates opportunities for socialising in ways that stretch beyond shake rattles and singing nursery rhymes — although those days aren't done yet.

Your toddler on screens

You can have all the online content, webinars and educational apps in the world to teach your toddler this and that, but what really gets a little person's brain going is contact with other people — most importantly, his parents. This needs to be shouted loud and clear: screens are not your friend, and they're not going to be good for your little guy's growing grey matter. You can download all the coolest apps to help your kiddo out, but nothing comes close to you being that intimate, personal, involved presence.

REMEMBER

Aim for a minimal screen experience for your little one and a maximal personal experience with *you* instead. The research evidence highlights that screens impact infants, toddlers and pre-schoolers in the following ways. Screens:

>> Kill social development

>> Undermine language development

>> Negatively impact cognitive development

>> Harm physical development

Screens impact sleep, eating, thinking, speaking, listening, attention, memory, movement, motor skills, thinking, relationships and more. It's a long list, and it's an important one.

This doesn't mean you should completely dump screens and hide your child from every laptop, TV, phone, tablet and more. At times, you may desperately need the screen so your kiddo will be quiet and you can use the toilet or take a shower in peace.

What it does mean, however, is that you want screens to be a last resort option rather than your go-to as soon as your little one gets antsy. Nearly every other option will be better than a screen, which may be tiring for you as a parent, but is great for your child and his growing brain and body.

REMEMBER

Helping your child to learn and thrive is all about your relationship and your interaction with him. The closer the relationship with the person he's learning from, the better he picks up new skills. Take language development as an example. TV and apps actually don't work. They teach children almost nothing about speaking and listening. But conversations with you? His brain goes nuts, and he learns in leaps and bounds.

Children need stimulation to grow and learn, and the first place they look for stimulation is with parents — not screens. Keep challenging your little one to try out new things — even though you may think he's not capable, let him have a go. Learning is about taking risks (within reason) and being challenged.

TIP

Everything you do around the house is an opportunity to learn, but don't get too caught up in your little guy 'learning' and 'getting ahead'. Instead, focus on involvement, conversation and supporting his autonomy in safe and appropriate ways. Activities such as washing the dishes can turn into a chance for your little one to practise pouring water and wiping down the bench, two simple activities he may be interested in and feel really good about when he masters them, particularly if you're there to watch him learn (without getting too controlling). You may find you have a budding chef in the house if you involve him in making his own lunch or getting dinner ready in the evening. Kids this age love having little tasks to do and want to contribute, so let your child, even if he makes a bit of a mess at times. It's about connection, building competence, and helping him have a sense of control.

REMEMBER

When your child is struggling with a task or activity, try to hang back and see what happens rather than stepping in to do it for him. Mums are (generally) more guilty of this than dads, but some dads are also just too keen to step in to help. If you're always stepping in, you deprive your child of the chance to figure things out for himself and overcome obstacles, and enjoy the confidence and self-esteem working out obstacles brings. Those psychological needs are met best when you're nearby and connected, but also letting your child grow in competence.

Developing skills and confidence

The third year of your child's life continues the staggering whirlwind of development of the past couple of years. If the second year was all about finding his feet, the third year is about finding his voice, and he will — usually in a shopping mall yelling 'No no no' at you, but that's another topic. His language skills are growing daily and so are his physical, emotional, social and cognitive skills.

You can help develop his skills by:

>> **Challenging:** Every day, give your child an opportunity to dress himself, walk up steps by himself, wash his own face and take other little steps towards

being independent. Of course, you can't expect him to master these skills all at once, but cheering on the progress he makes each day gives him the confidence to keep trying. Not long from now he'll be telling you he can do it all by himself, thank you very much. Just note, though, that you're not trying to push this. This process should be a natural opportunity for growth and development. On days when he isn't up for it, relax and support rather than going all drill-sergeant on him.

>> **Drawing:** Your toddler's fine motor skills are at work when he draws pictures, or rather, scribbles. And nothing is stopping you joining in. You can have little draw-offs with your child, where you challenge him to draw something for you and in return you draw something for him. Get your child to explain what his pictures are about, rather than giving empty praise for his work. Ask lots of questions about what he's drawing and repeat back to him in your own words what you're looking at; for example, 'Okay, I can see a house, a cat and a dog' (which will probably look like three circles on paper at this stage). Remember — the accuracy of his drawing doesn't matter; the effort and his explanations are what count.

>> **Hanging out:** If your child doesn't go to day care, you'll need to arrange some social situations for him to meet other children and play with them. This helps your child learn about sharing (which won't happen consistently and well until about age five), co-operating (which gets better from about age four), and language (which is exploding right about now). He'll also see other people his age. See Chapter 9 for information about playgroups and Chapter 10 for tips on handling toddlers' interactions.

>> **Making:** How many cereal boxes did you believe were rocket ships when you were a kid? Resurrect your imagination, that thing you gave up when you became an adult, and use it to help your child create all sorts of toys and playthings from everyday objects. See the following section for some ideas.

>> **Reading:** You can't read too much to a young child. Bringing your enthusiasm for reading to each story session encourages a love of words, stimulates your child's interest in the topic being read about and creates a warm, secure bond between the two of you. Your toddler will want you to read the same story over and over. That's totally fine. Go with it. It's about developing a love of reading. But I recommend taking a bunch of books to bed each night so you can mix it up a bit with different authors, styles and topics that challenge him. The key things to remember with reading include reading slower than you want to in order to aid comprehension, using lots of expression, asking questions about what characters are feeling and what that must be like, and reading books with lots of pictures so you can ask about the pictures too.

>> **Talking:** Your child learns his language from hearing you talk to him. Though he hasn't mastered getting his lips, mouth and tongue to do exactly what adults can do, he's on his way.

>> **Waiting:** Like time, toddlers wait for no man — or anything else. Patience doesn't come naturally, so provide examples of good things that take time, such as food cooking in the oven, or planting seeds and keeping tabs on their growth. Doing jigsaw puzzles is another excellent way to help him develop patience and persistence to complete a task. Self-control is a critical task for lifetime effectiveness and your toddler needs lots of patient and compassionate support as he tries to navigate this confusing world we live in.

TIP

Try not to get too hung up about having your child recite the alphabet or count to 100. You'll have plenty of time for all that when he gets closer to school age. In fact, nations that do best on academic things typically don't even start on this until kids are closer to six or even seven.

REMEMBER

Rather than diving in with bucketloads of praise when your child does something awesome, such as trying to say a new word when you point at a picture, or completing an activity like putting his cup on the bench, describe what he did and say thanks. 'Wow, you just put the cup on the bench to help me. I appreciate how helpful you are.' Gratitude and descriptive statements are far better for your little guy than praise (which is best avoided if you can help it — see the following section).

Swapping praise for gratitude

Common sense says that by praising our children for doing something, they'll do it more. Indeed, many psychologists and experts argue you should try to catch your child doing the right thing, and then praise him for it.

When children are under the age of four or five, this is probably true. But praising children is not a good habit to get into, because once they're older than five, their brains work differently, and they perceive praise differently too. Praise starts to have negative, rather than positive, effects.

Here's why praise can have negative effects:

>> **Praise is generally perceived as controlling.** When you praise your child, he perceives it as your attempt to manipulate his behaviour — which it very often is. When kids feel controlled, the first thing they'll often try to do is push against us. Have you ever noticed that if you praise your children for something they'll stop doing it? This is why.

>> **Praising your child can reduce his interest in doing whatever it is you praise them for.** This has been shown in *abundant* research. Whether it's cleaning something, eating something, sharing, helping or otherwise, praising kids makes them stop and think, *Gee, if Dad's making such a big deal about it, maybe I'm not supposed to like doing it.*

>> **Praising children reduces the quality of whatever is being praised.** Some specific research found that praising children for painting something nice led to less creativity next time they painted. Similarly, other research has found lack of motivation and effort in reading, problem-solving, drawing and helping after praise is offered. It seems that if praise isn't offered next time a child does that activity, they stop doing it.

>> **Praise, ultimately, is a judgment.** It's an evaluation, and your child doesn't like you to be his judge — because just as we can judge something as good (for example, 'good boy', 'good job', 'good work'), we can also be critical.

Some really cool research has shown that kids who are praised for being a 'clever boy' or a 'smart girl' can get caught up in defending that characteristic, which can lead to them making poor decisions around how they approach difficult tasks. Rather than enthusiastically embracing opportunities to learn, they fear failure — because it might show they're not really that 'smart' or 'clever' — and so they only approach what they're confident with, and avoid what they're not.

Perhaps the greatest issue with praise is that it can make your child feel as though you regard him conditionally. That is, he has to keep doing things that you evaluate positively to be considered 'worthy' to you, his parent. The idea that he has to earn praise makes it problematic. This is because the very idea of positive reinforcement promotes conditional love. And your child needs unconditional love and acceptance from you.

So, what do you do instead? You clearly need to give your child positive interactions. He needs to experience kindness and positivity. This is not about growling and grilling your child day in and day out. Instead of praise, however, try the following:

>> **Express gratitude:** When you see that your child has done something you value, say 'thanks'. For example:

- 'Hey, thanks for cleaning up your room. I appreciate it.'

- 'I'm really grateful you ate all your dinner tonight. It will help you grow even bigger and stronger.'

- 'When you share your toys with your friends, it makes me feel grateful, and it makes your friends grateful too.'

>> **Be supportive:** When your child does something you think is super, describe what you see. Ask them questions about their perception. Describe the effort you see them make. For example:

- 'Wow. When you played that song on the piano, your fingers seemed right, the louds and softs were in the right places. It sounded like you're really getting it. What did you think?'

- 'When your friend shouted at you, I heard you speak softly and kindly back. How do you think that made things better? How did you feel making that decision? How do you think your friend felt when you were kind to him?'

These alternatives are much more effective in helping your child feel encouraged, supported and appreciated. And they also help him form his own judgements of how he's actually doing, which is far more powerful than having judgements passed down from you.

Fun and games

Here are some more ideas for playing and having fun with your little one:

>> **Go camping in your living room.** If you've got a tent, you can set it up in your living room and fill it with pillows, toys and sleeping bags. Get snuggled up, watch some fun movies and eat some treat food. If you don't have a tent, organise a large cardboard box (your supermarket, retail stores or furniture shops may be able to provide you with one) or even a blanket, and make a little house out of it.

>> **Make a roll-around bottle together.** Cut two big plastic drink bottles in half and use the top end of each. Put some interesting shapes inside and thread a shoelace through the bottle tops on either end. Seal in the middle with tape. Knot the shoelaces together to make a line that your toddler can drag around.

>> **Make lunch.** Toddlers love to help, and seem especially drawn to helping out in the kitchen. If you get your toddler his own stool or box to stand on so he can reach the benchtop, he can help with simple tasks such as peeling boiled eggs and move up to using a knife (with your supervision, of course) to cut up firm fruit and vegetables like cucumbers and zucchini.

>> **Create an obstacle course.** Make tunnels by placing a blanket over the tops of two chairs with their backs facing each other. Add other elements with low tables to crawl under, stairs to climb and boxes to climb over.

>> **Get dizzy.** Have your toddler hold onto a towel and spin it around on a slippery floor (slowly enough so that your child doesn't fall but fast enough for it to be fun). You can also try sitting in a spinning chair like an office chair with your little guy on your lap whizzing around and around. These activities help your toddler's balance.

>> **Play chase.** Toddlers love being chased, peeking through curtains, and a bit of rough and tumble when they're caught.

>> **Sing!** So many great children's songs and nursery rhymes are available. Okay, they're probably not 'great', but they've been around for ages because they really work to teach language, expression and love of music. Little ones really love songs with hand actions, such as 'Two Little Dicky Birds', or 'Incy Wincy Spider'.

Some words for worried mums

If your partner has a seriously worried look on her face while watching you muck around with the little one, grab her and wrestle with her too. Mums can — and should — get involved in goofing off with your youngster.

No seriously. Do it. But remember that 'rough and tumble play' is healthy for kids, and research shows that it's often a Dad's natural way to engage with his child. Always remember to be mindful that your child is smiling and enjoying it. (Consent matters for things like this as well as for intimacy with your partner.) Rough and tumble play is good for kids — it develops their social and physical skills, uses their imaginations, and introduces the ideas of good and bad, justice and courage. It helps them understand limits and boundaries, and they also learn about consent and gentleness as you navigate what pinching and tickling is okay, and what isn't.

Dad, you have to make sure no-one gets too squished in a rough-housing session, including mum!

This Kid Keeps Getting Better!

Your child's brain is constantly developing, and it's happening rapidly. Some areas are coming along faster than others. Speaking and motor skills are getting up there, while emotional and social skills develop fully further down the line and over a long period.

Development update

As your child grows, the things he's capable of doing change, along with his behaviour. As a great dad, you really need to know about your child's development so you understand his behaviour and interests, and know how to respond to them.

Between the ages of two and three, your child:

>> Can feed himself, remove and put on clothing, and undo zips and large buttons

- >> Can remember people, places and stories
- >> Enjoys creating things
- >> Has a sense of ownership over his toys and belongings, saying things like 'mine!'
- >> Is able to use two- to three-word sentences, ask questions and follow an instruction with two steps
- >> Is confident enough on his feet to try running, jumping and hopping
- >> Is developing a sense of humour
- >> Likes to pretend to be someone else
- >> Knows his full name and gender
- >> Matches objects, such as shoes and animal pictures

Table 11-1 provides a guide to your toddler's speech development for his age.

TABLE 11-1   **Language Ages and Stages**

Age	Your child can
Two years	Use two words together; for example, 'Mummy gone', 'more drink', 'no shoes'
	Use words to request something, rather than just name it
	Ask questions ('Why?' is a favourite)
	Name objects without prompting
	Say no (a lot)
	Identify parts of the body when asked
Three years	Make a sentence of three or more words, such as 'me wear shoes'
	Use several hundred words (not all at once)
	Talk about things that happened in the past
	Use adjectives such as 'big' and 'fast'
	Talk about things that aren't present
	Ask even more questions (like 'Why?')
	Answer questions, such as 'What's Dad up to?'
	Say his whole name and gender
	Listen attentively for short periods

The way your toddler behaves is part of his growing up. One of the fundamental aspects of disciplining your child is to have realistic expectations of what he can and can't do. At two years old he can't manage his emotions well, express how he feels or remember all the rules. Consequently, during this stage you need to muster some extra patience. Getting him in strife for doing something wrong when he's developmentally immature and simply can't do as you're demanding is unfair. He'll get there in his own time!

Giving your toddler choices

Getting tired of saying 'no' yet? No, you can't open that cupboard! No, you can't go outside.

Imagine being in a relationship with your boss at work (or your partner) where all they did was tell you 'no'. Chances are, you'd start to dislike them pretty quickly.

The answer to avoiding being stuck in the 'no' loop is choices. Your toddler wants to go outside but it's pouring rain? Instead of saying no, offer him a couple of other activities he can do inside, such as drawing with crayons or playing with some blocks he's been tinkering away with. Tell him, 'We can't go outside because it's raining, but we can draw or play with blocks'. Offering your child a couple of things to choose from means you still have some control over what he does, but he also feels like he has some say in his life.

But another point to consider is that we often say 'no' because we don't want the inconvenience of what our toddler is asking. Are you saying 'no' because it's a bad idea? Or are you saying 'no' because you can't be bothered? Try saying yes to the things you can say yes to so no doesn't happen so often.

Distracting your child by giving him something else to do instead of the thing he can't do is a great technique for stopping the no's.

Say your child is pulling out clothes from the dresser to put on in the morning. Instead of saying no to the dressing gown he wants to wear to playgroup that day, give him the option of a green jumper or a blue one. He'll feel like you take his opinions into account and will be more receptive to putting on a jumper. Or, better yet, let him wear the dressing gown, but take the clothes he'll need to wear so he can change once you get there. (He will likely want to change once he sees everyone else left their dressing gown at home.) You can prevent a whole lot of angst by being creative and only sweating the stuff that really matters.

Giving your child a choice also works with eating. Instead of plying your toddler with lots of vegetables, give him a choice: Broccoli or carrots? He may even end up eating both. Also, not forcing a decision helps. Sometimes you can simply say, 'I'll do something else while you make up your mind whether you'd like broccoli or carrots'. In some cases, your little champ might start eating one of the choices when you're not looking — after all, he's hungry.

TIP

At bedtime, letting your child choose a couple of stories before bed gets him interested in the idea of stories and what he wants to hear, rather than having him focus on resisting bedtime.

Setting boundaries and rules to match

Imagine you've landed on planet Wafunkle and you have no idea about the local etiquette, the way people talk to each other, what the customs are, or the way people live. You don't know if smiling is considered rude, or doing underarm farts is a way of showing appreciation. You also don't speak the language well, so the best you can do is bumble around trying things out and being shown the rules until you get the hang of things.

This is the situation your toddler finds himself in right now. He doesn't know that wrenching your glasses off your face is wrong, or that sticking a knife in an electric socket is dangerous. He needs a guide to show him through the sometimes confusing maze that is modern life and society. And that guide is you. The method by which you guide him through that maze is called discipline. Discipline's about showing him the rules and having patience and strategies to help the rules stick.

REMEMBER

Discipline isn't about punishment, but about guiding your child to learn what the boundaries and rules in life are. You and your partner decide what the rules are depending on your personal beliefs, morals and way of life. Discipline is about finding a balance between letting your child run wild exploring things that can be dangerous for him or inappropriate, such as hitting and biting, and not letting him try anything out and hindering his ability to learn.

Here are some ideas for rules and boundaries you may want to instil in your child:

>> After two stories (or five — you decide), it's into bed.

>> No going on the road without dad or mum.

>> Plugs and appliances are off limits.

>> We're gentle to animals and other people.

>> We speak quietly and kindly.

>> We throw balls in the yard, not in the house.

>> When we make a mistake or hurt someone, we say sorry.

>> When we ask for something we say please, and when someone is nice to us we say thank you.

You may also like to come up with some rules and boundaries for yourself as a dad, including all of the preceding and a few more.

TIP

Be consistent with your rules and boundaries. Although you've told your little guy not to draw on the walls with crayon but only on paper and he keeps drawing on the walls, he'll understand and get the idea one day, so hang in there. At this point, you're not thinking getting your kiddo in trouble. You're gently reminding, redirecting or distracting.

REMEMBER

Telling your child for the millionth time not to run out onto the road can push your buttons, and make you angry and frustrated that the message isn't getting through. However scared and angry you are, hitting your child isn't the way to deal with it. Find another way to deal with *your* frustration — take a couple of deep breaths and make a mental note to use your favourite way to let off some steam later on. When you raise your voice to say 'STOP' (because he's about to run onto the street) give him a cuddle afterwards and explain to him why running onto the road isn't okay. The message *will* get through!

REMEMBER

A key aspect of effective discipline is consistency and appropriateness of your behaviour management to your child's developmental stage and temperament. So keep talking to your child about the same rules, help him understand by having him teach you the rules you're teaching them, and use the strategies outlined in this chapter and earlier chapters (refer to Chapter 10, for example).

Understanding why kids have such big tantrums

Kids can seem so irrational to us. Why are they having another tantrum? Why won't they listen? Why am I having to explain this thing to them again? You're up against some important developmental realities that can help you understand why this is universally such a challenging time.

Keep the following in mind when trying to understand your child's behaviour:

>> **Your child doesn't yet have a handle on emotional regulation.** When he feels it, he shows it. A 'no' from dad, regardless of how well-intended it is, feels like the end of the world to your kiddo. He can't understand how and why the big guy who loves him so much would stop him having what he wants! Emotional regulation grows bit by bit as your little one matures, but don't

expect him to have a solid handle on it until around age nine. (You probably know plenty of adults who still struggle with this, so go easy on your munchkin.)

» **Because your child can't regulate his emotions, he's going to have a hard time with his behaviour.** It makes sense, doesn't it? His form follows his feelings. Feel lousy, act lousy.

» **Your child has limited speech and language capacity.** This is why it's such a bad idea to say 'use your words'. They have very few words to use anyway but, at this point, their brain is in overdrive and the part of the brain that controls their 'words' is mostly switched off. Stop talking and stop making demands.

» **Your child is yet to develop something psychologists call 'theory of mind'.** This is the ability to see things from another person's point of view. When we say 'no', they lose the plot because it simply doesn't make sense to them that we have an opinion that differs from their own. They literally cannot conceive that our agenda is opposed to theirs. This confusion sets off big emotions (which they can't regulate), which cascades into big behaviours (which they can't regulate), which impacts their ability to use their words (because that part of their brain has switched off). Theory of mind develops somewhere around age five, although recent research suggests it continues to develop right through the lifespan.

REMEMBER

Never tell your child to calm down. First, they can't. Their emotional regulation is poor even when they're feeling okay. Right now, they feel lousy and they don't have the capacity to regulate. Second, they feel even worse because they're feeling incompetent — and they're feeling totally awful that they're disappointing you!

Talking to your child so he understands

Sometimes it feels as if you're beating your head against a wall as you try to communicate with your toddler. He won't listen, you get angry, and both of you end up frustrated and in a worse spot than you were before. Take heart — here are some techniques you can use now that will help to build good open communication between the two of you as your little one grows:

» **Acknowledge how he feels.** You can easily walk all over your little one's objections or opinions with your words when you're talking to him. As a dad, with all good intentions, you frequently think you know best. When your child falls over and cries, you say things like, 'Oh, it doesn't hurt', or 'You'll be right'. But this invalidates the fact that it *does* hurt and he *doesn't* feel right. Instead, say, 'Ouch, that must hurt' or 'Do you need a hug?'

>> **Describe the problem.** This avoids laying blame on your child for something he's done. Blaming can make your toddler feel helpless and wrong all the time, and he'll become defiant whenever you open your mouth. Say he's spilt milk on the carpet. Rather than berate him about the mess he's made, tell him there's milk on the carpet, which describes the problem, and that he'd better get a cloth to clean it up.

>> **Give information.** Your toddler has just drawn on the wall for the thousandth time. Instead of yelling at him for his misplaced art, show him that drawing is for paper, not walls — again.

>> **Offer choices.** You want your little one to clear up his toys, but rather than order him to clean up, offer him a choice of which toys to clean up first, and get involved to make it fun.

>> **Use a gentle reminder or gesture.** You've already asked every day for a year that toys be cleared up before bedtime, so your toddler should be getting the hang of that concept by now. Instead of a nightly, 'Clear up your toys, like I've asked you a million times', simply say, 'Your toys'.

Leaving out the blaming and ordering should get a better result. Kids dislike long explanations for things. Your tyke still has a very short attention span.

TIP

The underlying principle to most of these techniques is to avoid laying blame or criticism on your child. Making him feel wrong will make him defiant and scared, rather than open and willing to take risks. Ridiculing your child for a mistake is also unlikely to get him to take responsibility for his mistakes in the future because he'll be afraid of your mockery.

REMEMBER

When talking to your child, imagine the way that you would like to be talked to by an adult with some form of power — your boss, for example. You wouldn't like to be blamed, yelled at, taken the mickey out of or ordered around. Neither does your toddler.

To find out more about talking to your toddler, check out my books *The Parenting Revolution* and *10 Things Every Parent Needs to Know*.

Exploring Different Opportunities

Your role as a dad is simple — be there for your child with love, food and shelter. And until now, that's been enough. Traditionally this may well have meant that you take care of your child by 'bringing home the bacon'. But in our modern lives, you can explore other avenues as well.

The fathering road less travelled

If you're finding, like many dads do, that keeping all your plates in the air — work life, home life, time for yourself — is just too much, you can look at certain options to reduce some of the stress. These options include:

>> Become a stay-at-home dad (SAHD) while your partner works.

>> Reduce your hours and work a four-day week, or go part-time.

>> Start your own business, do what you love doing and organise your work life around your family (for example, by having a home office) — but be warned, this *may* make life busier.

>> Take a break from work, such as three months, especially if you feel you're stuck in a dead end career or job. Many career coaches recommend you change careers if your current job is a dead end, so use this time as a transition phase to spend some more time with the family.

>> Take up — or, more likely after COVID, continue — working from home options, which means you can have more flexible start and finish or break times, while remaining in work full-time.

WARNING

Money and your financial position dictate which of these options is available to you, so before you walk into your boss's office with your resignation letter, do your sums and work out what you can afford.

TIP

If you can work from home — as many of us do still can for at least some days a week following the COVID-19 pandemic — you can work quite flexibly by scheduling your work around nap times, or times when your partner or family can take care of your toddler.

Next stop — kindergarten

As your child gets closer to becoming a pre-schooler (when he turns three) you may want to start thinking about a more formal learning environment for him. Kindergarten is traditionally the place children go to transition from being at home with a parent or caregiver, or a step on from childcare before starting school. Kindergarten, or prep and pre-prep in parts of Australia, is a place where children continue to explore learning through play.

Kindergartens used to be for just those aged four, but some cater for children as young as 2½ years. Prep is generally for five-year-olds and pre-prep for four-year-olds. Unlike school, kindergarten, pre-prep aren't compulsory, while prep generally is.

Chapter **12**

Making More Babies: Brothers and Sisters

One of the questions fathers of one child are asked the most is, 'So when are you having number two?' Some dads might be ready with an answer — 'I've been planning on having seven children since I was little'. For others, it may be a question of asking whether number two will *ever* happen — fertility issues could be an issue. Or perhaps it's a case of 'One child is quite enough, thanks for asking'.

Adding another baby to your family changes the dynamic *completely* and can be a tricky adjustment period as everyone finds their feet. In this chapter, I take you through making the financial adjustment, juggling the needs of two children at demanding times in their development, and working out how to stop World War III from happening as toys, clothes and, most importantly, your love are shared between the two (or more) of them.

Having Another Child

Making the decision to have another child is almost a bigger decision than having the first. As well as all your concerns about being a father — the sleepless nights, supporting your partner, the trials and tribulations of daily life with a helpless baby or rambunctious toddler — you also must take into account your first child's needs, such as her need to be stimulated and cared for. You also now know how much time and work a baby takes, so the 'ignorance is bliss' attitude you may have had the first time round is probably gone.

Here are some of the things you might consider if you want to take the rational approach to making a decision about baby #2:

>> Are you are expecting life to get easier for you because the children can play with one another? This may be true, but not until your youngest child is two years or older.

>> Can you afford for you or your partner to not earn a living while caring for a new baby, as well as buying any new equipment you may need?

>> Do you have enough room in your house for four? Will you need to move? What about your transport and travel arrangements — will you need a larger vehicle?

>> How mentally prepared are you to cope with a new arrival? Would you be excited to have another baby, or is having another baby something you feel you have to do to complete your family?

>> How will the practical aspects, such as sleeping arrangements, routines and childcare work?

Asking these questions is important. It's a rational approach. But for most of us, if we only ask such questions, we'll typically decide that one is enough. From a purely logical point of view, having children is actually kind of nuts.

Some other questions are also important to consider. They include:

>> How does your partner feel about having another baby?

>> While some obvious costs are associated with bringing another human to your home and to the planet, costs to your psychology, your relationships and your family also exist if you choose *not* to have a baby when you and your partner really want one. What are those costs and are you prepared to wear them?

>> What is the impact that siblings might have on your first child, particularly as you (and they) age?

>> If money wasn't an issue, would there be hesitation?

>> Does the potential pain associated with having more children outweigh the pain of regret if you don't?

Ultimately, the emotional benefits of having another child can outweigh the rational negatives of doing so. Only you and your partner can make that decision — try to do so without being overly influenced by other people's expectations.

REMEMBER

Some parents (and people who try to influence them!) think that only children are often spoilt, antisocial and lonely. No good quality research evidence supports this old stereotype. Parents of only children can easily counterbalance by involving their child in lots of social settings, such as day care, playgroups, sleepovers and team sports. You needn't worry your child will turn into a spoilt brat just because she doesn't have any siblings. To the contrary, single children are likely to be as well-balanced (or a little entitled) as kids with siblings.

Is having another child worth it?

In the end, this is the question you and your partner have to resolve for yourselves. Having two (or more) children may not feel worthwhile when both kids are sick and up all night or terrorising each other by day. But it may be worth it when they are adults, have children of their own, and support each other in a way only family can.

Having additional children also gives you the opportunity to do things with your new baby differently if you feel you haven't done things the way you wanted the first time around. We get better at parenting when we practice.

REMEMBER

If your partner had a traumatic birth experience or difficulties breastfeeding early on last time, she'll need your support this time. You now have the opportunity to help your partner to see your second child as an opportunity to have a very different experience this time round.

What to expect

So you've decided you're ready for baby #2. Here's some more information you need to know.

With baby #2 you'll almost feel like a professional — after all, you've been there, done that. Many fathers of two say they don't feel as wound up and anxious about their baby the second time around, and that mothers are often more relaxed and confident. That said, here are some things you need to know:

>> Depending on the age gap between #1 and #2, you may need twice as many prams/buggies and car seats, which may mean you need a bigger car.

>> Your life will be more than twice as busy, with both children having different activities and sleep times, and twice as many nappies to change and clothes to wash. The level of activity doesn't add. It multiplies.

>> Your older child will not necessarily be particularly helpful with the younger child until she is a bit older, but will relish the responsibility of being in charge of the baby when the time comes . . . even if it's just in name only.

>> You'll need to be a lot more organised and may spend time lying in bed at night thinking about the laundry, getting lunch prepared for childcare, and pulling your weight with the housework.

Budgeting and finance

Raising a child is an expensive business. Estimates for how much it costs to raise a child through to 18 years are consistently updated in the media, although they're fairly loose and will depend on your income, your choices and your family's needs. When you look at the numbers (and I'm not including them here because they can be scary), it might be enough to put you off having kids forever! But week to week and month to month, it is manageable. Moreover, Australia's approach to taxation and wealth re-distribution is designed to support families with these costs. Family Tax Benefits exist precisely because raising a family can cost a lot. Means-tested income supplements are available for families in Australia because even the government wants you to have more kids! (Apparently it's good for the economy. Growth is good and all that stuff.)

The good news is that after having raised child #1 you now know what is really useful and essential, and what is just fluff. So my suggestion for #2 is cut out the fluff and focus on essentials. You may also take heart from an old Spanish saying: 'Every baby is born with a loaf of bread under their arm'. In other words, you'll find a way to make ends meet. (As a dad of six, I can attest to that. You find a way, and it's worth it.)

TIP

You can have another baby and not have to get a third job. Here are some ways to do so:

>> Stick to the essentials. You don't need another flash Moses basket or $40-a-tub nappy cream. And you didn't need half of all those clothes you had first time around, did you?

>> If you haven't still got your first child's stuff sitting in her wardrobe, ask for hand-me-downs, go to shwopping events (where you can swap clothes and toys), or check with friends who have kids.

>> Don't buy anything until after the baby shower, or register for baby shower gifts at a store. That way you won't double up on anything you already have.

>> Check out sites online that offer samples and coupons for baby and child-related products. Some supermarkets also have baby clubs you can join to get deals on nappies, food and other baby stuff.

>> Keep an eye on specials at supermarkets and baby stores to start stocking up on consumables. It always feels good to get nappies at half-price, even if the baby is still six months away.

TIP

In the coming years, childcare costs are going to be a major expense in your household. Think about how you could work flexibly, reduce your hours, enlist friends and family in a kind of group babysitting scheme, or work from home to reduce this cost.

Looking after Another Family Member

So you have another mouth to feed, another body to clothe and another bum to wipe. If you were stretched by one baby, two may seem impossible right now, but it's not.

Taking a practical approach

All babies really need is love, warmth, food, sleep and a clean bum. Though having colour co-ordinated outfits might have been mum's thing, when you've got two kids, this is likely no longer a top priority.

Read Chapters 6 to 9 about bub's first year to remind yourself of what's coming up, such as how to avoid nappy rash, how warm your newborn should be kept and which clothes you'll need.

Get into a routine with your new baby as soon as you can, but don't freak out if it all goes a little awry some days. With two children, you certainly won't get every-thing right every day, but don't beat yourself up about it.

TIP

Be as hands-on with this new baby as you were with the last. Remember how time flew by with the first one? Well, here's another chance to savour the unforgettable time when she's tiny. And remember photos! Take heaps of photos. Everyone focuses on photos with child #1, but subsequent kids often don't get the same special attention. Take those photos!

Keeping two or more healthy and safe

Having a second child is easier — and harder. It's easier in the sense that you have previous experience at handling a newborn, but harder in the sense that you now have to wrestle your toddler into her car seat with a baby demanding your attention at the same time.

Here are some ways you can avoid your life becoming a crazy house:

>> **Get organised.** Think about where the new baby will sleep. Do you need to get another cot, or is your older child ready to move into a bed? Organise chests of drawers and car seats, and work out where you're going to change the baby. Most importantly, look into changing your buggy/pram. Some manufacturers offer to swap or upgrade your one-seater pram to a two-seater (this service usually incurs a charge). Some prams can accommodate a two- or three-year-old as well as a newborn baby.

>> **Get your family and friends involved.** It takes a village to raise a child, so organise someone to take your older child on outings when you need a break, or to cook when you're too exhausted.

>> **Keep healthy.** The last thing you need with two little ones is to get ill. Inevitably your whole family will get sick and you'll be so busy looking after children all night long that you won't be able to get better yourself. Keep eating well and take every opportunity you can to get some exercise. A fantastic way to find time to exercise is to combine exercise with an activity with child #1.

>> **Prepare yourself to give child #1 some extra love.** This time can be a rough transition for her — suddenly she has to share your attention with another person in the house. You need to compensate for that. Read more about sibling rivalry later in this chapter.

>> **Try not to change your older child's routines too much.** If you're currently reading her five stories before bed every night, keep doing that. With a new person in the house, she's going through enough upheaval without losing her time with you too.

>> **Work as a team and make a schedule.** Divvy up chores around the house, talk about when you and your partner can have some time off, and don't forget to exercise!

Juggling activities

With two children now, both at challenging stages in their development, you'll need to fine-tune some of the activities you have in your life. You may be able to look at working from home more often, varying your start, finish or break times, banking hours, reducing your hours, or prioritising some of the things you do outside work and family. These options may not be feasible — that's the reality of trying to be a provider, provide the support your family needs, and still look after yourself. The central idea here is that you're going to need to be intentional and purposeful in what you choose to prioritise and what you do if you want to remain present as an involved and helpful influence in your children's lives.

Scheduling your tasks and making time with your family one of your top jobs helps to ensure you don't lose touch with what is really important — your partner and children.

Being the steady, stable, caring, positive presence in your children's lives is the most important thing you can do. When you are with your children, talk to them all the time. Let them share in what you do at work and be prepared to spend time reading stories, playing and doing all the dad stuff you've been doing so well anyway.

Working on Sibling Discipline

All children react differently to the news that another baby is coming along to usurp their throne as king or queen. Some rebel and get extremely upset when the new baby is even mentioned. Others relish the chance to meet their new sibling. Some children change overnight from angels into demons and others develop a new-found sense of responsibility and grown-upness that you never would have imagined. Your child may feel threatened, unloved or ignored. And some kids are completely unfazed. Once that new sibling arrives, though, expect everything to change — perhaps not all at once, but change is going to happen once the new bub comes home.

Understanding sibling rivalry

So far, your child has been the only apple of your eye, the centre of your world and the centre of her own world. Suddenly, a new baby is on the scene, taking away time and attention from her. You're busy with the new baby, which means her demands come second and she has to wait when she doesn't want to, share her stuff, and have the limelight shine somewhere else. No wonder she's a little grumpy and jealous right now. These changes don't necessarily happen all at once. They're more of a process. But expect challenges, particularly if your eldest child is still young. In Chapter 11, I talk about emotional and behavioural regulation. The older your child is, the more regulation she has. If she's younger, she's going to act like a toddler who wants attention because. . . well, she's a toddler who wants attention.

She's caught in a place where she's wanting things to happen one way, and she has no idea who this new kid is who's taking you away from her agenda. If you're giving too much of your time and attention to your new little one, she's going to let you know about it by being angry and jealous, and rebelling against you and her new sibling.

To prepare your child for the fact another baby is coming into your family, try these ideas:

>> Break the news to your child when the three of you are together. A good time to do this is when mum's belly is starting to stick out, or during the final trimester. Toddlers don't have a good grasp of time, so you'll be bombarded with cries of 'is the baby coming yet?'

>> Keep involving your eldest child in lots of things you do to prepare for the new arrival. For example, you can take her along to the scans and keep explaining things to her about how the baby develops. She may not understand everything but making her feel involved is important.

>> Offer some choices to your child when it comes to getting kitted out for the new baby, such as asking her to help pick clothes and gear for the new baby.

>> Let her know that the baby is not just for mum and dad, the baby is *her* brother or sister.

>> Prepare her for the demands a new baby will place on the family; that is, the baby will cry, will need to be fed (and how that feeding will happen — your child may get upset at mum and bub's new closeness if she's breastfeeding) and that the baby will not be able to play with her for a little while until he grows bigger. Invite her to problem-solve solutions so she can plan on how she'll act once the baby arrives.

Coping with jealousy and fighting

No matter how well your older child copes with the news that another baby is on the way and how brilliantly she accepts the new baby's arrival, she's still that same volatile mix of burgeoning independence and emotional immaturity, so inevitably she'll feel resentful and jealous from time to time.

Here are some techniques you can try to minimise bad feelings:

>> Balance the time that you spend with your newborn and toddler.

>> Encourage your toddler's pride in her new little brother by showing her how to hold the baby and taking lots of photos. Talk to your older child about when she was a baby and get some pictures out to look at.

- » Make special time to devote to your toddler that doesn't include the new baby.

- » Toddlers love to have 'tasks' to do, so you could enlist her help in getting baby's blanket and putting clothes away.

- » Try to keep your toddler's routine as much as possible so she doesn't feel lost in all the upheaval and resent her new sibling.

If your older child is uninterested in the baby, don't worry. She'll take an interest in her own time.

Fighting and setting boundaries

If you've got your toddler feeling pretty chuffed with her new sister, helping out with nappy changes and helping to settle her at night, you're doing really well. This is how it will go more often than not. But you're dealing with a toddler who hasn't quite worked out how to handle her emotions just yet. Anger, resentment and fighting are bound to break out at some stage. She's unlikely to fight with her little brother or sister — her anger is more likely to be directed at you. But now and then toddlers can hit or scratch or hurt their baby siblings, so here are some suggestions to help manage all of these potential challenges:

- » Should conflict break out, act fast. Hitting, snatching and acting roughly are unacceptable, whether it's hitting you or their sibling. Use those disciplinary options from Chapter 10 to diffuse the tantrum. Remember, your child is struggling. Don't add to her struggle.

- » Teach your older child how to touch the baby without hurting him, just like you do with a pet or with other children her own age. Say what you want to see, rather than what you don't want to see.

- » Don't try to teach, however, until your child feels safe and subdued. When emotions are high, intelligence is low, so teaching won't work. Help your toddler be calm. Then have the conversation about expectations and boundaries.

- » Until you feel that your toddler can safely be around the baby without incident, keep a close eye on them. Toddlers are notorious for snatching. If bub has a toy she wants, your toddler may snatch it straight out of your baby's mouth, which could result in some distress from bub.

- » Your behaviour is your child's greatest teacher and she'll copy what she sees you doing. If you're quick to anger and treat others with disrespect, she'll learn to do that too.

Behaviour management strategies need to relate to the developmental stage and temperament of your child. Try out a few things (and keep trying them as your child gets older) and use what works best for your child. In general, distraction techniques tend to work better with younger children. The solutions in Chapter 10 will be your best line of defence against ongoing challenging behaviour. But note, it takes a *long* time for your child to get this stuff right. (Even us dads still get it wrong from time to time, so don't be too hard on your child.) Just keep reminding, teaching, coaching and guiding — with patience and compassion.

Discovering different personalities

Take a look at your own siblings, if you have them. Are you into the same stuff? Do you have the same temperament or ideas? Chances are, although you were brought up by the same parents and share a heck of a lot of DNA, you've got your own interests and personality. After all, we're all individuals. And so it is with your children. Chances are both your kids are quite different kettles of fish and require different things from you as a father. Both your children are going to require different ways of stimulating them, encouraging them and building their confidence. A bit of trial and error may be required.

Rather than seeing different personalities as extra work for you, think of them as a good thing. You get to explore different interests with your children and they can learn from each other as they grow up, drawing on each other's strengths to get them through challenging times. Different personalities also keeps things interesting for you — never a dull day!

4

The Preschool Years

Chapter **13**

Fun and Games

Your walking, talking child is quite a different bundle from the newborn you first met three years ago. He's a dynamo of questions, words, stories and kooky ideas. And he needs you to keep up with him. Hang out with your child (a lot) and hang on for the ride!

In this chapter, I explore what your preschooler will be doing for the next couple of years as he nears school age. I share ideas for keeping that inquisitive little person busy and show you some ways to help your child get ready for learning at school and beyond.

Your Active Preschooler

With his third birthday, your child graduates from being a toddler to a preschooler. Preschooler isn't a great term because it describes what your child isn't, rather than what he is, but that's the most well-worn term to describe ages three and four years old. *Note:* Some people use 'young children' but that applies to a wide age range so I decided to stick with preschooler.

Mapping the next two years

As well as getting more of a grip on his language skills, being able to come up with more complex sentence structures and increasing his vocabulary, your child is developing in these ways:

>> He has more control over his emotions, is able to empathise more and shows concern for others.

>> He is able to express more complex emotions such as embarrassment, pride and guilt.

>> He likes to take part in imaginative games, such as playing doctor or schools, or pretending boxes are boats and rockets.

>> He can sort shapes, such as pegs and shells or buttons.

>> He can use alternate feet when climbing stairs or steps and, as he gets closer to five, to skip.

>> He starts understanding abstract concepts such as 'being a hero', confidence, or what it means to be the 'good guy/bad guy' in a play.

>> He can perform simple tasks and use scissors.

>> He can serve food, and eat and drink by himself.

>> His friendships become more important as he nears school age.

REMEMBER

Your child is also learning to count, the letters of the alphabet, the names of lots of animals, plants, objects and people, and more besides — provided you keep stimulating him with books, pictures, outings and opportunities. It's not a race. You don't have to get them reading early. But it's great to satisfy their curiosity and provide an enriching environment.

Building self-sufficiency and self-esteem

Like an athlete training for a big race, or a gymnast for a competition, practice makes perfect. The more you do something, the better you get at it. In order for a child to master a skill, he must do it again and again with lots of mistakes along the way so that he can improve and feel a sense of accomplishment. As a father, your role is to provide plenty of opportunities for your child to practise, make mistakes, improve and master a skill in order to build self-esteem and feel pride in his achievements. Satisfying and supporting this need for competence and (eventual) mastery is one of the most vital elements of helping your child build a successful life.

Letting your child fall, fail and pick himself up again can be difficult at times, especially because you can often see in advance what's going to happen and may not want to deal with the consequences of his fall. But giving him the space to mess up is important and your attitude that you believe he can get better rubs off too.

Between the ages of three and four, let your child take on more tasks that he might not get right at first, but with a little time and practice and patience from you, he will accomplish. A great example is giving your child little jobs around the house, or getting him to do personal hygiene jobs himself, such as washing his hands or brushing his teeth.

Praise

The idea that we're supposed to 'pump up our kids' tyres' through praise is pervasive. During the early years, research supports your use of praise — because your child's brain hasn't developed enough for it to be a problem until around the age of five). From around that age, avoiding praise is better. (Refer to Chapter 11 for the reasons.) If you are going to do it, remember that praise should never be about labelling your child ('you're such a good girl', 'you're a super runner', 'what a talent you are'). Instead, it should be about *how* your child did something well.

Careful research across the past few decades shows that it's even better to do something other than praise your kids. It's best to let them praise themselves. Here's how that looks.

Your child does something great. Perhaps they draw a picture, win an award, help around the house, or simply act like the legend you know they are. Rather than telling them, ask them questions like the following:

>> 'Can you tell me about what you did?'

>> 'How did it feel to do that the way you did it?'

>> 'You seem really excited about this! How come?'

>> 'That must have felt so great. How do you feel?'

When you say or ask these things, your little one has the chance to tell you all about why he's so awesome. He believes it and internalises it far more when he says it than when you say it, particularly as he gets older (from about the age of five or six). While it's not a big deal when your child is young, it's good to get into the habit of framing your conversations this way while he's young.

Another powerful strategy is to simply say 'thank you' rather than praising. 'Thanks for cleaning the mess. I appreciate it so much'. Some gratitude and a big hug can make an enormous difference for self-esteem, and it doesn't require that empty 'good boy' kind of praise.

Active movement

Active movement — that is, getting out there with your child and encouraging physical activities — is an important tool for building self-esteem and confidence.

Children (and adults) learn through repetition. When we do something over and over it seems to become locked in our brains. Learning things like climbing a ladder takes time and practice for little children to master, and some falls and spills will probably happen along the way. But without that practice, how will he ever get the chance to learn to climb a ladder? The best research shows that physical movement is key to helping the brain develop healthy and happy.

TIP

Embrace your inner child and get active with your children. Play on swings, go down the slide, do roly-polies. As a dad, you're a role model for your children, showing them how to master a skill. If you also become part of the activity and want to give it a try too, they'll love the activity all the more.

Even if you don't have a playground handy to your home where you can let your child practise swinging, jumping, climbing and balancing, you can encourage active movement at your own place. Here are some ideas:

» Create an obstacle course in your living room from chairs with sheets draped over them, and boxes and tables to crawl under.

» Dance in your front room. Keep a note of music your child enjoys; it will come in handy when he's fussy or bored. (*Hint:* At this age, it's not your music, although that can be changed over time. It's basically anything 'kiddy' that you're playing through the speakers.)

» Go on a walk in your area (not too far, you don't want a cranky, tired child) and check out letterboxes, flowers in gardens, birds on telephone wires and cracks in the pavement.

» Play chase. You probably know by now that little kids love to be chased, and will take off, wanting you to follow. Put a scarf in your child's trousers so it sticks out like a tail and chase him while trying to get the scarf.

» Play hide and seek. If your child can't count, use an egg timer to measure the time passed before he comes looking for you.

>> Roll down a gentle slope, or play helicopters where you spin around and around until you're dizzy. This helps your child's developing sense of balance, and is really great fun!

>> Show your child how to jump off low walls, and on and off surfaces you put on the floor for him, like a towel or piece of carpet. Be prepared for a few tumbles at first!

>> Walk like a bear around the house on all fours, play wheelbarrow walk and make a rope swing on a tree in your yard to encourage upper body development.

Classes

You can also consider enrolling your child in classes like junior soccer, swimming and water confidence, singing or music and movement. Follow your child's lead by paying attention to the activities he enjoys doing.

Father worries

Dads have been known to be somewhat competitive and to compare and measure children against one another. Raising children, however, is not a competitive sport, and you don't get a medal for having a child who is first to spell 'encyclopaedia' or count to 1,000. Every child moves and develops at his own pace.

Patience with your child's pace is one of the most important things you can give him right now. He's got to have space and time to develop and learn, and expecting him to do what others can do will leave you frustrated, and him less likely to figure it out for himself. It certainly doesn't boost his confidence to say something like, 'That little guy over here can already count to 100 (or kick the ball, and so on) — why can't you do that?'

Take a deep breath when he spills milk on the carpet for the hundredth time as he learns to master drinking from a glass, or drops his knife and fork as he tries to put his plate on the kitchen bench. He'll get there. By you helping, encouraging and gently challenging him, rather than getting frustrated and doing it for him, he'll learn he can do it by himself and have more confidence in his abilities.

REMEMBER

So you want your son to be a world-class golfer and have already got him swinging clubs in the backyard. But he's just not getting golf and wants to water the garden or help with the cooking instead. Follow his lead and ditch the clubs. Remember that old saying 'you can lead a horse to water but you can't make it drink'? It's the same with children. You can buy your child golf clubs but you can't make him like playing golf. You may have to get used to the idea that you've got a potential Jamie Oliver on your hands, not a golf champion.

During the preschool years, many children often switch from being very close to mum if she's been the primary caregiver, to wanting to be with dad all the time. If this happens for you, great! It means you have more opportunities to hang out with your kid and deepen that already awesome relationship you have with him. Make more of your time available to your little one and enjoy the attention you're getting! But if not, that's fine too. Mum at the top of the attachment hierarchy is a sign of good health, so long as mum can keep up.

Keeping Your Preschooler Busy

Some preschoolers are always on the move — they're always asking questions and always exploring the world. That's a great thing, but it can be a little tiring and on a rainy day, a high-energy preschooler may be a tantrum waiting to happen. Here I show you some ways to make the most of the time you and your preschooler have together that are fun and a little educational.

'Dad, I'm bored'

For years to come, you'll occasionally hear the refrain all fathers fear — 'Dad, I'm bored'. Not only is he bored, but he wants you to fix the problem. A couple of things here:

>> Although some people will tell you it's not your job to fix your child's boredom, this isn't altogether true. The younger your child, the more you really do need to provide a level of engagement and involvement for your kids. And an enriching environment is all on you!

>> You are totally within your rights to tell your kiddo to figure out what to do about his boredom — so long as he has someone to play with. Kids are relational. They rely on having someone to be involved with them. As our society has become more 'indoors' and screen-focused (and we've decided it's not safe to be outside in the street or the park), kids have lost access to the community they need so much.

So if you don't want your child to be 'bored' (and research shows it's not good for them because it's associated with depression, anxiety, loneliness and even deviance), make sure they've got stuff to do and someone to do it with.

REMEMBER

Fobbing off your child with a computer game or putting a movie on is a friction-free, easy option, but the best activities for your preschooler are the ones that involve the two of you being together. These are opportunities to read, play, explore and learn together, or to introduce your child to a hobby or passion of yours that he may be interested in.

Here are some ideas for banishing the 'I'm bored' blues:

>> Stop, drop, and roll. Just get down on the floor and wrestle.

>> Jump on the trampoline, kick a ball, go for a walk — be active. It's what dads do best.

>> Have a mini adventure in the kitchen. What can you make that's tasty and easy to make? Jelly is as easy as it gets. And the tidy up is another activity too!

>> Pop a song on and dance for five minutes.

>> Read some books. If you're sick of reading the same books over and over, head to the library for some new ones.

The key word is *involvement*. The more you're involved and connecting, the better the outcomes for you and for your kiddo.

If you're a dad who's eager to go the extra mile, who has some spare time, or who has more energy than most, the following ideas could be even more exciting:

>> Ask a question about a concept your child wouldn't have come across, like 'Do you know how bats can fly in the dark without bumping into things?', then offer to find out together with him. Do some research together and make it into a 'solving the mystery' quest.

>> Build something together, such as a swing, bird feeder or a wooden seat, but be clear about safety around tools. Three-year-olds and saws are not a good mix without careful supervision.

>> Encourage a love of gardening and growing his own food by starting a garden in the backyard. Pumpkins and peas are pretty easy to grow and your child will be encouraged to eat them at dinnertime knowing he's grown the food himself! (Chillies are easy too, but . . .)

>> Hide something in the house or garden that he has to find by asking you for clues.

>> Involve your child in a chore you have to do, such as vacuuming or washing the car. Let him be in charge of lifting rugs for you to clean under or washing the tyres. Helping with tasks such as hanging out the washing develops fine motor skills and can make a dull job more enjoyable.

>> Remember all the games you used to play as a child like 'I spy with my little eye'? Play them with your child.

>> Take a trip to the beach to play in the sand, go for a bike ride, visit the local playground, take a child-friendly bush walk, or wander around the botanic gardens, museum, sportsground or zoo. Keep talking with your child all the time about what you see and hear, and ask him questions about what he thinks about things you come across.

>> Visit your local children's farm. Some farmers in rural and even semi-city locations have opened up their gates and offer tours and hands-on experiences. Search online for children's farms near you, along with opening hours and ticketing information.

>> Visit some pals. Arrange a play date with other kids your child's age from playgroup, kindergarten, your antenatal group or other friends with children.

WARNING

Sometimes saying he's bored is your child's code for 'I want to watch TV or play on the computer'. It can be easy just to let him, especially if you have chores you need to do or you're tired. But try to resist. Perhaps just a quick trip to the local park will give him enough lift to come home and be entertained with doing his own thing for the rest of the afternoon.

TIP

Encourage your child to come up with activities he would like to try to keep on hand when the 'I'm bored' blues hit. You act as a circuit-breaker, rather than the Commissioner for the Department for Fun.

Bad weather busters

Adults find it difficult not to go stir-crazy with cabin fever when it's raining and cold outside. For children, who have energy to burn — and parents who are willing to invest time being involved — here are some ideas:

>> Board games are always good fun for an emergency. Perhaps invite some friends over to play. Make sure the games are designed for pre-schoolers. And watch out for games where winning and losing are expected — they typically don't work out so well without lots of preparation and guidance.

>> Get hands-on by getting out the craft supplies or playing with play dough, all cheap and cheerful activities that encourage creativity and fine motor skills. See the sidebar 'How to make your own play dough' for a play dough recipe.

>> Get out some old photos from when you were a child, teen or student. Organise a family photo session, which can be even better if you have some old slides and a projector. Create a fabulous home cinema experience for your child.

>> Get your little one involved in baking and cooking.

>> Have a singing and dancing competition in your lounge.

>> Make up stories, and then draw pictures to go with them.

>> Organise a trip to a nearby airport, train station, harbour or docks. Young children are typically fascinated by the hustle and bustle that can be observed at these places.

>> Pretend you're outdoors by making a tent out of chairs or a table and some sheets and blankets. You could camp out all day in your tent, with snacks, toys, books and pillows for lounging on.

>> Visit the local museum or indoor play centre.

Bringing out your child's talents without going OTT

Expecting your child to be super-skilled at something at this age is unreasonable, although you may think the way he kicks a ball means he's the next David Beckham. Rather, this is a time for giving your child lots of opportunities to discover what he's good at and what he enjoys doing. How will your child discover if he loves gardening if he never sees a garden, or enjoys fishing if you never show him what fishing is all about? I don't mean spending thousands on fishing gear, but by exposing your child to ideas, telling him what others are doing and showing him in books, you'll see what your child takes a fancy to.

Sometimes you can use this opportunity to try out something new yourself and share that experience with your little one. Remember the saying 'do something that scares you every day'. Doing something new with your children is a great way to step outside your own comfort zone.

REMEMBER

You want to go for breadth, not depth, when it comes to your child's experiences. Don't push. Instead, exposure to lots of fun, good things is all you're looking for here. Experiencing loads of different activities is going to do him better in the long run than being the best at just one thing. You don't want him to peak too early!

Being a dad is also about showing your children that you too have to learn new things and that you're keen to try something new. Take a keen interest in what your children like doing, even if they're not interested in your favourite sport or activity.

TIP

Follow your child's interests. Let him choose which books he's interested in, what games he likes and which activities he's into, even if you hate it and it's not what you want for him. Forcing your values on him or making his decisions for him isn't going to help build his relationship with you, or let him become his own person. This is not a huge issue just now, but it's going to become one as he gets older.

HOW TO MAKE YOUR OWN PLAY DOUGH

Here's everything you need to make play dough:

2 cups plain flour

2 cups warm water

1 cup salt

2 tablespoons vegetable oil

1 tablespoon cream of tartar

Food colouring

1. Mix all the ingredients together in a pot over a low heat. Stir.

2. When the mixtures thickens, clumps in the middle and feels dry rather than sticky, remove from the heat and allow to cool.

3. Turn out onto a bench or tray and knead until the dough's silky smooth.

4. Divide into as many balls as you want to make colours.

5. Poke a finger into each ball and add a drop of your desired colour into the hole. This protects your hands from coming into contact with the concentrated food colouring, which can stain your skin. Knead the colour through the ball.

This dough keeps for a few days and is best kept in the fridge. Wrap the dough in cling film to stop it drying out. If the dough does dry out, it can be dampened with a little water.

Voila! Now you can get really creative. Watch out Michelangelo!

Being a good sport

Preschoolers are more interested in other people than toddlers are, but still struggle to control their emotions and impulses. Theory of mind (the ability to see things from another person's point of view) still hasn't kicked in, and that emotional and behavioural regulation still has a way to go until it's developed to a level of maturity that makes it seem like your child is getting it together.

While your child may love playing with others, it can be hard for him to accept not having his own way all the time, and playing sports or games with winners and losers can be really tricky for a preschooler to deal with. Learning to lose without losing your cool is a skill, like learning to ride a bike. Being able to cope with losing is a step towards being able to admit making mistakes, or accepting not getting your way, which are emotions that even adults struggle with. Being a good winner and not gloating is also an important skill to learn.

General advice for kids this age is to minimise games and activities with winners and losers. (This isn't namby-pamby, bubble-wrap parenting. It's recognising kids just don't get it yet.) You can introduce them to competitive sports when they're a little older, but for now they're most likely to get upset. Developmentally, they're simply not there yet.

Even if you try to reduce competitive experiences, they'll still come in contact with games and scenarios where there isn't enough for everyone, or only one person can win (like pass-the-parcel at a party). Here are some ideas you can instil in your child to help him become a good sport:

>> **Be a good sport as a father.** You're a role model, and accepting defeat gracefully encourages the same behaviour in your child.

>> **Congratulate the winner.** It takes grace to admit someone else played better on the day. If you're the winner, be gracious about winning by not rubbing it in the other team's face.

>> **Focus on the fact that the performance, not the person, lost.** Your child is not a 'loser' because he lost. He's the same person and may beat his opponent next time. He lost because of the way he played, not because of who he is. And at this age, it's usually not about skill. It's all luck!

>> **Don't make excuses for why your child lost.** Blaming others like referees or cheating from the other side only makes you look desperate, and means your child has no chance to analyse why he lost and improve on his performance for next time.

TIP

Don't get your kids involved in competitive activities until they're at least eight or nine, perhaps even older. Competition can be great once kids understand the concepts of winning and losing, but it takes years for these ideas to really sink in.

REMEMBER

Social skills and an understanding of teamwork take a long time to develop. Younger children can generally only focus on one thing at a time (that's why three-year-olds playing football all chase after the ball and don't keep their positions). So be realistic about your expectations when it comes to team sports.

The great outdoors

Preschoolers are naturally curious, active and imaginative. And what better place to hook into all those parts of themselves than out in nature? Nature is fuel for the soul, for our kids and for us.

For a fun day out that will charge his batteries and get those brain connections whirring, try taking your child to:

>> **The beach.** Parks and day cares have sandpits for a reason — sand is a blank canvas for a child to play on. Your child can create castles, words, faces and shapes. Or he can just feel the sand and scoop it up for hours. Most little kids also love the water, so keep a look out to make sure he's safe — and remember the sun block. And the rocks on the headlands! So much fun (but make sure the surf is small and you're well away from any waves that could sneak across and cause harm).

>> **The bush.** Try taking a walk through the bush for a few hours to get your child's body and mind fit and healthy. Take along a book about native plants or birds and animals and see what you can find.

Another great thing about using the outdoors and nature is that they're usually free of charge. #outsideisfree

REMEMBER

Encouraging an appreciation of the great outdoors also encourages an appreciation of our environment. Remember to take only pictures and leave only footprints when you're out and about.

Lifelong Learning Starts Here

The first years of a child's life are critical to his development as a thinking, feeling human being. Forming an attachment to you and your partner, and forming connections between different parts of his brain is your child's main function at this age.

School is on your child's horizon, and with it comes a more formal way of learning than you've been practising at home with books, toys and talk.

Fathers as first teachers

As a father, you are your child's role model and teacher. He'll learn more from you than how to tie his shoelace or use a knife and fork. Giving your child the opportunity to spend time with you, doing puzzles, climbing trees and reading together, all makes you his first teacher.

Kindergarten happiness

If your child hasn't gone to creche or day care, the first time he leaves home for periods of time away from you may be to go to kindergarten. In Chapter 11, I discuss how kindergartens prepare your child for school and teach skills through play.

REMEMBER

If your child is already in day care or a creche, have a chat with the teachers there about whether they have sessions that prepare children for school as they turn three and four. Many centres will already have something in place.

When selecting a kindergarten or preschool for your child, ask yourself these questions:

» What are the staff like? Do I feel confident in their abilities?

» What is the kindergarten's philosophy on learning? What skills do they encourage the children to have?

» How much is the curriculum play-based so my child can enjoy childhood as much as possible?

» What social opportunities and community building experiences does the service provide?

» How will the kindergarten's style of learning suit my child?

» What preparation is there for going to school?

REMEMBER

Leaving your child at a kindergarten or preschool can be tough at first as he settles in, but don't feel guilty. Feel confident that the staff have seen it all before and know how to handle it. If your child is upset about you leaving, give him to a teacher, give him a kiss, tell him you love him and you'll see him later. Give him a wave and let the staff get on with their job. If you come back two minutes later you may find your child happily absorbed in an activity, having completely forgotten you were ever there.

Learning objectives

Finding out what your child is capable of learning at this age is a bit tricky because all children develop at their own speed. People have all kinds of ideas for helping kids to develop. But this is not useful or important at this age. The best way for you to encourage his learning is through play, through reading together, and with one-on-one time with you.

At this stage, forget learning the alphabet, don't worry about learning to count, and ignore anything academic. Let him enjoy the outdoors, his continually developing skills, his relationship with you and other important people in his life, and the thrill of being alive. That's it!

TIP

Lots of schools push kids to be semi-literate before school even begins. This is not important at all. Your child can learn everything he needs to know once he arrives *at school*. That's what school is for. Your job is to help your child feel safe, explore and love life. School's job is to work on the three Rs. And research shows that the healthy balance I'm describing plays out great for kids.

Learning for the whole family

Even though you're the father and you're the one role modelling and passing on your knowledge to your kids, learning is a two-way street. You can learn a lot from your child too. Your child can teach you:

>> **How to be totally in the moment.** Watch your son's delight at running sand through his fingers.

>> **How to see the world for the first time again.** Enjoy the moment with your son when he sees an animal at the zoo he's never seen before.

>> **How to translate the world (a bit later in life).** Just like you did for your parents, your child will be able to explain why what's in fashion looks good and why music on the latest and greatest app is popular (or maybe you'll be explaining why your favourite bands are somehow trending again on the future's version of TikTok).

>> **How to make the best out of every situation.** For example, you'll learn how unimportant it is that your son is rubbing his snotty nose on your suit pants before work.

>> **Patience.** When your little one thinks a dragon is under his bed at 3 am, you can muster the patience to convince him he's going to be okay.

>> **What really matters in life.** Is it impressing the boss with long hours, or being home in time to read *Green Eggs and Ham* with your son?

TIP

Another fun activity is to switch roles with your children. Ask them to play 'dad' and you play 'child'. The outcome can be hilarious as they play back your own behaviour to you. It can also give you interesting clues about what you might want to change in how you treat your child. You can of course also get your own back by throwing yourself on the floor, screaming and shouting to explain what your son looks like when he's in tantrum mode. (But don't do that if your child doesn't. You want to model for your child the best you see in them.)

Chapter **14**

Health and Nutrition

Your health is the most important thing you have. Surely the health of your child is equally important or even more important to you? She doesn't yet know how to maintain her health, so you need to ensure that she stays in tiptop shape. The health she enjoys now, and the healthy eating and exercise she does, are good habits to instil in the early years and will stay with her for life.

In this chapter, I show you how to encourage and maintain those good habits, not just for her but for you too. I guide you through the difficulties of picky eaters, allergies and introducing new foods. I also bring you up to speed with the multiple bugs and illnesses your child will inevitably pick up from her environment, which is a rather challenging part of fatherhood.

Food, Nutritious Food

Like you, young children need three meals plus snacks and plenty to drink every day to keep healthy and active.

Over the years, the food pyramid (which shows recommended servings of each food type) continues to change. This change is driven, in part, by research. But it's also driven by the food industry and lobbyists. Being aware of what your child *really* needs is important so you can help her grow up healthy and strong.

Your child needs a variety of foods from each of these groups:

>> Breads and cereals — at least four servings a day

>> Dairy products and milk — two to three servings a day

>> Meat, pulses and other sources of protein such as eggs or tofu — one to two servings a day

>> Vegetables and fruit — at least five servings a day (two fruit, three vegetable)

REMEMBER

A serving is usually the size of your child's palm, or a piece of bread, glass of milk or tub of yoghurt.

Cooking and baking for busy dads

Getting all these 'servings' into your child may seem daunting, but it's not. Don't panic if your child hasn't had exactly what's in the guidelines; her appetite will guide you for the most part. Don't force-feed your child, because she may develop an aversion to the food you're trying to get into her. She may also get very upset and throw up, which means you've achieved the opposite of what you were trying to do.

If you're stuck for ideas, try these:

>> **Breads and cereals:** Muffins, sandwiches, fried rice, risotto, pikelets, filled rolls, pasta, couscous or quinoa in a salad

>> **Fruit and vegetables:** Try dried fruit (only occasionally, because the sugars in them can harm teeth), frozen or tinned fruit and vegetables, and fruit and vegetables in muffins or sandwiches

>> **Meat, pulses and protein:** Sliced lunch meats, baked beans, kidney or pinto beans, nuts (only if she's three years or older) or nut spread, tuna in a sandwich or salad, tofu, chickpeas

>> **Milk and dairy products:** Cheese slices in a sandwich, yoghurt, a fruit smoothie or milkshake

TIP

A simple strategy to inspire kids to eat a variety of fruit and veg is to point out the colours to them; for example, 'You've eaten lots of orange food, how about some green (peas), red (tomatoes) and yellow (sweet corn) food?' Some dieticians recommend encouraging your kids to 'eat the rainbow'. A wide variety of natural foods in a range of colours usually indicates a healthy diet. (Yellow and white — which kids seem to gravitate towards — are not much of a rainbow.)

Kids need fluid just like we do, so keep your child topped up with a cup of milk or water in a bottle.

WARNING

Drinking juice is not recommended because the sugar content is so high. If you do want to give your child juice, dilute it, and avoid giving it after she's brushed her teeth at night.

CHECK THE NET

You'll find more recipes, dietary guidelines and nutrition information at `www.nutritionaustralia.org`.

Avoiding the wrong foods

You may be familiar with the healthy food pyramid, but just in case the rigours of parenting have ousted it from your memory, foods high in salt, sugar and fat are right at the top of the pyramid, which means you should have them only as treats. Just as foods at the top of the healthy food pyramid are 'sometimes' foods for dads, so they are 'sometimes' foods for your child, and should be eaten a few times a week at the most.

Occasional treat foods include foods that are:

>> Heavy in sugars, such as lollies, biscuits, chocolate and dried fruit

>> Heavily processed, such as microwave ready-meals, frozen ready-meals such as pizza or pies, fruit roll-ups and sweet cereals

>> Laden with saturated fats, such as fish and chips, or burgers

>> High in salt and flavourings, such as crackers and chips

We've also become increasingly aware of how food additives, flavourings and colourings can affect our children, how processing can take away nutritional value, and how cruel some farming practices can be to animals. Many people are moving towards eating more organic, less processed foods in order to avoid pesticide residues and get more nutritional value from what they eat. You may want to consider doing the same.

WARNING

If your child is under three, avoid foods that may choke her, such as nuts, olives or popcorn. Even after three, discourage eating while on the move, watching TV or doing anything that may distract her. Keep cutting food into small pieces to avoid an airway blockage.

Telling your child 'no' for the hundredth time to the lollies or biscuits you have stashed in the pantry is easier said than done, and even if you don't have a private supply that your child knows about, she's going to discover treat foods at day care or kindy, or at friends' houses. So you probably won't be able to keep your child as pure as the day she was born. That's okay. A few animal crackers every now and then aren't going to be a problem. Just keep remembering to fill her full of good stuff whenever you can and continue to live an active, outdoors lifestyle.

TIP

Completely banning 'bad' foods makes them objects of desire, so let your little one have a few treats now and then, just like you would treat yourself. Children need fat in their diet, but things like chips should be limited to infrequent occasions.

If your child is overweight, it's important that you don't make a big deal about it, and you definitely do NOT want to tell her about it. Research has shown that our children don't need to be told they're overweight, and when we do tell them it increases the likelihood that they'll have ongoing weight issues. Instead, our role is to be kind and patient in helping them develop a healthy relationship with food, and encourage active living.

Introducing different foods

Putting a plate of never-seen-before food in front of your child can be a little disconcerting for her. She may turn her nose up at something you think she'll love just because it looks funny. So take some time to introduce new tastes and textures thoughtfully. Here are some ideas:

>> **Do it yourself.** You are your child's role model, and if you tuck into your food with gusto, chances are she will too.

>> **Get creative with your presentation.** Make a face, shapes or patterns with food.

>> **Give her something to dip into.** Low-fat dressing, tomato sauce or a mild salsa, hummus and yoghurt dip all provide a fun way of testing out new foods.

>> **Get sneaky.** Put finely chopped pieces of new foods into stews, omelettes, mashed spuds or rice.

>> **Grow your own.** One way to get children into fruits and vegetables is to take part in growing it themselves. She'll be enormously proud to tuck into those beans she's seen grow from seed and watered every night.

TIP

Forcing children to eat something they don't like is counterproductive. If she tries a new meal and doesn't like it, that's okay. She'll make up for it by eating others. Punishing your child for not eating makes her more defiant and creates an unhealthy approach to food. Remember also that children take time to develop a taste for something. The fact that she turned down broccoli the first time she tried it doesn't mean she'll never like it. Some research says kids need to be exposed to specific tastes between 7 and 15 times before they approach the food willingly.

Leading by example

You are your child's role model, and what you eat and how you live sets the scene for how your child will eat and live.

Children who have one obese parent have a 40 per cent chance of becoming obese themselves, and children with two obese parents have an 80 per cent chance of facing obesity. Much of this may be genetic, but it's impossible to discount lifestyle factors as well. This means you and your child have the opportunity to choose (and it means you have the personal responsibility).

If you've already fallen into the trap of giving your child whatever sugary and fatty processed foods she wants, now's an opportunity to consider a change of course and swap unhealthy food options with healthy ones.

Simple ways to make meals healthier include:

» **Avoid processed and pre-prepared foods.** Generally, the less time food's spent going through a factory, the better it is for you. This also goes for basic ingredients such as sugar, flour or rice. Use raw or brown sugar, wholemeal flour and brown rice.

» **Eat meals as a family when you can.** Turn off the TV and use dinner time to catch up on your day and enjoy each other's company. Sharing food is an important social interaction for humans and enjoying food together should be special.

» **Exercise restraint.** If you habitually have dessert, keep the portions small and eat it less frequently.

» **Find out about healthy substitutes to sugar- and fat-laden foods.** Try natural yoghurt with fruit added rather than tubs of sweetened yoghurt, for example. Honey (especially Manuka honey) is an excellent replacement for refined, white sugar. Honey is a natural product and complex food that is easier to digest and produces less of a 'sugar high' than white sugar.

» **Prepare meals together.** Let your child have some responsibility over what goes into her food. Get her involved in where your food comes from and how easy it is to prepare. As we get older, making food for each other is another social interaction that shows our family and friends how much we love and care for each other, and this can be a positive activity for your child to enjoy right now.

Curbing fussy eaters

Children may go through a fussy eating period. This stage is annoying and exhausting, and all you want your child to do is eat! It's enough to make a grown man cry. There can sometimes be a reason behind it, such as mealtimes falling at a time when she's tired, too much distraction when she should be eating, or snacking before mealtimes. In all circumstances, patience with fussy eating results in better eating than getting angry and annoyed.

Here are some ways to deal with fussy eaters:

>> Avoid arguing about food. Forcing your child to eat mushrooms is unlikely to encourage a love of them in the future, so you're no further ahead next time you serve them up.

>> Avoid giving snacks in the hour before a meal, so she's still hungry when mealtime arrives.

>> Offer a variety of small servings of food in a meal, with lots of vegetables and other goodies to choose from, so if she doesn't like one food she has others to choose from.

>> Don't make a big deal about the fact that your child ate something. Treat eating as just what we do, even when it's a new food.

>> Try some of the suggestions from the section 'Leading by example' earlier in this chapter, such as getting your child involved in food preparation, making meal times a family time and growing your own vegies. Finish all (or most) of what's on your plate whenever you eat. If you leave lots of food on your plate and walk away halfway through a meal your little one will copy exactly what you do.

Try to avoid:

>> Cooking another meal to feed her if she turns up her nose at the first

>> Giving your child a treat to make her stop whining

>> Having meals in front of TV or while doing something else, such as reading, playing games or walking around the house

If you're concerned your fussy eater isn't getting enough to eat to grow, play and be active, talk to your GP.

REMEMBER

Coping with special dietary requirements

More and more children seem to be developing allergies to certain foods, such as wheat, gluten, eggs, nuts, milk, shellfish and even some types of fruits and vegetables. Some children may grow out of them, others won't. Managing an allergy can be a matter of life or death.

The recommended practice of introducing new foods one at a time helps with detecting reactions to certain foods. If your baby shows symptoms of an allergic reaction take her to your GP to have her tested.

What is an allergy?

An *allergy* is a reaction by the immune system when it thinks the food you're eating is harmful. It produces *histamines*, which can cause hives, breathing difficulties, a tight throat, nausea, vomiting and diarrhoea. The most dangerous reaction the body can have is called *anaphylaxis* in which the tongue swells, air passages narrow and blood pressure drops. Anaphylaxis can cause death.

How do you manage an allergy?

Avoiding the foods that cause the body to overreact is the best way to avoid an allergic reaction. The jury is still out on what causes allergies, and while some thinking seems to be that *the later* potentially harmful foods are introduced, the less likely your child is to develop a reaction to them, other research suggests precisely the opposite. So . . . it's tricky.

Luckily, more people are learning about food allergies and food producers are hopping on the bandwagon too. You can now find many substitutes for common food *allergens*, those foods that cause an allergy. Wheat-free breads, pastas and baking products are available, you can buy egg substitute for baking, and cow's milk can be easily replaced by soy or rice milk. Many day care centres, kindergartens and schools have banned nuts and nut products from the premises in a move to ensure the safety of children with nut allergies.

If your child is allergic to certain foods, you'll have to be more vigilant about reading labels on food packets, as well as making other parents and caregivers aware of your child's allergy so that at day care, on play dates or at birthday parties, your child isn't given food that may cause a reaction.

Some people think that just having a small amount of an allergen is okay, but this has been shown to be very dangerous. Small amounts or even being in the same room as an allergen is enough to make some children seriously ill. For severe cases of allergies, children may have to carry an EpiPen, which administers medicine in the event of an allergic reaction. Talk to your GP about allergies, and discuss ways of managing your child's allergy, including EpiPens. It may also be helpful to speak with a dietitian, who can help manage the allergy and teach you and your child what you need to do to avoid allergic reactions.

WARNING

Smooth peanut butter can be given to children from eight to nine months of age, but watch them closely for any signs of a reaction. If your family has a strong history of nut allergies, seek medical advice before trying nuts. If your child has any breathing difficulties, call an ambulance.

CHECK THE NET

Being informed about what you're dealing with when your child has a food allergy helps you stay on top of it. See these sites for tips on managing your child's allergy and contacting support networks:

>> Allergy & Anaphylaxis Australia www.allergyfacts.org.au

>> Australasian Society of Clinical Immunology and Allery www.allergy.org.au

Vegetarian children

A vegetarian diet is becoming a lifestyle choice for more and more parents, be it to save the planet or on moral grounds. If you want to bring up your child on a vegetarian diet, you have to pay a bit more attention to where she gets her iron and protein from, especially because children have higher iron needs than adults. Good sources of iron include:

>> Most dark green (leafy) vegetables such as broccoli, spinach, silverbeet and kale

>> Dried fruit such as apricots and raisins

>> Lentils, chickpeas and dried peas

>> Wholegrain cereal and bread

TIP

Vitamin C helps the body absorb iron, so make having fruit such as citrus or kiwifruit with a meal part of your routine.

You can help your child get plenty of protein by feeding her:

>> Dairy products

>> Eggs

>> Grains such as brown rice, oatmeal, buckwheat and millet

>> Hummus, chickpeas and most legumes, such as soy beans and lentils

>> Peanut butter and nuts (for children aged three years and over)

>> Tofu and tempeh

>> Vegetables such as eggplant, courgettes (zucchini), beetroot, cabbage

TIP

A great way of getting protein into your child is adding puffed-up grains to muesli or cereal. Puffed-up grains that are available include millet, rye or quinoa (they're all healthy alternatives to wheat).

A vegetarian diet can be bulkier and more filling than a non-vegetarian diet, so your child may feel fuller with less food. Offer smaller meals more frequently throughout the day to ensure she gets enough energy and nutrients to get through her day.

Keeping Up the Exercise

I talk a lot about how being active from birth helps to develop your child's brain. And, this may not be earth-shattering news — exercise is quite good for her body too!

Getting your child (and yourself) into exercise

An amazing fact of human biology is that, just by being active with our bodies, we grow our brains. So keeping active and exercising can help your child develop her mental powers!

But the balancing act of life at work, home and getting time for yourself may mean exercise falls to the bottom of the priority list, never to be seen again. When it comes to your body, you either use it or lose it.

By this stage of your life and parenting journey, your belly might be larger than it once was. So time once more to man up to a big task and get on with it.

Try the following:

>> Check out gyms that offer childcare.

>> Get off the bus a few stops early and walk the rest of the way home. Park your car further away from work, or walk or cycle to work. Skip the elevator and walk up and down the stairs.

>> Involve your child in your exercise program. Stroller jogs, swimming lessons at the local pool, or exercising at home using your child as a weight, sitting on you while you do sit-ups or push-ups are all great ways to incorporate her into your exercise program.

>> Schedule some time into your week for exercise. Make exercise a priority, and a promise to yourself that you can't break. Take turns with your partner; one day she exercises, the next day you do.

>> Team up with a few other mates and get a personal trainer. Nothing is like peer pressure and professional advice from a coach to get you in shape.

REMEMBER

You are your child's role model, so by making exercise and activity normal and a high priority in your own life, you're making exercise normal and a high priority in her life.

Exercise with your little one by:

>> Clambering over the monkey bars and climbing walls at your local playground with her.

>> Doing chores around the house. Unfortunately, you're officially old enough (and potentially unfit enough) that vacuuming, mowing the lawn and washing the car can help you get a sweat up. Get your child to help.

>> Getting a trampoline for the front or back yard. Jumping around for 15 minutes gets your pulse up.

>> Going for walks (short ones at the beginning). Encourage your child to walk by themselves rather than be carried.

>> Having a pillow fight or a bit of rough-housing to get all the muscles working!

>> Showing her how to climb trees.

>> Signing up to coach a sport at your local school and having your child come along to play too.

Working-out routines

Can you imagine your toddler or preschooler doing aerobics, or being able to follow what a weights class instructor is saying? Not likely. Working out with your child should be fun, not a stream of complicated instructions to follow. Kids don't need an exercise program, particularly at young ages. Instead, use the activities listed earlier as your workout routines, or try for more traditional exercises with weights (for you, teddies for your child) and set moves. Here are some tips to make working out work out smoothly:

>> Don't eat just before exercise and especially not before swimming.

>> Explain how important it is to warm up, stretch and stay hydrated — water is the ultimate ergogenic aid.

>> Make movement a regular activity you're both involved in together — say, after day care or before dinner — so that your child looks forward to exercise and it becomes part of her routine.

>> With kids, it's not about exercise. It's about them being with you and enjoying physical activity and your great company — preferably in nature.

Practising yoga and meditation

Yoga is an ancient method of not only strengthening the body and maintaining physical wellbeing, but also maintaining mental wellbeing. The practice consists of moving into *poses* by using breath and movement. Yoga encourages flexibility, stamina and relaxation for general good health, including stress relief.

And what better time to start practising yoga than when you have a frisky toddler or preschooler to entertain? Though a young child's attention span may not cater for long sessions of yoga or deep meditation, there are a lot of poses you and your child can do at home, or you may want to enrol her in a class specialising in children's yoga. Plenty of YouTube videos can guide you too.

Many yoga poses are named after animals or things found in nature. Children often enjoy imagining they really are a dog when doing the downward dog pose, or have the roots of a hundred year old eucalypt when practising the tree pose.

Don't think for a minute that yoga for children is too easy for you. Many poses have variations or more advanced options, and you can do lots of poses along with your child that are just as challenging for you to do. In fact, your child will probably do many poses better than you, which is a great source of motivation. Keep up with your toddler so she doesn't call you 'old man' (just yet).

Preparing for Common Health Problems

No time is scarier than when your little one comes down with something and you're not sure what's happening. Before your child can speak and tell you what the matter is, you have only your innate dad-sense to tell you what the trouble is. So in these sections I make it a little easier, by laying out for you some basic health issues you'll probably have to delve into some time or another.

Childhood illnesses

At times, it may seem that every couple of weeks your child is struck down with a cold or, worse, an ear or a chest infection. As your child's immunity is still developing and she spends more time in the company of other children, she's going to pick up a lot of nasties. The list in this chapter covers the 'usual suspects' of childhood illnesses. Chapter 17 examines what to do when you find out your child may have a serious or rare illness.

Following are some of the most common childhood illnesses to watch out for and what you can do about them.

Bronchiolitis

An acute (usually viral) chest infection, bronchiolitis usually comes after a cold, ear infection or tonsillitis. It affects the small airways in the lungs called *bronchioles*.

>> **Symptoms:** A hacking cough, difficulty breathing and wheezing. Sometimes a child's lips or tongue turn blue. Some children vomit. Children can be ill for seven to ten days.

>> **Treatment:** Keep your child well hydrated. Because bronchiolitis is viral, in mild cases no drug treatment is available. Severe cases may require hospitalisation. See your doctor if you're concerned.

>> **Precautions:** Watch for secondary bacterial infections, which can be treated with antibiotics. If the bronchiolitis symptoms don't go away as quickly as predicted by your GP, or new symptoms, such as flu symptoms, appear, go back to your GP or hospital. They may diagnose a secondary infection.

Chickenpox

Chickenpox usually affects children and is a viral illness that can be transmitted through coughing and sneezing, or from touching one of the fluid blisters that appear on the skin of a patient. Having chickenpox usually provides long-lasting immunity to the disease and only rarely have people had chickenpox twice. In adults, chickenpox can result in complications such as shingles.

>> **Symptoms:** Cold and flu-like symptoms — runny nose, cough, tiredness and fever. A rash of small round lumps appears that a few days later are replaced by itchy, fluid-filled blisters. The blisters tend to appear more on the torso, stomach and back, but can also form on the inside of the mouth, scalp and face.

>> **Treatment:** Applying topical lotions to the blisters can help with the itch, but bed rest, paracetamol for pain and fever and not scratching are recommended.

>> **Precautions:** Let your day care or preschool, friends and family know that your child has chickenpox because it's contagious for about five days before the first symptoms appear.

TIP

You can now get your child immunised against chickenpox. Looking after a child with chickenpox is horrendous and is quite a nasty experience for her too, so consider having her immunised, even if you have to pay for it.

WARNING

You may have heard of the concept of a 'chickenpox party'. The idea behind these parties is to purposefully expose children to another child who has chickenpox to get the inevitable infection out of the way. It's a lousy idea. Chickenpox can be severe so should not be treated light-heartedly. Immunisation is a better alternative.

Common cold

A cold is a viral infection, mainly affecting the nose and throat and lasting from two to three days to a week.

>> **Symptoms:** Runny nose, nasal congestion, weepy eyes, sore throat, tiredness, cough, sneezing and fever.

>> **Treatment:** Bed rest and fluids. You can help nasal congestion by placing a few drops of eucalyptus oil in the bath (use as per label or pharmacist's advice). Lots of cuddles, rest and keeping fluids up are also recommended. Paracetamol can be used for pain and fever. Chest rubs can be used in children over two years old to alleviate coughing.

>> **Precautions:** If your child doesn't get better over three to four days, see your GP. A secondary infection such as an ear infection or worse may be on the way. If your child has a high fever (more than 37.4 degrees Celsius when measured under the arm or 38 degrees Celsius measured elsewhere, such as in the ear), a strange cry or a very sore throat, go to the GP straightaway.

Conjunctivitis

Also known as pink eye, conjunctivitis is an inflammation of the tissue that lines the eyes. A range of things cause conjunctivitis — allergens in the air, bacterial or viral infection, food allergies or a blocked tear duct. If your child's case of conjunctivitis is caused by an infection, it can be very contagious, so wash your hands after touching your child so you don't come down with it as well! Keep your child away from day care and tell staff about the infection.

>> **Symptoms:** Red, sore eyes and possibly green or yellow mucus at the corners.

>> **Treatment:** Wash your child's eyes with a disposable cotton bud dipped in cooled, boiled water. Wash and dry your hands after doing this to curb infection spreading to you. A doctor can prescribe eye drops or ointment.

>> **Precautions:** Wash bedding, clothing, towels and flannels in hot water with some disinfectant to curb further infection or reinfection.

Ear infection

Children under seven years old are particularly prone to ear infections, which occur when germs get into the middle ear. Pus and fluid can build up in the eardrum, making your wee champ pretty miserable.

Deal with ear infections promptly because fluid can remain in the ear, causing a condition known as 'glue ear', which can make it hard for your child to hear, and therefore listen and learn.

>> **Symptoms:** Ear infections are pretty distressing for young ones. Your child will be cranky, rub her ears and not want to lie down for sleeps or nappy changes. Ear infections can coincide with colds, flu and chest infections. Older children will tell you the ear feels full and in severe cases the eardrum can burst. Don't waste time — see your GP because you need to get confirmation of an ear infection from a health care professional.

>> **Treatment:** Pain relief like ibuprofen and paracetamol can help. Antibiotics can help when the infection is caused by bacteria, but not with viral ear infections, so see your GP. Raising the head of the bed slightly can help too. Your child won't be able to hear well, so keep background noise down so she can hear you.

>> **Precautions:** Recurring ear infections may mean more drastic action needs to be taken. Doctors can put *grommets* in children's ears to prevent fluid build-up. Grommets are small tubes inserted in the eardrum to allow airflow and drainage between the inner and outer ear.

Gastroenteritis

Bacteria and viruses can attack the gut, causing a tummy bug. Gastroenteritis can happen because of a range of causes, from not washing hands properly after using the toilet or changing a nappy, to food poisoning.

>> **Symptoms:** Vomiting, diarrhoea, stomach cramps, body pains, fever, nausea, and in extreme cases, diarrhoea with blood or mucus.

>> **Treatment:** Losing fluids through vomiting and diarrhoea means you have to be careful dehydration doesn't occur, so make sure your child is drinking plenty of fluids.

>> **Precautions:** Refusing to eat is less of a worry (in medical terms) than dehydration. However, refusing to eat is an indicator that something may not be right. Monitoring your child's temperature and ensuring she has plenty of fluid intake when she's ill is always the priority.

WARNING

See your doctor straightaway if your child becomes very weak, is overly sleepy, has difficulty breathing, vomits, develops a high fever, has very dry skin, sunken eyes, doesn't want to eat her favourite food or stops passing urine.

Meningitis

Meningitis is a very serious disease in which the *meninges*, or protective membranes of the brain and spinal cord, become infected and inflamed (swollen). Meningitis often comes on very fast and can be fatal or cause severe disability if not treated. There are different kinds of meningitis, but the most well known is caused by the meningococcal bacteria. Meningitis is passed through coughing, sharing eating utensils or cups and glasses, or being in close contact with a carrier. Many people carry the meningococcal bacteria, but don't develop symptoms. Familiarise yourself with the symptoms of meningitis. You'll need to be on the watch for these symptoms because the disease develops so quickly and is potentially fatal.

>> **Symptoms:** Severe headache, neck stiffness, sensitivity to light and loud noises, frequent crying with high-pitched cry, refusing food or feeds, vomiting, fever, rash with blotchy skin or red and purple spots. The onset of symptoms can be very fast. Your child may have an unusual cry, or be very sleepy.

>> **Treatment:** See your doctor immediately if you suspect meningitis. Call an ambulance if you can't see your doctor immediately. Your child can become seriously ill very quickly, so don't second-guess yourself — get to the doctor or hospital!

>> **Precautions:** For more info visit Meningitis Centre Australia www.meningitis. com.au. This centre also provides a helpline — call 1800 250 223 in Australia.

Pneumonia

Pneumonia is a disease in which the air sacs of the lungs become infected.

>> **Symptoms:** Wheezy or rattly cough, rapid breathing, making a noise when breathing, or having a hard time breathing. Your child may be very tired and look really unwell. Viral pneumonia starts out like a cold, while bacterial pneumonia can cause a fever as well.

>> **Treatment:** Go to your GP. Keep your child hydrated with fluids.

>> **Precautions:** Pneumonia makes it hard for people suffering from the disease to get oxygen, so your child may look very pale, even a little blue, and be very sleepy. If this happens, see your doctor immediately, because your child needs more oxygen urgently.

Tonsillitis

This is an inflammation of the tonsils, which are two little slits at the back of the throat, one on each side. Tonsils can become extremely sore and covered in pus. Symptoms can go on for four to six days. Tonsillitis can be caused by the streptococcus bacteria and can be highly contagious.

>> **Symptoms:** Tonsils become red, sore, swollen and sometimes secrete pus. Your child may also have flu symptoms like tiredness, fever, muscle aches and swollen glands in the neck.

>> **Treatment:** Visit your GP. Antibiotics can sort out a case of strep-caused tonsillitis. However, if the disease is viral, bed rest, fluids and paracetamol for pain relief are your best bet. Since your child's throat will be very sore, eating cold soft foods like jelly is best. Gargling with warm salt water can clear any pus build-up.

>> **Precautions:** Some children have recurring bouts of tonsillitis, which may result in having their tonsils removed surgically.

Whooping cough

Also known as *pertussis*, this disease is easily preventable because vaccines have been available in most communities for decades. Whooping cough has three stages and can last many weeks, even up to three months. The defining characteristic of whooping cough is the cough with a 'whoop' at the end, but it's no whooping matter — the cough is nasty and will make your child pretty miserable for the duration of the illness.

>> **Symptoms:** The first stage, which lasts about a week, includes a hacking cough at night, loss of appetite, sneezing and possibly a slight fever. The second stage lasts about another week and is characterised by the horrendous coughing spells ending with the loud 'whoop'. Your child may cough up lots of mucus, which may make her vomit. Sometimes children can stop breathing during these spells, so keep them close to you for monitoring. The third stage is usually when things are on the mend, though watch for secondary infections like ear and chest infections.

>> **Treatment:** Go to the GP. Some children need to be hospitalised. Small meals and lots of fluids are important, as is lots of love for your little one while she gets through the illness. Antibiotics may be prescribed. Steam and humidifiers can be used, but talk to your doctor.

>> **Precautions:** Keep your child at home for three weeks from the start of the illness, or for five days after starting antibiotics to prevent infecting other children.

WARNING

Infants too young to have been vaccinated against whooping cough may become very ill, so if your child or someone else in your family has whooping cough, stay away from infants.

TIP

If your child is treated at home, take turns with family and friends to stay up at night to monitor your child because the cough is often worse at night.

Immunisation

Immunisation is a provocative topic for some people, but it's vitally important to mention it here. Most immunisations for children have been available (and improved upon) for several decades at least. And while a *lot* of scary information is out there warning people about dangers associated with immunisation, the overwhelming majority of scientific evidence is powerfully supportive of having your children immunised. Our world, today, is safer than it has ever been before because of the impact of these medicines.

Recurring health problems: Where to from here?

Children under five have an average of six to eight respiratory tract infections (or colds) a year. The range in the number of infections children will have is huge though; while some children can get away with no infections at all, other children can have many.

Kids get sick so often because they:

>> Catch bugs from other children, and their immune system is still developing and getting up to speed trying to fight all the bugs around

>> Could have an overactive or an underactive immune system

>> May have problems with the way they are put together anatomically, such as circulation problems, broken skin, and obstructions in the ears and lungs

You can't influence some of the factors just listed, but you can do your bit to help your little one stay healthy. For example:

>> Check that your child is adequately dressed for the weather when playing outside. For example, in windy weather make sure she wears a hat. Take an extra set of clothes so you can change them quickly if they get wet or put on an extra layer if the temperature drops suddenly.

>> Ensure room temperatures at home (and in her bedroom) are close to the World Health Organization (WHO) recommendation — 19 degrees Celsius. Go easy on air conditioning near children and avoid drafts.

>> Keep up general hygiene standards such as washing hands after going to the toilet or petting animals, and especially before touching food or eating. Teach your child not to pick up things from the floor and put them in her mouth.

REMEMBER

If you think the number of times your child is ill, or the severity of your child's recurring illness is unusual or excessive, talk to your GP. There may be an anatomical or immune issue here that you can treat.

Alternative medicines and remedies

Some dads seeking help with their children's illnesses sometimes turn to the less beaten track by checking out alternative medicine. Many of these treatments look at preventing illness, or curing illness through looking at the whole person rather than just the disease. Types of alternative care include:

>> **Acupuncture:** An ancient Chinese technique where special needles are inserted at pressure points in the body.

>> **Homeopathy:** Using plant extracts to treat illness and promote wellbeing.

>> **Massage:** Using touch to relax muscles and stimulate blood flow around the body.

>> **Naturopathy:** An alternative medical system that uses the body's ability to heal itself.

>> **Osteopathy:** Treats the body using manipulation of the musculoskeletal system.

Many of these techniques can be beneficial for your child. However, they're generally not designed to replace primary care, so a trip to your GP is still a good idea even if you swear by the benefits of the various alternative approaches. You should also be aware of the following when turning to alternative medicine to treat your child:

>> Check the use of alternative medicine beforehand with your GP or hospital. Many alternative therapies are unproven and unregulated.

>> Some herbal remedies may contain allergens. Read labels carefully. Some can cause high blood pressure and liver damage. Check with a GP if in doubt.

WARNING

I have listed the previous techniques and remedies for the sake of completeness and because some of them are very common. The effectiveness of alternative medicines and remedies in many cases has not been scientifically proven.

Child obesity: Honey, we're spoiling the kid

A 2007 study of nearly 5000 Australian four- to five-year-old children revealed dads play a crucial role in their kids becoming obese. About 15 per cent of the children studied were overweight, another 5 per cent were obese. Parents in the study were classified according to their parenting styles:

>> **Authoritarian:** The old 'children are seen but not heard' style of parenting.

>> **Authoritative:** Warm but with high expectations for their children's behaviour.

>> **Permissive or indulgent:** What little princess wants, she gets. Children aren't given clear boundaries for their behaviour.

>> **Neglectful:** The child is not loved, not cared for and not seen.

Children of authoritarian dads — that's 'eat what you're given and don't leave anything on the plate' parenting — were 11 per cent more likely to become obese or overweight than children of authoritative dads. Children of permissive fathers were 59 per cent more likely to be obese or overweight, while children of neglectful fathers were 35 per cent more likely to be overweight or obese. The parenting style of mothers appeared to have little or no influence on whether their child was obese or overweight.

A word on health insurance

Health care in Australia is technically 'free' for young children. However, you may want to investigate health insurance for your child. This means you pay a premium to an insurance company and, in return, you can claim certain medical expenses and have access to private hospital care, avoiding the waiting lists of the public health-care system. Health insurance can cover treatments such as putting in ear grommets (refer to the section 'Ear infection', earlier in this chapter), depending on the type of policy.

If you have medical insurance for yourself already, talk to your insurer about adding your child to your policy. You may also want to check what cover you can get if your child is seriously ill and you need to take time off work to look after her.

Chapter **15**

Education

School is a major part of your child's life for the next 13 years. Into adulthood, his school days shape his decisions, his values and his way of thinking, not just the qualifications he earns or the things he knows. As a dad, you obviously want to get the best schooling for your children. This may mean a focus on academic achievement, on a holistic view of the child as a well-rounded individual, or on spiritual and religious elements important to your cultural or ethnic background.

Your child's school should also be somewhere you feel comfortable so that you can stay connected to your child and involved in his school life as much as possible. Research shows that the better the student's family support and involvement, the better he performs at school. And, ultimately, a thing called 'school belonging' is vitally important for your child to do well at school. This means you can see your child feel like he is integrated into his school community — like he really does fit in and belong.

In this chapter, I lay out all the options you have in navigating the education landscape, from single-sex schools to Montessori and Steiner (based on imagination and creative thinking), and give you some tools to help decide which is best for your child.

Exploring Education Philosophies

Over the years, school has changed enormously. Expectations of how schools will support our children have lifted. Teachers are expected to do more than ever, and many parents want school to be a holistic, enriching experience from day one through to graduation to give their children every advantage in what often feels like a dog-eat-dog world.

These days, we know a lot more about how a good education can impact the path your child's life will take, and therefore a lot more pressure is on parents, and in some cases on dads, to get it right. It doesn't need to be like that. You can adopt a healthier approach. This chapter will point to how to get the balance right.

Getting your head around education choices

School choice is a central tenet of the Australian education system. But this means that trying to pick the best school for your child can be baffling — and the stakes can feel high. The school your child attends isn't just about academics. It's about who your child will socialise with and develop friendships with (that might affect the rest of their lives). It's about what resources your child will have access to, what extra-curricular and enrichment pursuits will be available, and so much more.

Here's a look at what you have to choose from in Aussie education:

>> **Government schools:** Publicly funded schools in your local area.

>> **Non-government schools:** Schools where you pay fees for your child's tuition. These schools include Catholic, Christian, Anglican, Islamic and other religious schools. Some non-government schools are non-denominational and are usually known as independent schools, and while some do not have any religious orientation, many of these schools also retain a special religious character. First Nations schools can fall into this category.

>> **Single-sex** (either all-boys or all-girls schools) or **co-educational** (both girls and boys at the same school): These can be either government or non-government (religious or non-denominational/independent) schools.

>> **Alternative schools:** Schools in the non-government categories can also include those such as Montessori or Waldorf/Rudolf Steiner.

To help you make your decision about which school your child should go to, it may help to ask yourself these questions:

>> Can you afford to send your child to a private school?

>> Besides getting good marks, what else is important at this school? Are there sports teams, language classes or music facilities that you would like to encourage your child to get involved with?

>> Do you feel happy and confident about coming in to talk to teachers and the principal?

>> How practical is it to get your child to the school and back? Are long journeys by car, bus or train involved? Is the school en route to work or a long way out of your work travel route?

>> What are the school's values and teaching philosophies? Do they match your values and philosophies?

Many parents make school decisions based on my version of the 3 Rs: *Reputation*, *Results* and *Resources.* Using these when choosing a school has a certain logic and obvious appeal. I recommend an alternative framework, however. Instead of looking at issues of prestige and external acclaim, consider if your child's *friends* will be there, if the school is a good *fit* for your child and his needs, and whether the school's *philosophy* is aligned with what you hope education will do for your child (ideally, that it makes learning *fun* so it becomes a lifelong passion.)

TIP

Spend some time at the school if you can. Ask yourself if you like the atmosphere, the way the teachers and children respond to each other and if you like the children there. Are the children precocious, spoiled, respectful or meek? Culture doesn't show up in NAPLAN scores or the My School website, but it's far more important.

Alternative education philosophies

If traditional school philosophies, with their emphasis on reading, writing and 'rithmetic, aren't your thing, you do have alternatives. Both Montessori and Rudolf Steiner methods aim to educate children in a holistic way, shaping the child to be a good person with strong values and senses of themselves.

Montessori

Developed by Dr Maria Montessori in 1907, this approach involves observing and following the child's interests and encouraging him to explore and learn at his own pace. The main principles are as follows:

>> Children are separated into age groups 0–3, 3–6, 6–9, 9–12 and 12–14 years.

>> Learning environments are designed so children can explore and have lots of specially designed materials to encourage skills and development that are

easily manipulated by children. Classrooms are very calm, ordered places, where children learn to respect the space and needs of their classmates. Children are taught to put things back where they belong so others can use them.

>> Montessori believed that with the right environment and freedom to explore, children develop a love of work, order and silence, and grow to become independent, self-disciplined adults who are true to their natures.

>> Older children are encouraged to be role models and support younger children.

To find out more, go to Montessori Australia www.montessori.org.au.

Waldorf/Rudolf Steiner

Rudolf Steiner was an Austrian philosopher who founded the school of thought called anthroposophy. Without getting too technical here, Steiner's schools (sometimes called Waldorf because that was the name of the first school) use the concept of imagination and creative thinking to develop children into free-thinking adults. Steiner schools regard the child's inner life as being as important as learning to read, write and do maths.

The main principles of Steiner schools are as follows:

>> Childhood is divided into three parts: Early childhood, where emphasis is put on learning through experience; elementary age, where emphasis is put on the child's spirit; and adolescence, where emphasis is on developing analytical and abstract thinking skills.

>> Foreign languages and crafts such as knitting, art and artistic movement are used to teach staple subjects such as reading, maths and science.

>> The first lesson of the day is called 'main lesson' and it lasts for about two hours. During main lesson, a particular curriculum area is taught using art, stories, recitation or physical movement. Main lesson has a theme, which continues for about a month.

>> The same teacher stays with children as they progress through school for the first six years.

To find out more, go to Steiner Education Australia www.steinereducation.edu.au.

Private versus public

For some fathers, whether you send your child to private or public school will be all down to finances — you can either afford the fees, or you can't.

But the push for private schooling is often not so much about education and more about other factors. Perhaps you were a private school student and you are philosophically aligned with this approach. Or maybe you always loved the idea of public education, and you disagree with the multi-tiered system private schools risk creating. It may simply be that you have religious or cultural reasons for preferring one school over another.

Does it really matter if you select private or public for your child? Do kids from one educational background do better than kids from another?

At a population level, we can probably draw out some statistics to support one perspective over another. But research indicates there's not a whole lot in it. Kids from private schools *and* kids from public schools tend to get on about the same in life if we only look at educational factors. Some thrive. Some don't.

REMEMBER

You usually can't tell whether the adult you're working with, living next door to, or buying something from has a private or a public education. It's just not that obvious.

The most important factor is your child's background — the place he comes from, and the support he receives from family and the community. It's true that more children from well-off backgrounds attend independent schools and those schools often perform better than some government schools on a variety of educational measures. And it's also generally true that private schools have a better record for children going onto tertiary education, whereas government schools have higher rates of students entering the workforce and taking up apprenticeships. But this is often less about the schooling and more about the family values, family modelling, and life experience of the child and his parents, and less about educational facilities. (And be aware that plenty of public school kids get fancy degrees while plenty of private school kids don't go on to university study at all.)

School does matter. Let's not quibble over that fact. But what matters more than anything is how you value education in your family, and what you teach your kids about their educational goals, aspirations, and journey.

When considering which school to send your child to, ask yourself these questions:

>> Do I want my child to be educated in a religious setting? If yes, private schools of your denomination are for you.

>> Do I want my child to have access to a large range of extracurricular activities? If yes, a private school may be for you. Private schools tend to have more emphasis on extracurricular activities and sports, and may have scholarships for young people who excel in sports. Many public schools have selected specialties too, though, so don't discount your options here.

>> What value do I place on cultural diversity? Private schools are typically going to have less diversity, and will therefore be more homogenous than public schools.

TIP

Talk to other parents and students at the school you're looking at. They are the best gauge of a school. Even then, however, what works for their child may not work for yours.

Same-sex versus co-ed

Girls and boys learn in different ways. Boys often learn better when they stand up and are active, girls often learn well in a structured or formal setting. Remember what it was like for you when you were young? Perhaps a little bundle of activity just bursting to get out of the classroom and onto the footy field? (Or perhaps not?) So the idea of separating boys and girls to have a more effective learning experience can seem pretty straightforward.

That said, experts are divided on the effectiveness of single-sex schools. Data clearly show that girls tend to do better academically than boys regardless of the academic setting, but they absolutely thrive academically at girls' schools. (This doesn't mean girls schools are better, but only that girls do better academically). Once again, school is less important than what's happening at home. Adjusted for social background, the variances are minimal. Principals at single-sex schools claim that without the distraction of the opposite sex around, students get on with learning and girls are more likely to come out of their shells a bit. Those who champion co-educational schools say that social advantages exist in having the opposite sex around on a daily basis.

That doesn't help you dads, though, does it? If you're in the position where you can afford the privilege of choosing which school your kids go to, perhaps this is something you'd like to talk about with your child. He may have a preference and you can always check with parents whose children attend single-sex or co-ed schools. Ask yourself the same questions I suggested for checking out schools in general: Does this school reflect your family values? How comfortable are you about this school? And keep in mind that, while we hope that they're the exception, sometimes single-sex schools are in the media for all the wrong reasons, churning out culturally revolting kids who have simmered in toxic cultures without the balance of the other sex to help them.

Other options for schooling are becoming increasingly popular over time. Distance education (where kids have a teacher but stay home to study) is happening more and more, even with kids who have a school down the road. It's particularly popular for children with anxiety or other mental health challenges. Home school is also more and more common, with parents taking on the role of teacher and guiding their kids through an academic curriculum with lots more freedom for exploration and child-centred learning. And there's the un-schooling movement, which is a rebellion against formalised schooling more generally.

School Begins This Summer

Welcome to a whole new world — the world of school! Going to school is a big milestone in any child's life. Be sure to take lots of pictures and enjoy seeing your child in his new environment. As his role model, if you enjoy school and being there with him, he'll love it too.

In Australia, the school year runs from late January or early February to December, and the academic year is divided into four terms depending on where you live. Short breaks occur between terms, with a longer break of roughly six weeks over the summer.

Preparing for school

If your child has been to day care, kindergarten or preschool, he has some experience with being around lots of other children and teachers without you, and the transition to school may be quite straightforward. On the other hand, going to school is also a new environment. Bigger kids will be there and your child may be quite scared about all the changes in his life right now. This is also *school*, which is such a big milestone in his life that you'll undoubtedly be feeling all sorts of emotions — your little man is growing up!

Many day care centres, preschools and kindergartens have contacts with local schools and will take a part in getting your child prepared for school. They may initiate visits to the school with other children in your child's peer group so that your child will feel this is an adventure like an outing, rather than a big, scary institution. Just like when you were settling your child into day care or kindy, taking your child to school and staying with him for visits will help him adjust and become familiar with his new surroundings. The more predictable things are, the more secure your child will feel, and it's likely that his adjustment will be better as well. Talking together about what happens at school, what playtime is, what happens at lunchtime and where his bag goes will also help him be less overwhelmed by the change in his life.

TIP

Tell your little one what it was like for you when you were in school (hopefully you still remember some details!). Show him photos if you have some and get him excited about school by telling a few tall tales of your own school days.

Most schools have an orientation day for new entrants in the last term of the year before your child starts school. As well as helping your child, the orientation day also helps you be more at home in his new school, which is important. Studies show that fathers who are comfortable at a school are more likely to be actively involved in their child's education.

REMEMBER

School holidays come round quickly and you will need a plan for when your little guy doesn't have to go to school for a while. Plan well ahead by arranging with your partner or family who will look after him during the holidays, and where possible, work from home or take time off to be there for him during these long breaks.

Checklist: Things kids need to know

Imagine you're starting a new job. You turn up at your new office and are shown your desk and a stack of work to do. And that's it. Maybe you've been shown where the loos are, where to make a cup of coffee, what time lunch is, where meetings are held, and what time you knock off for the day. But on day two, how are you going to remember it all — let alone all the new people you met yesterday? What were their names again? Most likely you would be feeling pretty out to sea if this happened to you, and your child will feel the same.

He may find going to school and settling into a new environment overwhelming if he doesn't get a heads-up from you about what's going to happen, so here are a few things you may have overlooked that your child needs to know:

» Let him know that asking questions if he's not sure of anything is okay. Teachers and teacher aides are always around who can help.

» Explain the school rules — no hitting, running with scissors, stealing and other good rules.

» Give your child a rough guide to the day's structure: There'll be a playtime and lunchtime, and play lunch (morning tea) should be eaten at playtime, not lunch!

» Explain that only the people he knows well, such as dad, mum and special relatives and friends, should take him home from school.

» Tell him that school is on every day except weekends. Some kids feel like having been there once or twice means they're done!

>> Make sure he knows that looking after his bag, clothing and lunch box is his responsibility. Dad won't be able to run around finding stuff for him at going-home time.

>> Show him how to go to the toilet and wash his hands by himself.

>> Show him how to put on his uniform and how to look after it.

>> Be sure he understands that the teacher is in charge of the class. If he needs something, your little one should ask the teacher.

You can help the transition to school by saying hello to the teacher every morning, and stopping to talk to any children or parents that you know. But keep goodbyes short. Say 'goodbye' and 'I love you', give a quick kiss and let the teacher — a trained professional in these matters — take over. (Many schools do a drop-off in the school carpark to make this daily farewell easier.)

Once your child is big enough, you might encourage him to walk or ride to school, ideally with some friends. It's great for confidence, social time, getting physical activity in, and spending time in nature. All of this builds a whole child who can be resilient and independent.

REMEMBER

Your child will be really tired from school in the first few weeks, so let him have some time to himself and a snack after school before making him do any chores. Show lots of interest though and be prepared to listen when your little one is ready to tell you about his exciting day at school.

TIP

Just as when you leave your child with a babysitter, or when you've taken him to day care or kindergarten, your child may be a bit clingy when you leave him at school on the first day. To get around this 'return of the separation anxiety', make sure your child is with an adult, such as a teacher or teacher aide, or an older child like a cousin or friend when you leave. Give him a big kiss and a cuddle, and tell him you love him. Say something like 'I'll be back after school', or 'see you later' and walk away. Don't draw out the goodbye. Your child is in good hands in school and he'll be just fine starting his journey to becoming an independent adult. Be there for your child when he needs you — walk him into class and be there to pick him up — but remember that you don't have to be all stoic. It's okay to offer gentle compassion and kindness — and you don't have to rush the process. If he thinks you're trying to get away from him, it might make him feel worse! It's a fine line to tread, but you've got this. Kind, compassionate and clear.

Homework with dad

Along with schoolwork comes homework, and this is where we get a little provocative again.

Many schools will have children from the youngest grades assigned homework. The idea is that it's supposed to be a time where the day's learning is reinforced.

Often, however, homework turns the dining table into a battleground. Loads of kids hate it, and so do parents (and teachers!). So here's the deal with homework:

>> No reliable research supports the use of homework as an effective learning tool for kids in primary school.

>> In 2014 the Victorian Parliament conducted an inquiry into the effectiveness of homework, and failed to find clear evidence for its promotion, especially in primary school — but despite that, they didn't end up removing it from their guidelines.

>> Homework often causes stress for students who don't understand the work (so repetition doesn't teach them anything except they're dumb), and it causes stress for parents who aren't trained teachers but are trying to be the teacher anyway.

>> Homework is often boring for kids who know how to do the work and understand it.

>> Homework interferes with family time, socialising time, extra-curricular activities, physical activity, shopping, down time, and more.

>> Homework is one of the most reliable ways to crush a child's curiosity when it's handed out the way most homework is distributed in Aussie schools.

In short, no justification or rationale passes the evidence or logic test when it comes to your kids doing homework in primary school. (That changes in high school, though.)

In spite of all of this, you do need to consider the following:

>> First, many schools will demand that your child do homework anyway, regardless of the lack of scientific support for it. They'll tell you that it will teach your child discipline, that repetition is important, and that they'll be doing it later so they may as well get used to it now. These are crappy reasons, but it's going to be up to you to decide if you want to put your foot down on this topic or not. (If you'd like to have some help here, google my name and 'homework letter' for a template of a letter I sent to my children's teachers each year when the kids were in primary school.)

>> Second, if your kiddo is going to come home and sit in front of the Xbox or a screen all afternoon, maybe homework isn't such a bad idea after all. My opposition to it is aligned with the lack of evidence that it helps, and the fact

that it displaces other worthwhile activities. If your child isn't doing anything worthwhile, perhaps it's the better option.

» Finally — and this is the big one — when I'm talking about homework, I'm talking about those homework sheets, cards, and so on. I'm not talking about reading. Reading matters. A lot.

Research shows that the best thing your little ones can do is read. All the time. Reading isn't homework. Reading is just what we do because it's great to read! Academic outcomes go up when kids read a lot. It's so good for them.

WARNING

When it comes to reading, don't ask your kids to read a certain number of pages (because they'll just choose books with big font sizes). And don't ask your kids to read for a certain number of minutes (because they'll stare at the clock more than they read the book). And never tell them you'll buy them a treat or surprise if they finish a book (unless it's *another* book).

Just give them books to read. Read with them. Read to them. Have them read to you. Just read. In primary school, it's the best thing you can do for them.

Special dads for additional needs

The term 'additional needs' covers a wide range of issues that some children face, from physical difficulties such as disease or disability, to mental, behavioural and emotional issues that affect the way they learn. Just as all children are unique, so too the problems they may face are unique. No one-size-fits-all approach exists when it comes to children with additional needs.

Some examples of disorders and disabilities that may require special education include:

» Children who are hearing or visually impaired, who are wheelchair bound, or who have chronic illnesses such as cystic fibrosis

» Children on the autism spectrum (ASD), attention deficit/hyperactivity disorder (ADHD), foetal alcohol syndrome (FASD), developmental delay, Down Syndrome or Tourette Syndrome

For some fathers, your child needing additional help with his education will be obvious. For others, it may just be a feeling that something isn't quite right. As always, talk to your child health nurse, your GP or teachers.

In most instances, schools will make allowances and provide support for your child so he can flourish in mainstream schooling. NDIS funding is available for many disorders, delays and difficulties. Your school's wellbeing officer will be your most important port of call.

As dad, you must be a strong advocate for your child. Don't just shrug and tell him to toughen up and deal with it. Instead, be informed and willing to go the extra distance to get your child the educational opportunities he deserves.

CHECK THE NET

If you're concerned about your child's education and feel he may need access to special education services, here are some places to start:

➤ ACT www.education.act.gov.au/public-school-life/public-schools-in-the-act/special_schools_act_government

➤ New South Wales education.nsw.gov.au/teaching-and-learning/disability-learning-and-support/programs-and-services/special-schools-ssps

➤ Northern Territory nt.gov.au/learning/special-education/about-special-education-and-disability

➤ Queensland education.qld.gov.au/students/students-with-disability

➤ South Australia www.education.sa.gov.au/parents-and-families/student-health-and-disability-support/disability-support-school

➤ Tasmania www.decyp.tas.gov.au/supporting-student-need/support-students-disability/

➤ Victoria www.education.vic.gov.au/pal/enrolment/guidance/enrolment-specialist-schools

➤ Western Australia www.education.wa.edu.au/children-with-special-educational-needs

When schools don't meet your expectations

If you have any concerns about the education your child is receiving, there are issues with how your child is settling in, or any concerns at all with your child's school, make an appointment to see his teacher or principal. Talking it through may bring to light some issues you weren't aware of that you can address, or vice versa for the school.

If issues such as bullying or questionable standards of teaching continue, or your child's additional needs aren't being appropriately supported, and you still aren't happy with the school, it may be time to look at what other schooling options are out there that may be a better fit for your child. This is a big decision. Upending your child's social context, interrupting their routines, and trying to start all over again can be deeply disruptive, and it can reinforce to your child (rightly or wrongly) that there's something 'faulty' with him! Tread carefully with this option, but recognise it always has to be an option worth considering when things get too rough.

Wherever your child goes to school, your attitude and role modelling are most important as a father. Keep reading to your child and encouraging him to read. Make sure you stay connected by talking about his day, and become a part of your child's education. You're still the most important part of his learning.

Complementary Education

Many people had a whole lot of extracurricular activities going on when they were growing up. Today more and more classes and courses are available that your child can participate in to complement the learning he does at school.

The best time to start on subjects like language and music is now. As they get older and don't have the absorbent brain they used to have (or the time they used to have), many adults have regretted not learning in their youth an extra skill such as music. But before you enrol your child into every class under the sun, ask him what he would like to do and follow whatever his interests are, rather than your own. (And make sure you have the financial and the time resources to do this, particularly if more kids are in the pipeline!)

Languages

Languages other than English form part of the school curriculum depending on where you live. But the languages taught at your school may not be what your child wants to learn, or you may have a passion for a particular place and will be visiting there a lot, making learning that language important.

Depending on where you live, private tutors are available to teach your child a language other than English. Many primary schools offer language classes. And once your kids make it to high school, language class options will almost certainly be available.

Music

Starting school age is a great time to start music lessons (recorder, anyone?). But go with something like music appreciation rather than hard-core music lessons. Once your child is around age eight, start the solo stuff. (If you can, expose your child to several instruments over the course of a few years so he can have basic proficiency in each, and then choose the one he enjoys most.

Be mindful of your investment too, though. Start small. Don't expect your child to be able to handle a full drum kit or stand-up double bass just yet. Piano, guitar, violin and wind instruments may be up your child's alley. See what he would like to play. One or two terms on several instruments will be the way to go. Perhaps even a year! But don't spend up big until he knows what he loves. (Oh, and going into a music store and tinkling on the drums, the piano, the guitar and percussion won't give them *any* idea of what they're going to enjoy. The only way to know is to start to teach them.)

Sport

Getting your child involved in the sport of his choice is a great way to keep him active, give him goals and show him how to play with others. Your child should decide which sport he wants to get involved with, because the main thing at this age is to enjoy the sport. If he's not sure or can't decide, watch some games, research the sport on the internet, or if you happen to know how, show him how the sport's played.

Remember, however, that in the early school years, sport should be about three things and three things only:

>> Physical activity and fun

>> Friendships and relationships

>> Building skills and competencies

Take the emphasis *completely* off competition. Don't try to have the under eights world champion. Don't even discuss what he needs to do better in defence or attack. Just make sure he's having fun with his buddies. When he gets into high school and understands the psychology of competition, you *might* start to emphasise performance and goals.

5

What Happens When

IN THIS PART . . .

Understand what's involved with being a stay-at-home dad and primary caregiver, and how you might be able to juggle any paid work you take on.

Find help when dealing with miscarriage, serious illness, injury or a terminal illness.

Adapt to your child having different abilities or additional needs.

Look after your child as you cope with separation or divorce.

Chapter **16**

Stay-at-Home Dad

You and your partner have made a decision — and it's pretty radical. *You* are going to be the one who stays home with the baby while your partner heads back to work or study. You'll be the number one caregiver, taking care of your baby's needs for the majority of the time. You're about to board a new, scary roller-coaster and, as any stay-at-home mum will tell you, a really rewarding one.

Stay-at-home dads (SAHDs) are far more mainstream than at any time in our modern culture's history. That said, for some a stigma exists about being a SAHD. Respect isn't always there — as though it's not masculine to care for your kids. That's slowly changing, and that's a good thing. Just as women pursue careers and take on formerly male-dominated roles, men can make a change to what was once firmly female territory.

In this chapter, I give you a list of the reasons dads make great primary caregivers — you may want to carry it around with you to shoot down any naysayers — and give you some food for thought on balancing your new full-time job with a little paid work or a side-hustle. I also give you the low-down on making the transition into your new role as smooth a ride as possible.

Daddy's in Da House

Data from the Australian Institute of Family Studies shows that the proportion of SAHDs has actually been fairly stable since 1991, hovering around the 3 to 4 per cent mark across that time. However, the number of families where both adults are working has increased from 54 per cent in 1991, to 58 per cent in 2001, to 66 per cent in 2016. More fathers are engaging in part-time work, increasing from 6 per cent in 1991, to 10 per cent in 2016. Flexible and work from home arrangements have also seen an uptick, particularly in families where the mother works full-time. Across gender, the number of parents who are unemployed has plummeted in households with dependent children, from around the 7 to 8 per cent mark in 1991, to only 2 per cent in 2022.

What this means is that, on the whole, fewer parents are home with the kids than ever before, whether male or female. But dads are taking on more responsibility with child care, and they're arranging their work schedules to participate in the home more than ever before.

Debunking some myths about guys as primary caregivers

Even with a few decades of dads being home in this capacity, SAHDs are still a recent phenomenon in terms of the way that our modern society operates, and some people don't really understand what 'stay-at-home dad' means. Or they do know what it means but they perceive it as somehow less masculine. People can make judgements about you and your family, which can be hard to swallow some-times. Here are some of the myths you may encounter:

>> Fathers can't parent as well as mothers.

>> Fathers can't breastfeed babies, so the baby will miss out on breastmilk.

>> Fathers can't handle looking after a baby without causing chaos in the house and leaving a mess wherever they go.

>> Fathers won't be able to handle being a SAHD at all.

>> Fathers will forget practical things such as food, nappy changes and appropriate clothing.

>> Fathers don't have a 'mother's intuition' and won't be able to tell if their child is unwell.

Other issues may arise, and they perhaps have greater weight to them, with greater potential impact on your wellbeing. These issues include:

>> Being a SAHD may feel like it lacks purpose (which can also be the case for some mums)

>> Being a SAHD may feel isolating and lead to loneliness (which can also be the case for some mums)

>> Being a SAHD may lead to skills becoming redundant (which can also be the case for some mums)

Some of the challenges of being a SAHD are easily waved away. Others less so, but each challenge probably applies as much to mums as it does to us dads. Although fathers parent differently from mothers, it doesn't mean dad's way is wrong. To the sceptics, consider the following:

>> Showing love and wanting the best for their kids makes fathers just as qualified to look after their little ones as their mothers.

>> Mothers can express breastmilk for dad to give feeds, or top up with formula if appropriate.

>> Fathers can do everything mums can do, such as looking after the household in addition to looking after bub, even if they haven't been doing it for as long as mums.

>> Dads make fantastic parents. Active father involvement has been linked to improved performance at school and fewer problems during teen years such as teen pregnancy or binge drinking.

>> Fathers aren't thick. We can remember nappy changes and to do the washing. Nutting out our own way of doing things may take some work, but we get there.

>> Fathers who spend time with their babies will learn everything there is to know about their little ones, and will be able to use their common sense and the tips they learn in this book to tell when baby is ill.

>> Guys are very practical and often good at things that mums can struggle with (and vice versa, of course). So dads have got lots of useful skills they can transfer to raising their offspring from an early age.

The other issues such as meaning, purpose, isolation and maintaining skill relevance are all challenges you'll need to use your resourcefulness and initiative to work your way through. But you have infinite creative options for you to chase as you navigate being a star dad. You've got this!

Coping with your new career

Models of masculinity are changing in substantial ways as the 21st century continues its march. While there's been a historical approach to masculinity that argues that men ought to be the breadwinner and to provide financially for their children, society is structured in such a way that this doesn't always need to be the case. Plenty of women have the capacity to out-earn their husbands or they just want to work. And the option of splitting household and earning roles more equitably than it has been done historically is an attractive option for many couples.

But if you're going to stay home with bub, even if it's just part-time, be warned: going from a full-on career to staying home with a baby is a big change — ask any first-time mum how she coped with it! And as a guy, you don't have the physical changes of pregnancy to prepare for how weird the whole parenthood thing is. (But that could also be a blessing, of course!)

Having a support system in place helps when it comes to your new career. Family, friends who have children and other men who can remind you it's not all about nappies, bottles and crying can all provide support.

Being out of the politics of your office, without a demanding boss or several people to report to, can be nice. You don't have any deadlines for reports or projects to manage. But, on the other hand, you might miss the adult-to-adult interaction, and the way you bumped up against ideas and people at work all the time.

With that said, the small new boss is a pretty demanding one, and if you don't get the work done right — if you don't burp that gas out, if you let her get overtired, or if you don't have enough formula on hand — you're going to be rapped over the knuckles pretty quickly! You can't clock off at five o'clock, no-one is waiting to take over the late shift and, hardest of all, you don't get sick leave. When you're the primary caregiver, the buck stops with you. And you'll need to get used to that question most mums have learned to detest: 'What's for dinner, sweetheart?'

So how do you go from being a career man to being the main man? Remember that what you're doing is a privilege and doing so will bring you much closer to your little person than you could ever have imagined. Why would you ever want to go back to work? The time that your child is small is so short, and she'll never be this age again. Looking after a baby or toddler is tough work and your career may have been important to you; however, not many men out there have the same opportunity to be this close to their children. Enjoy it!

REMEMBER

You're never alone. Set up your own group of fathers and create a network of people you can call on. (See the section 'Catching Up with Other Dads', later in this chapter, for more.)

Getting organised

Being organised when you have a child is essential. Having systems and routines in place that save you time and effort make life a lot easier, giving you time for the things you like to do rather than have to do.

Your morning begins the night before. Checking every night at bedtime that you've got the essentials for the next day will prevent you finding you've run out of something really important.

Here's a quick run-down on the essentials that you may want to have on hand:

>> Clean nappies

>> Food, whether it be expressed breastmilk or formula for babies under six months, or solids and finger food for older babies

>> Wipes or cloths for nappy changing

>> Bum cream

>> Any medicine or ointments your child needs

>> At least two changes of clothes

TIP

If you get out and about a lot, which I recommend, keep the nappy bag stocked at all times so loading up the pram and going isn't a big deal.

REMEMBER

Always take your nappy bag with you everywhere. Even a short trip to do the grocery shopping may require a nappy change, or circumstances may mean you're away longer than you planned.

Most SAHD duties don't usually start for the first few months of your child's life. Even if your partner is the one heading back to the office, she'll typically take an extended period of leave. Nevertheless, if you're up for it, you may as well be involved in everything you can and take the load off her as soon as it's practical. This means that from the first few weeks of life it could be on! Your baby may have a very busy appointment book — check-ups with your midwife or doctor, vaccinations, child health nurse visits or trips to a specialist. Keep a list or calendar of appointments in the early weeks so you don't forget. Chances are, you'll be too tired to remember your own name, let alone when the nurse is coming.

All that organisation may sound boring right now, but children keep things interesting and generally respond well to a change of plan. Even if you're adhering to a strict routine or schedule, children like to mix things up a bit. So what if you miss a swim lesson or don't make it to music? If something else turns up that means you'll have to change plans. It's not worth panicking over.

My Daddy Just Cares for Me

If you're the primary caregiver, the buck stops with you. Being primary caregiver is like being the head of a major corporation, only you have one very demanding, unforgiving, but utterly cute client who pays you in smiles and love.

Upskilling

Trying to figure out what your baby is saying to you when she arches her back or screws up her face in a certain way is daunting. It can be baffling when she's grumpy and cranky and nothing seems to settle her. You're not a bad father if you're struggling with this. Rather, it probably means you just don't have the skills to deal with each stage of your child's life yet. By the way, stay-at-home mums face the same challenges. It's called being a parent, and you'll experience it together, one way or another, for much of the rest of your life.

Parenting is not one of those things you want to simply be 'winging it' with. We make sure we receive adequate training for work. We follow instructions in one way or another for almost everything we do in life. Yet when it comes to parenting, we seem to believe we can simply figure it out as we go along. Ironically, we also claim that it's the most important job we'll ever do and the most critical role we'll ever be involved in. Surely it's worth a little professional development (PD).

Fortunately, PD for dads is relatively easy to access these days! Grab a great quality parenting book as soon as you're done here, and keep the investment in your parenting going. Such an investment will be good for you and for your family. Books that I've written have been popular and helpful for countless families. Try *The Parenting Revolution* straight out of the gate. You'll also find *The Whole Brain Child* by Daniel Siegel a powerful tool to get you started.

In addition, parenting classes are available to help you decipher your baby's many cues and help you act on them. Parenting classes can also be an invaluable support network. Find them online — check out www.happyfamilies.com.au/join) or google what's available in your local area (recognising that some substantial differences in quality exist with many of these options).

Through these classes, you'll meet other dads, hear what they've been experiencing and get tips on how to deal with any issues you have with your fatherhood experience.

Building healthy bodies and active minds

Just as your child needs food to grow her body, active movement and experiences feed her mind. When she was first born, her brain was about 15 per cent developed, but by three years of age, her brain's well on its way to being fully developed. The first three years in particular shape your child's life like no other period. By making a great connection with your child — remember, connection means feeling seen, heard and valued — and by giving her lots of opportunities to explore and learn, and lots of encouragement, you're doing the best job a dad can do.

All those little things children do when they play — feeling textures, judging distances, figuring out what's hot and cold, pouring water from one cup to another, and making those raucous noises and squeals — is all about practising skills that we adults have (almost) perfected. By offering lots of things to touch and play with, you're giving your child lots of opportunities to get some practice in for the real deal — growing up and adulthood. Refer to other chapters on specific age groups for ways to get active with kids.

REMEMBER

To ensure your child's body stays as healthy as it can be, give your child lots of healthy and nutritious foods. You may also need to improve your cooking and baking skills in case you're not the natural-born Naked Chef. Remember the basics — avoid fatty, sugary foods, establish a feeding and eating routine, avoid distractions during eating and ensure bub gets lots of rest and good sleep. For more on nutrition see Chapter 14.

Keeping mum in the loop

In a busy household, where you're at home with your child and your partner is out at work, it's easy to fall into a trap where you're so absorbed by the hectic lives you lead you have no time for each other. You're tired from chasing after a small human all day and can't wait to hand her over to your partner, who's exhausted from meetings and deadlines. You may fall into a trap of thinking that spending time with your child is a chore, or expecting that your partner is supposed to pull a second shift once she comes home from work when she's totally spent.

Remembering that the three of you need to spend time together as a family and enjoy each other's company is really important. If your partner is away at the office and your child does something that would be of interest to her, let her know — a quick video message is a delightful pick-me-up for your partner, and it keeps everyone connected. And when she comes home, rather than plonking the child on her lap the instant she walks through the door, have a family meal or a general catch-up on what the three of you have been doing all day.

TIP

As your child gets older, encourage her to do something special for her mum when she gets home, such as taking her bag or showing her a drawing she made.

Working from home

You may decide to be a SAHD who works from home. Flexible options in the workplace continue to evolve (one thing we can thank COVID for). Video calls (via platforms such as Zoom, Teams and WebEx) are a daily reality even for people who are in an office. And the desire for workplaces to be accommodating to people who request alternative employment arrangements continues to make SAHD and work an increasingly attractive option for many who are in the privileged position to take something like this on.

Knowledge workers (or those who use a computer all day at work) can work from home more easily than ever before. Concerns about the fear of missing out (FOMO) or reduced productivity have essentially been allayed due to the enormous shift in working from home that occurred during the COVID pandemic. Nevertheless, if you're used to working with a lot of people or in a busy environment, suddenly finding yourself at home with a child and a laptop to work with can be strange, lonely and perhaps even a little boring. You may be tempted to make yourself a cup of coffee every ten minutes, or feel unmotivated because you don't have a work environment around you to keep that energy going. If you're not self-disciplined or motivated, chances are working from home is not going to be easy for you.

You can do things to stop yourself going mental, or being so lonely you invite the meter reader in for coffee:

>> Have a routine for you and your child, so you can slot work in around when she sleeps. Having a structured routine allows you to more easily make appointments, schedule phone calls or take part in online meetings. If possible, be flexible to allow for those days when your child's unsettled.

>> Don't be too ambitious with what you can achieve. You'll have days when you can't get any work done and other days when your princess is a dream who sleeps for hours at a time. Overcommitting yourself to your boss will just stress you out and make your fathering life more difficult.

>> Give yourself a few hours each day to get out and about — go to a Babes in Arms movie session, go for a walk, or attend a planned activity like playgroup or swimming lessons. Most of all, use that time to see other people! And remember that nature is fuel for the soul — yours and your baby's.

>> If you have face-to-face meetings to attend, check ahead to see if you can take your child, or arrange for a sitter, friend or relative to cover for you.

>> Be enthusiastic about the work you're doing. Otherwise, you have to ask yourself is it worth the stress of trying to do your job *and* be a SAHD (which is also a full-time job)?

>> Make a work space in your house that's just for your work. By having your own work space, you don't have to set up your gear every time you want to work. You're more likely to settle into productive work if you don't have to clear the breakfast dishes away from the dining table to work at it while bub is sleeping. When your child gets older, explain to her that this is daddy's office and not an indoor playground.

Catching Up with Other Dads

New mums join mother's groups and hold similar types of catch-ups in the weeks and months following birth for a reason. Sometimes you just want to meet up with others who are in the same boat as you, sharing similar joys and — yes — experiencing similar bad days.

As a SAHD you're on the front line of parenting, taking the hits (dirty nappies), outwitting the enemy (playing chase), fighting the good fight (rough-housing) and going the extra mile (in the buggy, when junior won't go to sleep). Of course, you can go to the mother's group with bub as well, but finding a network of dads is all about finding that camaraderie between fathers, and ensuring that dads gather together and get through any good and bad times they might be experiencing.

Being at home means that you might become slightly isolated, but you can call on your fellow dads. See the following section for the various ways you can get in touch.

Networking as a SAHD

So how do you find this mythical network of dads, who are going to be your rocks when you need them? SAHDs are more common than they used to be, but they're still a rare beast, so keep your eyes peeled at the local library, music sessions, playgroups and coffee groups. Or just stroll up to other blokes pushing buggies — you don't need an excuse to start a conversation. You can also ask your midwife or child health nurse if they have other SAHDs on their books.

Basically, just do what the mums do (but in a man kind of way). Get together with other SAHDs at a local coffee shop, go to child-friendly movie sessions or take turns for meeting at home. Mums do this all the time and they are pretty good at it — no reason why dads can't network too. In fact many SAHDs are meeting all over Australia. To find a dads group close to where you live, check out `www.dadsgroup.org`.

Being the only guy in the room

Since most primary caregivers are women, most of the activities that you take your child to, especially in her first year of life, are bound to be full of mums and babies. Being the only guy in the room can be a bit weird. Then again . . . it can be really cool because you'll get lots of attention — most mums love the fact a SAHD is in the group to add some variety and dad-perspective. You may even be overrun with mums keen to find out about the male approach to parenting. Single mums may be especially grateful for being able to expose their child to male parenting. So enjoy the attention and show you can keep up with the best of the mums!

Chapter **17**

Serious Illness and Losing Your Baby

In an ideal world, I wouldn't be writing this chapter and you wouldn't be reading it. Your child should always be well, happy and carefree. But, unfortunately, life's not that simple. Children do get ill, they get hurt and, sometimes, tragically, they die.

When your child isn't well, you find yourself in uncomfortable and sometimes scary territory. As a dad, you find that your baby's comfort and safety becomes all-consuming. And you often feel completely helpless as your tiny kiddo screams, wails and tries to communicate that, 'Yes, Dad, something's wrong with me.' It will throw you off balance, and leave you wondering how you're supposed to make it right. The trouble is that being a human means this is a reality of life. Sometimes illness is avoidable, sometimes it isn't.

In this chapter, I show you ways to minimise the risk of illness, starting with pregnancy, and how to cope should serious illness strike. Lastly, I discuss disability and what support organisations exist to help you on your fatherhood journey with a child who has additional needs.

Avoiding Health Problems

What you put in your body plays a big part in your health. Make your home a smoke-free, drug-free environment. Reduce alcohol intake and be responsible if grog's around. If you're a little tipsy and you trip and fall while you're carrying bub, you'll never forgive yourself. And snoozing through a hangover while the baby feeds himself that two-day-old piece of icky food he found on the floor may have serious health consequences.

The following sections run through some more ways to ensure bub starts off on the front foot and as healthy as possible.

Protecting against diseases

Having your child immunised against diseases such as whooping cough, meningitis and diphtheria protects him from these illnesses, which can cause death or serious long-term harm to a child. Talk to your child's GP about the right ages to be vaccinated.

Providing a violence-free home

Shaking your baby or hitting your young child may cause serious physical harm or death in extreme cases. The message is simple — never, ever, shake your baby, and consider smack-free discipline.

Beyond the physical harm shaking and hitting can cause, in the first years of your child's life he's learning to form a safe and secure attachment to you, his father, and this attachment plays a big part in how well he acts and forms relationships as an adult. If you're violent towards him, you're creating a serious risk of attachment challenges, trust issues and psychological difficulty when he is older. More immediate is the serious risk of harm. Adopt the policy that the only time you should place your hands on your child is to help, and never to hurt.

REMEMBER

If you're at the end of your tether and just feel like making your baby or child shut up, take a deep breath and count to ten, or leave him in a safe place and get some air for a minute. Stress is the distance between the situation in front of you and how well you think you can deal with that situation. Tell yourself you can handle it and see how much better you feel. He's a baby. He's acting like one. You're an adult. Act like one.

CHECK THE NET

If you're often angry at your child, your partner or the situations you're in, it may be time to get help dealing with your emotions and anger. Check out Relationships Australia (`relationships.org.au`), which has links to services and courses in your state or territory.

Keeping accidents at bay

Keeping your child physically safe around your home, in the street and in your car is also really important. Here's a short checklist for things to keep in mind when you've got a baby in the house:

>> Keep your cups of tea and coffee (and any other hot drinks or food) well away from the baby. Your baby might accidentally touch them or knock them over (and so could you). Scalding is a serious health risk to babies and young children.

>> Whenever you leave your baby somewhere, make sure nothing can fall on top of him and he can't fall off anywhere. A soft blanket on the floor is the perfect place to keep your baby safe.

>> If you give your little champ a bottle feed, check the temperature of the formula or milk carefully. Using your mouth is the best temperature guide. Give your baby warm fluids only. If it feels hot to you, it's too hot for your baby.

Refer to Chapter 4 for car seat safety and safety around animals in the house.

Keeping up to date with household chores while looking after a small child can sometimes seem like brushing your teeth while you're simultaneously munching on Oreo biscuits. You wash and clean all the nappies, only to have junior need changing twice as often. Or he's suddenly power-spewing all over the place. You may have your hands full just tending to bub. But washing your hands after nappy changes, cleaning up spew or dealing with laundry is absolutely essential, and helps cut down the risk of bacterial infection from nappies and stomach bugs. If a global pandemic has taught us anything, it's good hand hygiene. So get the soap going consistently, count to 20 while you wash, and keep things clean.

You can also keep the following in mind:

>> Have a bottle of hand steriliser in your nappy bag.

>> Empty rubbish bins with disposable nappies and wipes in them regularly — at least once per day.

>> Wash toys regularly. Most plastic toys can be scrubbed in a basin, while soft toys can go in the washing machine.

>> Air your rooms regularly, to reduce the risk of respiratory infections caused by damp, dusty houses.

>> Keep baby's room at a temperature of 22 degrees Celsius, as recommended by the World Health Organization, and avoid any draughts. (And be sure you have enough clothing on your little one.)

>> Avoid tummy bugs by not reheating food for your child that's been in the fridge more than 24 hours. Cook fresh food, or food that's been safely frozen and thawed. If you need to keep food in the fridge, make sure it's covered; for example, with cling wrap.

WARNING

Don't store left over food in tins. The CSIRO explains that food stored in an open metal means 'tin and iron will dissolve from the can walls and the food may develop a metallic taste. Food containing high concentrations of tin can cause nausea, vomiting, diarrhoea, abdominal cramps, abdominal bloating, fever or headache.' Not what you want for your precious kiddo.

Keeping your child physically safe around your home, in the street and in your car is also really important. See Chapter 8 on child-proofing your home and Chapter 4 for car seat safety.

Keep your child safe around roads by teaching him to hold your hand crossing the road on footpath crossings, when you're near driveways and to never go on the road without an adult.

Creating a healthy start to life

Doesn't every child deserve the best start in life you can possibly provide? Keeping mum tanked up with healthy food, lots of fresh air and exercise from when you first know you're going to be a dad goes a long way towards keeping your baby healthy in the long run.

REMEMBER

You're not the boss of your partner. Stay healthy yourself, create a healthy life-style, move and be active together, and watch the difference it makes for you and your soon-to-be family. Some research suggests that dads being active and healthy increases the likelihood that their kids will follow in their footsteps.

Avoiding risks during pregnancy

Creating a whole new person is an enormous task, and pregnancy can make a woman's body vulnerable to infection and conditions such as high blood pressure. Pregnancy can affect bones, teeth, blood flow, muscles and joints, and so much more. What goes into your partner's body — and how she uses her body — can be associated with the level of risk she and the baby experience during that 40 weeks of baby-growing.

REMEMBER

If your partner has any chronic health issues, such as diabetes or asthma, make sure both of you are happy with the way that your medical professional or health carer is monitoring the progress of the pregnancy. If not, find a health provider you are confident in.

These are some of the things your partner should be aware of during her pregnancy:

>> **Alcohol:** Experts are unsure of what a 'safe' level of alcohol is for pregnant mums, so avoiding all alcohol is best. *Foetal alcohol syndrome* is caused by alcohol crossing the placenta and affecting the baby's developing brain, and it doesn't take heavy drinking to do the damage. Light drinking from time to time still poses a risk. Children with foetal alcohol syndrome can have problems with learning, concentration, hyperactivity and speech. For more information, check out www.nofasd.org.au. And consider taking a 'pregnant pause' from alcohol during pregnancy and breastfeeding — together. (Refer to Chapter 2 for more on making this commitment.)

>> **Chickenpox:** When we're kids, chickenpox (also called varicella) is much like any other illness, and the only long-lasting effect of the disease may be a few pock scars. But in adults, chickenpox is a serious illness. If your partner gets chickenpox when she's pregnant, the virus can be transmitted to your growing baby. Though rare, the baby's development can be affected, causing limb deformities, mental retardation, or even miscarriage or stillbirth. If you haven't had chickenpox and you're planning to get pregnant, consider being vaccinated now.

>> **Listeriosis:** Pregnant women are much more vulnerable to an infection from bacteria living in certain foods called *Listeria*. The infection, listeriosis, can be caused by eating deli meats, soft cheeses, unpasteurised milk, unwashed fruit and vegetables, raw meat, pâté, ready-made salads, smoked seafood and smoked shellfish. It's best if your partner avoids these foods while pregnant. Listeriosis can cause miscarriage and stillbirth.

>> **Rubella (German measles):** If a pregnant woman contracts rubella, the virus can seriously harm the developing baby, including causing severe mental retardation and blindness. Most women are vaccinated against rubella as teenagers, but if your partner hasn't been vaccinated and you're planning to get pregnant, talk to your GP about being vaccinated now.

WARNING

Being vaccinated against rubella doesn't always guarantee lifetime immunity against the virus. Women planning pregnancy should have their immunity status checked.

- **Smoking:** Pregnancy is a great time to quit smoking. Poisons from the smoke are passed to the baby through the placenta. Babies born to mothers who smoke are at risk of developing breathing problems, having a lower birth weight and being twice as likely to die from SIDS (*Sudden Infant Death Syndrome*, also known as cot death — see the section 'Reducing the risk of SUDI and SIDS', later in this chapter). However, quitting smoking is tough and not made much easier by having a preachy dad-to-be around, or one who is continuing to smoke himself. Instead, give your partner your wholehearted support and contact a helpline in your area, not just for your partner, but for both of you to quit smoking.

- **Toxoplasmosis:** This is an infection that can be caused by a bacteria living in the guts of animals. The bacteria can be carried in raw meat and in cat poo, so pregnant women should avoid dealing with kitty litter boxes, and take care when gardening because cats may have used the soil for a toilet. Cook all meat thoroughly.

- **Unprescribed drugs:** In case it needs to be said, the risk to mum and bub is significant if any other drugs are consumed during pregnancy (other than those prescribed by a suitably qualified medical practitioner and used as directed in relation to her pregnancy). Risks are present if your partner uses marijuana (or other drugs containing THC and cannabinoids), ecstasy (or other stimulant pills), cocaine, heroin, methamphetamine (ice), or any other illicit drugs.

- **Vaping (e-cigarettes):** At the time of writing, insufficient studies are available to allow me to draw solid conclusions about the effects of vaping in pregnancy. However, I'm probably safe in saying that since e-cigarettes have any number of chemicals in them (often, though not always, including nicotine) any decision to vape during pregnancy would be risky. Even if your partner is trying to quit smoking and sees e-cigarettes as an alternative, my cautiously conservative advice is to stay away from vapes.

CHECK THE NET

If you want to give up smoking, go to www.quit.org.au or phone their Quitline on 137 848.

Encouraging breastfeeding

Encouraging and supporting breastfeeding in the first months of life boosts your baby's immunity and gives him the very best nutrition he needs to grow and thrive. Experts have highlighted that, for your baby, breastfeeding is associated with:

- Better vision

- Fewer cases of bacterial meningitis

- Fewer colds and respiratory illnesses such as pneumonia and whooping cough

>> Fewer ear infections, especially those that damage hearing

>> Less diarrhoea, constipation and reflux

>> Less illness overall and less hospitalisation

>> Lower rates of infant mortality

>> Lower rates of Sudden Infant Death Syndrome (SIDS)

>> Stronger immune systems

And that's just getting started on the health benefits. Breast milk also contains substances that naturally soothe your little one. The positive health impacts have been found to extend even into adolescence.

For mum, breastfeeding is associated with faster weight loss (her body burns up to 500 calories a day just to keep creating that milk supply), improved post-pregnancy-related health (reduced postpartum bleeding and better uterine health), and reduced risk of postpartum depression. Breastfeeding releases feel-good hormones, helps with bonding, and builds trust between mum and bub.

I could go on for a while yet, but it's worth highlighting one more list of benefits to breastfeeding. Mums who can breastfeed are likely to experience:

>> Less cardiovascular disease

>> Less diabetes

>> Less endometriosis

>> Less osteoporosis with age

>> Lower risk of breast cancer

>> Lower risk of ovarian cancer

>> Lower risk of rheumatoid arthritis and lupus

Now that you've read all that, applying pressure to your partner to make sure she puts bubba on the boob might be tempting. Please don't. She already knows these benefits but, for a reasonable portion of women, breastfeeding isn't viable. These reasons include the following:

>> Breast reduction surgery

>> Depression or anxiety, or high stress

>> Insufficient milk supply

>> Medications that flow into breast milk and are bad for baby (such as antithy-roid medication and some mood altering drugs — although this is an area that has a lot of mixed evidence)

>> Radiation therapy

>> Serious illness or other medical issues

Even if those just listed aren't the reason/s, your partner needs to be allowed to make her own decision. While it might be your baby, it is *her* body and *her* wellbeing.

REMEMBER

Breastfeeding can be difficult in the beginning, and your partner may be pretty exhausted and frustrated at times, so give her all the help you can.

DEALING WITH THE GRIEF OF MISCARRIAGE

A miscarriage is the death of a baby before 20 weeks gestation. Many women don't even know they're pregnant when they miscarry, but many others lose much-wanted and cherished babies. In the past, people have had the attitude that miscarriages are something to be gotten over, and that everything is fixed by trying for another baby. As men, we'll never understand just how deeply a miscarriage affects the baby's mother — our partner. The effects of miscarriage can be profound. While I would never engage in a comparison game, we do need to recognise that fathers can also be deeply impacted by the loss of a baby they'll never have the opportunity to hold and to raise. The grief that comes with the lost future of that child can be overwhelming. Having healthy ways to grieve is important for men as well as women. One thing to be aware of is that some-one just getting 'over it' is rare. Give yourself and your partner the time necessary to grieve.

If you grapple with this devastating loss, you will also likely feel you have to be strong for your partner . . . and in a sense you do. You need to advocate for your partner at a time when she's confused, angry, vulnerable and grieving. But you also need to be empa-thetic and caring, and one way to do that is to talk openly about your feelings with your partner. You also need to acknowledge your feelings of loss and sadness, rather than pretend to keep a stiff upper lip. You may have heard the phrase, 'If it's mentionable, it's manageable'. If you can mention how painful things are, you can start to process them more effectively. Talking also offers what psychologists call 'psychological distance', and allows you the space you need to step back and see your pain for what it is, rather than living in it. Remember, though, that your focus may need to be on your partner and her grief for a time.

Having a ceremony or funeral for your lost baby may be comforting and give you a chance to express your grief and let others support you. The ceremony can be anything from a few people lighting a candle, to a funeral with a minister or religious leader. Just do what comes naturally to you and your partner. Naming your baby can also help you heal — acknowledging your baby as a real person, not a 'loss' or an 'it' can really help.

If you need to talk to someone outside your family and friends, support is available. You just have to ask for it.

In Australia, contact the following:

- **Bears of Hope:** An organisation that offers grief wellness groups in your local area and grief counsellors, free of charge, for people who have lost a baby during pregnancy, birth or infancy. Visit www.bearsofhope.org.au or call 1300 114 673.

- **SANDS:** An independent organisation that provides support for miscarriage, stillbirth and newborn death. Go to www.sands.org.au or call them on 1300 308 307.

Birth options to reduce the risk of fatality

Approximately one per cent of babies die between 20 weeks gestation and up to 28 days after birth. This is referred to as a *perinatal* death. Most of these babies die because they're born too early and their bodies aren't developed enough for life outside the womb. Others die from congenital abnormalities and, in some cases, there is no known reason. Completely normal, healthy pregnancies can end in stillbirths.

The World Health Organization and various UN agencies estimate that 11 in 1,000 Australian mothers die because of complications in pregnancy and childbirth. We're lucky that we have access to good health-care facilities, skilled maternity carers and plenty of nutritious food for pregnant women and their growing babies.

To reduce the risk of complications during pregnancy and childbirth, find a carer you trust, whether it be an obstetrician, GP or midwife, and attend regular checkups with them. Your carer will monitor for conditions such as pre-eclampsia, gestational diabetes and other factors that may cause complications during pregnancy and childbirth. If you're not familiar with these terms, check the Glossary and read up on them.

Home birth

You may be wondering whether having your baby at home is riskier than having your baby in a hospital. While being nearer to medical facilities should something go wrong during your child's birth may help, babies can still die in hospitals with experienced carers, even after mum-to-be took great care of her health during pregnancy and excellent health care was provided to her during her pregnancy.

Home birth is a contentious issue in Australia. Talk with your carer about your birthing options.

But women with high-risk pregnancies, who are at risk of pre-term labour, have pre-eclampsia, gestational diabetes or any other medical complication during pregnancy are not advised to have a planned home birth.

Caesarean birth

You may think that avoiding a vaginal birth and the stress on baby and the mother's body may be the way to go, but risks are associated with elective caesareans too. After all, a caesarean is major surgery and the mother may experience haemorrhaging and infection.

A 2007 British study also showed that babies born by caesarean can have breathing difficulties because fluid in the lungs is not squeezed out as it is in a vaginal birth. Emergency caesareans are performed when the condition of the baby or mother is deteriorating, such as *cord prolapse*, when the umbilical cord comes out of the uterus before the baby, blocking off his lifeline. In those cases, you often don't have a choice about having an emergency caesarean because the life of the mother or child is at risk.

REMEMBER

If your partner has had a textbook pregnancy, I suggest *not* worrying about the risks of fatality. Concentrate instead on creating a peaceful and calm environment for your baby to be born into, with lots of support for your partner. Relax and enjoy this momentous time in your life.

Reducing the risk of SUDI and SIDS

SUDI stands for *Sudden Unexplained Death of Infants*. In some cases, death is caused by smothering or some other known cause. SIDS is a type of SUDI and stands for *Sudden Infant Death Syndrome*, where the baby, for reasons unknown, stops breathing. Experts believe babies who have been around cigarette smoke are more at risk. SIDS used to be commonly known as 'cot death'.

Simple ways you can reduce your baby's risk of SUDI/SIDS include the following:

>> Keep your baby's environment smoke-free. If you both gave up smoking when your partner was pregnant, your home is now smoke-free. If you still need

help with quitting the habit, call the Quit helpline in your area (refer to the section 'Avoiding risks during pregnancy', earlier in this chapter, for contact details).

>> Sleep your baby on her back, not on her side or front.

>> Keep your baby's cot or bassinet free from bumpers, duvets and doonas, cuddly toys and sheepskins that could smother her.

>> If you do share your bed with your baby (known as co-sleeping) only do so when neither you nor your partner has been drinking or is excessively tired to avoid the risk of rolling onto your baby. Co-sleeping is also safe only if you haven't been smoking, because exposure to smoke puts your baby at risk.

TIP

You can buy baskets that allow you to co-sleep with your child and prevent you rolling onto her or smothering her with a blanket. Check with your local baby supply store.

TIP

If you're worried about your baby's risk of SUDI or SIDS, consider buying an advanced baby monitor that constantly checks the baby's heartbeat and breathing. Check your local baby supply store for these monitors.

CHECK THE NET

To find out more about SUDI and SIDS, go to www.healthdirect.gov.au/sudden-infant-death-syndrome-sids. Also check out rednose.org.au and click on the Safe Sleeping icon.

Coping with Illness and Injury

Having a sick or injured baby or child is no fun. As well as feeling pretty darn terrible, your child may have trouble understanding what's wrong with him, not be able to communicate well with you about what's wrong, and be scared of the treatments he's receiving.

Spotting injury

The likelihood of your infant being injured is very small, and if it happens you or mum will probably be nearby. An immobile baby doesn't do much without a parent being nearby. But accidents do happen, and if you're not there when they do, it can be hard to know how to help.

A few pointers:

>> Never leave baby unattended on a chair, lounge, change-table, kitchen bench, car roof, or anything at all that he could roll off. Full stop. End of story. Your kiddo can't fall off the floor, so that's the only place he can be left unsupervised.

>> Never leave baby unattended in a bath, sink or any body of water. You have to be there.

>> Never leave baby close to anything that he can reach out, grab and pull down on top of himself. Tablecloths, or perhaps that doily with a vase on top? Danger.

REMEMBER

If your little one is hurt, the most important thing is to stay calm yourself. Hitting panic stations results in poor decision-making. Remember — high emotions, low intelligence. Keep it level and balanced. You can think more clearly.

Here's a rundown on some unlikely, but possible, injury problems and how to deal with them:

>> **Burns and scalds:** Run cold water on a burn for 20 minutes. If your child has scalded himself with hot liquid, take his wet clothes off because the heat in the clothes can continue to burn his skin. If material is sticking to the skin, don't try to take it off. If the burn is serious and you see redness and blistering, get someone to call an ambulance while you take care of your child. Once you've finished pouring cold water over the area and if a trip to hospital isn't necessary, cover it with a clean cloth or tea towel and see your doctor. Your child is likely to be very cold from the cold water, so make sure he's dressed warmly.

>> **Concussion:** Babies have knocks and bumps regularly. Things can fall on them easily. A bump to the head can result in more than just a lump and bruise. Concussion is a temporary loss of brain function, from the brain banging against the skull. Your child may have hit his head so hard he lost consciousness, or has a headache, seems disoriented and may vomit repeatedly. Being irritable and sensitive to light can also be a sign of concussion. Take your child to the hospital immediately.

>> **Elbow and joint dislocation:** Some dads aren't aware of how delicate a baby is. In some ways your child is really robust. In other ways, things break or get damaged. And elbows and joints are one of those other ways. When you move your baby, never pull him up by the hand. His wrist, elbow and shoulder aren't strong enough to cope with the strain of being pulled, and dislocation and even fracturing can occur. (One of my kids was the unfortunate recipient of this when I danced a little exuberantly with her and dislocated her elbow!) Always lift a baby with one arm underneath the bub, and the hand supporting

the neck and shoulders. As your baby grows more strength, head support is less necessary. But even when they're older, swinging a toddler by his arms can cause serious injury.

>> **Squished fingers:** Your little one might reach out as you close a door or drawer. Hands and fingers can be easily crushed — or at least squished — so take care when closing anything with baby in reach.

>> **Swallowing foreign objects:** Your little one is guaranteed to pick things up and put them in his mouth. It's what babies do. Swallowed objects, choking, accidental poisoning, and even objects lodged in the ears and nose can cause serious injury and even death. Small batteries, a pin or needle, or even cat food (or, worse, cat litter) can all find their way into baby tummies or intestines. Keep stuff clear of your baby. Maintain a clean space. And watch what your bub is picking up and mouthing. And if you're worried, get medical help right away.

REMEMBER

If in doubt about anything to do with your child's health, being safe rather than sorry is best, so visit your GP. For any of the following injuries, get yourself to the hospital quickly:

>> Anaphylactic shock from food allergy or bee sting, where the face or mouth swells and your child has trouble breathing

>> Bite from a snake, spider or another animal

>> Car accident

>> Convulsions

>> Eye injuries

>> Electric shocks

>> Swallowing of poisons, toxic material or prescription medicines that were not prescribed for your child

Emergency phone numbers

Make sure you have the emergency numbers for your state or territory handy:

>> **Ambulance:** 000 (112 will also work from a mobile)

>> **healthdirect (ACT, NSW, NT, SA, TAS, WA):** 1800 022 222 (24 hours, seven days per week)

>> **Nurse-on-call (VIC):** 1300 60 60 24 (24 hours, seven days per week)

>> **13 HEALTH (QLD):** 13 HEALTH or 13 43 25 84 (24 hours, seven days per week)

>> **Poisons Information Hotline:** 13 11 26 (24 hours, seven days per week)

>> **Parentline (NT and QLD):** 1300 30 1300 (8 am to 10 pm, seven days per week) to talk anonymously about any concerns regarding parenting and children; also check the website — www.parentline.com.au

>> **Parentline (VIC):** 13 22 89 (8 am to midnight, seven days per week) for parents and carers of children from birth to 18 years old, offering confidential and anonymous counselling and support on parenting issues

First aid kit

Keep a well-stocked first aid kit to deal with injuries. If you haven't got a first aid kit, check with your health care provider or ambulance service such as St Johns for sources where you can buy certified kits.

TIP

If you haven't done so, consider taking an infant and child first aid and CPR course. It can literally save the life of your child or the lives of others. If you haven't done a general CPR course for a while, getting a refresher by attending an infant and baby CPR course may also be a good idea.

Diagnosing a serious illness

The good news is that the worst illnesses most children cop are colds, the odd ear infection or a tummy bug. But some children have to cope with much worse. As an involved dad, you can probably spot the first signs of a serious illness, because you know your child inside out and can tell when something's not right. But now and then you might not notice a thing — until . . .

REMEMBER

If you miss the signs of illness in your child, don't beat yourself up. Unless you're a medical doctor, some signs are hard to spot. (And if you are a medical doctor, still be gentle with yourself. We all make mistakes now and then.)

Confirming your child has a chronic illness, such as asthma or diabetes, a genetic disorder or a disease such as cancer takes a doctor's diagnosis. Seeing your little child being admitted to hospital is stressful and anxiety-inducing, but fortunately lots of support is available.

If this kind of thing happens when your child is older, your child may be very frightened or blaming himself for the chaos his illness is causing in your lives. Try to be as open and honest with him as you can about his health and how you feel, and be available to answer any questions he puts to you.

CHECK
THE NET

The following organisations can help you in the event of your child being diagnosed with a serious illness. Don't be afraid to ask for help if you need it — think of the good it might do your child.

In Australia, you can contact the following:

» Cancer Connect (available via the Cancer Council) on 13 11 20 or www.cancer. org.au/support-and-services/support-groups/cancer-connect

» Diabetes Australia at www.diabetesaustralia.com.au and National Diabetes Services Scheme at www.ndss.com.au

» National Asthma Council Australia at www.nationalasthma.org.au

Preparing for the End

To learn that your precious child has a life-limiting illness is possibly the toughest thing you may have to go through in your life. Anger, confusion, denial, helplessness, despair — you may experience every negative emotion you can imagine. The impact it might have on your relationship is enormous too. Staying strong for your partner and child when you feel like falling apart will be hard, but with little steps you *can* do it. Take things one day at a time. Just remember that staying strong doesn't mean showing no emotion. Instead, it means being vulnerable, and always being available to provide support and a shoulder to cry on.

Taking care till the end

Some may think it's a good idea not to frighten a child with a terminal illness with the knowledge that he's going to die. But *palliative care* professionals — those who care for people at the end of their lives — say communicating with your child honestly and openly will help allay some of his fears rather than cause them. Your child may be very confused about what's going on, and talking honestly and planning for the future can help put your child's mind at rest. He may be concerned about why you and your partner are so sad, may blame himself for your sadness, or be worried about his pets or schoolwork. Reassure him that it's not his fault that you're upset and be open to answering any questions he may have.

For inspiration, have a look at an amazing blog that documents the journey of Kyah, who passed away after a 500-day battle against cancer at the age of nearly three: kyahsjourney.livejournal.com.

Talk to your health care team about palliative care options for your child. Care can be at home, in hospital or in a children's hospice (in Australia only). These health professionals can help you talk to your child about what he's facing in an age-appropriate manner.

These ideas may also help you get through this seemingly impossible time:

>> Enlist the support of family and friends to help with tasks such as laundry, food preparation, feeding pets and so on. They can also babysit your other children if you have them, when you need to be at the hospital or hospice.

>> Look after yourself, rest and eat well when you can.

>> Talk to counsellors or chaplains at your hospital. Your care team can put you in touch with them. Involve your partner and other children if you like.

>> Find out if you child has any special activities they would like to do. Perhaps you can take a trip to the beach together as a family, or visit a special place together.

>> Write in a journal, take photographs and revisit old photographs with your child. Make memories.

>> Cry, shout, stamp your feet. It's okay to be angry, to need time to yourself and to grieve.

>> Don't let anyone hurry you into making any decisions about anything. Take your time and do things at your own pace.

Where to care for your little one

Palliative care is specialised care for people who have a terminal or life-limiting illness. Palliative care professionals not only take into account the stages that the body goes through as it shuts down, but also how the patient and his family are coping and dealing with this most traumatic event. For adults, most palliative care takes place in a hospital or hospice, which is a special facility for palliative care.

Hospices

Hospices sound like they are scary places, but the staff make every effort to make them comfortable, safe places for families in times of great stress, and crying out loud in a corridor is considered quite normal!

Australia has three hospices just for children — Bear Cottage in Sydney, Very Special Kids in Melbourne and Hummingbird House in Brisbane. Each is specially set up to deal with children and their families in a warm, loving environment where kids' needs come first. They often organise activities for kids with their families.

**CHECK
THE NET**

See more about these hospices at their websites:

>> Bear Cottage www.bearcottage.chw.edu.au

>> Very Special Kids www.vsk.org.au

>> Hummingbird House www.hummingbirdhouse.org.au

Home

Of course, you can also consider caring for your child at home, with assistance from palliative care workers, depending on the type of illness or injury your child has, and which services are available to you.

REMEMBER

You may be overwhelmed by having to make a decision about where your child will spend his last days. Take your time. Talk it through with your partner. Don't hurry into a decision.

Letting family and friends know

Dealing with the devastating news that your child has a life-limiting illness is hard enough without having to tell friends and family. Ultimately, this is something only you'll know how to do and when the time is right to tell others.

Once you have told them, people will usually be only too happy to help out with any errands that need to be done, and with cooking, laundry and the like, which may be in the too-hard basket for you right now.

REMEMBER

If it's just too hard to tell people, perhaps you could tell someone in your immediate family who can do this for you. Don't force yourself to do anything you don't want to do right now. Just getting through each moment is challenging enough.

You may have to break the news to your other children or nieces and nephews, and here I give you some pointers:

>> Be honest. Only tell your children what you believe to be true.

>> Be somewhere safe where you won't be interrupted (put your phone on silent), and be sure you have the children's full attention. They'll know it's important just by the way you carry yourself.

>> Anticipate that there will be tough questions to answer, but answer them as honestly as you can. Trying to soften the blow may mean your children are upset even more when things get messy.

>> Give small pieces of information that the children can chew over. They don't need to know all the ins and outs of cancer treatment, for example, or anything too detailed.

>> It may take a while for the information to get through. Give the children time to digest what they've heard, and be available to answer any other questions they may have in the coming days and weeks.

>> Give lots of cuddles, and let your children know it's okay to be upset.

>> Reassure your children that it's not their fault that this is happening to their sibling or cousin.

Seeking help

You'll have a lot of questions and be feeling all over the place. Knowing someone is available who can guide you and your partner through your grief helps. While everyone grieves in a different way, it can help to talk it through with people who can share their knowledge and help you on your journey.

In Australia, these organisations can help:

>> The Compassionate Friends Australia (with chapters in every state and territory) www.tcfa.org.au

>> Grief Australia www.grief.org.au

>> SANDS (Stillbirth and Newborn Death Support) www.sands.org.au

>> National Association of Loss and Grief www.nalag.org.au

>> Feel the Magic (support for kids and teenagers when a parent dies) www.feelthemagic.org.au

Dealing with the Unthinkable

When a child dies, we lose more than a person we loved — we lose the promise that person brought with him. It can threaten our identity as fathers. We blame ourselves, because as fathers we're supposed to protect our children and look after them, ensuring they're well. The death of a child cannot be approached rationally. You can only acknowledge your feelings and thoughts, many of which may not make any sense.

What to do, what not to do

Men grieve differently from women, so while our partners may find it easy to go to friends or family for support, it may not be so easy for you (or vice versa). It may take a little longer for some dads to really process feelings or some may not know how life is supposed to carry on without their child.

Here are some suggestions for getting through this difficult time:

>> Talk to your partner — even if it's just to say you don't want to talk. Let her know if you need some space, or a hug, or to just sit together.

>> Being physical can help. Go for a long walk, a bike ride, or play some sport. Being outdoors close to nature can be restorative and help you process your feelings too.

>> Try not to let yourself become isolated. Sure, you want space, but shutting everyone out is not going to help you in the long run. Let people know you need space for a bit.

>> Keeping busy really works for some guys who are grieving. Creating a memorial or starting a project can distract you from the all-encompassing nature of grief.

>> Try to look after yourself. Eat, sleep and shower. Though they may make you feel good in the short term, avoid drugs and alcohol.

>> Get counselling. Seriously do this. It takes a real man to own the fact that he needs help. So own up to it and get the counsel you need.

Saying goodbye

Take time with your child to say goodbye, to hold him, and to let other members of your family see and hold him too. You can ask your funeral director to arrange to have photographs of your child taken by a tasteful, sensitive photographer. You'll probably feel a bit hesitant about this, but it can be a healing experience for you to look back and remember holding your child.

All cultures have a funeral tradition for good reason — the ritual of saying good-bye to a loved one who has died is a very powerful and healing process. Funerals encourage us to confront our grief and to express how we feel about our loved one. A funeral also marks that child's place among his family.

When a baby is stillborn (dies *in utero* after 20 weeks gestation) or dies shortly after birth, the law requires that a funeral must take place and that the baby be buried in a cemetery or cremated. In Australia, some hospitals can arrange the funeral for you. However, SANDS (Stillbirth And Newborn Death Support) recommend having a family arranged funeral because hospital arranged funerals sometimes take control out of the family's hands, leaving the family little choice about what happens at the funeral, or even when the funeral's held.

For your baby's funeral, consider music to be played, songs, poems or other readings. You can have your baby's funeral at home, and can transport your baby from the hospital, home and to the cemetery.

REMEMBER

There's no hurry to do anything. Don't feel forced into doing anything you don't want to do. Take your time and decide when you feel you're ready.

CHECK THE NET

For more help, see www.sands.org.au. The organisation provides peer-to-peer counselling — that's people who have been through the death of a baby supporting others.

Is there such a thing as 'moving on'?

Each parent and person grieves differently for the child they've lost. The term 'moving on' implies that the intensity of feeling you had for the child you've lost fades and the significance of that child also fades. Organisations helping parents grieve report that no parent ever forgets the loss of a child. Some parents report that for them, they haven't moved on, but the way they feel is different. The child they've lost, whether he be 12 weeks gestation, stillborn or a teenager when he died, is still a big part of his parents' lives and a part of their family, and they celebrate the impact he had on their hearts.

Chapter **18**

Disabilities, Disorders and Special Conditions

E very father wants his child to be happy and healthy. Fathers want their children to experience everything, to have every opportunity and to be able to do anything they want to do. But for some children, that world of possibilities is limited by illness, injury, or an inherited disorder or condition.

Although medical science and technology can help improve the mobility, hearing and sight of a disabled child, and our more enlightened society can give children with disabilities the same rights and advantages that non-disabled children have, it's still a hard road for many dads.

But where to start? How do you discover your child has a disability? And what do you do about it? Once you have a diagnosis, what do you do then? In this chapter, I offer some suggestions along the way, with tips for finding help and knowing your speech pathologist from your occupational therapist. I also give you a heads-up on how having a child with a disability may change your lifestyle.

What Is a Disability, Anyway?

A *disability* is a condition, disorder or disease that disables the person from taking part in one or more life activities. The disability stops the person from doing what other people can do, whether it be walking, listening, grasping ideas or talking. Disabilities can be physical or mental. Children with disabilities are sometimes called *special (or additional) needs* children.

Knowing when something is wrong with your baby

Some children are born with a noticeable disability. Congenital abnormalities (also known as birth defects) or genetic disorders that manifest themselves physically, such as Down Syndrome, will be pretty obvious when the child is born. These problems may have been picked up during the pregnancy.

But other disabilities aren't so obvious and it may be a while before they make themselves known. Disabilities such as visual and hearing impairment, learning disabilities and neuro-divergence won't be apparent for months, sometimes years.

Sometimes you can just tell when something's not right. Perhaps your baby doesn't recognise toys or shapes, perhaps she doesn't seem to hear or respond to your voice the way other babies respond to their dads. Perhaps she doesn't try to crawl or move when other kids her age are already running. Or perhaps it's just a feeling you get, your intuition telling you things aren't quite right.

Your first port of call should be your child health nurse or GP. Discuss your concerns and see if you can be referred to a specialist such as a paediatrician or psychologist to pinpoint what the problem might be. If your GP or child nurse tries to fob you off with an 'I think she looks fine', and you're sure she's not, stand your ground. Your child isn't able to stick up for herself the way you are. Your job is to advocate for your child and get her the help you feel she needs. If you don't trust and have confidence in your GP or child nurse to take your concerns seriously, try another GP until you find one you feel comfortable with.

It may pay to track your child's progress before going to see your child nurse or GP, so you have something concrete to show them when you have your appointment. Keep doing this until you've spoken to a specialist and have decided on a course of action or had a diagnosis made.

Waiting for a diagnosis can be stressful, but try to stay positive for your little one. Don't blame yourself or your partner for any perceived problems — neither of you is at fault.

Once a diagnosis is made, you and your specialist can decide on a course of action and get your child started on medication or treatment if required.

Physical disabilities

A physical disability is a permanent disability that restricts body movement or mobility in some way. Some physical disabilities are caused by genetic disorders, a *congenital abnormality* or birth defect that has developed while growing in the womb, an illness such as meningitis, or as the result of an injury to the spine, brain or limbs.

The main forms of physical disability include:

>> **Brain and spinal injuries:** These injuries are mainly caused by an accident that breaks or damages the spinal cord, or causes damage to the brain. They can cause paralysis or mental impairment.

>> **Cerebral palsy:** This is a condition where parts of the brain are damaged either during pregnancy, during birth, or as the result of a lack of oxygen.

>> **Disabilities of the senses:** Children can be born with visual or hearing impairments because of congenital abnormality or a genetic disorder. These senses can also be affected by disease after birth.

>> **Muscular dystrophy:** This is a genetic disorder in which muscle strength and function deteriorate over time. Most commonly seen in babies and young boys, some forms aren't diagnosed until early adulthood. Duchenne muscular dystrophy is the most common form and it affects mainly boys (Duchenne muscular dystrophy is rare in girls). About one-third of those affected also have some sort of learning difficulty. Not only are muscles in the limbs affected, but also heart muscles, which eventually affects life expectancy.

>> **Spina bifida:** A congenital abnormality, which means it happens while the baby is growing in the womb, spina bifida literally means 'split spine' and happens in the early weeks of pregnancy. As the spine develops, vertebrae grow and close around the spinal cord, protecting it. In the case of spina bifida, the vertebrae don't close completely and in some types of spina bifida, the spinal cord and *meninges* (a system of membranes which envelop the central nervous system) protrude from the back. As a result, the spinal cord can be damaged and messages sent to and from the brain get confused. Paralysis, incontinence, loss of sensation and a build-up of fluid on the brain called *hydrocephalus* can occur.

CHECK THE NET

To find out more about any of these physical disabilities, see these websites.

>> Association Children with a Disability www.acd.org.au

>> Cerebral Palsy Australia www.cpaustralia.com.au

>> Deaf Children Australia www.deafchildrenaustralia.org.au

>> Muscular Dystrophy Foundation Australia mdaustralia.org.au

>> Vision Australia www.visionaustralia.org

REMEMBER

Australia also has associations in individual states and territories that you can find on the internet using a search engine, and there are plenty more. The ones listed here are just a starting point. Organisations exist for every challenging condition your child might experience, from ADHD to eczema.

Intellectual disabilities

Just as congenital abnormalities and genetic disorders can affect a child's body, they can also affect a child's intellectual abilities — the ability to think, reason, communicate, control emotions and grasp ideas. Increasingly people with intellectual disabilities are being integrated into mainstream society, where they're appreciated for their individual attributes rather than judged by their disability.

Some intellectual disabilities can be diagnosed at birth, or even before. Others won't be obvious until your child is a few years old, or at school.

Some of the most common syndromes and disorders that can cause intellectual disability include the following:

>> **Autism**, which is also known as autism spectrum disorder because the range of severity differs from person to person. A person with autism may have trouble making sense of the world, and find it difficult to communicate, cope in social situations, or control her emotions. The causes of autism are unknown.

>> **Down Syndrome**, which is caused by an extra bit of chromosome being replicated in cell division very early on after the mother's ovum has been fertilised, means that a child with Down Syndrome has an extra chromosome in her body. Children with Down Syndrome have varying degrees of mental and sometimes physical disability.

Intellectual disability can also be caused by drinking, drug abuse or illness during pregnancy, an infection such as meningitis, head injuries, a lack of oxygen during birth or during an accident like a near-drowning. Other rare genetic conditions such as Prader-Willi Syndrome can also cause intellectual disability.

With a very small child, doctors and health professionals often use the term *developmental delay* rather than labelling the child as intellectually disabled.

CHECK THE NET

For more about specific intellectual disabilities, see these websites:

>> Autism Spectrum Australia www.autismspectrum.org.au

>> The Brain Foundation site has links to common and not so common brain disorders, with support information www.brainaustralia.org.au

Multiple disabilities

Most disorders, illnesses or injuries are rarely limited to only one part of the body, so in some cases a child with a particular problem will have more than one disability. For example, Down Syndrome affects cognitive abilities as well as physical growth. Children with Down Syndrome also have a higher risk of having congenital heart defects, recurrent ear infections and thyroid dysfunctions as well as other conditions.

Getting formal confirmation

In some cases, the specialist you've been referred to will be able to tell you if your child has a specific disability or a range of disabilities, and may be able to tell you how the disabilities were caused.

In other cases, a diagnosis isn't clear and your child may continue to undergo tests, which can be a fairly traumatic time.

Once you have confirmation about a disability, it's time to put a plan in place to manage the condition, through medication, physical treatment or getting any equipment you may need like a wheelchair. In some situations, you'll be given a case worker to help you.

TIP

Support groups and organisations for almost every condition, illness and disability that exists are available. Contact the organisations listed earlier in this chapter, or consult your specialist or care worker. Having support from people who've been through what you're going through now, who may be able to share information and strategies, or help you get access to specialist services is invaluable. Sometimes even just knowing that you are not alone with a condition and discussing what it was like for other parents can be a huge help.

What comes next?

You're in for yet another journey as part of your fatherhood experience. Treatment, therapy and learning about the fathering your additional needs child will probably require is going to take some extra effort. A positive reframe is that your child is more capable than you know, and there are real opportunities for you to support your child to develop. Additionally, this is going to lead to your own personal growth and development. Chances are, it could help you become a more compassionate person, and an amazing father.

REMEMBER

You can find so many inspiring stories from fathers whose children have additional needs. Common themes include the fact that looking after a child with additional needs is in many ways no different from looking after typically developing child. Babies and children with additional needs all cry, laugh, eat, soil their nappies and want to be loved. When dealing with the limiting factors of their children's condition, these dads have often challenged doctors or therapists about their expectations of what children with a particular disability may or may not be able to do. In other words, they've found their children are not nearly as limited as professionals often suggest. Often parents have managed to achieve amazing results with their children by finding alternative ways around barriers that have allowed their children to participate in what life has to offer, just like any other child would. This doesn't mean they've become world-class coaches, driving their children to success. Rather, they've offered love and support, and given their kids the encouragement they need to develop mastery over their condition, their environment and their circumstances, often showing more resilience than typically developing children in the same circumstance.

Here are some general tips on living with a child with additional needs for both you and your family:

>> **Work with your child's strengths and interests.** What does your child like doing? You can incorporate dancing, art, footy and water play into your child's therapy or treatment plan. Does she like to be hands-on? Or does your child need a strict routine to give her security? Being aware of the way your child learns best and the routines she needs is a key dad-skill to develop.

>> **Involve your child whenever you can with simple tasks.** This could include food preparation, doing the vacuuming or making the bed. Break instructions down into simple bite-sized pieces and give heaps of praise for her efforts. Involvement continues to be a key word throughout your fathering. So does competence-building.

>> **Get support.** A lot of support organisations out there can put you in touch with other fathers and guide you to find funding, treatments and even respite care.

>> **Give lots of encouragement and support for your child.** For example, encourage her when she accomplishes a new skill or takes on a new challenge.

>> **Focus on the things your child can do, rather than what she can't.**

>> **Learn as much as you can about your child's disability.** Knowledge is power.

>> **Have realistic expectations about your child's development**. This also might mean challenging any preconceived limitations people place on your child about what she can and can't do. Perhaps there's a way she can accomplish a task — after all, you know your child best.

Help, My Child Has Additional Needs!

In the past, many people used words such as 'disabled' for children with additional needs. But these days, things have become more inclusive and oriented towards focusing on what people can do, rather than what they can't. If your child has additional needs, you'll probably become more sensitive to the way you speak about people with additional challenges or needs. In general, the use of terms such as 'handicapped', 'disabled', 'physically challenged' or 'special needs' is unhelpful and stigmatising. Instead, saying your child has some 'additional needs' is preferable. Another preferred term is that your child is experiencing 'non-typical' development.

Finding out that your child does have additional needs — whether physical or intellectual — can bring out all sorts of frustrations and disappointments. This is normal. Talk to a compassionate advisor about how you're feeling.

Imagining the hard road ahead of you can be devastating, and you may even blame yourself for whatever the problem is. But another way to look at your child's disability is as a way to motivate yourself to help your child develop in creative and unexpected ways. You can have moments of 'what if?' and occasional self-pity. But it's not about you. It's about your child, and helping her thrive.

Adjusting your expectations

When you first find out you're going to be a father, thinking of your child as a way to fix all the things that went wrong in your own life, or wanting your child to have more opportunities or career options than you did, is tempting. Perhaps you imagined your child becoming an astronaut, concert pianist or anything that she may dream of being.

So getting used to the idea that your blind child is never going to see the world, your face or her own children (unless amazing leaps forward occur in technology) may take some time. But then again, would Stevie Wonder have become the amazing artist he is if he wasn't blind? You never know what's in store for your offspring, which is really no different from the experience all other parents have.

Going into fatherhood, we also expect that our children grow up and one day leave home. Living an independent life may not be possible for children with a severe intellectual disability who need one-on-one care, 24 hours per day. This realisation can take quite a while to sink in, so cut yourself some slack and allow emotions and frustration to come and go. And find someone — a professional if necessary — to talk to. Talking your thoughts and emotions through can make a world of difference.

DISABLED IN ONE WAY — VERY ABLE IN OTHERS

Disabled is a misleading term. For one thing, it defines a person by what they're not able to do.

What do we most remember about Beethoven, Louis Braille or Stephen Hawking? They've all achieved incredible things, far beyond what many folk without their challenges have done! The great composer Beethoven gradually went deaf, but was still able to create incredible music — eventually without any sense of hearing. Louis Braille was blinded by an accident as a young child and went on to create a way for the blind to read with their fingers. Stephen Hawking had a form of motor neurone disease called *amyotrophic lateral sclerosis* and was given only a few years to live when his condition was diagnosed in his early twenties in 1963. (He died in 2018 at age 76.) As the disease progressed, Hawking became wheelchair bound and needed a computer to communicate. Despite these breathtaking barriers, he produced ground-breaking work in the field of theoretical physics.

Other famous people who have shown that the difficulties life threw their way don't stop success include actress Marlee Matlin, who went deaf from a childhood illness; Helen Keller, who proved being deaf, blind and mute couldn't stop her getting a university degree; and Dylan Alcott, who despite being born with a tumour wrapped around his spinal cord that left him a paraplegic, went on win multiple Grand Slams in singles tennis (among many other achievements).

But incredible things can be said for accomplishing outcomes that are relevant to your child's world. The triumph of an autistic child who, with time, patience and the right support, is able to communicate her needs and ideas to a range of people, feels like a huge achievement. Kids with additional needs can teach us some of life's most valuable lessons — that life isn't always a competition, for example.

And who's to say that your child won't be able to do what most experts think she can't do? You may find that your little one completely shatters your ideas of what it means to have additional needs and achieves much more than you ever imagined.

Finding help, assistance and resources

Knowing where to go to find assistance is a minefield. Start with your case worker, paediatrician or GP, the support organisations listed earlier in this chapter, and the following resources:

>> To access emotional, practical and financial support for carers of children with additional needs, go to www.carergateway.gov.au.

>> To learn about support programs and payments, check out www.servicesaustralia.gov.au/caring-for-child-with-disability.

>> The Association for Children with a Disability is an organisation based in Victoria, but their advice is universal: www.acd.org.au.

>> My Time supports parents of children with disabilities through forums and links to specific sites for disabilities: www.mytime.net.au.

>> The Raising Children Network, supported by the Australian Government and other agencies, has some great resources on bringing up a child with a disability: raisingchildren.net.au/disability.

Also see the health department in your state or territory for more information.

Working with Disabilities and Additional Needs

Now that you know what you're dealing with, it's time to get into solution mode — something dads are great at! You can shine as dad for your disabled child in numerous ways, such as by making a little ramp for the wheelchair or coming up with a computer program that assists your child's communication. No doubt you'll have many skills you can readily use to create a better experience for your baby and child.

Caring for your special baby

You're bringing your baby home from the hospital for the first time. It should be a time of great excitement, but you're probably overwhelmed with the challenges of not only looking after a new, small human being, but also a new small human being with additional needs. These tips may help you get through this time:

>> While you may still experience an emotional roller-coaster, try not to forget that you have a small child who needs all the love and nurturing you can give her as she becomes aware of her world. As for any newborn child, this time is fleeting, so take some time to admire those little fingers, those chubby little legs, and enjoy the new addition to your lives.

>> Get family or close friends to support you, by perhaps fending off unwanted visitors, organising appointments with health workers, or just doing your laundry. Let someone look after you for a while, just as you need to look after your baby.

>> Ask for help if you need it. Struggling on bravely because you can't ask for a hand is pointless. Plenty of people are around to help you.

>> Keep records of health visits, of your baby's daily progress or any notes you need in one central place so you can grab them next time you need to talk to your health workers.

Getting help from health professionals

Some of the health professionals you might meet when caring for your special needs child include:

>> An *audiologist*, who assesses your child's hearing and can recommend treatment or hearing aids.

>> An *occupational therapist*, or OT, who assesses how well your child is able to perform day-to-day tasks, such as dressing or brushing teeth. Your OT may also assess how you'll manage getting from place to place if transport is a bit more complicated with your little one. The aim of an OT is to help your child become involved in all aspects of day-to-day life, and increase her independence and wellbeing.

>> A *psychologist*, who assesses your child's mental health and cognitive skills. Psychologists may help with strategies for managing emotional and behavioural problems.

>> *Speech therapists* and *speech pathologists,* who assess how well your child can communicate with others, and figure out ways to either improve her speech, or find alternative ways of communicating, such as electronic devices or sign language.

Other health professionals you may need include physiotherapists, neurodevelopmental therapists and dietitians.

Living with a disability

It doesn't matter what the condition, illness, injury or syndrome your child has, finding out that your child is not the child you had hoped she would be can be devastating. On top of managing your own feelings and frustration, you may also be sensitive to what other people's reactions are when they see your child. As with all feelings, give yourself time to work through them (rather than ignore or suppress them) and seek help if you need to. Most importantly, keep communicating with your partner, who's likely to be feeling the same thing.

TIP

Be aware of what triggers negative feelings, such as going to doctor's appointments or seeing friends' children. Then you can prepare yourself and work out strategies for coping with any negative emotions.

Living with a non-typically developing child is often a bit more involved than living with a typically developing child, but you can do things to make it easier. Keep the following in mind:

>> Do your own research. Knowledge is power. Use online sources to find out if any devices, techniques or therapies are available that could help your child (or you) become more independent or make life easier.

>> Set small achievable goals for your child, as you would any child. Pushing her too hard will only leave both of you frustrated. Competence needs are fragile.

>> If your child is going to day care or school, talk to teachers and administration staff well in advance, so they can build ramps, obtain resources and apply for any special teacher aide staff that may be required.

>> Keep in touch with teaching staff about your child's progress. This helps you, your child and the teachers, who can personalise a program for your child.

Changing your lifestyle

Having a child with additional needs will probably mean you have to adjust your lifestyle to suit her development. For example:

>> Depending on the level of care your child needs, you or your partner may have to give up working outside the home.

>> If your child uses a wheelchair, you'll need to renovate your home to make doors wide enough to get the wheelchair through, install ramps rather than steps, and fit equipment for lifting the chair in and out of vehicles.

>> With one less income and more expenses, your family may be under extra financial pressure, so seek out any subsidies or allowances you can from government agencies. See 'Finding help, assistance and resources', earlier in this chapter, for links.

>> You may need to go to more doctors' appointments and trips to the hospital. If you live far from a hospital, it may mean you need to move house to be closer to medical facilities.

>> Some children need 24-hour, seven days a week care, which is hard work. You may need a dedicated carer or specialist assistance to organise care in your home.

REMEMBER

If your child is disabled and needs a lot of care, you must take some time to take care of yourself and your partner. Talk to your health workers about respite care, or get support from family and friends so you have a little time off every now and then.

Sharing the love

If I've used one word over and over again in this book, it's *support*. Nothing beats having people to help share not only your problems, but also the love. When your child is disabled, small victories are to be had along the way. With other parents in similar situations, you have a whole lot more people to share those successes with.

IN THIS CHAPTER

» Saving a failing relationship — what you can do

» Realising that your marriage has gone under — what next?

» Coping as a single dad

» Looking after your children as the primary caregiver

» Explaining a new love in your life to your kids

Chapter **19**

Divorce and Separation

C reating a strong, stable, healthy long-term relationship is hard. As time has passed, the nature of our marriages and partnerships has changed. Today's marriages and long-term relationships demand more of us as partners than ever before. We're expected to be all things to our partner — and we expect that of them too. We want them to be our confidante, our lover, our financial adviser, our friend, our walking and sporting partner, our travel guide, our cook and cleaner, and more. (And, once again, that's reciprocated). We look to our partners to fill a lot of roles others once did.

Additionally, society has increased its demands on us and who we are. For many of us, work comes home. Emails are expected to be answered at all hours. Once the kids are in bed and dinner is cleaned up, an expectation often exists that more work will be done. And the continued financial pressures that young families experience as they try to get a foothold in the property market or simply provide a roof over their family's head are substantial. All of this pressure (and more) puts strain on you and your relationships.

Besides all of that, consistently being nice, compassionate, helpful, forgiving and understanding of what's going on for your partner can be difficult — and, again, just as difficult for your partner to do the same for you. It's hard not to be selfish, biased and demanding. Marriages and relationships aren't easy — even the best of them. As a result, some marriages and relationships won't survive the stresses of parenting, financial worry, the frenetic pace of life and the need for your own space.

Kindness and compassion is needed during this time. A relationship that breaks down is devastating for everyone, particularly when children are involved. As a father in this situation, life can feel pretty rough and frustrating. But being a great father doesn't end with your relationship ceasing. In fact, you're needed *even more* here — so long as you can be a safe, healthy influence in your child's life.

You're the adult here, the dad, and where you have control and the power to make decisions for your family, your children don't. They may be confused, blaming themselves and frightened about what the future brings for them. They may be hoping you and their mother can patch things up. It's important to tread carefully, for their sakes.

In this chapter, I offer some ways to help save an ailing marriage or relationship and avoid the devastation a breakup causes. But if your relationship's beyond help and it's time to call it a day, I guide you through the separation and divorce process in terms of how it impacts you as a dad. And I give you some advice on surviving your new life as a single dad, whether you're primary caregiver or not.

Marriage on the Rocks!

A myth has been perpetuated since divorce laws changed in the 1970s that divorce is too easy and people can walk away from their relationships whenever they want these days. While divorce did become easier to obtain (which wasn't necessarily a bad thing, based on what too many people had to endure in toxic relationships), I've not met anyone yet who shrugged their shoulders and walked away from a marriage or long-term commitment as if it were nothing — and even more so when children are involved.

Every relationship goes through difficult times, but knowing what you can do about it can mean the difference between calling it quits or building a better relationship than you and your partner had before.

What you can do

If your marriage or relationship is going through a rough patch, it's time for some honesty and a whopping dose of humility. Take a close look at yourself and your part in the difficulties the two of you are experiencing. Of course, it takes two to tango and two to make a relationship work, but here you need to focus on the part you as an individual play in it. You need to be able to take full responsibility for your actions in the relationship. Ultimately, you have full control only over your own actions. You can't make someone else do what you want. So to avoid further frustration, start looking at the man in the mirror to see what he can change before pointing the finger at your partner.

To be able to look at your role in the relationship objectively, let go of negative emotions such as anger and blame. Being righteously indignant, or holding on to the feeling that you've been wronged, doesn't help you fix whatever the problem is. If you're feeling guilty or ashamed, try to let that go as well. Clear your head, sit down and make a list of what you really want from your relationship. Are you being fair in your expectations? Do you even know what you want?

Now, ask your partner to make a similar list of what she wants from the relationship. Are you aligned? Do you have the same values? Are you heading in the same direction? Are you able to provide that for her? If she wants to be a world champion sport star and you want her to be a stay-at-home mum, chances are this isn't going to work so well. It could be that you want to raise your children with a strong faith and she is firming up in her atheism. These types of challenges will be harder to work through and overcome.

However, maybe she just wants a guy who is present and involved with her and the family more than a guy who's really great at *Grand Theft Auto.* Many differences are reconcilable once you both get really clear on what matters most to you and the relationship. Perhaps she wants a guy who prioritises hugs and connection more than beers with the boys. It could be that the shifts you each need to make are actually going to make you better people, and your life better as a family. Be open, listen gently and speak truthfully (and kindly).

Look at what you've both written in your lists of what you want from the relationship. If you've got a level of alignment, consider and keep these lists in mind as an inspirational goal for your relationship. Once you're clear about what you want, discuss your list (and her list) with your partner regularly — perhaps every Sunday morning over brekky. Remember that you and your partner are on the same side of the mediation table and the 'problem' in your relationship is on the other side. The process of getting your relationship back on track is much more productive if you work together, rather than getting wound up in a blame game.

TIP

Asking others for some feedback may also help. This can be pretty tough but a close friend will tell you straight up how he sees things. Keeping a clear head and seeing things objectively when your relationship is in a tailspin can be tricky. A third-party perspective may give you a more unbiased view of yourself and your relationship.

REMEMBER

Repairing a marriage takes time. If it took two years for things to deteriorate to the nasty place they are now, recognise that it's going to take more than two minutes or two hours (or even two days or two weeks) to get back on track. Vulnerability is tricky to show when you've been hurt. Trust is hard to rebuild when it's been broken. Try to be patient and realise things aren't going to magically happen overnight. Be conscious of, and patient about, how things are changing as a result of your efforts.

WARNING

You're an adult and a dad who is in the process of bringing up a child or children to be responsible, able to deal with their emotions, and have self-control. It, therefore, makes sense to demonstrate those qualities in yourself and not fight or bad mouth your partner in front of your children. Ever. Under any circumstances. This sort of behaviour places a lot of stress on a child and forces him to take sides, which isn't fair. If you need to let off some steam, find a place where you can be alone and do whatever helps you release some tension (in a safe way). Ideally, do something that's physically exhausting.

What you can both do

You can only change yourself — but if you get your partner working with you, the two of you can agree on ways to rebuild your relationship. Both of you have to be willing and able to make changes.

Here are some ideas:

>> Talk openly about what is and isn't working in your relationship. Rather than blaming the other person for what's wrong, try to explain things in terms of how you feel or think. If talking between yourselves about the relationship gets you nowhere, consider involving a relationship coach or relationship counsellor.

>> As a couple, come up with strategies for making things better. Write down your strategy. Assess how well you're sticking to it and figure out if you need to make some adjustments.

I recommend asking the following questions:

>> What's working?

>> What's not?

>> What's one thing we can work on over the next week or two?

Have this conversation every week. You can help each other stay on track with the following:

>> Make it a rule to emphasise gratitude for your partner.

>> Eat together at night, so you have a chance to talk about your day and catch up a little bit — without screens. Maybe go out for lunch or dinner every now and then.

>> Listen without interrupting your partner, even if you strongly disagree with what she's saying. When she says something you disagree with, get curious, not furious. Say something like, 'I'm seeing it so differently. Can you help me get what you mean a little more?'

>> Don't get complacent. Your relationship isn't going to fix itself without a little work from both of you. You both need to work on your relationship and keep at it.

CHECK THE NET

For relationship counselling contact Family & Relationship Services Australia (frsa.org.au) or Relationships Australia (relationships.org.au).

Where to go if all fails

Sometimes, despite all the efforts you've made to hold onto your relationship, it still fails.

The best-case scenario when a relationship comes to an end is that your relationship is amicable and you're both a daily feature of your children's lives, with that same loving bond with them.

However, if the relationship has ended badly or you've had to leave the family home, it can be very easy to slide into despair. Sure, you're not going to be the life of the party right now, and feeling rotten is normal, but if you have trouble getting out of that dark place and feel hopeless, you need to get help climbing back out. Feeling depressed and frustrated only holds you back from moving on and being a great dad. Your kids will be feeling confused, anxious and, if they're still young, potentially blaming themselves for what's happened. They need you right now and your job is to be there for them.

REMEMBER

Your role as a lover and partner is over, and it may hurt and be a painful blow to your ego and your feelings of competence as a human! But you're still the father of your children and this will always be the case. Your fatherhood journey doesn't end here, although you may have to take a different route.

You can access the following options for support and advice when your relationship's gone pear-shaped:

>> **Counsellor:** Get help dealing with the grief and emotions you have about the end of your relationship or marriage.

>> **Lawyer or legal aid:** Find out where you stand legally with regards to seeing your children, and what rights and obligations you have.

>> **Mediator:** Talk to someone who can assist with family group counselling sessions.

>> **Men's group:** Get support from men who have been through the same thing as you. (Men's groups are a bit rare and can be hard to find. Unfortunately, some have reputations for sowing seeds of contention and entitlement, so tread carefully here.)

Splitting Up

Your relationship, sad as it is, is beyond help. You and your partner can't see a way to stay together and have decided to split. Whether it's amicable or not, the end of a relationship means the start of a whole new world for you, your former partner and your children.

Moving out of the family home

You may find your relationship has taken a turn for the worse and you've had to leave the family home. As some men experience, you may end up haggling over shared assets and personal possessions and, of course, the tricky question of how best to manage your children's care.

Sorting out childcare arrangements and the distribution of assets is best done when the dust has settled at bit, not in the heat of the moment. Wait until you and your estranged are able to talk without antagonising each other, or ending the discussion in tears.

Understanding the divorce process

Now that you are separated, you may be thinking about getting divorced or dissolving your civil union, which puts a permanent end to your legal relationship. Get legal advice here. Don't try to do it on your own. And, if you can, agree with your ex that the needs of the kids will come first.

Making separation easier on your children

A separation can be quite tough as you struggle with all your feelings about the relationship ending, but your kids also need you. Try to offer them support and continue to nurture that loving relationship you've worked so hard at all this time.

Children react to separation and divorce in different ways. Some act out and will go 'off the rails'. Others become clingy and need reassurance you're not abandoning them. Some children blame themselves for what's happening. Others hide how they really feel and appear to be coping well.

However your child reacts to the news that you and your spouse aren't together any more, these tips will help get them through this traumatic time:

>> **Fighting in front of your kids is not okay.** Fighting in front of your kids is stressful, puts them in the middle of your fight and can dent their trust in you. Leave your kids out of any conflict you have with their mum — don't ask them which parent they'd like to live with, don't ask them to lock her out, and don't ask them for information about what she's doing.

>> **Don't lie to your child.** When you tell your child about what's going on, use neutral language, rather than blaming their mum or getting angry. Take the emotion out of what you're saying. Be honest and genuine with your children.

>> **Make sure they absolutely and completely understand that this was not their fault.** Reinforce with them that this was an issue that mummy and daddy couldn't work out. It can never, ever, be about them.

>> **Let your children know you're there for them.** You may be living away from home right now, but make it clear you're always able to talk to them. Be open and honest with any questions they may have and remember to take the emotion — anger, frustration, animosity — out of what you're saying, so you leave your children out of the conflict you're having.

CHECK THE NET

In Australia, the Family Relationships Online website provides help with family relationship issues, including advice on mediation for families who are separating or splitting up — go to www.familyrelationships.gov.au.

You're not just another statistic

Marriage and relationship breakdown is, sadly, quite common. In Australia, two in five marriages end in divorce. Note, however, that this is *all* marriages. Second, third and subsequent marriages are at significantly higher risk of divorce than first marriages. In fact, first marriages dissolve at a rate of a little under one in three. Second and subsequent marriages can break up at levels as high as two in three!

With these rates of divorce, you're clearly on a well-trodden path, but that doesn't mean it hurts any less, or that your kids aren't going to be hurt by it too. It may help you to know that many people are going about their ordinary day, having gotten over a divorce and having found great solutions to what was once a very messy situation for them.

On the other hand, even though separation and divorce aren't uncommon, every relationship breakdown, just like every relationship itself, is unique. The way that you cope with, and help your kids cope with, this tricky time in your lives is unique to your family.

REMEMBER

You may be able to find a support group near you. However, it's important that the group is a positive influence and not just an angry men's club. As tempting as it may be to rant and see yourself as a victim, it generally does nothing towards being a successful role model for your children. Separation and divorce are yet another opportunity for you to be the bigger man and for your own personal growth.

Finding good support

Finding someone to support you through this time is essential — a kind of 'breakup buddy'. You're probably getting all sorts of advice from all sorts of people, but they don't necessarily know what's best for you or your kids. You need someone who:

>> Can be honest with you, perhaps even a bit blunt at times

>> Is 100 per cent there for you when you need it

>> Isn't vindictive towards your ex

>> Knows how important it is you stay a strong role model and loving father to your children

REMEMBER

You can also turn to a counsellor or a men's group for advice and support. If you can't find a men's group in your area, try joining an online group.

WARNING

Avoid any group or professional who makes you feel like you're not being heard. Try to avoid groups who foster negative action towards any or particular organisation such as the family court.

When you find great support, hang onto it. The process of separation and divorce can take several years or more to get through, and you'll need ongoing support to keep you focused and moving forward.

Separating being a husband from being a father

Though the relationship with your partner is over, your relationship with your kids continues and will last for as long as you live. For many years to come, frustrations and difficulties may arise when dealing with your ex, but it helps no-one if you voice these feelings to your kids, who still have a loving relationship and bond with their mum, even if you don't.

At the same time, lying to your children isn't helpful. They deserve to know what's going on between the two most important people in their lives, but try not to couch the conflict in terms of who's at fault, or what one person did to another.

Instead, try to explain the situation to your kids by taking out the emotion. This, of course, is easier said than done and takes some practice. The trick is in choosing your words carefully. You may find it helpful thinking about or even writing down things before you talk to your children. Try hard to describe the situation in neutral terms.

This leaves your children to make up their own minds about what is happening, and it fosters a safe and stress-free environment for them to share their own concerns about what's happening. They'll be more likely to feel comfortable about asking questions and voicing how they feel about the situation.

Remembering You're Still Dad

With your family split in half you may be asking yourself how you can continue to be the stellar father you've been so far. Now you're either living away from your kids, which is the most common post-breakup situation, or their mother is away from the family home, what new responsibilities and roles do you have?

Who'll look after the kids?

Now that you and your partner are no longer living together, you'll need to work out who the children will live with as their primary caregiver and how the day-to-day care of your children will be managed.

You'll need to think about:

>> Who will your children live with most of the time?

>> How will your children get to and from school and other activities? Who will pick up a younger child from day care or kindergarten?

>> How often will the other parent be able to see the children?

>> Who will look after the children at weekends, school holidays and Christmas?

Day-to-day or *parental care*, which used to be called custody, can be shared between the two of you, with time spent at both houses equally, or mainly at one parent's house with visits to the other's house.

If you can agree with your former partner amicably about day-to-day care and time spent with the other parent — called *contact* — then you don't need to go to court, you can work it out between you. You can write a non- binding *parenting plan* or *parenting agreement*, so both of you are singing from the same song sheet and your children know what's going on too. The court will also be satisfied that your children are in good hands as you go through the legal process of divorce.

But if you can't agree about day-to-day care and contact that the other parent has with the children, you'll need to get legal advice and take the matter to the Family Law Court and get a *parenting order* or *court order*. This is an order made by the court deciding who will take care of the children on a day-to-day basis, and when other people, which may include you, can see your kids. Even if you and your former partner have agreed amicably about the care of your children with a parenting agreement or parenting plan, you can take it one step further and have it formalised by the court with a parenting order.

Being a remote or part-time father

An unfortunate consequence of separation and divorce is that a large number of fathers are separated from their children. Separation should be no barrier to continuing to be a great dad and role model for your child or children.

Very little difference exists in your responsibilities as a father between being a non-resident father and being a living-at-home father.

REMEMBER

You don't have to be going through separation to be regarded as a remote father. Fathers who are away overseas on military service, fathers who are in prison, and dads who are very busy or travel often can also be considered remote fathers.

Here are some tips for continuing to be a great dad, even though you can't be there for every bedtime:

>> **Be punctual.** If you're expected at noon, be there at 11:55 am sharp. Waiting around for you can be very hard on a young child, especially one who doesn't understand why you don't live at home anymore. (But don't go crook at mum if she's a few minutes late. Compassion is king in these situations — so long as the lateness isn't intentionally divisive.)

>> **Don't slack off on all those fatherly duties you may have had when you were still living with your kids.** This includes discipline and encouraging their development. Be consistent with your rules and boundaries. As difficult as it may be, you also need to work hard to agree to some basic principles for disciplining your children with your ex. And, of course, keep going with the principles of parenting — provide your child with love and warmth, a secure and safe environment, and do lots of listening and talking with him.

>> **Foster a good working relationship with your child's mother.** Your child will pick up when things aren't going well between you two, so work hard at putting the anger, bitterness or frustrations behind you. If this is too hard, treat her like a valued client or colleague at work. You don't send them angry text messages when they get something wrong! Don't do that with your ex either.

>> **Keep your promises.** If you told your child that you'd be there on Thursday to pick him up after school, then do it.

>> **Take care of yourself, mentally and physically.** Being positive and happy is rough after separation and divorce, but it makes you a positive role model for your kids. Neglecting your basic needs (eating decent food, showering every day, getting some exercise and keeping your place tidy), or turning your place into a new bachelor pad is not a great situation for your children to spend time with you.

>> **Try to avoid falling into the trap of buying your kids special presents or taking them on special outings all the time.** This might be in an attempt to be the favourite parent or to ensure they love you, but 'Disneyland Dad' (the dad who does all the fun stuff all the time) can create challenges for mum if she's the only one doing the 'real' parenting. Remember, your kids love you unconditionally and the best gift you can give them is your time, your respect and your unconditional love.

>> **When you drop your child back to his mother's house, try not to draw out the goodbyes.** Don't act like you're about to go to the moon for a month. Normalise the situation by saying goodnight, that you love him and you'll see him very soon.

REMEMBER

Your child may be feeling abandoned, or resentful that you've left, or just plain confused about when he'll see you again. Being on time and a man of your word means your little one can trust in you and believe in what you say. Remind him that even though you don't live at his home anymore, you'll always be there for him.

Understanding contact arrangements

When you're not granted day-to-day care of your child or children, or it just works out better for your family situation that your children live with their mother, you'll have contact time with your kids.

Contact arrangements range from shared 50/50 (though you're not listed as the primary caregiver) to strict supervised access with time restraints in an enclosed area if the children are believed to be at risk.

At first it can be tough to accept you need to put special time aside to see your kids when you used to be around them all the time. Work hard to make the most of the time you've got with your little ones.

Here are some tips to make contact arrangements work smoothly for both parents and children:

» Communicate with anyone you need to about how the contact arrangements are working out. If they're not working, talk to your ex or lawyer about changing them.

» Don't complain to your children about the time or circumstances around your contact arrangements. They can't do anything about the arrangements and your complaining will just make them feel bad.

» If the time you have together is limited, plan what you're going to do well in advance by asking your children what they would like to do a few days beforehand.

» If you're going to be late or there's a change of plans, let people affected know as soon as you can.

» Keep a good working relationship with their mum. Your kids will pick up on any tensions between you and your ex and it will dampen their excitement.

» Keep your word. Don't let your kids down by not showing up, or by promising something you can't commit to, like a weekend at the beach, or a special gift.

» Do not ask your kids to spy on their mother for you. She's getting on with her life and so are you! Asking them to spy puts your kids in the middle of your conflict, which isn't fair for such little people to cope with. Your children love both of you — don't ask them to choose.

>> Do not bad mouth your former partner, even if you find out your partner does this about you — again, be the bigger man. Your children still love their mum. Blaming your ex may eventually make your children defend your ex's actions.

>> When making special arrangements for yourself or your child(ren), remember to notify your ex-partner and any persons or organisation involved in the access arrangements of your intentions. Give them plenty of notice.

REMEMBER

The most important thing, whether you're in charge of day-to-day care or have limited contact with your children, is that you enjoy the time you have together. Be safe. Be strong. Be attentive. Be involved.

Paying child support

Though you and your former partner have split up, both of you still have to pay for your children's food, clothes, housing, school fees, and all those other expenses such as pocket money and sports fees. It usually falls on the shoulders of the guardian or custodian — that's whoever manages the children's day-to-day care — but between the two of you, you can work out a mechanism so both of you pay your way.

If you're the guardian or custodian of your child or children, ask yourself these things when making a child support agreement with your former partner:

>> What costs are involved in bringing up children? What special expenses do your children incur, such as extracurricular activities, medical expenses, or special dietary requirements?

>> Have you captured all costs accurately and fairly, such as by keeping receipts, so you can explain how you got to a total figure?

>> Are you on any benefits that may affect the amount of child support you are entitled to? How will child support payments affect your eligibility for benefits?

In some cases, where the split has been nasty, or reaching an agreement without resorting to other means isn't possible, the guardian parent can get child support from their ex-partner with the help of government agencies.

In Australia, the government agency that deals with child support is Child Support, via Services Australia. How much child support you'll either pay or receive is usually determined using a formula that takes into account the cost of raising a child at a certain age, both parents' incomes and the amount of time your child is in your care.

CHECK
THE NET

Services Australia provides lots of information for newly separated parents in its website — go to www.servicesaustralia.gov.au/guide-for-newly-separated-parents to get started.

Seeking guardianship of your children

The care of your child used to be called custody, but is now called sole parenting or day-to-day care of your child or children. If you and your former partner can't agree who'll be the main caregiver for your child, and you're determined that it should be you, you'll have to apply for a parenting order through the Family Law Court (Australia). If you're successful, you'll be named the guardian or custodian of your child. Applying for a parenting order can be a very challenging, emotional and stressful endeavour, as well as being very time-consuming and expensive. The process of applying for a parenting order depends on your expectations and your former partner's expectations, and the ability to meet an agreement that serves the best interests of the child(ren) involved. You'll need to get a lawyer who specialises in family law.

When you set out to gain guardianship of your children, ask yourself if what you're doing is in the best interests of the kids, or yourself. Be honest about your motivation for doing all this. As tempting as it may seem, try hard not to use guardianship of your child as a way of getting back at your ex. Guardianship and contact arrangements are always done for the maximum benefits of the child(ren), not either of the parents.

Before you start the process to claim guardianship, check the following. Are you:

>> Able to commit to being in charge of your children by yourself? Bear in mind that at times you'll be sick, have a stressful period at work or start seeing another person. Are you sure you're up for having the day-to-day care of your children?

>> Concerned about your children's safety if they stay in your former partner's care? Then you're totally justified in attempting to get a parenting order.

>> Trying to have the children with you because you don't want your ex to have them? This is not a good reason for trying to get a parenting order.

REMEMBER

Gaining guardianship of children should only be about what is best for the children and never about personal gain and pride. Be honest and real about your expectations, and try never to lose your cool and get angry during the process.

Also ask yourself these questions:

>> Have you worked out what child support you might be eligible for? Are you financially able to take care of your children by yourself if child support isn't forthcoming?

>> How practical is it for you to be the guardian? What help do you need from your former partner to pick up your kids from school or day care?

>> Would your children be happy living with you? Are you living near their friends, other relations and familiar haunts?

The following may help you on your path to guardianship:

>> Ensure you're well set-up to look after your child or children, with a clean and child-friendly home, close to their school.

>> Dress well when going to any appointments or hearings with family court judges.

>> Always keep in mind that you're seeking day-to-day care of your children because it's in the best interests of your kids. That will help you keep motivated when things get rough.

>> Keep a record of the time you spend with your kids at the moment, with receipts and notes on interactions with your former partner.

If you really think about and decide that being your children's guardian isn't in their best interests after all, don't be afraid to stand up and say it. Be upfront with your lawyer and your former partner. Finding out now is better than when your children do come to live with you. Perhaps after admitting it, you'll be able to reach an amicable voluntary agreement with your former partner about shared arrangements or contact time.

REMEMBER

At all times act with dignity and integrity. Think of how your children will remember you during these trying times when they've grown up and have a family of their own.

Getting advice

You probably know from when your child was a newborn baby that every man and his dog likes to give you advice. Sometimes the advice is helpful, sometimes it's not. Ultimately you have to make the decisions. Do what you can to avoid poor choices because you got carried away.

The advice that will be truly useful and beneficial to you is anything that gets you through this time and onto happier, greener pastures, even if the advice is hard to hear — such as being told to get off the couch, stop wallowing in misery and have a shave. Sometimes that's just what you need to hear to move you forward. Anyone who allows you (or encourages you) to keep resenting and blaming your former partner for everything is not doing you any favours.

Counselling and support

If you're struggling to deal with day-to-day tasks or feeling hopeless about your future, get some professional help and quick! It's easy — search online, pick up the phone and call a counsellor.

CHECK THE NET

Check the following to get started:

>> Australian Counselling Association www.theaca.net.au/find-registered-counsellor.php

>> Parents Beyond Breakup, Dads in Distress parentsbeyondbreakup.com/dids/

>> Family & Relationship Services Australia frsa.org.au

>> Lone Fathers Association of Australia www.lonefathers.com.au

>> Relationships Australia relationships.com.au

Finding a lawyer

Navigating the legal system is tricky, but a good lawyer can help you negotiate your way through parenting orders, contact agreements and your divorce. They know the legal system and have experience in dealing with these matters. Many specialise in family matters such as parenting orders and divorce.

When looking for a lawyer, ask yourself these things:

>> Does your lawyer explain proceedings and your part in them adequately?

>> Does your lawyer advise you what to do rather than tell you?

>> Are you bamboozled by what your lawyer says or feel fully informed?

REMEMBER

This is about the future of your family and you should feel comfortable that your lawyer is representing *you* skilfully in a way you're comfortable with.

CHECK THE NET

If you're looking for legal advice, contact the Law Council of Australia Family Law section at `www.familylawsection.org.au/need-legal-assistance`.

Becoming the Primary Caregiver

You have either been granted a parenting order by the courts, or negotiated with your former partner that you're primary caregiver. Dads being primary caregivers is more unusual than it is for mums, so take pride that you're blazing a trail for dads everywhere! As the primary caregiver, you're in charge of your kids. Whenever you have to make a decision about your family, keep in mind that the kids come first.

Getting to grips with being a primary caregiver

Having day-to-day care of your children on your own can be both exciting and terrifying. Being primary caregiver is a huge responsibility and you need to take a lot into consideration:

>> How do you look after yourself in all this?

>> How will you handle contact arrangements with your former partner? How often will your children see your former partner's family?

>> Where will you find the money for mortgage payments or rent, food, clothes and school uniforms, school fees, doctor's visits, transport, school supplies, extracurricular activities and sports fees? Will you work, or receive welfare or child support payments?

>> How much time will you have for paid employment? How will you juggle your children's school and sports schedules?

>> How are you going to sort out life with your children if you've got a new partner?

At times it may seem daunting to be a single dad, but plenty of single mums are out there looking after children and doing a top-notch job. As I've always maintained, a dad can do just as good a job as mum — but in an ideal world, they'll have the positive, healthy and safe influence of both of you in their lives! Having a routine and making sure your kids know what's happening helps. Enlisting family (both yours and, if practical, your former partner's) to give you some space or help with pick-ups or babysitting from time to time also helps.

Chapter 16 is all about stay-at-home dads, and is a good place to start for more information about all the things you need to know/do/remember when being the primary caregiver.

REMEMBER

Being primary caregiver for your children is a great thing, as well as a big responsibility. But just think — your children will learn the sort of man they want to be or want in their lives from the examples you provide as you bring them up. How cool is that!

Supporting your children's mother

Even though you're not partners in a romantic sense, you and your children's mother are still partners in a parenting sense. Whatever happened during the marriage or partnership that caused the breakdown and separation, it's time to work through and grow from the negative feelings — the hurt, the resentment, the anger — and get on with raising your children as best you can.

Your children need their mother around. And they need you around. Your continued positive, safe, healthy involvement will be vital in their health, wellbeing and resilience. At a practical level, you can make this happen simply by staying in close proximity to your ex, if possible. Living in the same suburb or nearby will facilitate convenient transport, social and schooling practicalities.

If the kids are with you and not mum (or even when they're just visiting you), you can do some easy things to support the relationship between your kids and their mum:

>> Just like bedtime and dinnertime, you might like to make mum time a daily ritual. Mum could call at the same time each night to say goodnight, or read a bedtime story on the phone. If she lives nearby, she could come over for half an hour at the same time each night to tuck the children in.

>> Keep your children's mother up to date with your children's progress at school or kindergarten, any special events that are coming up, or parent–teacher evenings she should attend.

>> Keep your negative comments about your kids' mum to yourself — bad mouthing her to your children is not okay. They love their mother and have trust in her, and eroding those feelings helps no-one.

>> Realise your former partner may be feeling inadequate as a mother (or even irresponsible) if the kids are with you most of the time. Appreciate that this arrangement is probably quite tough for her.

>> Share pictures and stories, artwork and school successes with your former partner so she still feels a part of what the children are up to when she's not there.

>> Try not to be too rigid with contact arrangements. Go easy on your ex-partner if she's a little late. At the beginning she may be a bit nervous, or unsure of how her relationship with her kids is going to work out. Make sure the kids are ready to go when she arrives and pack their bags so she's not caught out without nappies or drink bottles.

Seeking help and assistance

As the primary caregiver of the child(ren), you may require some (or loads of) help and assistance. You shouldn't hold back from making use of what is available. This book, for example, is written with the idea that dads are just as good parents as mums and can do everything mums can do (except breastfeed and be pregnant, of course). No part of this book relies on mum to do anything — you can do it all!

Financial help

Contact the appropriate government department to see if you're eligible for any benefits or tax credits.

In Australia, Centrelink runs the Family Tax Benefit payments, childcare assistance and other payments that help you raise your children (www.my.gov.au).

Getting out and about

Just knowing you're part of a wider network of dads raising their kids alone and well is invaluable. It's also really healthy for your kids to know they're not the only ones dealing with mum and dad apart. If parent's groups or dad's groups are close to where you are, join in so you can network with other parents.

Personal help

The end of a relationship can bring up some personal issues. You may realise you need help with anger management, self-esteem or managing stress. Don't procrastinate — if you feel you could benefit from a coach, therapist or other specialist, pick up the phone or search the internet. Your kids need you to be the best dad you can be, so if that means getting a bit of help, just do it. Refer to 'Finding good support' and 'Getting advice', earlier in this chapter.

Having fun

Despite everything that's happened, spending time with your children is still generally great fun. But, you may encounter some times when it isn't so much fun. When you're having a rough day in the office, get home to bills in the mail and children who turn their noses up at their dinner, just stop for a moment and clear your head. Take a look at your children's faces. Remember how much you love them, and how they make you smile and laugh. Your children are worth every bit of extra effort in the end.

REMEMBER

Your children will bring you more joy than frustration if you're open to it.

Play and interact with your children as much as you can. Read books together, give them lots of cuddles and let yourself be a bit silly with them. Children can learn so much from an involved and caring father.

TIP

If you're an older dad, constant playing can take a toll on you, so get other family members involved, set up play dates and share the fun, while you spend time with adults watching the children have fun. Actually, you don't need to be an older parent to do this — it's highly recommended!

Introducing a New Partner

Wanting to find yourself another partner, or at least have a romantic relationship with someone new, is natural. Your life doesn't have to be all about being a father and working to support your family. But beware — you're not the carefree single man you used to be. You now come with extras.

TIP

When you go on dates, or meet someone you'd like to be more than friends with, be honest from the outset that you have children. With the high rates of relationship break-up, it's no longer unusual to be single with kids, so you needn't feel self-conscious about it. By letting this person know you have kids from the outset, you're letting her know how important your children are to you. Some women may not want to get involved with a man who has children — that's okay, their loss.

Talking about a new partner to your children

The idea of a new special person in your life after all the mess and trauma of their parents' break-up may be tough for your children to deal with at first. Initially your children may be confused when they think of how you used to be with their mum and now they're seeing you with another woman. When you start dating or have met someone special, talk to your children about why you want to date and what it means for your family. Take things slowly and don't rush your children into anything they're not comfortable about. Thinking this new person is going to replace their mother may be very painful for your children. The reality is that children are likely to think of their birth mum as 'mum', but over time they can get used to the idea of having two mums.

So give your children lots of time and let them know they can ask you lots of questions about your new partner. Be aware that your children may be resistant to the idea of your new partner. If possible, get their ideas for the first meeting and involve them somehow. It may be easier for your children to deal with the situation if they feel they have some sort of say over what happens.

REMEMBER

Your children may be secretly hoping that you and their mum are going to get back together. The idea of a new romance in your life will mean that's not going to happen and can be tough for your kids to deal with. This can be crushing. Go gently. Be kind, patient and compassionate.

Meet and greet

When you have found the right person, she (or he or they) will one day need to meet your children and your children will want to meet that special someone. The meeting doesn't have to be stressful — it can be as simple as having any of your friends over to visit. You may want to choose this first meeting to happen in a neutral area, such as a park, playground or café. Keep it short, sweet and casual, and don't push your kids into liking this new person.

After a few visits, chances are your children will get used to having your new partner around. Again, never push them into liking this person. It can take years for children to accept that a new person is around and going to become part of the family.

REMEMBER

If your new special someone changes your sexual status (from straight to gay, trans, or any other sexuality), you may need to spend some additional time helping your children understand what this means for you, them, and your new partner. Approach these issues sensitively, recognising that most children will be immediately accepting but that some children may struggle in deep ways for a long time. Love and acceptance will be your central and most powerful approach.

TIP

Make it clear to your kids that your new partner isn't replacing their mother, but is an addition to the family. Continue to support the relationship between your kids and former partner, and make her a priority in your kids' lives. Ask her to do the same if she gets involved with another partner as well.

This situation is probably pretty intense for your new partner too. Listen to the concerns they may have. Just like any good relationship, you should foster an environment of open communication, where all of you can talk openly about anything, including feelings.

Getting remarried

If the time comes that you and your new partner decide to get married, get your kids involved with the whole shebang. Ask them what they would like to do. Tell them that this is a very special day for you and it would be even more special if they helped. Cut them some slack if they're not hugely enthusiastic about you getting remarried. After all, they may still be clinging on to the way things used to be with you and their mum being married.

TIP

Make sure you don't get so wrapped up in the event on the day that you don't notice your children looking lost and feeling sidelined. It can be helpful to have family dedicated to looking out for them, to give them loads of hugs and kisses, because the wedding's a big day for them too. They now have a stepparent!

6

The Part of Tens

Work out some important ways to make your partner's life much more bearable — and even pleasurable — during pregnancy.

Understand how to improve your baby's and your family's wellbeing through being a connected dad, and creating more engagement and bonding with your baby and your partner.

Fire up your toddler's already active mind with activities and strategies for getting in some serious dad-time.

Chapter **20**

Ten Ways to Improve Your Partner's Pregnancy

Pregnancy looks easy when it's happening to someone else. As men, you don't have to endure what's going on in a pregnant woman's body 24/7 — and a lot is going on. Media depictions of pregnancy have led us to believe that a woman demurely throws up a few times, and then swells elegantly into a glowing, radiant Venus figure, à la Gal Gadot (that's Wonder Woman for those who don't keep up with the most glamourous movie stars). Finally, birth is quick with a few deep breaths, some loud screams and — voila, a beautiful baby is here.

Not so. Read Chapter 3 for what really happens when your partner is pregnant, and then help her get through the experience by trying a few of these tips.

Take Care of Your Lady

Growing a baby is hard work and takes quite a physical toll on a woman's body. Sure, some women climb mountains and run marathons up to the day they give birth, but those are exceptions rather than your average woman's pregnancy experience. For starters, morning sickness can be debilitating and, for some women, the morning sickness doesn't ease off until the pregnancy is over.

The tiredness and carrying of all that blood, fluid and an extra person around puts all sorts of strains on the female body. Look after your partner 24/7 if need be, especially if she's having a difficult pregnancy, and do all you can to make life easier for her. This may mean looking after the household for nine months all by yourself and, for sure, you're going to get sick of it. But, let's face it — would you prefer to squeeze a baby out of your body? So, be decent, and do whatever needs doing in the house. You can take it one step further and really pamper your mum-to-be by painting her toenails, giving her a foot rub or helping her rub oil onto her belly.

TIP

The best thing you can do for your pregnant partner is do the thinking. The cognitive load of running the house often falls to the woman in the partnership. Let her focus on the stuff that only she can do. Step up here and plan a few meals, organise the house, use the vacuum, and make a phone call or two to keep things moving.

Get on the Wagon

Your partner will ensure the safety and health of your baby best if she chooses to stay off alcohol, drugs, cigarettes, blue cheese, seafood and a whole lot more. Seeing you downing a pint of beer and enough salami to sink a small ship could be enough to send her over the edge, or at least send her a message that you don't quite understand empathy and compassion. Staying off alcohol and cigarettes, not to mention anything heavier you may be into, and eating what she can eat is not only better for you, but also sets a precedent for how you intend to live as a father. Plus, it shows you have a heart. So be considerate of her — it will strengthen your relationship.

Give Your Partner Some 'Me' Time Every Now and Then

The prospect of becoming a mother, while really exciting for your partner, is also a daunting one, both mentally and physically. For most mothers, the first few months after birth end up being a 24-hour, seven-days-per-week job. They may have traded in their old life of meetings, schedules, work commitments and deadlines (which they may have varying degrees of sentimental attachment to) for the care of a tiny, helpless baby who they love. However, the role can be overwhelming.

During pregnancy, your partner is bound to have some trepidation about her new responsibility and how she's going to cope. Over the next few years, even perhaps until your child has left home, your partner's always going to have one eye on what she's doing and one eye on your child. So, in the months before this all kicks off, let her have some time that's just for her.

Be There for the Medical Stuff

Go along to all the medical appointments, scans and meetings with your midwife or obstetrician. Your partner wants you to be there to share in it. The first time you hear your baby's heartbeat or see your baby moving and bouncing around in your partner's belly during an ultrasound scan, you'll be glad you came along.

REMEMBER

Although you're not carrying the baby right now, that tiny growing cluster of cells in there is your child, too. Your place is to know about how well your baby is developing, any potential health issues, and what options you as a couple have for welcoming your child into the world. Going to appointments also supports your partner because, in the event of any unwelcome news, you're there to help her.

Get with the Program

Start skilling-up on essential baby knowledge and skills. Mums-to-be love to see their partners getting excited about their new life as parents, and what better way to show your excitement than to throw yourself into the preparations? You have so much to learn about looking after a newborn baby and the months after that, so why not find out all you can about it now?

Ask your midwife, GP or obstetrician about antenatal classes in your area, and discuss which one you think would suit you and your partner best. Make never missing a class a priority, even in the face of work commitments. Let's face it — your work is there for a long time. Preparing for your first child happens only once in your life. And if your partner has any special preferences for learning about birth, practising for the birth, or doing whatever it takes to make things work better, be supportive. The investment of your time (and money) is worth it.

Go on a Babymoon

As a couple, now is the perfect time to take a relaxing and indulgent holiday somewhere. I'm not talking about backpacking through India or somewhere hot, with wild animals and tonnes of people (although if that's your thing and you can do it safely and healthily, why not). Somewhere low-key might work better given what is coming for you though — I'm going to suggest somewhere sun lounges and swimming pools are more common than office blocks. Somewhere the two of you can just hang out, sleep late, read books and do whatever you want when you want . . . because those days are about to be properly limited! If budget allows, a getaway in the mid-trimester might be nice.

Be Excited about Becoming a Dad

Finding out you're going to be a dad can be a little daunting for some. And for others, well, you may have some reservations because of your own childhood, your financial situation, or the responsibility you're going to have. Your partner may also share some of those worries and concerns, but burying your head in the sand and pretending the baby's not going to happen doesn't help. Even if the impending change of lifestyle takes a while to sink in, you can definitely make the pregnancy experience more enjoyable for your partner if you show a bit of excitement about becoming a dad. Showing your partner that you're excited gets her excited and happy about becoming a mum. You want her to be happy and excited.

A lot of parenting is about attitude. The anecdote about dealing with picky eaters really sums this up. One father complains that his daughter is a terrible eater and doesn't eat anything unless it's got cheese on it. He's really stressed out about it and is pulling his hair out thinking of a solution. On the other hand, another father happily tells the first guy that his son is a terrific eater because, as long as it's got cheese on it, he eats anything. It's all about attitude.

Celebrate!

In a few months when the baby is born, you're going to be celebrating a new person's presence in your life. Not just any new person, but the person who is on this Earth because of you. That's pretty special! But the arrival does come with a price — temporary sleep deprivation and a restricted social life.

So make the most of your quiet nights and unlimited access to the outside world now! Take your partner for a flash dinner somewhere fancy, visit a special place together — do whatever spins your wheels as a couple.

One dad-to-be surprised his partner with a picnic lunch at the local zoo in the weeks before their baby was born. He'd even packed non-alcoholic sparkling wine to toast their health and a pillow for her to sit on. She spent some of her picnic time moving back and forth from the ladies, but the gesture was most appreciated.

Record That Beautiful Belly

In our great-grandmothers' and grandmothers' days, having a whole litter of children was common, and in some cases the pregnant belly was hidden away as if it were some kind of obscenity. These days, having more than three or four children is rare, and a woman having one to three children in her lifetime is more usual.

Celebrating the physical changes that take place during pregnancy (not the heartburn and piles, mind you), such as the voluptuous new shape of a pregnant belly and those plus-sized bosoms that you'll no doubt love, is now common. Most pregnant women, while not loving the weight they put on, love their bellies, so get out your phone from week one and snap some pics regularly. You laugh when you look back and see how your baby grew even before you got to meet your little one.

TIP

Even better than snapping shots on your mobile, hire a professional photographer to take some photos of your partner's gorgeous shape. For some women, an album of professional photos helps her feel sexy and beautiful, and boosts her confidence.

Tell Her You Love Her

For many women, the hardest part of pregnancy is near the due date. Your partner may be having a difficult time getting comfortable at night and suffering from heartburn and piles. She may have stretch marks, and her legs and feet may be sausage-shaped. Your partner's tired all the time but can't sleep. She wants her body back but is frightened about how she's going to handle giving birth.

You, as your partner's great ally, her support and her rock, can show her that the changes she's experiencing only make you love her more by actually saying the words. She wants to know you still find her attractive and that she's still, despite everything going on in her body, the woman you fell in love with — not just because of the way she looks, but because of who she is — and that she's going to make a wonderful mother. Say it by using your words. Show it by helping her. And be it through selfless action.

Chapter **21**

Ten Ways Dads Build Baby's — and Family's — Wellbeing

I f you've made it this far into the book, you're planning on being an engaged, committed and present dad. The baby is either almost here or has already arrived. It's an exciting time, either way.

But you may have some nagging doubts. Being a first-time dad is a bit like being a first-time driver. You know what all the buttons and pedals do. You know the wheel turns. But the first time you try to do it, you're probably going to be pretty clunky and clumsy. And you're almost certain to make a handful of mistakes.

Raising a child is a lot like learning to drive a car, or picking up a language or musical instrument. To get good at it, you have to make a lot of mistakes. Millions, perhaps. Yet it's the consistent effort applied over time — the practice — that leads to mastery. The mistakes make you better, if you learn from them.

Unfortunately, a lot of dads feel like once the baby is born, they're sidelined. They may feel they don't have much to do except earn the money, pay the bills, and try to be supportive while mum and bub bond. And now and then, mums go along with that because it's easier. They're the ones spending more time with the baby. They've had most of the practice with the nappies, the late nights and dinner time (since dads don't breastfeed so well).

But most dads want to be involved, positive fathers. And that's a good thing. Numerous studies show that dad creating a solid attachment bond with bub in the early days increases the wellbeing of the whole family. The research shows family functioning improves and relationship satisfaction between partners goes up (which is usually pretty good for sexual satisfaction too, so long as those first six weeks are over and your partner feels good about getting it going again).

REMEMBER

Involved dads influence more than just family function and relationship satisfaction. Researchers from the UK investigated dads' interactions with their three-month-old babies and found that by age two, the littlies with the most engaged and interactive dads were doing better on a range of cognitive tests than the ones whose dads were less 'there'. The presence or absence of an engaged father influenced mental development.

So in this chapter, I outline ten things you can do to create more engagement and bonding with your newborn baby, and with your partner.

On your fatherhood journey, I wish you luck.

Get Skin to Skin

We already know that skin-to-skin contact is great for mum and your new baby. But dads can do it too — even if you're covered in manly chest hair. That physical contact releases bonding hormones in you, and makes you more crazy about your baby. If you're worried about messes, just keep their nappy on. You can still have skin-to-skin contact without total nakedness.

Work on Your Baby Talk

For decades, scientists have known that mums often speak in a more sing-song, high-pitched voice when talking to their babies. You may call it 'baby talk'. (People used to call it 'motherese', but these days we're more inclusive so we call it 'parentese'.) And for a lot of us guys, it can be a bit off-putting, and not many dads do it. Perhaps don't start off when you're in public, but have fun with your baby by trying some baby talk out. Watch their reaction. Talking to bub in this kind of sing-song voice often ups the engagement and delight your baby feels. And when that kiddo smiles at you, you'll have to hold yourself back from trying to eat him!

Sing

We all have different singing abilities, I know. But researchers have found that in the animal kingdom, singing is good for family life. A specific example: nightingales. Researchers have found that the better a male nightingale sings, the more supportive and protective he is of his family. The same research doesn't exist in humans, but the idea carries across regardless. When you sing to your little cherub, you'll look into their eyes, smile, connect and touch. You'll actually be supportive and protective. And you will bond when you do that.

Play

The world is teeming with data that shows that dads are uniquely more likely to play with their kids than mums. Of course, mums play. But dads do it more, they do it more naturally, and they tend to do it with more rough and tumble fun. You need to be really careful when your infant is new, but as he grows, this rough and tumble fun should become a staple part of your relationship. It helps with bonding, and it creates an understanding of risk, limits, consent and more. And it leads to endless giggles and laughter that you'll cherish for the rest of your life.

Feed

This is the bit where you can integrate all of your best attributes as dads. You can play, sing, talk in funny voices — and channel your very best choo-choo train or airplane to get that food into our child's mouth! And, yes, you can keep your cool when food ends up on the floor or all over you.

Bathe

When you spend time with a baby, time stands still and you get to completely immerse yourself in the moment. And perhaps one of the coolest bonding moments you can have every couple of days is bath time. True, you sometimes have to deal with unwanted bodily fluids or waste products prior to the bath. (Make sure you clean up their bum properly before bath time. No-one wants to bathe in their poop.) But once they're in that warm water, kicking their legs, splashing and laughing their heads off while they smile up at you, you'll be a goner; completely smitten and lost in the moment.

Sleep

Everyone wants a good night's sleep. But babies aren't designed for that. They're supposed to wake up every few hours. It's just what they do. But with some clever design you can create a space for your baby to sleep close to you in your bedroom (or maybe in your bed if you're up for co-sleeping). Having their bassinet within arm's reach so you can hear their gentle breathing as they snooze creates that amazing calm that feels so good I don't really have words to describe it.

Pray

While a large percentage of Aussie blokes are ticking the 'no religion' box on the census (about 32 per cent in Australia), still a large percentage of the population claim a religious faith. If that's not you, this tip won't be so useful, but if it is, consider what praying with your little one close by can do for the bonds you feel towards him. When you ask God, the Universe — or whatever your faith directs you to pray to — for favours and goodness for your child, your heart feels like it grows ten sizes.

Be Still

Most of the tips in this chapter encourage you to be actively involved with your new baby in some small way. They demand you do something. This second-to-last idea goes entirely the opposite way. Sometimes, when you're with your baby, do nothing but stare. Soak it all up. Breathe in that brand new baby fragrance.

Feel the softness of his hands as he grasps your pinky when you put it in his palm. Take in the perfection of his skin, the tiny lips, and the wide-open, trusting eyes. Engorge your eyes on the little tufts of hair on his head and the stilted, jerky movements he makes as he tries to make sense of his surroundings. And be still. Bask in the breathtaking miracle of the tiny wonder you've helped create and bring into the world. If you want to feel like a dad, sometimes it's best to stand in the majesty of the moment — even if it's in the lounge room while you're in your undies — and consider the potential of the little life in front of you.

Love Your Baby's Mum

Hopefully your relationship with your little baby's mumma is rock solid. Put her first. Be there for her. Support her. Think about how you can help her. In some strange way, this will build more bonding into your relationship with your baby.

But even if your relationship's not solid, take a step back and realise that this child is half you and half her. Acknowledge the good that's in her, because it has likely passed through to your child. You can't love the child without loving the part that she has played in your child's life right now.

Chapter **22**

Ten Ways to Engage with a Toddler

Toddlers are funny little creatures. They're curious and cute, interested yet impulsive, and are like little learning sponges soaking up everything they see, hear and do. Playing with toddlers is really fun and interacting with you is great for both you and your child. One of nature's best tricks is that playing with you is a way of learning and developing for your child. In this chapter, I give you a handful of great ideas for having fun with your little one.

Obstacle Course

My top pick for busting boredom on a rainy day, or just for fun and everything in between, is to set up an obstacle course. Use chairs with a sheet draped over the top, coffee tables to crawl under, big cardboard boxes to crawl through, toys or suitcases to manoeuvre around and bean bags to shimmy over. Of course, getting through the obstacle course is all the more fun for having to avoid the dad'o'saurus who threatens to tickle the hide off any toddler who doesn't avoid him in time!

Get Handy

Playing hand games like 'Under the Bam Bushes' and 'Two Little Dicky Birds' are more than just a good time, they encourage the development of hand–eye co-ordination, gross motor skills, language and memory.

Playing Chase and Tag

Have you noticed that your little one loves it when you run after her, and will encourage you to run after her by taking off in the middle of a crowded street, or near a busy road? Near a highway isn't the best place to play tag or chase, but your backyard and home are. Chasing your toddler into another room, then having her hide when you come looking for her is an advanced form of peek-a-boo — it never fails to delight toddlers.

And what's wrong with a little running around the house anyway? Running's good for the heart and lungs and ensures your toddler sleeps well that night. And hey — it may even help you burn a few extra calories!

Jigsaws

Fitting shapes into a jigsaw puzzle is pretty easy for dads, but it wasn't always. A lot's going on in your brain when you do a jigsaw. You need to identify colours and patterns and visualise the piece in a bigger picture, as well as having the motor skills necessary to make that piece fit. Doing a jigsaw is almost like rocket science for toddlers. Best of all, jigsaws help your toddler develop her patience. What many parents don't realise is that patience is a skill that needs to be learnt, just like riding a bike or learning to swim. Patience is not something that some people have and others don't — it needs to be learnt and practised regularly. Doing puzzles with your little one is the perfect way to practise patience.

Balloons

When's the last time you bought a bag of balloons and blew them up? Back in the 1980s at the 99 red luftballon party? Well, that's about to change. Though your toddler may not understand how to blow up balloons, nothing is stopping you from doing it — and then letting them go so they whiz around the room in a crazy freefall. Toddlers love to look at balloons, play with balloons, have air come out of balloons in their faces, and watch balloons float into the sky. Balloons should be part of every great dad's kit. Same goes for bubbles.

Balls

Like balloons, balls are an endless source of fascination for toddlers. The unpredictability of where a ball is going to bounce, roll or fall can keep a toddler engaged for whole . . . minutes. Show your toddler how to throw a ball and watch how excited she becomes. Then try throwing the ball gently to her. She probably won't catch it, but will try again and again. And that's how skills are learned — by repetition. At the beginning you can start engaging with your child by rolling a ball to her and getting her to roll it back to you. As your child gets older you can do trickier stuff with balls, until finally you can teach her (or learn with her) the art of juggling.

Water Games

Who would have thought that an old bucket, some empty drink bottles and a little watering can could be a great investment for engaging with your child? Most children are fascinated by water play — the simple acts of pouring, splashing and swishing develop their motor skills and their spatial awareness. Have a water play 'set' ready to go on warm days, and show bub how to water the garden or the balcony plants.

You may want to take this a step further and enrol your toddler in swimming lessons. Swimming lessons for toddlers are usually just having a play in the water and building up confidence in the pool.

Art

Every culture in the world has a concept of art as a way of expressing themselves. Children do too. Get messy with finger paints, crayons, pencils and felt pens. This lets your children explore *schema* — repetitive patterns and shapes that develop a child's brain. She'll also get the hang of the idea of writing and holding a pen in a certain way, and you'll begin to see more recognisable shapes and themes as she grows.

Reading

You can't read enough to your child. As time passes, you'll find story time before bed, whether you're perched in bed together or sitting in a favourite armchair, one of the highlights of your day. Many a father knows *The Gruffalo*, *The Very Hungry Caterpillar*, or *The Cat in the Hat* by heart from his many story times with his children.

Reading together isn't just about the words on the page, just as eating together isn't just about food. Reading together is about spending time together, exploring a new world together, and providing a safe, secure place for your child to be.

Children learn by repetition, and often want you to read to them the same story over and over again. So go with it, and soon your little one will be reciting *The Gruffalo* back to you. Don't forget to stop at each page and see which things your child can point out or name as you go.

Stacking Blocks and Building

Most toddlers are fascinated by textures, colours and stacking things. Sit down with your child on a rainy day with a bucket of blocks, and you may not get up again for an hour or so. Not only will you get a kick out of making the perfect Lego spaceship, but you might also discover that your child has just built the Eiffel Tower.

You can build all sorts of things from basic wooden blocks — garages for toy cars to be parked in, tunnels for trains to rumble through, houses for cuddly toys to sleep in. You're limited only by your imagination.

Glossary

To help you understand the medical mumbo jumbo you may be exposed to during pregnancy or when visiting a paediatrician, I've compiled a list of the most commonly used terms.

active movement: Developing your child's fine and gross motor skills, cognitive skills and senses by doing things such as rolling on the floor, crawling, playing finger games and climbing.

active phase: A phase of the first stage of labour, in which contractions are increasingly painful because the cervix is nearly completely dilated and your partner's body is getting ready to start pushing your baby out.

acute illness: A short-term illness.

allergens: Substances or materials that cause an allergic reaction or allergy. Examples include certain foods, grass and animals; see also *anaphylaxis.*

allergy: When the body has an overactive immune system and reacts to particular substances, such as certain foods, grass and animals, which are called *allergens.*

amniocentesis: A test to check for genetic birth defects such as Down syndrome. The test involves inserting a large needle into the amniotic sac and drawing some amniotic fluid for testing. Amniocentesis is usually performed around 16–20 weeks into the pregnancy; see also *Down syndrome.*

amniotic fluid: Also called *liquor amnii,* this is the fluid that surrounds your baby in the amniotic sac while in the womb. When your partner's waters break, amniotic fluid is what comes out.

amniotic sac: The thin membrane that holds the amniotic fluid. When the 'waters break', the amniotic sac is what leaks fluid.

anaphylaxis: A life-threatening reaction to an allergen, in which parts of the face and body swell up and block airways; see also *allergens.*

antenatal: Also known as prenatal, this is the period before the baby is born.

Apgar score: A score from one to ten given to a newborn baby at one and five minutes after birth to determine health and wellbeing.

artificial insemination (AI): Using donor sperm to fertilise a woman's egg inside the uterus.

assisted reproductive technologies: Using technologies such as *in vitro fertilisation (IVF)* and *artificial insemination (AI)* to get pregnant.

attachment parenting: A style of parenting in which close contact with the child is maintained at all times. Attachment parents co-sleep with their baby, breastfeed and carry their baby in a *sling* or *baby carrier* rather than a buggy or stroller.

Attention Deficit/Hyperactivity Disorder (ADHD): A condition in which children have trouble concentrating, and are easily distracted, hyperactive and impulsive.

authoritarian parenting: A style of parenting in which children are told what to do, parents are to be obeyed and rules must be observed.

authoritative parenting: A style of parenting in which children and parents have a give and take relationship. Parents have high expectations of children, and children have an open and honest relationship with parents.

autism: Also known as *autism spectrum disorder* because the range of severity differs from person to person. A person with autism may have trouble making sense of the world, and find it difficult to communicate, cope in social situations or control emotions.

baby carrier: A back or front pack in which you carry a baby or small child on the body. *Slings* are another form of baby carrier.

barrier cream: A cream you apply to a child's bottom and genitals to prevent nappy rash.

bassinet: A kind of mini cot or basket for newborns to sleep in.

birth canal: A term used to describe your partner's vagina during childbirth and labour.

birth centre: A specialised birthing unit run by midwives. Some birth centres are attached to a hospital, others aren't. Birth centres aren't available in all areas.

birth plan: A document in which you and your partner make clear how you prefer the birth of your child to go in the best case scenario. A birth plan should also include which forms of pain relief your partner is open to or would like available, whether or not you want to cut the umbilical cord, who you want to have in the room with you, and which kinds of intervention you're open to, if any.

bodysuit: A T-shirt that does up at the crotch with domes (clips) that's suitable for babies and young children.

Braxton Hicks contractions: The false contractions that many women experience in the weeks, days or hours leading up to real labour starting.

breech: When your baby is 'upside down', meaning the feet rather than the head are pointing down, ready for birth.

bronchiolitis: An inflammation of the lungs' airways. Your child will develop a nasty cough and may have trouble breathing. Go to your GP.

buggy: A large pram, usually with three or four wheels, that can be folded down either in half or lengthwise.

burping: The process of getting your baby to bring up wind by rubbing or patting the back.

caesarean: A baby born by caesarean is removed from the uterus through an incision in your partner's belly. Caesareans are performed when labour has been going on too long, or some condition in which the baby must be born immediately is apparent, or vaginal birth is too dangerous.

cerebral palsy: A condition where parts of the brain are damaged during pregnancy or birth, or as the result of a lack of oxygen.

cervix: The opening between the uterus and vagina. The cervix is sealed shut during pregnancy and must widen far enough to let the baby through during labour.

chickenpox: An infection that starts with a fever and cold symptoms. After a day or two, your child starts getting red, itchy blisters. You can calm the itch with calamine lotion from your pharmacy and give your child lots of soothing baths.

chloasma: Darkish patches that appear on a pregnant woman's face, also known as the *mask of pregnancy*.

chronic illness: A long-term illness, such as asthma or diabetes.

cognitive skills: Thinking skills and the ability to grasp concepts.

colic: Persistent crying at certain times of the day, usually the early evening, for babies under three months. The cause of colic is unknown.

conjunctivitis: A highly contagious eye infection in which the linings of the eye are inflamed.

conscious fathering: Actively developing parenting skills and researching to understand why babies and children behave the way they do. Respond to your children by using these skills and knowledge, rather than with a reaction picked up from your parents or others.

controlled crying: A technique in which a crying baby is comforted at regular intervals in an effort to help the baby learn to fall asleep independently.

cord prolapse: A rare event in which the umbilical cord blocks the baby from being born.

cradle cap: A type of dermatitis that causes flakes on the scalp in young babies, similar to dandruff in adults.

crèche: A kind of day care centre.

croup: A viral infection that starts out as a cold but becomes a pretty nasty and wheezy cough that comes on suddenly. Go to your GP.

crowning: A term used to describe the baby's head showing in the birth canal, meaning birth is near.

cry-it-out: A technique in which a baby is left to cry and fall asleep independently.

cystic fibrosis: An inherited chronic disease affecting the lungs and digestive system.

day care: A facility where children under five years old are cared for, with programs to assist their learning and development. Day care centres are staffed by qualified early childhood teachers and aides.

demand feeding: Feeding a baby when she shows hunger cues such as turning her head to search for a nipple, crying or sucking her fists.

developmental delay: Professionals say that a child has a developmental delay, rather than labelling the child intellectually disabled, when a child's development lags behind average statistics on developmental milestones.

dilation: A term used to describe the widening of the cervix ready for the baby to leave the uterus and enter the birth canal.

discipline: A term used to describe the way you show your children clear boundaries, rules and consequences. It doesn't mean punishing your child.

dizygotic twins: Twins from two different eggs, also known as fraternal twins. These twins do not share identical genetic material as identical twins do; see also *monozygotic twins*.

Doppler: An instrument that allows you to hear the baby's heart beating in the womb.

doula: A paid attendant, usually a woman, who helps support and coach a woman through labour and childbirth. Doulas are also called childbirth assistants.

Down syndrome: A genetic disorder caused by an extra bit of chromosome being replicated in cell division very early after conception. Children with Down syndrome have varying degrees of mental and sometimes physical disability.

due date: The date your baby should arrive, though this is not for certain, because only around 5 per cent of babies arrive on their due date. In Australia, the due date is technically called an EDC, or expected date of confinement.

ear infection: An infection of the ear, in which your child will be grizzly and tug at the ears, or rub them. A trip to your GP to check your child's ears thoroughly and prescribe antibiotics is in order.

eczema: Also known as *dermatitis*. The skin is sensitive to certain materials and can become itchy and blotchy.

elimination communication: Rather than using nappies to catch poos and wees, parents watch their baby for signs they need to go to the toilet. The baby is then held over a potty.

embryo: What your unborn baby is from the time it implants into the uterine wall to about 8 to 12 weeks into the pregnancy.

endometrium: Lining of the uterus wall.

engaging: Engaging is when an unborn baby is getting in position for birth.

epidural: A pain relief method that involves a needle going into the spinal column with local anaesthetic. Epidurals are used in caesareans so that mum can stay awake while the baby is being born; see also *caesarean*.

episiotomy: Cutting the perineum to make the vaginal opening bigger during labour.

estrogen: Though estrogen's coursing through the bodies of both men and women, the hormone is found in much higher levels in women. Estrogen's known as the female sex hormone in the same way that testosterone is the male sex hormone. It's responsible for the growth of breasts and contributes to the menstrual cycle in women.

extrusion reflex: A reflex in which a young baby pushes an object out of his mouth with his tongue. One of the signs that your baby's ready to eat solids is when he stops automatically pushing things like spoons out of his mouth.

fallopian tubes: The tubes that connect the ovary with the uterus. An egg is often fertilised in one of the fallopian tubes and travels down the uterus to become an embryo.

family day care: A paid carer looking after your child at her home under the supervision of an early childhood organisation.

fertilisation: When egg meets sperm, and the beginnings of a new child are formed.

finger food: When your baby is about eight to nine months old, she becomes interested in small snacks such as pieces of toast and crackers that she can eat with her fingers.

foetal alcohol syndrome: Condition caused by a woman drinking alcohol in pregnancy. Foetal alcohol syndrome manifests itself as a number of intellectual and behavioural problems in the child.

foetal monitor: A device that monitors heartbeat, movement and contractions of the uterus to determine the unborn baby's wellbeing. Foetal monitors are used in antenatal check-ups and in the early stages of labour.

foetus: What your unborn baby is called from the time it stops being an embryo, about 8 to 12 weeks into the pregnancy, until birth.

folic acid/folate: A vitamin that helps prevent neural tube defects such as spina bifida.

forceps: An instrument like a pair of tongs designed to help with the baby's birth, easing her out of the birth canal.

formula: A substance, primarily of milk powder, which is given to babies.

fundal height: Measurement of how far the uterus has progressed into the abdomen as your baby grows.

gas: A mix of nitrous oxide and oxygen that can be inhaled during labour as pain relief.

gastroenteritis: Infection of the gastrointestinal tract that can be caused by bacteria from infected water, poor hygiene or bad food.

gestation: Another word for the time your baby spends in the womb. You hear your carer say things such as '30 weeks gestation', which means 30 weeks in the womb.

gestational diabetes: A form of diabetes that can be contracted during pregnancy. Your midwife, obstetrician or GP is on the lookout for it with tests throughout the pregnancy.

group B strep: A life-threatening bacterial infection in newborns.

hCG: Also known as *human chorionic gonadotropin*, a hormone made by the embryo to ensure its survival. Most pregnancy tests look for the presence of hCG.

homebirth: Your partner labours and gives birth at home rather than in a delivery suite at a hospital.

hospice: A palliative care facility, where people who are in the final stages of a terminal illness are cared for.

hydrocephalus: Also known as 'water on the brain', hydrocephalus is a condition in which fluid collects in the brain. It can cause intellectual disability and death.

hyperemesis gravidarum: Extreme sickness during pregnancy, with continual nausea and vomiting, weight loss and dehydration.

hypnobirthing: Using hypnotherapy to control pain during labour.

in utero: Latin for 'in the womb'.

in vitro fertilisation (IVF): A technique in which a harvested egg is fertilised by sperm outside the womb.

induction: The process of artificially starting labour. Substances and procedures that mimic the body's natural actions are used with a pregnant woman to kickstart labour.

infant acne: A newborn baby's acne, caused by pregnancy hormones that are present in the baby's body.

intracytoplasmic sperm injection: A process in which a harvested egg is injected with sperm to ensure fertilisation outside the womb.

kindergarten: A type of preschool.

lactation consultant: A carer specially trained in breastfeeding who can give one-on-one advice and care in getting breastfeeding up and running. She can also provide support when breastfeeding's not going so well.

last menstrual period: The first day of your partner's period before getting pregnant is the date that the length of the pregnancy is calculated by. So even though you may have conceived your baby on the 15th day after your partner's period, your baby is already considered two weeks along or at two weeks *gestation*.

latent phase: The first phase of the first stage of labour, when the cervix is starting to dilate. Contractions shouldn't be too painful and can be managed with natural techniques such as heat packs and moving around.

linea nigra: A darkish line appearing on a pregnant woman's belly as her pregnancy progresses. It's caused by melanin marking where the abdominal muscles are parting to make way for junior. It fades a few weeks after birth.

Listeria monocytogenes Bacteria that live in some foods, such as soft cheese, cold meats and raw seafood. The illness *Listeria* infection causes, listeriosis, is dangerous to an unborn child and can cause miscarriage or stillbirth.

long day care: A day care facility outside the home, such as a preschool for young children.

meconium: Thick, tar-like poos your baby does in the first few days of life.

meningitis: An illness that can cause death. Symptoms include a severe headache, stiff neck and fever.

midwife: A health professional who specialises in pregnancy, labour, birth and newborn care.

miscarriage: When an unborn child dies before 20 weeks gestation.

monozygotic twins: Twins who are formed when one fertilised egg splits. These twins are identical; see also *dizygotic twins*.

morning sickness: A side effect of pregnancy, usually in the first trimester, in which your partner feels nauseated and is hypersensitive to foods and smells.

Moro reflex: A reflex in which newborn babies seem to suddenly flinch in their sleep.

Moses basket: A basket that newborn babies can sleep in for the first few months of life.

multiple birth: A set of children born at one time, such as twins, triplets or more.

muscular dystrophy: A genetic disorder, in which muscle strength and function deteriorates over time. Most commonly seen in male babies and young boys, some forms aren't diagnosed until early adulthood.

nanny: A person trained in baby and child care hired to look after children.

nappy rash: A skin condition caused by the ammonia in wees and poos on your baby's bottom and genitals. Nappy rash is usually red, flat and quite sore.

neglectful parenting: A parenting style in which children are ignored, abused or left to fend for themselves.

neural tube defect: The neural tube is an embryo's developing central nervous system and it closes at around 15 to 28 days after conception. If the neural tube doesn't close, the condition can cause a birth defect such as spina bifida, where the spinal cord is not fully formed or not enclosed by the vertebrae.

nuchal fold test: An ultrasound scan done at about 12 weeks to scan for birth defects such as spina bifida by checking how the vertebrae are developing around the spinal cord.

obstetrician: A specialist in reproduction.

obstetrics: The arm of medicine to do with reproduction.

occupational therapist: A specialist in helping people regain skills and mobility.

ovaries: A part of female anatomy where eggs are formed.

overdue: Any date past the baby's due date.

overtired: When your baby can't get to sleep and is too tired, she becomes overtired and more difficult to settle.

ovulation: When an egg is released from an ovary, ready for fertilisation from a sperm.

oxytocin: The hormone that causes your partner's uterus to contract, and is responsible for the let-down reflex when she's breastfeeding.

paediatrician: A doctor specialising in paediatrics, or care of children.

palliative care: Care of a person in the final stages of a terminal illness.

peritoneal cavity: the space within the abdomen that contains the intestines, the stomach and the liver, and is bound by thin membranes.

permissive parenting: Parents let their children do anything and children have no clear boundaries, rules or understanding of consequences.

pethidine: A drug used commonly in labour, similar to morphine.

physical disability: A condition, disease or injury that prevents someone from undertaking normal day-to-day activities, such as getting dressed, eating or walking.

placenta: The lifeline between your baby and her mum, a dinner plate–sized gloop of blood and tissue that is attached to the uterine wall and absorbs nutrients and toxins from the mother. The placenta's connected to the baby by the umbilical cord, and is 'born' shortly after your baby.

placenta previa: When the placenta covers or is close to the cervix. It can cause bleeding, and your baby will have to be delivered by *caesarean*.

playcentre: Parent and family run day care groups.

playgroup: Parent and family run activities for children held in a community centre or hall that is open to everyone.

pneumonia: An infection of the lungs.

posterior: Where your baby is positioned head down but facing mum's abdomen, so baby's skull is against the back of your partner's pelvis.

postnatal: Also known as *postpartum*. The period after birth, usually one year.

postnatal depression (PND): A kind of mental illness after the birth of a child, usually in the early months. People with PND feel hopeless and detached from their baby.

postpartum: The period after your baby is born (usually a year). Also known as *postnatal*.

potty: A small plastic seat and bowl for teaching a baby or young child about going to the toilet.

pre-eclampsia: A very serious condition that can occur during pregnancy, pre-eclampsia can cause stroke, organ failure and seizures in the pregnant woman, or cause the placenta to come away from the uterine wall. Symptoms include high blood pressure and protein in urine, so your midwife, obstetrician or GP may test for these symptoms at each check-up.

premature: A baby born before 37 weeks.

preschooler: A child aged three to four years old.

primigravida: A Latin term for a woman who's pregnant for the first time.

progesterone: A pregnancy hormone that helps prepare tissue on the uterine wall for its special star, the egg, to implant. Throughout the pregnancy, progesterone helps get breasts ready for milk production and may be responsible for your partner's mood swings.

prolactin: The hormone that stimulates milk-making cells in the breast to produce milk.

prostaglandin: A substance that helps to make the cervix soft so that it can dilate and efface (or shorten) during labour.

psychologist: A health professional specialising in mental health.

pull-ups: Nappies that pull up and down like underpants.

reflux: A condition in which a young baby can't keep food in the stomach and brings up painful stomach acid in the throat.

ripening the cervix: When the cervix becomes soft and ready to dilate. Prostaglandins do this job.

round ligament pain: Pain endured by pregnant women as the pelvis widens.

rubella: Also known as German measles. If a pregnant woman contracts rubella, the virus can cause birth defects in her unborn child.

SAHD: Stay-at-home dad.

separation anxiety: Distress at being away from a parent or main caregiver.

show: During pregnancy, material that makes up the 'show' has plugged up the cervix, keeping the uterus free from infection. The show may come out and make an appearance in the days, or hours, leading up to your child's birth.

sleepsuit: An outfit with trousers and top in one piece, usually with long sleeves and legs.

sling: A piece of material or simple carrier that allows a baby or toddler to be carried around on a caregiver's body.

solids: First foods that babies eat after breastmilk or formula. Solids are usually introduced at about six months of age.

special needs: A term describing children who have a physical or intellectual disability.

spill: When a baby has a milk feed, the baby may spill, or vomit a small amount.

spina bifida: A congenital abnormality caused by the vertebrae not closing around the spinal cord while in the womb.

spinal block: An American term for an epidural, or spinal anaesthesia during childbirth and labour.

stillbirth: When a child dies in utero after 20 weeks gestation, or dies in childbirth.

strep throat: A throat infection accompanied by a high temperature.

stroller: A pram that can be folded easily widthways, and can be carried by the handle with one hand. The child faces outwards.

Sudden Infant Death Syndrome (SIDS): When a baby dies during sleep for unknown reasons; also known as cot death.

Sudden Unexplained Death of Infants (SUDI): Can have a known cause, such as smothering, or be unexplained, such as in the case of Sudden Infant Death Syndrome (SIDS).

swaddle: A term to describe wrapping a baby in a light cloth for sleeping, as well as the name of the cloth used to wrap the baby.

synapses: Connections in the brain.

Syntocinon: A synthetic version of oxytocin, a naturally occurring substance that triggers breastmilk let-down and contractions.

teething: The process of baby teeth coming up through the gums.

TENS: A machine that delivers an electric current during labour as pain relief.

thrush: A fungal infection that babies can get on their bottoms and in their mouths.

toddler: A child who walks, or toddles, up until about age three.

toilet training: The process of teaching your child to use the toilet.

tonsillitis: An infection of the tonsils, which are inside the throat. Can be very painful.

toxoplasmosis: An infection caused by a bacteria that lives in the intestines of animals, particularly cats. Humans can also be infected by eating very rare meat. Pregnant women are particularly vulnerable to toxoplasmosis.

transition: A phase of labour between the cervix dilating (first stage) and pushing the baby out of the birth canal (second stage).

tummy time: Having a baby spend time on the tummy to develop head, neck and back muscles, as well as stimulate eyes and brain.

ultrasound scan: A handheld scanner run over your partner's belly to see inside. A picture appears on a TV screen nearby showing a grainy black and white image of your baby in the womb. Scans are used in the *nuchal fold test* to check for the possibility of birth defects, the development of your baby's body at 20 weeks, or the presence of twins. If you like, you can find out the baby's sex before the birth. 3D and even 4D scans are now available.

umbilical cord: The cord that connects the unborn child to the mother via the *placenta*.

uterine wall: The wall of the uterus, in which the fertilised egg nestles.

uterus: The organ in which an unborn child grows.

varicocele: Varicose veins in the scrotum that may lead to male infertility.

vena cava: The vena cava is the largest vein in the body and consists of two parts: the superior vena cava and the inferior vena cava. The superior vena cava carries blood from the head, neck, arms, and chest. The inferior vena cava carries blood from the legs, feet and organs in the abdomen and pelvis.

ventouse: An instrument with a suction cup to help baby be born.

vernix: A waxy coating that protects baby's skin in the womb.

vitamin K: A substance needed for the body's production of blood clotting agents. Some babies are at risk of a deficiency and can be given a dose at birth.

water birth: When your baby is born in a birthing pool or water.

whooping cough: Also known as *pertussis*, this is a serious and distressing respiratory tract illness in babies and young children.

wind: Air that becomes trapped in your baby's stomach. You need to get that air out by burping your baby by rubbing or patting his back.

word spurt: A stage in toddler development where language skills really take off and seem to progress rapidly.

Index

A

accessories, 75–76
accidents, avoiding, 317–318
acne, 146
active movement, 258–259, 387
active phase, of labour, 93–94, 100, 103–104, 387
activities, 54, 168–169
acupressure, 99
acupuncture, 99, 286
acute illness, 387
Adams, John, 76
'additional needs,' 299–300, 343–346
adoption, 42–43
advice, getting for divorce/separation, 361–363
aftershock, of birth, 116–120
alcohol, during pregnancy, 319
allergens, 387
allergies, 275–276, 387
Allergy & Anaphylaxis Australia, 276
almond oil, 83
alternative medicines/remedies, 286–287
alternative schools, 290
ambulance, 327
amniocentesis, 387
amniotic fluid, 387
amniotic sac, 95, 387
anaphylaxis, 387
animals, in the home, 80
antenatal, 387
antibacterial cream, 83
Apgar score, 63, 110, 387
apps, for labour, 97
armchair, 78–79
arnica cream, 83
arousal stage, of sex, 34
art, 385
artificial insemination (AI), 41, 388
asking for directions, 27
assisted reproductive technologies, 388

Association for Children with a Disability, 338, 343
attachment parenting, 23, 130, 388
attachment relationships, 119
attachment theory, 23
Attention Deficit/Hyperactivity Disorder (ADHD), 299, 388, 395
audiologist, 344
Australasian Society of Clinical Immunology and Allergy, 276
Australian Capital Territory (ACT), 43, 161, 300
Australian Competition and Consumer Commission (ACCC), 75
Australian Counselling Association, 362
Australian Nappy Association, 82
Australian/New Zealand standard AS/NZS 2088:2000, 75
authoritarian parenting, 388
authoritative parenting, 388
autism, 338, 388
autism spectrum (ASD), 299
Autism Spectrum Australia, 339
autonomy, for toddlers, 211

B

babies
    activities for, 150
    development of, 55, 59–60
    losing, 315–334
    meeting, 109
baby bath, 75–76
baby brain, during third trimester, 65
baby capsule, 74
baby carriers, 167–168, 388
baby chair, 76
baby massage, 149–150
baby nail scissors, 84
baby showers, 80
baby talk, 378–379
babymoons, 374
baby-proofing, 169–171, 209
babysitters, leaving baby with, 176

cloth nappies, 78

clothing, 78, 87, 89

co-ed schools, 294–295

cognitive skills, 389

colds, 145–146, 281

colic, 142–144, 389

colleagues, for help, 29–30

common colds, 281

communication, with toddlers, 239–240

community health organisations, 161

The Compassionate Friends Australia, 332

complementary education, 301–302

conception, 37–38, 40–41

concussions, 326

confidence, developing, 229–231

confirmation, of pregnancy, 44–45

congenital abnormality, 337

conjunctivitis, 281–282, 389

connection, for toddlers, 210

connection stage, of sex, 34

conscious fathering, 389

consent, getting for sex, 34–37

constipation, during second trimester, 58–59

consumables, 81–85

contact, 356, 358–359

container, for placenta, 85

controlled crying, 130, 389

cooking, 270–271

cord, cutting the, 108–109

cord prolapse, 324, 389

co-sleeping crib, 77

cot, 77

counsellors, for relationship advice, 352, 362

couple activities, during three to six month period, 172–173

court order, 356

cradle cap, 144, 389

cravings, during third trimester, 66

crawling, during months six to twelve, 187–189

crèche, 389

croup, 208, 389

crowning, 389

crying, 132–133

cry-it-out approach, 130, 390

cutting the cord, 108–109

cystic fibrosis, 390

D

dad
experience of being a, 14–15, 30–31
as first teachers, 266
imagining what type you want to be, 10–12
new-generation, 21–24
seven habits of highly successful, 24–26

dad groups, 30

daddy time, 133

dads groups, 314

Dadvice, 27, 28

dairy, during first trimester, 51

day care, 390

day care centres, leaving baby with, 176–178

day-to-day care, 356

Deaf Children Australia, 338

death, of children, 332–334

decorations, for baby's room, 79

demand feeding, 129, 390

desire stage, of sex, 34

development, 151–155, 211–217, 234–236

developmental delay, 299, 339, 390

Diabetes Australia, 329

diet, 50–51, 182–185, 206–207

digital thermometer, 84

dilation, 94–95, 390

directions, asking for, 27

disabilities and disorders
about, 335
adjusting expectations, 341–343
education and, 299–300
getting formal confirmation of, 339
intellectual disabilities, 338–339
knowing something is wrong, 336–337
multiple disabilities, 339
physical disabilities, 337–338
resources for, 343
tips for managing, 340–341
working with, 343–346

discipline, 186–187, 218–220, 249–252, 390

disease protection, 316

dislocations, joint, 326–327

disorders. *See* disabilities and disorders

disposable nappies, 81–82

About the Author

Dr Justin Coulson and his wife, Kylie, have been married since the late 1990s and are the parents of six daughters. (Yes, they do own a TV and, no, they weren't trying for a boy.)

After struggling — and subsequently failing — during high school, Justin became a radio announcer, eventually working at Brisbane's B105. But while he was good at his job, he was struggling in his role as husband and father to two little girls, aged three and newborn.

Following a temper tantrum (his) that resulted in deep introspection, Justin left his media career and returned to school to study psychology so he could learn to dad. He completed a TAFE course, then a four-year psychology degree (graduating with first-class honours), before he spent another (almost) four years earning a PhD in psychology, focusing on what makes families flourish.

Subsequently, Justin worked for a short time as a lecturer and researcher in academia before starting one of Australia's most recognised organisations promoting healthy parenting: happyfamilies.com.au.

These days, in addition to working on his parenting skills, Justin and Kylie host the #1 podcast in Australia for parents, the Happy Families podcast. He is also the parenting expert and co-host of Channel 9's hit TV show *Parental Guidance*. Justin is a popular keynote speaker at corporate events, conferences and in schools.

Dedication

This book is dedicated to every dad who is working to 'dad' with kindness, gentleness and love.

Authors' Acknowledgements

I wouldn't be a dad without my wife, Kylie. And I wouldn't have become the dad I am without Kylie's patience and breathtaking support. To Kylie, my love and my indescribable gratitude, forever. Everything else is dust.

I also wouldn't be a dad without Chanel, Abbie, Ella, Annie, Lilli and Emilie. To our six girls, I'm grateful for what you've taught me. Being a father is one of the greatest gifts I've been given.

Wonderful appreciation to my publisher, Wiley. This is a team effort and I am grateful to Lucy and Leigh, in particular, for being such supportive, understanding, patient people.

To the worldwide community of dads who show up — again, and again, and again — with kindness, patience and unconditional love for partners and spouses, and particularly for their kids. You are making a lifelong difference in the lives of the ones who matter most.

And, lastly, I acknowledge the noble father I follow. Dad, your example and foundation of unconditional love and support has been the bedrock on which I've built my life. I could never have asked for more.

Publisher's Acknowledgements

Some of the people who helped bring this book to market include the following:

Acquisitions, Editorial and Media Development

Project Editor: Tamilmani Varadharaj

Acquisitions Editor: Lucy Raymond

Editorial Manager: Ingrid Bond

Copy Editor: Charlotte Duff

Production

Proofreader: Evelyn Wellborn

Indexer: Estalita Slivoskey

Every effort has been made to trace the ownership of copyright material. Information that will enable the publisher to rectify any error or omission in subsequent editions will be welcome. In such cases, please contact the Permissions Section of John Wiley & Sons Australia, Ltd.

Printed and bound by CPI Group (UK) Ltd, Croydon, CR0 4YY

19/12/2024

14615703-0001